Harpole

The landscape of a Roman villa at Panattoni Park, Northamptonshire

by Andrew Simmonds and Steve Lawrence

with contributions by
*Martyn Allen, Enid Allison, Edward Biddulph, Paul Booth, Alex Davies,
Mandy Kingdom, Tom Lawrence, Julia Meen, Rebecca Nicholson, Cynthia Poole,
Mairead Rutherford, Ian R Scott and Ruth Shaffrey*

Illustrated by
Charles Rousseaux, Aidan Farnan, Sophie Lamb and Magdalena Wachnik

Oxford Archaeology Monograph No. 34
2022

The publication of this volume was generously funded by M1dway Devco Ltd
Published by Oxford Archaeology as part of the Oxford Archaeology Monograph series

Designed by Oxford Archaeology Graphics Office

Edited by Chris Hayden

This book is part of a series of monographs that can be bought from all good bookshops and internet bookshops.
For more information visit www.oxfordarchaeology.com

Front cover: Corndrying oven 2039
Back cover: Plan of the crop-processing area with the millstone reused in corndrying oven 2039

ISBN 978-0-904220-90-2

Typeset by Production Line, Oxford
Printed in Great Britain by Short Run Press, Exeter, England

Contents

Chapter 1: Introduction

Chapter 2: Evolution of the Panattoni Park landscape from early prehistory to the early Roman period

Chapter 3: The villa landscape, *c* AD 150–400

Chapter 4: Artefactual evidence

Chapter 5: Environmental and osteological evidence and radiocarbon dating

Chapter 6: Discussion

List of Figures

Chapter 6

List of Tables

Summary

Excavations in advance of construction of a complex of logistics and industrial spaces at Panattoni Park, adjacent to Junction 16 of the M1 motorway, *c* 5km west of Northampton, uncovered part of a Roman villa and evidence for preceding prehistoric and early Roman settlement. The development area lay on the north side of the Nene Valley, and the sloping topography of the site necessitated the creation of landscaped terraces for construction by cutting some areas of the slope and infilling other regions with soil. Following an extensive geophysical survey and trial-trench evaluation, five areas of open excavation were undertaken where these cut operations would impact on the identified archaeological remains, as well as a watching brief on an area where archaeological features were exposed during topsoil stripping in one of the intervening preservation areas.

The period before the Iron Age was represented mainly by unstratified flintwork and a small number of pits, but a key find was an *in situ* knapping cluster dating from the Mesolithic period, where locally available flint cobbles were worked into blanks that were then used to produce a range of tools, some of which were utilised at the site while others may have been taken away for use elsewhere.

A pit alignment running down the side of the valley, perpendicular to the river, was constructed during the early Iron Age or at the start of the middle Iron Age. The Nene Valley around Northampton is the location of a particularly dense concentration of such boundaries, which may have been used in the context of pastoral farming. Some were particularly long lived, and the boundary at Panattoni Park was no exception, continuing in use into the late Iron Age, when the northern part was recut as a ditch that defined the western limit of an enclosure complex.

While the pit alignment boundary was still in use, a settlement comprising at least seven roundhouses was constructed at the edge of the floodplain, 450m to the east. No evidence was found for cultivation of arable crops, either in the form of charred plant remains, quernstones or other processing tools, or storage pits, and the settlement may have been entirely pastoral, engaged in grazing livestock, predominantly cattle, on the grasslands of the floodplain. Occupation may have been seasonal, and the roundhouses may not all have been occupied contemporaneously but instead may represent a longer sequence, with only a few houses in occupation at any one time.

An enclosure complex was constructed against the pit alignment boundary during the late Iron Age and was occupied into the early part of the Roman period. No certain domestic focus was identified, although two successive enclosures at the south-west corner of the complex were defined by substantially larger ditches and may have served this function. Alternatively, the complex may have been the fields and paddocks of an enclosed settlement immediately to the north, at the top of the valley slope, that was excavated in 1966. This phase exhibited the first evidence for the adoption of a mixed farming regime. Cattle contined to be the most numerous species but were joined by arable cultivation, and the wider range of activities evidenced probably represent more permanent occupation. Activity here ended *c* AD 50/70 and a hiatus of about a century passed before occupation resumed with the establishment of the villa.

The site was recognised from the outset as having significant archaeological potential due to the proximity of a Roman villa that had been identified during the 1840s, when a mosaic was discovered. Most of the villa building complex was probably destroyed by widening of the A45 (now the A4500) in 1966, when limited trenching recorded the south-east corner of the main building and a stone-lined cistern, as well as a stone-lined drain that indicated the probable presence of a bath house somewhere near the east end of the main house. The Panattoni Park excavation uncovered an aisled building that was probably the southernmost structure in the main complex, as well as a large area of the associated agricultural landscape to the south and south-east. The villa was occupied continuously from the mid-2nd century until the end of the 4th century, if not into the 5th, although the 1966 excavation indicated that the final phase of occupation may have been in reduced circumstances since the cistern building was demolished and reused as a tannery. The villa was probably sited to take advantage of the grazing land that was available within the valley, and the predominance of cattle among the livestock continued, while spelt wheat was the main cereal crop. The pasture land within the valley may have functioned with little or no requirement for ditched boundaries, but the landscape immediately surrounding the villa was enclosed and divided into clearly distinct zones. These comprised an enclosure complex around the villa that probably served a range of agricultural functions, a rather isolated building adjacent to a spring channel that was interpreted as a temple or mausoleum, an area dedicated to crop-processing and, separated from the main complex by the spring channel, a large enclosure complex. Geophysical survey by CLASP has indicated that a similar landscape developed to the north of the A4500. The temple-mausoleum had been severely affected by stone-robbing and truncation by ploughing, as a result of which little stonework remained in place. The robber trenches indicated a possible concentric ground plan analogous to a Romano-Celtic temple, and associated pits contained the burials of (sacrificed?) animals and deposits of calcined animal bone that may have been the deliberately burnt debris of ritual banquets, as well as a charred stone pine cone scale. Pollen evidence from the adjacent spring channel suggested that the building was associated with a walnut grove and may be the earliest definite evidence for cultivation of walnut trees in Britain. The crop-processing area was in use from the 2nd century until the late 4th century and comprised four certain and one possible corndrying ovens and four stone-lined pits. It is argued that these features were used primarily for malting, either as a cash-crop to supplement the income from the villa's more conventional produce or to provide ale for the workforce. The eastern enclosure complex was reorganised several times, forming a construction sequence that extended well into the late 4th century and possibly beyond. From the late 3rd century until the mid-4th it took the form of a large circular enclosure with subdivisions and a smaller central enclosure, possibly representing a compound for livestock with a central roundhouse, although such an arrangement would be extremely unusual at this late date. This arrangement was replaced in the second half of the 4th century by an extensive complex of rectilinear enclosures interpreted as a stockyard for handling and processing livestock. Hay was evidently grown within or close to the complex, since one of the ditches produced a notable group of mower's tools comprising a field anvil, hammer and spud.

No Anglo-Saxon material was found, either at Panattoni Park or during the 1960s trenching of the villa buildings, and it would appear that when the villa was abandoned it was simply forgotten. Ridge and furrow earthworks and the historic Harpole Mill, which formerly stood on the adjacent part of the Nene, attest to the exclusively agricultural use of the area during the historic period, when it lay at the edge of the fields attached to Harpole parish.

Acknowledgements

The authors would like to thank M1dway Devco Ltd for funding the archaeological fieldwork, post-excavation programme and publication. Thanks are also extended to Ian Anderson of First Panattoni for his help in making the project run smoothly and to Philip Bethell of RPS Consulting (formerly CgMs) as the client's consultants overseeing the programme of works.

The project was managed by Steve Lawrence. The fieldwork was directed in the field by Paul Murray and Guy Cockin, assisted by Natalie Anderson, Robert Backhouse, Alexander Batey, Simon Batsman, Liberty Bennett, Phoebe Burrows, Diana Chard, Elizabeth Connelly, Rebecca Coombes, Rachel Daniel, Grace Davies, Barbara Dziuraweic, Aidan Farnan, Adam Fellingham, Emma Forber, Rose Grant, Victoria Green, Leah Hewerdine, Tamsin Jones, Rowan Hendrick, Tom Lawrence, Rachel Legge, Ben McAndrew, Andrew McGuire, Michael McLean, Adam Moffat, Emma Morgan, Jim Mumford, Muhammed Quadir, Adam Rapiejko, Henry Rayment-Pickard, Chris Richardson, Rachel Sisman, Benjamin Slader, Andrew Smith, Jacob Spriggs, Dan Sykes, Edward Tolley, Jack Traill and Emma Winter. The post-excavation programme was managed by Andrew Simmonds. Support was provided by Leigh Allen (finds management), Matt Bradley (geomatics management), Louise Loe (burials management), Rebecca Nicholson (environmental management), Nicola Scott (archives management) and Magdalena Wachnik (graphics management).

The project could not have been completed without the hard work of the many other Oxford Archaeology staff who contributed to the project, both in the field and during the post-excavation analysis. Survey and digitising were carried out by Aidan Farnan. The illustrations were drawn by Aidan Farnan, Charles Rousseaux and Magdalena Wachnik. The authors would like to thank Charlotte Walker of Northamptonshire Historic Environment Record and Ben Donnelly-Symes of Northamptonshire Archives for providing access to Gwen Brown's draft site report and associated correspondence. Thanks are also due to Dana Goodburn Brown of CSI: Sittingbourne for cleaning and conservation of the Roman coins. The report was edited for publication by Chris Hayden.

The authors are especially grateful to Dr Alex Smith for reading and commenting on the original text. Any errors, however, remain the responsibility of the authors alone.

Chapter 1

Introduction

PROJECT BACKGROUND

This volume presents the results of a programme of archaeological excavation undertaken by Oxford Archaeology (OA) in advance of construction of a complex of logistics and industrial spaces at Panattoni Park, adjacent to Junction 16 of the M1 motorway, *c* 5km west of Northampton (Fig. 1.1). The site of the development (known as M1dway during the development stage) was recognised from the outset as having significant archaeological potential due to the proximity of a Roman villa that had been identified during the 1840s and partly excavated in advance of the widening of the A45 (now the A4500) in 1966, although the villa's precise location was not certain. The historic Harpole Mill, demolished in 1970, was located just beyond the site's south-eastern limit. The site did not disappoint, and the excavations uncovered the southern part of the villa's main building complex and recorded extensive areas of the agricultural landscape around it, including a dedicated crop-processing area and a building that was probably either a temple or mausoleum, as well as remains from earlier periods including a rare instance of an *in situ* Mesolithic flint scatter, a long-lived Iron Age boundary and nearby settlement, and a settlement that was established at the end of the Iron Age and apparently swept away when the villa landscape was set out in the 2nd century. Together, this evidence has provided an opportunity to explore the development of farming in this part of the Nene Valley over a period of several centuries during the late prehistoric and Roman periods, and to greatly increase knowledge of the villa and explore its surrounding landscape.

In view of the evident archaeological potential of the development area, a historic environment desk-based assessment (DBA) was produced for the initial wider area of the proposed allocation by Iain Soden Heritage Services Ltd (Walker 2014). The site area was subsequently reduced following allocation as a strategic employment site as part of the West Northamptonshire Joint Core Strategy, following which a series of preliminary investigations was undertaken by Museum of London Archaeology. Central to this was a revised DBA designed to address the reduced site area, comprising a reworking of the original DBA that incorporated a reconsultation of the Historic Environment Record and selected cartographic sources (MOLA 2015a). The revised DBA was also informed by the results of a magnetometer survey (MOLA 2015b) that identi-fied potential archaeological features in the eastern part of the site, east of the Red Lion truck stop. West of this the survey indicated only ridge and furrow, palaeochannels associated with the adjacent River Nene, and other natural anomalies (Fig. 1.2).

A subsequent trial-trench evaluation of the entire development area, involving the excavation of 75 trenches, confirmed the date of many of the features and enabled several areas of archaeological signifi-cance to be defined (MOLA 2015c). The western-most area contained a late Iron Age to Romano-British rectilinear settlement comprising a series of ditched enclosures abutting a pit alignment, the latter poorly dated due to the scarcity of artefactual material. To the north, close to the A4500 and the location of the villa, lay a rectilinear field system defined by a series of parallel linear ditches aligned east–west, with some internal divisions, and associ-ated with Roman pottery. It was noted that the pottery assemblage from this area contained greater quantities of fineware and samian ware pottery than would be expected for a typical rural site, and the foundations of two stone-built rectangular structures were identified that were interpreted as the remains of a smokehouse for preserving food products, similar to an example found at Pineham Barn in 2013 (ULAS 2014). The final area was located on the southern edge of the site, near the river, and comprised a small area of middle Iron Age ditches and ring ditches of varying sizes, at least one of which was thought likely to relate to a roundhouse.

A written scheme of investigation (WSI) was produced that presented site-specific research aims and proposed a mitigation strategy designed to investigate those areas of archaeology identified during the evaluation which were considered to be at risk from the development (MOLA 2016). The sloping topography of the site necessitated the creation of landscaped terraces for construction by cutting some areas of the slope and infilling other regions with the arising soil. Excavation was to be targeted on nine areas where these cut operations would impact on the areas of archaeological signifi-cance identified by the geophysical survey and trial-trench evaluation. Archaeological features which lay outside these cut areas were to be preserved *in situ* by the build-up of fill as part of the terracing works and would therefore not be excavated.

OA's involvement in the project began in 2017, when they were commissioned to undertake excavation of the nine areas defined in the MOLA

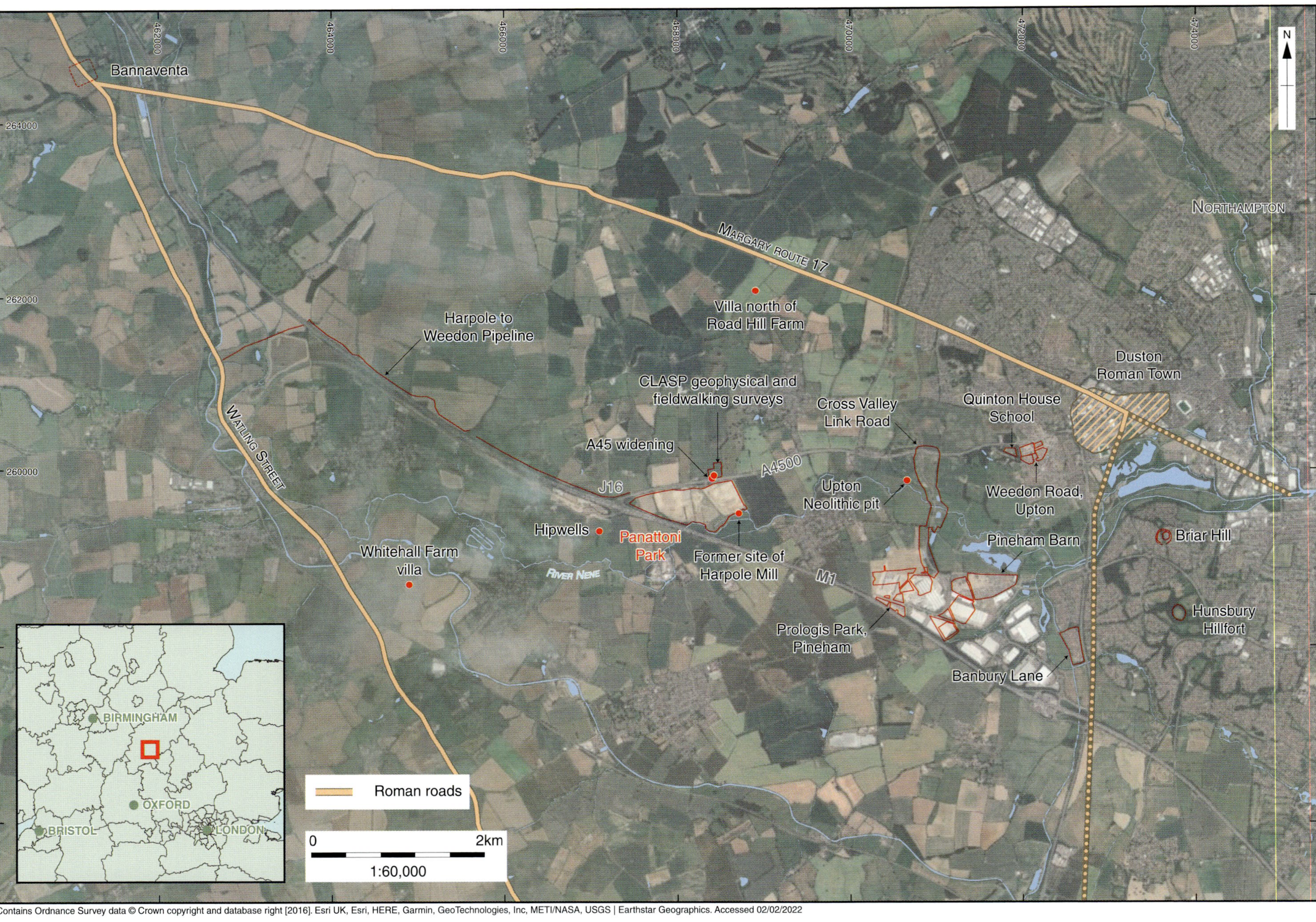

Fig. 1.1 Site location and previous excavations

Fig. 1.2 Geophysical survey results and evaluation trenches

WSI. Following consultation with the developer and their consultant, Philip Bethal of RPS Consulting (formerly CgMs), the nine areas were consolidated into five larger areas, so as to create larger, contiguous areas which would allow the various areas of archaeological significance to be excavated within single areas, and which, logistically, were easier to strip and excavate (Fig. 1.3). Area 1 was also extended to the east to include the full extent of the temple or mausoleum, and Area 2 was extended to the west to encompass that side of the crop-processing area. A watching brief was subsequently also carried out during the initial groundworks phase of construction in the area which was to be preserved *in situ* between Areas 3 and 4 to ensure that such areas were not truncated (Fig. 1.7).

Following the completion of the fieldwork, a post-excavation assessment was produced that presented the preliminary findings, assessed the potential of the results to address current research agendas, and set out a programme for analysis and dissemination (OA 2018). This volume is the product of the consequent analysis.

LOCATION, TOPOGRAPHY AND GEOLOGY

The development area lay on the north side of the Nene Valley and comprised a roughly triangular area of former farmland between the M1 motorway and the A4500 Northampton to Daventry road, centred at NGR SP 6825 5963 (Fig. 1.1). The apex of this area was formed by Junction 6, where the two roads meet, and it extended east as far as a track that branched off the A4500 and led south to the location of the former Harpole Mill, beyond which it was adjoined by further agricultural fields. Most of the site lay within the historic parish of Harpole, but the western tip was within the adjoining parish of Upper Heyford, the boundary between the two running along a small stream that flowed through the site from north to south. The excavation areas, however, lay exclusively within Harpole parish. Part of the south-east boundary of the development

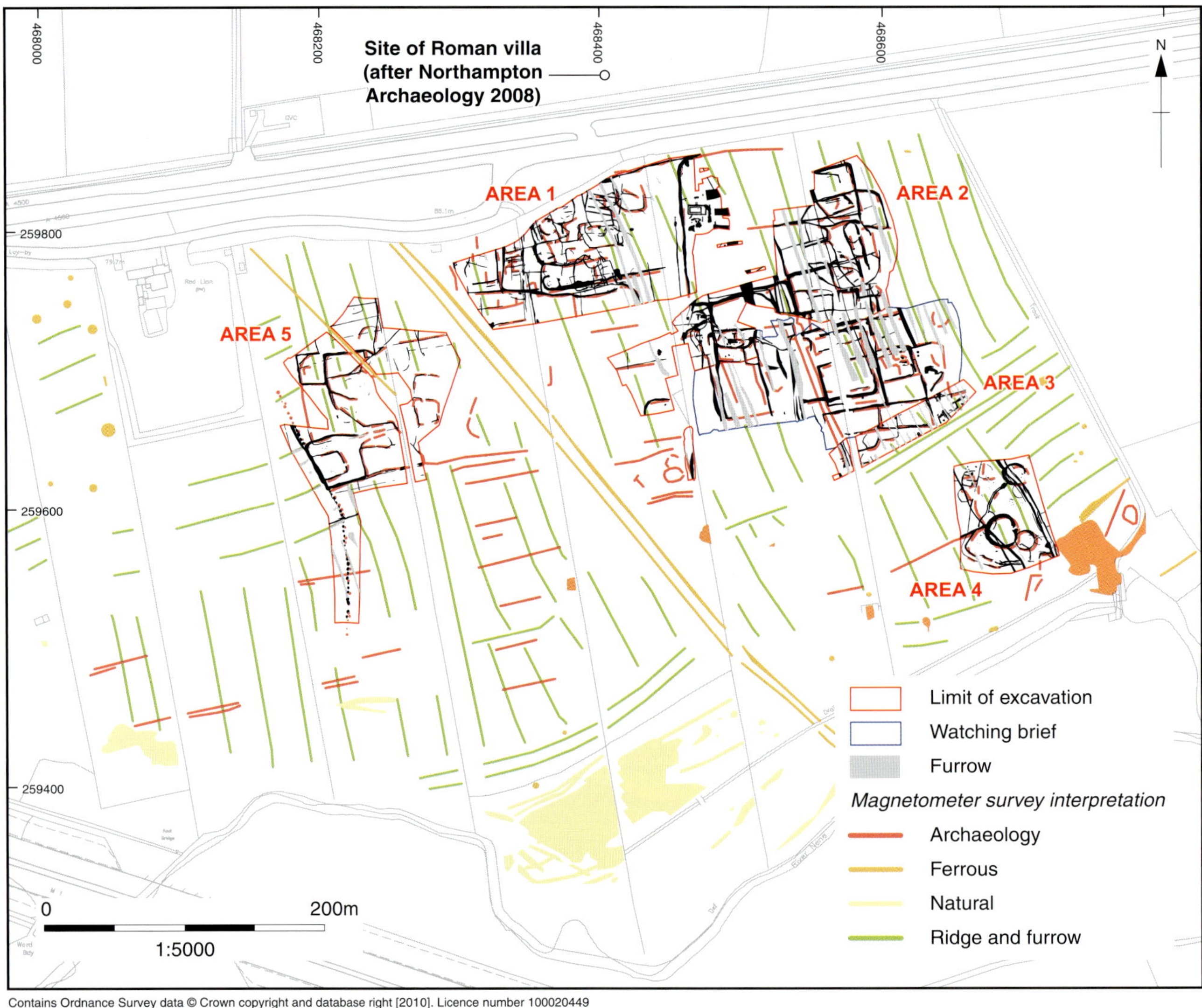

Fig. 1.3 Plan of excavation and watching brief areas, with interpretation of the geophysical survey results

ran along the River Nene, and the entire site lay on a slope that ran gently down towards the river from a maximum elevation of *c* 85m above Ordnance Datum (aOD) beside the A4500 to *c* 65m aOD close to the river in Area 4.

The underlying geology is mapped as Dyrham Formation siltstone and mudstone (BGS nd). To the north, this is overlain by ferruginous limestone of the Marlstone Rock Formation, the boundary following approximately the same line as the A4500 apart from a small spur of limestone that projects to the south immediately east of the Red Lion truck-stop. Above this is further mudstone of the Whitby Formation, and the sequence of relatively porous limestone interstratified between layers of impermeable mudstone has created a spring line, as indicated by the springs on the north side of the road marked on the 1st edition OS map. The eroding effect of water flowing from an unlocated spring somewhere close to the road near the east end of Excavation Area 1 is the most likely explanation for a linear band running from north to south across the site that obscured the ridge and furrow earthworks that were otherwise ubiquitous within the development area. In the lower-lying areas of the site, close to the River Nene, the Dyrham mudstone is overlain by deposits of alluvium, clay, silt, sand and gravel, but these deposits did not extend into the excavation areas.

ARCHAEOLOGICAL BACKGROUND

Previous investigations

The Nene is one of the longest rivers in England, and its valley has a long history of antiquarian and archaeological investigation. Much of this work, particularly downstream from Northampton as far as Peterborough, has been carried out in advance of gravel quarrying (Meadows *et al.* 2009, 6), but west of Northampton the deposits of gravel are smaller and their extraction less commercially viable. As a consequence, the main driver of archaeological investigation here, at least during the late 20th and early 21st centuries, has been the expansion of the conurbation of Northampton. Of particular significance to the current project are a series of excavations at Upton (Foard-Colby and Walker 2010; Walker and Maull 2010; MOLA 2012), extensive excavations associated with the construction of the distribution park at Prologis Park, Pineham (Brown and Carlyle 2007; MOLA 2017) and the adjacent residential development at Pineham Barn (ULAS 2014; 2015), and a watching brief and excavation during construction between these areas of the Cross Valley Link Road (Carlyle 2010), since renamed Upton Valley Way.

The Roman villa was first identified in the 1840s, when a mosaic was exposed, and further excavations were undertaken in 1899, when the mosaic was re-exposed and part of it removed, and in 1966 when the site was threatened by widening of the A45 (now the A4500). Information on the original exposure of the mosaic is preserved only in three short contemporary notices in the *Journal of the British Archaeological Association*, based on information provided to the journal by a Mr Edward Pretty (Anon. 1850; 1851; White and Baily 1847), and a brief account of the 1899 excavation appeared in the *Journal of the Northamptonshire Natural History Society and Field Club* (Northamptonshire Exploration Committee 1901–2). The most recent excavation, carried out when this part of the road was straightened to run north of the previous alignment, was directed by Gwen Brown for Northamptonshire County Council, but the only published accounts of the findings are very short notes in the *Journal of Roman Studies* (Wilson and Wright 1967, 186) and the RCHME volume on south-west Northamptonshire (RCHME 1982, 73–4). An unfinished draft report and associated correspondence are at the Northamptonshire Archive and were consulted for this project, but the draft report is of a very summary nature and much uncertainty remains. More recently, the villa was one of eleven Roman sites in this and the surrounding parishes that were subject to non-invasive investigations undertaken by the Community Landscape Archaeology Survey Projects (CLASP) as part of their Heritage Lottery-funded project 'Local People: Local Past' (CLASP nd a) with the aim of assessing archaeological survival across this narrowly defined study area. CLASP's fieldwork comprised an intensive fieldwalking survey in 2000 followed by two phases of geophysical survey (Pre-Construct Geophysics 2003; Northamptonshire Archaeology 2008b).

Prehistoric

Evidence for activity before the establishment of more archaeologically visible (and perhaps more permanent) settlements in the Iron Age is relatively sparse, but rivers such as the Nene would have provided important corridors of communication as well as a supply of water and other resources. This period is often represented in excavations only by flintwork, although communal monuments and funerary sites are also known. The earliest of these in the local area was the early Neolithic causewayed enclosure at Briar Hill, on the south side of the river, 5km east of Panattoni Park (Bamford 1985). It was discovered during aerial survey in 1972 and excavated in 1974 to 1978 in advance of housing development, revealing two circuits of ditches and a smaller, more circular inner circuit that may have been later, but still early Neolithic, in date. Recent Bayesian modelling of radiocarbon dating has indicated that construction probably took place in *3760–3415 cal BC* and that the site was occupied for *150–505 years* (Whittle *et al.* 2011, 293–300), although the presence of later Neolithic pits and a small group of Bronze Age cremation burials shows that it continued to be a significant monument in subsequent centuries. A substantial middle Neolithic funerary monument was found at Banbury Lane, Northampton, comprising three concentric ditch circuits, the entrance to the innermost of which had been blocked by the digging of an elongated pit that contained the disarticulated remains of at least 130 individuals. Radiocarbon dating indicated a date of 3360–3100 cal BC (Holmes *et al.* 2012). Episodes of Neolithic occupation are commonly represented by small clusters of pits, an example of which has been excavated at Weedon Road, Upton (MOLA 2012).

In the wider landscape many Bronze Age barrows have been recorded along the Nene Valley, although they are largely concentrated downstream from Northampton. A cropmark complex to the north-west of Panattoni Park includes a ring ditch that has been interpreted as a round barrow, and an isolated Bronze Age cremation burial within a Collared Urn was discovered during flood attenuation works between Upton and Kislingbury *c* 2.5km to the east (Foard-Colby 2008), while a possible barrow ditch and a Bronze Age cremation cemetery have been excavated at Pineham Barn (Brown and Carlyle 2007).

Pit alignments like the one at Panattoni Park appear to have been particularly common in this part of the Nene Valley and are typically ascribed to the late Bronze Age and early to middle Iron Age. An alignment to the west at Hipwells, Upper Heyford, yielded a single sherd of late Bronze Age pottery (Seddon and Murray 2000), and to the east three sites lie on an approximately E–W alignment at Weedon Road (Walker and Maull 2010), Quinton House School (Foard-Colby and Walker 2010) and near the A45 on the Cross Valley Link Road (Carlyle 2010). Further north, a further cluster of alignments has been identified from cropmark evidence around Harlestone and Dallington Gateway, one of which was excavated at Harlestone Quarry (Chapman *et al.* 2017). South of the river, an alignment at Wootton Fields was at least 130m long (Chapman *et al.* 2005), and a complex of four alignments at Prologis Park appears to branch off an E–W boundary ditch to divide up a large area of land on either side (MOLA 2017).

The Nene Valley was extensively settled between the early to middle Iron Age and Roman period because of its productive agricultural land. It is likely that during the middle Iron Age Hunsbury hillfort, 5km to the east of Panattoni Park, acted as an important centre for this part of the valley. Most of the interior of the fort and much of the surrounding land was quarried for ironstone in the late 19th century and, as a result, a vast amount of archaeological material was recovered, making Hunsbury extremely important to the study of Iron Age material. More than 300 pits were uncovered, and the finds included weapons, tools, currency bars, brooches and more than 150 querns, as well as glass and pottery (RCHME 1985). The hillfort may have been superseded as the predominant centre in the local area by an extensive settlement at Duston, *c* 4.5km east of Panattoni Park on the north side of

the river (RCHME 1985). Unfortunately, as with the hillfort, most of the site was destroyed by ironstone quarrying during the 19th century, and interpretation relies mainly on casual finds reported during the works. At least 20 Iron Age coins are known, as well as 13 Colchester-type brooches and 'Belgic' pottery, which were produced during the 1st centuries BC and AD. The evidence certainly points to fairly extensive settlement before AD 60 and at least some occupation before AD 43, although the nature and extent of the pre-Conquest settlement is uncertain. Smaller, farmstead-sized settlements would have been the most numerous elements of the settlement pattern. Brown's excavation in advance of widening of the A45 (now the A4500) in 1966 uncovered an enclosed settlement of Bronze Age or Iron Age date, but the precise location is not known, and the rescue conditions and adverse weather allowed little detail of the interior to be recorded. The enclosure ditch was 54m in diameter and 2.1 to 2.7m deep, and several pits up to 1.3m deep were identified in the interior, as well as small hearths both within and outside the enclosure. Dating evidence from the ditch was limited to a sherd of possibly Bronze Age pottery, although animal bone, slag and some fragments of 'crucible-like containers' were also recovered, and the pits produced red and black butt beakers of Iron Age date (Brown 1967). The circular shape of the enclosure and the possible Bronze Age date may indicate that it was a ring ditch or ringwork, but there is insufficient evidence to be certain. Several other Iron Age farmsteads have been excavated in the surrounding area. These include a middle Iron Age settlement at Pineham Barn which comprised several roundhouses situated within a square enclosure, representing at least two phases of construction (Brown and Carlyle 2007). The boundary defined by one of the pit alignments at Prologis Park was subsequently incorporated into a recti-linear late Iron Age enclosure within which stood a single roundhouse (MOLA 2017). A particularly interesting sequence was excavated at Weedon Road, Upton, where a series of small, discrete enclosures which stood beside a linear boundary ditch from the 2nd century BC, forming part of a wider pastoral landscape, were replaced in the late Iron Age by a single enclosure with a substantial ditch and possibly a central roundhouse (Walker and Maull 2010).

Roman

The original archaeological interest in the site derived from the discovery of a mosaic in 1846, which was reported to the *Journal of the British Archaeological Association* by a Mr Edward Pretty, although precisely how it came to be discovered was not reported (White and Baily 1847). It is possible that it had been accidentally exposed during ploughing, since this was how it came to be uncov-ered for a second time in 1849, when Pretty provided the *Journal* with a more detailed description (Anon. 1850). Pretty took the opportunity presented by this second exposure to have a measured drawing made, which the *Journal* published in a third note (Anon. 1851). This drawing provides a fortuitous record of the mosaic, since the ongoing damage resulting from further ploughing, evidenced by the large number of tesserae that were being brought to the surface, prompted Northamptonshire Exploration Committee to undertake an excavation in 1899. The Committee's account of the investigation (Northamptonshire Exploration Committee 1901–2) indicates that part of the mosaic was removed at this time and that there was an intention to lift the entire floor for display at Northampton Museum, although there is no subsequent record of this having happened. Pretty specifically stated that the foundations of the building in which the mosaic was situated were not exposed in the excavations he witnessed, although he opined that the site was likely to be more extensive than the observed remains since 'tesserae and other relics are discovered to a considerable extent beyond the spot' (Anon. 1850, 375), and although the 1899 excavation was evidently more extensive it was not possible to recover the ground plan of the villa because the wall foundations had been comprehensively robbed (Northamptonshire Exploration Committee 1901–2, 8).

In 1966, one of Brown's trial trenches exposed the south-east corner of the main villa building, and a separate open area excavation investigated a cistern 12m further east that may have been part of a nymphaeum, but the locations of neither are precisely recorded. The area of the villa buildings was much disturbed from the previous investigations, but two phases of construction were identified, the earlier, dated to the 2nd century, mostly destroyed when it was replaced by the larger, later building. The outline of the robbed walls was defined, inside which was the outer edge of a tesselated pavement of grey limestone; it is not clear from her account whether this was the same floor that had been exposed during the previous century. In addition to the limestone tesserae, ceramic pieces and others made in stone of different colours were recovered from the overburden. Wall plaster dating from the 2nd and 4th centuries was also found, the former painted yellow and green. The later plaster was dark red with black transverse lines. A considerable quantity of *opus signinum* was also found, as well as much roof tile. Beyond the building, the trench uncovered a cobbled yard and boundary wall, and small areas of burning interpreted as hearths. The cistern to the east was built of faced limestone on a pitched stone foundation that contained a coin of Hadrian (117–38). It measured 6m by 3m and 1.2m deep and was fed by water pipes. Like the main building, it exhibited evidence for two phases, the later of which was dated by a coin of Julian the Apostate (361–3). On the north side was an entrance consisting of a fan-shaped limestone surface into which were cemented three

inverted ox skulls, two of them with hooves beside them. Brown noted that Professor Toynbee (presumably Jocelyn Toynbee, former Professor of Classical Archaeology at Cambridge University) considered this to be a dedicatory threshold and that the building was 'a small temple to a water god' (ie a nymphaeum). Brown reported that a small spring bubbled up immediately north of the cistern, and may have fed it, and close to this was part of a stone plinth with a small circle cut into it that contained a fragment of lead, possibly a pedestal for a statue. The lower part of the cistern was filled with plaster and roof tiles from the building that had stood over it, and above this the fill contained much lime, animal bone and bone skiving tools, which Brown interpreted as evidence for reuse of the cistern as a tannery. This activity was attributed to the 5th century, but the evidence for this date was not specified. South-west of the cistern, and believed to be contemporary with the reuse of the cistern as a tannery, were the postholes of a large circular timber building that contained several hearths, and a cobbled yard that had been built around it to the south. It should be noted that neither the 19th-century excavation accounts, nor Brown's draft report, provide an accurate location for the remains of the villa

The fieldwalking carried out in 2000 by CLASP in the field adjacent to the north side of the A4500, where the villa was believed to be located, resulted in the recovery of 4970 pottery sherds, 1432 tesserae, 221kg of tile and four coins over an area of *c* 2ha. The distribution of this material, and particularly the building material, was concentrated in the south-west part of the field, immediately adjacent to the road, which may represent the location of the villa building(s). A gradiometer survey in 2003 indicated that this concentration lay within a large subrectangular enclosure which was surrounded by associated ditched fields (Pre-Construct Geophysics 2003). A second programme of geophysics extended the surveyed area to the north and also included a resistivity survey of the putative building location. The results of this were not clearly defined, although possible walls and areas of collapse or flooring were tentatively identified (Northamptonshire Archaeology 2008b).

The villa is in fact one of two such establishments that have been identified within Harpole parish, the other lying *c* 2.5km away, directly north of the modern village. This prompts some difficulties regarding nomenclature since, although both sites have been known since the 1840s, neither has a commonly accepted name. When first discovered, the mosaic adjacent to Panattoni Park was described simply as 'at Harpole', and a similar terminology was used in the account of the 1966 excavation. The county Historic Environment Record refers to it by the rather ugly designation 'Romano-British villa near Red Lion Pub', and Scott's gazetteer of villas in Britain eschews names altogether and refers to both sites simply by their

NGR co-ordinates (Scott 1993, 144). CLASP term the Panattoni villa 'Harpole 1' and the other 'Harpole 2', although the geophysics surveys they commissioned refer to the sites as 'Harpit' (after the field in which it is situated) and 'Barns Close' respectively. To add to the confusion, the other villa has been scheduled under the name 'Roman villa north of Road Hill Farm' (EH list entry no. 1003901).

The location of both villas within the Upper Nene Valley places them within one of the most densely populated parts of Roman Britain, where the Nene and Great Ouse drained across the productive agricultural land of the East Midland Plain. Locally, there is another villa at Whitehall Farm, Nether Heyford (CLASP 2012), 3.5km to the west, as well as examples at Wootton Fields (Chapman *et al.* 2005) and Piddington (Friendship-Taylor and Friendship-Taylor 2013) near Northampton, and others further downstream including Redlands Farm (OAU 1992) and Stanwick (Neal 1989). The late Iron Age settlement at Duston developed into a roadside settlement at the junction of two Roman roads that lead south to Towcester and north-west to a junction with Watling Street near Daventry. Due to the ironstone quarrying, much of the site has been lost and consequently its layout and character are very poorly understood, although it appears to have extended over some 8ha (RCHME 1985). Finds of pottery and large numbers of coins have been reported over the years, as well as a possible cemetery to the north and a burial in a stone sarcophagus within a stone building that was most likely a mausoleum. The road north-west from Duston, Margary's route 17 (Margary 1967, 187–8), followed the higher ground north of the Nene to a junction with Watling Street at *Bannaventa* near Whilton Lodge, the nearest walled town, some 8.5km north-west of Panattoni

Park. Its continuation south-east beyond Duston is lost, although Margary speculated that it continued to a crossing point of the Nene south of Northampton city centre. A second road, less well understood, is believed to have extended south from the town.

Post-Roman

During the historic period, the site lay within agricultural land between the villages of Harpole, which lies *c* 900m to the north, Upper Heyford, 1.8km to the west, and Kislingbury, *c* 750m to the south-east on the opposite side of the Nene. Evidence for cultivation during this period was provided by the remains of ridge and furrow, which survived as earthworks (Fig. 1.6) and were recorded by the magnetometer survey (Figs 1.2–1.3). The preservation was variable, ranging from moderate to good, and in some places varied strikingly between the modern fields into which the area was divided, demonstrating that the survival of the earthworks was dependent on the modern land use. The best-preserved earthworks lay in the eastern half of the site where the excavation areas were located. A number of furlongs could be identified, lying on differing alignments and separated by headlands, and their location in relation to the parish boundaries indicates that they formed part of the fields of Harpole.

The historic Harpole Mill would also have been a significant element of the local landscape throughout these periods, standing beside the Nene, just outside the south-eastern limit of the site, where only the mill pond and leat now survive (Fig. 1.1). The first mention of a mill at Harpole dates from the early 13th century, when it was referred to as *Molendino de Horepol* (Starmer 2002). The next

Fig. 1.4 Area 5 during excavation, view to south-west across the Nene Valley toward Heygates Flour Mill and the M1 bridge

record does not appear until 1777, when Joseph and John Davis were named as millers, but it is likely that the mill was continuously active throughout this period. The final mill was working until at least 1919 but was labelled on the 1950 OS map as disused and was demolished in 1970, when the surviving machinery was recorded (Starmer 1970, 27; 1971, 9–10). A wooden beam over the mill race bore an inscription that commemorated its construction in 1823 – 'new bilt by W P Milright and W D M…son for the [?glory of God]' – and was removed for donation to the Billing Mill Museum. Brick foundations at the former mill site were noted during a site walkover undertaken in 2015 as part of the desk-based assessment (MOLA 2015a, 17), and disturbance recorded here by the magnetometer survey (Fig. 1.2) was interpreted as rubble from its demolition and other associated drainage channels (MOLA 2015b, 5). Similar mills would have been situated throughout the local landscape, including Bugbrooke Mill, across the Nene on the site now occupied by Heygates Flour Mill, a well-known modern landmark (Fig. 1.4).

The common fields of Harpole were enclosed by Act of Parliament in 1778, and by the time of the 1813 OS map the site was divided into a series of small fields or paddocks. This map shows the course of the river Nene as rather different from its current position (and that shown on all subsequent maps), flowing further north and passing through the southern part of the development area, but it is uncertain whether this was due to a surveying error or indicates that the river has since been altered, perhaps when the mill was rebuilt in 1823. The first edition 6" OS map was published in 1884 and shows that the fields of the 1813 map had been rationalised into a more regular arrangement with straighter boundaries, comprising a series of parallel boundaries defining long, rectangular fields between the A4500 and the river in the eastern part of the site, where the excavation areas were situated, and larger fields in the western part. With the exception of the removal of a few subdivisions to consolidate smaller fields into larger ones, this arrangement remained unchanged until the construction of Panattoni Park.

Fig. 1.5 Excavation in progress on the south side of late Iron Age/early Roman enclosure 5448/5449, view to east

Fig. 1.6 Ridge and furrow in baulk of Area 4, view to west

FIELDWORK METHODOLOGY

Open area excavation was undertaken to investigate those areas of archaeology that the MOLA WSI (MOLA 2016) had identified as being at risk from the development, based on the results of the geophysical survey and trial-trench evaluation and the disposition of the cut and fill areas of the development (Figs 1.3–1.6). A watching brief was also maintained on the stripping and backfilling of the preservation area between Areas 3 and 4 (Figs 1.7–1.8).

Fig. 1.7 Features exposed in the Watching Brief Area: a) view to north; b) west end of the Preservation Area, view to south

The overburden, comprising topsoil and subsoil, was removed to the top of the archaeological deposits by a machine using a toothless bucket operating under archaeological supervision. The exposed area was hand-cleaned to define all archaeological features present, which were mapped using GPS/GNSS in order to establish a pre-excavation plan. All archaeological deposits were then excavated by hand and recorded stratigraphically in accordance with OA's standard recording system (Wilkinson 1992) and the WSI. Linear features associated with settlement were investigated by means of a 10% sample by length and other linear features were sufficiently sampled to allow an informed interpretation of their date and function, the excavated slots in both instances being a minimum of 1m wide and targeted to investigate all stratigraphic relationships to determine the sequence of activity. A sample of 35% of the pits in the pit alignment was investigated by hand excavation (comprising 13 of the 37 pits exposed), 10 being half-sectioned and the others having smaller interventions excavated to investigate specific stratigraphic relationships. All other discrete features (ie pits and postholes) were half-sectioned with the exception of burials (below). All features and deposits were given unique context numbers and recorded on *pro forma* sheets. Planning of excavated features was conducted using a combination of GPS/GNSS and hand-drawing, and photogrammetry was used to record more complex structures such as the corndrying ovens. Sections were recorded by measured drawing at an appropriate scale, usually 1:20. Spot-heights and levels of individual features and artefacts were recorded relative to Ordnance Datum (OD). High-resolution digital photographs were taken of each feature and related groups of features, and to record the process of the excavation more generally.

Artefacts were recovered by context and those allocated a small find number were recorded in three dimensions. All features and spoil heaps were scanned with a metal detector in order to enhance recovery of metal artefacts. This was supplemented by a targeted programme of environmental sampling. Priority was given to the basal fills of features and to those deposits showing visible evidence for charred plant remains. A monolith sample for pollen was collected from the sequence of deposits filling the spring outwash channel, and a series of 20 litre bulk samples was taken incrementally through the organic channel fills, from each of which a subsample of one litre was processed for waterlogged plant remains and of two litres for insects. Similar incremental samples were recovered from middle Roman ditch 2511.

The watching brief monitored the removal of earth from the area between Areas 3 and 4 which was to be preserved *in situ* to ensure that this area was not truncated. The turf and topsoil in this area was removed under supervision and the features exposed were planned. It was ensured that the machines did not track across exposed areas so that the exposed features could be recorded. No excavation was planned (although an inhumation grave and a cremation burial were excavated) and finds were collected only from the surfaces of features. The initial backfilling was also carried out under archaeological supervision to ensure that a suitable depth of made-ground was in place before wheeled vehicles accessed the area. The backfilling was carried out using spoil arising from the cut areas which was compacted into spits, starting from the edge of the stripped areas to ensure that no machines tracked across exposed features (Fig. 1.8).

The excavation and watching brief uncovered four inhumation graves and a single cremation burial. These were excavated under a Home Office licence under the supervision of an experienced osteoarchaeologist in accordance with OA standard guidelines (Wilkinson 1992). All human remains were cleaned and placed in boxes following the

Fig. 1.8 Backfilling the watching brief area

methods detailed in the Chartered Institute for Archaeologists' technical paper *Excavation and post-excavation treatment of cremated and inhumed human remains* (McKinley and Roberts 1993).

STRUCTURE OF THE REPORT

Following this introductory chapter, which describes the background to the project and the methodology adopted in the investigations, the volume is divided between a description of the data recovered during the investigations, in Chapters 2 to 5, and a synthetic discussion in Chapter 6. The prehistoric and early Roman features are described in Chapter 2 and the middle and late Roman features, associated with the adjacent villa, in Chapter 3. Within each phase, the description progresses chronologically and broadly from west to east. Figures 3.1 and 3.25 present general plans of the middle and late Roman features, these being the phases when activity was spread most widely throughout the entire site, and more localised phase plans are used throughout the text to illustrate individual areas of activity. Selected section drawings are shown to aid the understanding and interpretation of the site sequence.

The subsequent chapters present the artefactual evidence (Chapter 4) and the palaeoenvironmental evidence and human remains (Chapter 5). The overall discussion in Chapter 6 brings together the various strands of stratigraphic, artefactual, environmental and dating evidence and considers them in relation to the research objectives defined in the post-excavation assessment.

Presentation of the site sequence and phasing

The stratigraphic sequence has been divided into broad phases of activity on the basis of stratigraphic relationships, ceramic dating, evidence from coins and other objects, and radiocarbon dating. Features investigated by more than one intervention (mostly ditches) have been given a subgroup number for ease of analysis and description. In all other cases, the intervention or cut number has been used as the principal feature reference. The phase numbers were allocated during the assessment stage (OA 2018) and revised where possible in the light of closer dating evidence obtained during the subsequent analysis. Significant changes from the assessment phasing include the expansion of Phase 1 to include Neolithic and Bronze Age features in addition to Mesolithic activity, and the removal of the late Bronze Age–early Iron Age phase, the pottery from which has been redated as middle Iron Age. In some cases, where there was clear stratigraphic justification, phases have been divided into subphases. Thus, two subphases (2a and 2b) were defined in the middle Iron Age settlement in Excavation Area 4 on

stratigraphic grounds and three subphases (3a–c) are recorded in the late Iron Age to early Roman settlement in Areas 1 and 5. The middle Roman sequence was only divided into subphases in Area 2 (4a and 4b), but there are three late Roman subphases (5a–c) in both Area 1 and Area 2. It should be noted that the subphases are specific to the stratigraphic sequences in individual excavation areas and do not correlate across the site, due to the almost complete absence of features that extended across adjacent areas, linking the individual area sequences. Thus, features of subphase 5a in Area 1 need not have been contemporary with those of subphase 5a in Area 2.

The phases used in the report are as follows:

Phase 1: Mesolithic, Neolithic and Bronze Age activity

In situ Mesolithic flint scatter, isolated pits and residual or unstratified flint.

Phase 2: Middle Iron Age

Small feature group in Area 2, settlement in Area 4, pit alignment in Area 5.

Phase 3: Late Iron Age to early Roman

Settlement straddling Areas 1 and 5.

Phase 4: Middle Roman

Establishment of the landscape associated with the adjacent villa, comprising an enclosure complex adjacent to the villa in Area 1, a temple/mausoleum adjacent to the spring channel between Areas 1 and 2, a field system and crop-processing area west of the spring channel, and some indication of agricultural enclosures east of the spring channel.

Phase 5: Late Roman

Further development of the enclosure complex adjacent to the villa in Area 1, possible abandonment of the temple/mausoleum, intensification of use of the crop-processing area, and three phases of activity at the field system east of the spring channel.

Post-Roman features were limited to furrows and modern field boundaries and are not discussed in detail but are mentioned in passing where relevant.

LOCATION OF THE ARCHIVE

The finds, paper records and digital archive will be deposited with the Northamptonshire Archaeological Resource Centre at Chester Farm Heritage Park, Irchester. Northamptonshire Historic Environment Archive has allocated the investigations the event number ENN108879. The digital archive will also be deposited with the Archaeological Data Service.

Chapter 2

Evolution of the Panattoni Park landscape
from early prehistory to the early Roman period

PHASE 1: MESOLITHIC, NEOLITHIC AND BRONZE AGE ACTIVITY

Early Mesolithic flint scatter in Area 4

Excavation of middle Iron Age features in the southern part of the excavation area uncovered a small concentration of early Mesolithic flint preserved within a shallow hollow (Fig. 2.1). The hollow was *c* 4m across and 0.05m deep and was investigated by means of a single 1m-wide sondage across the middle. The fill of the hollow comprised a firm mid-yellowish brown sandy clay (4235) that presumably represented the remains of a truncated soil layer. The flints within the layer appear to represent the *in situ* debris from a knapping event in which cores were worked to produce blades and tools (see Lawrence, Chapter 4).

Early prehistoric pits in Area 4

No early prehistoric pottery was recovered during the excavation but two pits in Area 4 (4224 and 4226) were attributed to this period on the basis of their small lithic assemblages (Fig. 2.1).

Pit 4224, near the northern end of the excavation area, was a shallow bowl-shaped feature, 0.96m across and 0.28m deep, that had been backfilled with a mixture of fire-cracked stone and black, charcoal-rich soil (4223; Fig. 2.2). Three flint flakes and some chips and burnt unworked flint were also recovered from a soil sample. Three undated pits of similar size were situated close to this feature but lacked the charcoal-rich backfill or any artefactual material and may not have been contemporary.

Pit 4226 was situated in the southern part of the area and was the only other feature which contained worked flint that was not certainly residual in a later feature, although the date of the pit is far from certain. The pit was oval, measuring 1.64m by 1.02m and 0.28m deep, and contained a single bladelet and one piece of burnt unworked flint.

Late Bronze Age pit 5129

The only feature that produced Bronze Age material was shallow subrectangular pit 5129, located in the north-eastern part of Area 5 (see Fig. 2.14). The pit was 1.4m long and 0.2m deep and contained sherds from two vessels, comprising a rim sherd from a vessel with an in-curved rim and body and rim sherds from a shouldered jar with an out-turned rim.

PHASE 2: MIDDLE IRON AGE

Middle Iron Age activity was represented by part of an enclosure in Area 2 West, a settlement in Area 4 that included at least eight roundhouses, and a pit alignment in Area 5 (Fig. 2.3).

Features in Area 2

At the south-western limit of Area 2, part of a curved ditch (2455) was uncovered that continued beyond the excavated area and probably represented the north and west sides of a small enclosure, although whether this was circular or subrectangular is uncertain (Fig. 2.4). The ditch was quite substantial, with a depth of 0.88m, and nine small sherds (30g) from a middle Iron Age globular vessel were recovered from its lower fill (2454), as well as five sherds (71g) in an Iron Age fabric that could not be dated more precisely.

Within the area enclosed by the ditch were a tightly clustered group of two pits (2472 and 2474) and a short linear feature (2477). All three features were shallow, measuring no more than 0.18–0.24m deep. The fill of pit 2472 mostly comprised cobble-sized stones that were heat-discoloured and friable, and this feature and the linear feature both contained further small sherds of Iron Age pottery but no other finds.

Settlement in Area 4

The settlement comprised at least eight round-houses, several posthole groups that evidently represent structures of some description although none could be resolved into a definitive form, and an L-shaped ditched boundary. The boundary does not appear to have formed a complete circuit enclosing the settlement and may instead have formed part of an arrangement of broadly recti-linear boundaries that was indicated by geophys-ical anomalies extending to the south of the excavation area (Figs 1.3 and 2.1). It is unlikely that the settlement extended significantly to the west, north or east of the excavated area since no contemporary features were recorded in the evaluation trenches in these locations. Stratigraphic relationships enabled the features, including the boundary ditch, to be resolved broadly into two subphases (2a and 2b, Fig. 2.1), although a sequence of intersecting ring gullies in the south-eastern part of the settlement hinted at a more complex development. Some features, including all the posthole groups, shared no stratigraphic relationships with other features and so could not be assigned to a specific subphase.

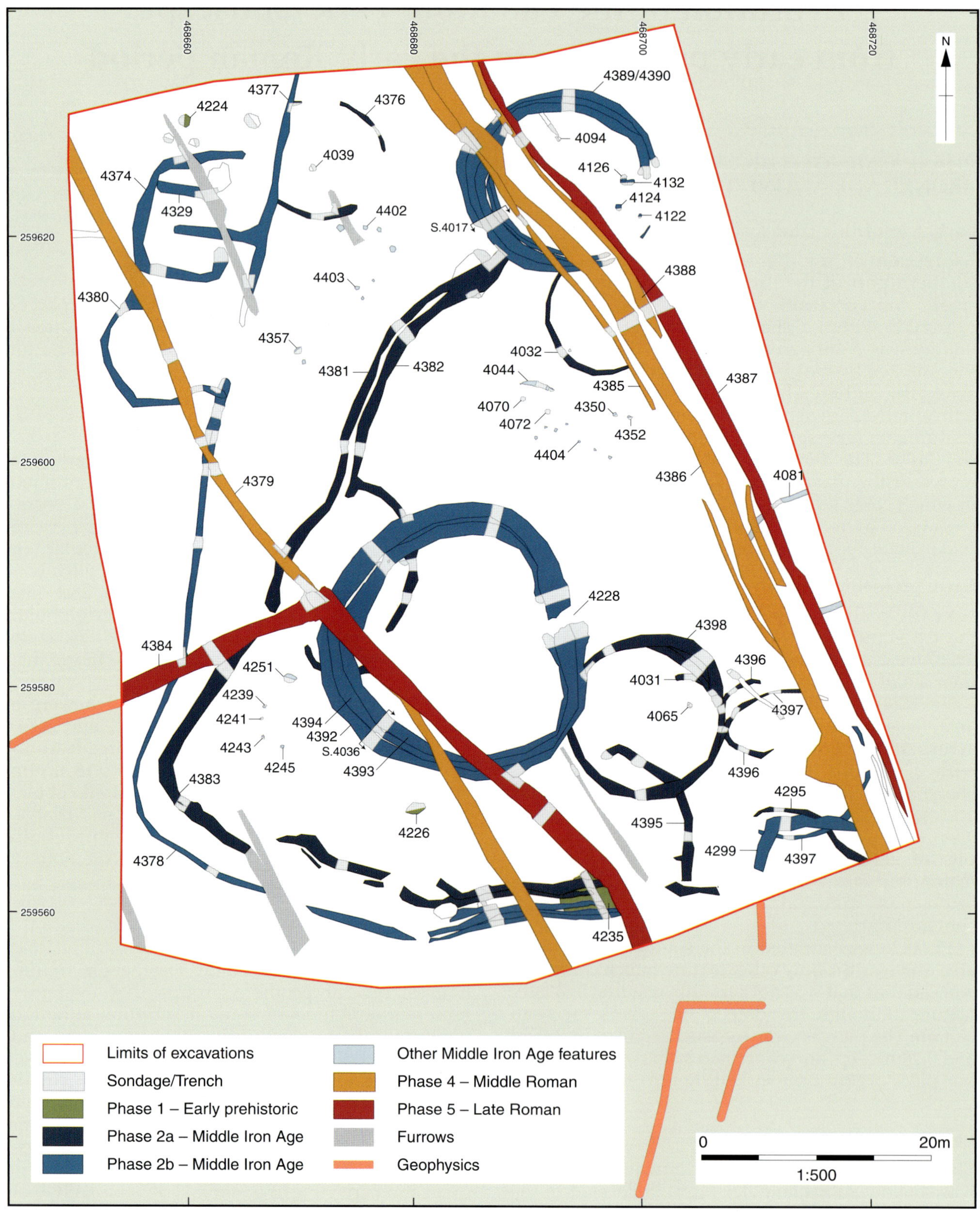

Fig. 2.1 Plan of features in Area 4

Fig. 2.2 Early prehistoric pit 4224, view to east, scale 1m

Artefactual evidence comprised only small groups of pottery and animal bone; the composition of the pottery assemblages from the two subphases was identical.

Subphase 2a

The features allocated to this subphase comprised the original iteration of the ditched boundary (4381, 4382 and 4383) and four ring gullies (4032, 4376, 4396 and 4398).

L-shaped boundary ditch

The ditch was not substantial, ranging from 0.25m to 0.4m in depth, and the boundary extended for *c* 55m from north-east to south-west before turning eastward and extending for a further *c* 50m. To the north-east it was cut by a subphase 2b ring gully and its extent to the east was indistinct due to truncation by later features and medieval furrows. Two curving ditches (4295 and 4395) near the south-eastern limit of the excavation area may have been associated boundaries, perhaps representing small sub-enclosures since they were clearly not ring gullies. A break in the western part of the main boundary may represent an original entrance but had been largely obscured by a Roman ditch, only the north side surviving. The southern part of the boundary was represented by a single ditch (4383), but north of the entrance it comprised two closely spaced ditches (4381 and 4382). Adjacent to the entrance ditch 4382 diverged from its partner to form an oval enclosure adjoining the boundary. The enclosure measured 15m by 10m. It was significantly truncated by later features but appeared to have had two entrances: one to the south-west, adjacent to the entrance through the main boundary, and the other to the south-east.

Ring gullies

The boundary evidently did not represent the limit of the settlement since a ring gully (4376) was situated beyond it in the north-western part of the excavation area. The gully measured 10m in diameter and 0.2m deep and was discontinuous, with substantial breaks to the north, west and south-east. A single shallow feature (4089), which

may have been a pit or a posthole, was situated within its footprint.

Ring gully 4032 was also situated in the northern part of the excavation area, albeit further east, within the area encompassed by the boundary ditch. Much of the feature had been destroyed by a sequence of Roman boundary ditches and only the south-east side survived. The remaining part of the gully was 0.23m deep and its curvature indicated an original circuit with a diameter of *c* 10m.

Two intersecting ring gullies (4396 and 4398) were recorded near the south-east limit of the excavation area. Gully 4396 was the earlier of these and was also by far the smallest such feature on the site. Only the western half of the circuit survived and was nowhere more than 0.1m deep, its projected diameter amounting to a little over 6m. The east side of gully 4396 was cut by gully 4398, which was the only ring gully in this subphase to exhibit evidence for recutting. It measured 12.5–13m in diameter and was slightly elongated to the north-east, where three successive cuts were identified, the earliest only 0.48m deep but the later versions quite steep-sided and 0.55–0.70m deep. Within the ring gully was a single pit or posthole (4065) and part of a curving gully (4031) that may represent a small ring gully similar to gully 4396, although not enough survived to be certain.

Subphase 2b

This subphase comprised a realignment of the boundary ditch and three further ring gullies.

L-shaped boundary ditch

The boundary was re-established on a somewhat different alignment (4377 and 4378), the east–west branch being moved 2–2.5m to the south and the northern part moved from the north-eastern orientation of its original form to a more northerly alignment. The ditch was of similar proportions to its predecessor and again was interrupted by a single entrance, 4.7m wide. The entrance was associated with a pair of enclosures (4374 and 4380) adjoining the west side of the ditch, which presumably served as replacements for the enclosure, defined by ditch 4382, that was formerly attached to the east side. Enclosure 4374 was roughly rectangular and measured 10.0m by 6.2m. It was enclosed on the north, west and south sides by a shallow ditch, with ditch 4377 apparently serving as the east side. A short return at the south-east corner of the enclosure and a ditch that branched off ditch 4377 combined to form what appeared to be a complex entrance from the south, and a further short ditch (4329) may have been an internal division. This enclosure was adjoined to the south by curvilinear enclosure 4380, which was *c* 10m across. Traffic accessing the entrance through the main boundary would have had to pass between the two enclosures.

At the south-eastern limit of the excavation area was an L-shaped ditch (4299), 0.5m deep, that had

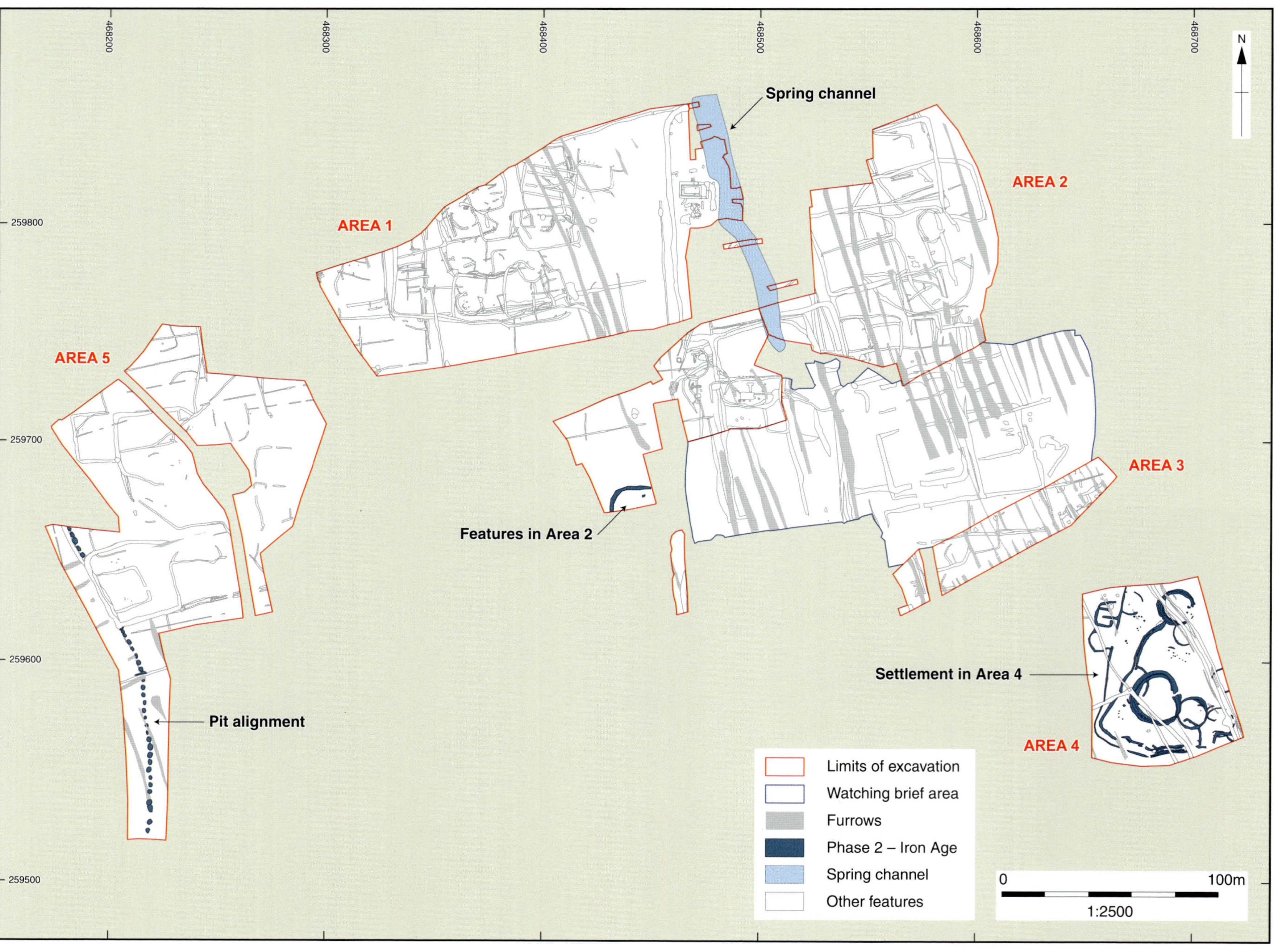

Fig. 2.3 Plan of all middle Iron Age (Phase 2) features

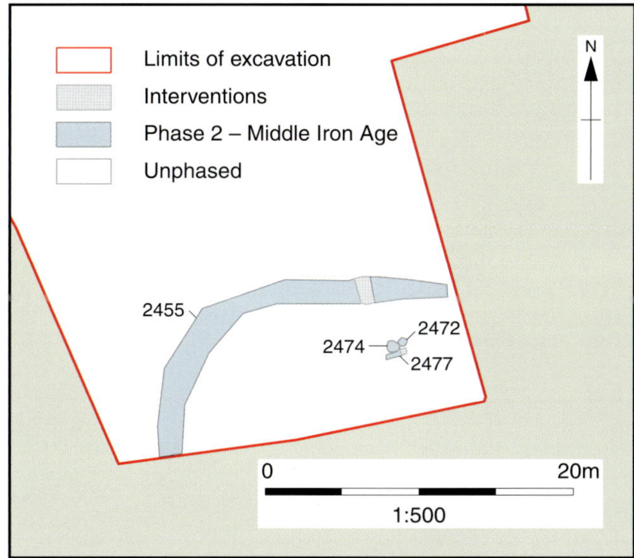

Fig. 2.4 Middle Iron Age features in Area 2

Fig. 2.6 Section through the west side of ring gully 4389/4390, view to north-west, scale 1m

been identified by the geophysical survey. The geophysical anomaly continued beyond the southern edge of the excavation where, with a further L-shaped ditch, it appeared to form part of an arrangement of broadly rectilinear boundaries.

Ring gullies

Two of the ring gullies in this subphase exhibited evidence for repeated recutting. Five successive phases were identified on the west side of the north-ernmost gully (4389/4390), although elsewhere only three were present, the later iterations having

presumably completely truncated their predecessors at these locations (Fig. 2.5, section 4017 and Fig. 2.6). The diameters of the various phases ranged from 12–15m, and the depths from 0.1–0.5m. In all its phases, the structure had a south-east-facing entrance, *c* 7.5m wide, which was associated with three postholes (4122, 4124 and 4126/4132) that probably repre-sented a rectangular porch structure 2.1m wide. One of the post settings was formed of two intersecting sockets (4126 and 4132), indicating that the post had been replaced during the lifetime of the building. Otherwise, the only structural element within the gully was a single posthole (4094).

Ring gully 4392/4393/4394 cut subphase 2a ring gully 4398 and the enclosure associated with the entrance through the subphase 2a L-shaped boundary ditch (Fig. 2.7). Three phases were identified, the earliest gully (4394), 0.3–0.4m deep, being largely truncated by the two subsequent cuts

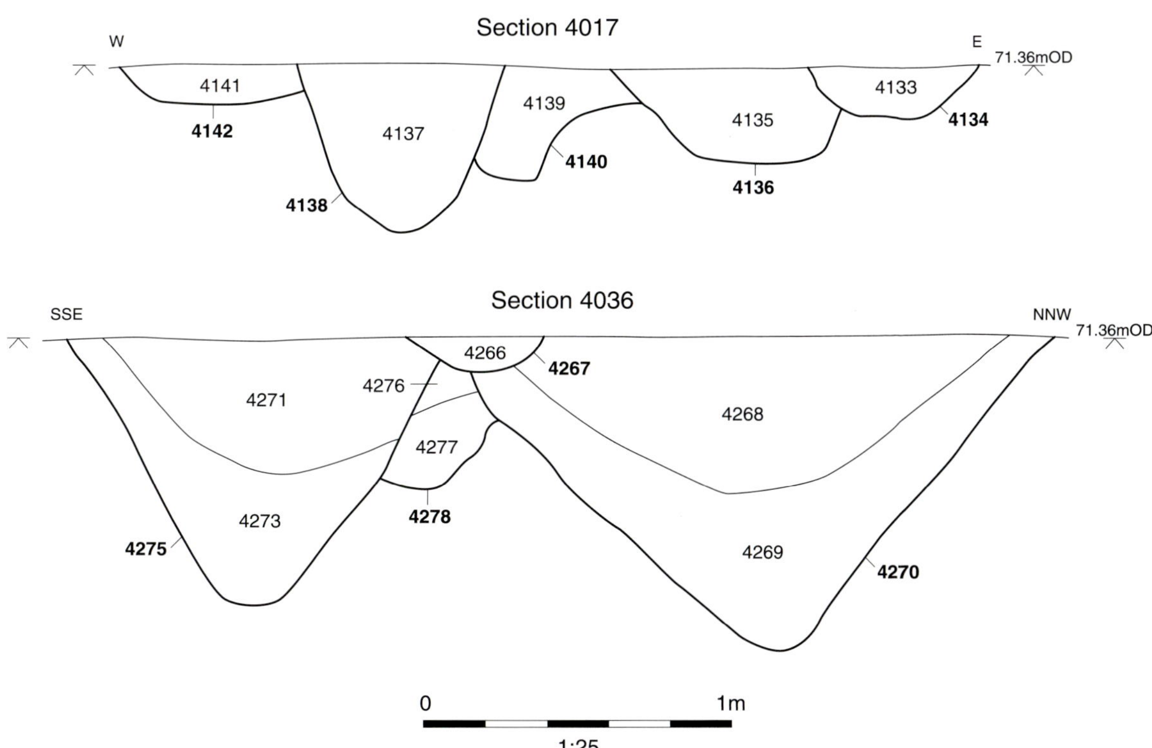

Fig. 2.5 Sections through middle Iron Age ring gullies

Fig. 2.7 Section through the south-west quadrant of ring gully 4392/4393/4394, view to north-west

(4392 and 4393), which were relatively substantial V-shaped gullies up to 1.15m deep (Fig. 2.5, section 4036). In all three iterations the gully had an unusual shape, measuring 19.75–22.50m by 17.5-19.5m with a rather flattened east side at the centre of which was an entrance a little over 1m wide. Fuel ash slag, perhaps from a hearth within the building, was recovered from the northern terminal of the final phase of the ditch, and a roughly constructed metalled surface (4228) lay within the entrance (Fig. 2.8).

South-east of ring gully 4392/4393/4394 lay ring gully 4397, which cut subphase 2a ring gullies 4396 and 4398. It had a diameter of 12.5m and was repre-

Fig. 2.8 Metalling 4226 in entrance to ring gully 4392/4393/4394, view to west, scales 1m and 2m

sented by a gully that was typically 0.1–0.16m deep but in one location measured 0.4m deep, with two breaks on the east side and a much larger one on the west.

Other middle Iron Age features

Ring gully 4081

Ring gully 4081 was situated at the eastern edge of the excavation area, lying partly under the baulk, and much of it had been destroyed by Roman ditches. The remaining part was 0.14m deep and had a diameter of 10m.

Posthole groups and pits

Four posthole groups were identified, and although none produced any artefactual material, their location within the settlement strongly suggests that they were contemporary with it. Posthole group 4402 was a curved alignment of four features, extending over 5.2m, located in the northern part of the excavation area, immediately south of ring gully 4376. None of the postholes was excavated. A short distance south of this was a group of three postholes (4403) whose arrangement suggests they may have formed three elements of a small rectangular four-post structure measuring 1.75m by 0.95m. Again, the postholes were not excavated. Further south again was pit 4357, a somewhat isolated bowl-shaped feature, 0.85m by 0.75m across and 0.28m deep, that was lined by a thin basal layer of charcoal and may have been the remains of a hearth. Further east, posthole group 4404 comprised an L-shaped arrangement of unexcavated postholes that extended for 6.3m NW–SE and 1.2m NE–SW. Two pairs of postholes located immediately to the north-west (4070 and 4072) and north-east (4350 and 4352) may have been associated with this structure, as may a short gully (4044) to the north. An arc of four postholes (4239, 4241, 4243 and 4245) was excavated in the south-western part of the settlement. Pit 4251, a shallow feature only 0.28m deep with a flat base and a dark grey fill, lay close by.

Pit alignment in Area 5

The dating of the pit alignment is problematic (as discussed below), but it has been assigned broadly to the middle Iron Age. The alignment was first identified by the geophysical survey, extending for at least 200m on a dog-legged north–south orientation, and its character was confirmed by excavation of two pits during the evaluation. The shape of Area 5 was designed to expose the alignment for a length of 150m, where it would be impacted by cutting as part of the development groundworks; the northern end of the alignment lay in an area that was retained *in situ* and the southern end in an area subject only to fill operations (Fig. 2.9).

A total of 37 pits were identified within the excavation area, and more had certainly been present in the northern half, where the alignment was obscured by a late Iron Age/early Roman ditch that superseded the pits as the boundary marker. Thirteen pits were sampled by excavation, ten being half-sectioned and the others having smaller interventions excavated to investigate specific stratigraphic relationships. The pits were typically oval or sub-circular in shape with steep sides and flattish, sometimes slightly concave bases, and ranged in size from 1.7m by 1.4m to 2.5m by 2.1m and 0.48–0.86m deep (Figs 2.9–2.13). The various pits were recorded as having between one and three fills, although the fills were generally quite homogeneous and probably all represent the same gradual silting process.

Artefactual material was limited to small scraps of pottery and animal bone from a handful of pits, and dating the alignment has been hampered by the undiagnostic character of the sherds, as well as the possibility that such small groups may be residual. Furthermore, most of the material came from middle and upper fills, where it may have been deposited during silting some considerable time after the pits were actually dug. The only pottery recovered from a bottom fill was also possibly the earliest sherd, part of a vessel with a slightly flared neck in a possibly early Iron Age fabric with leached shell or limestone voids, found with two undiagnostic sherds in fill 5125 of pit 5095 (Fig. 2.10, section 5006). Two sherds from a possible shouldered jar in the same fabric (Fig. 4.4, no. 3) were recovered from the main fill (5208) of pit 5207, but its position within the pit is not known (Fig. 2.10, section 5023). No such shouldered jars were identified from the middle Iron Age features in

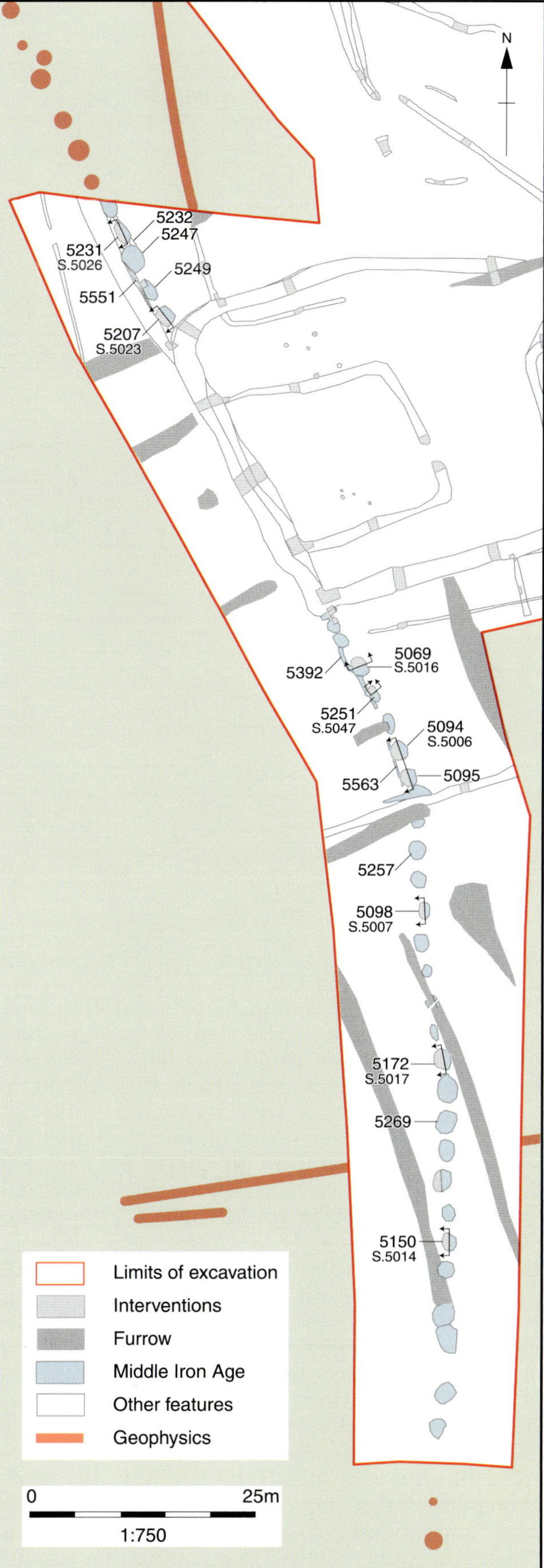

Fig. 2.9 Pit alignment in Area 5

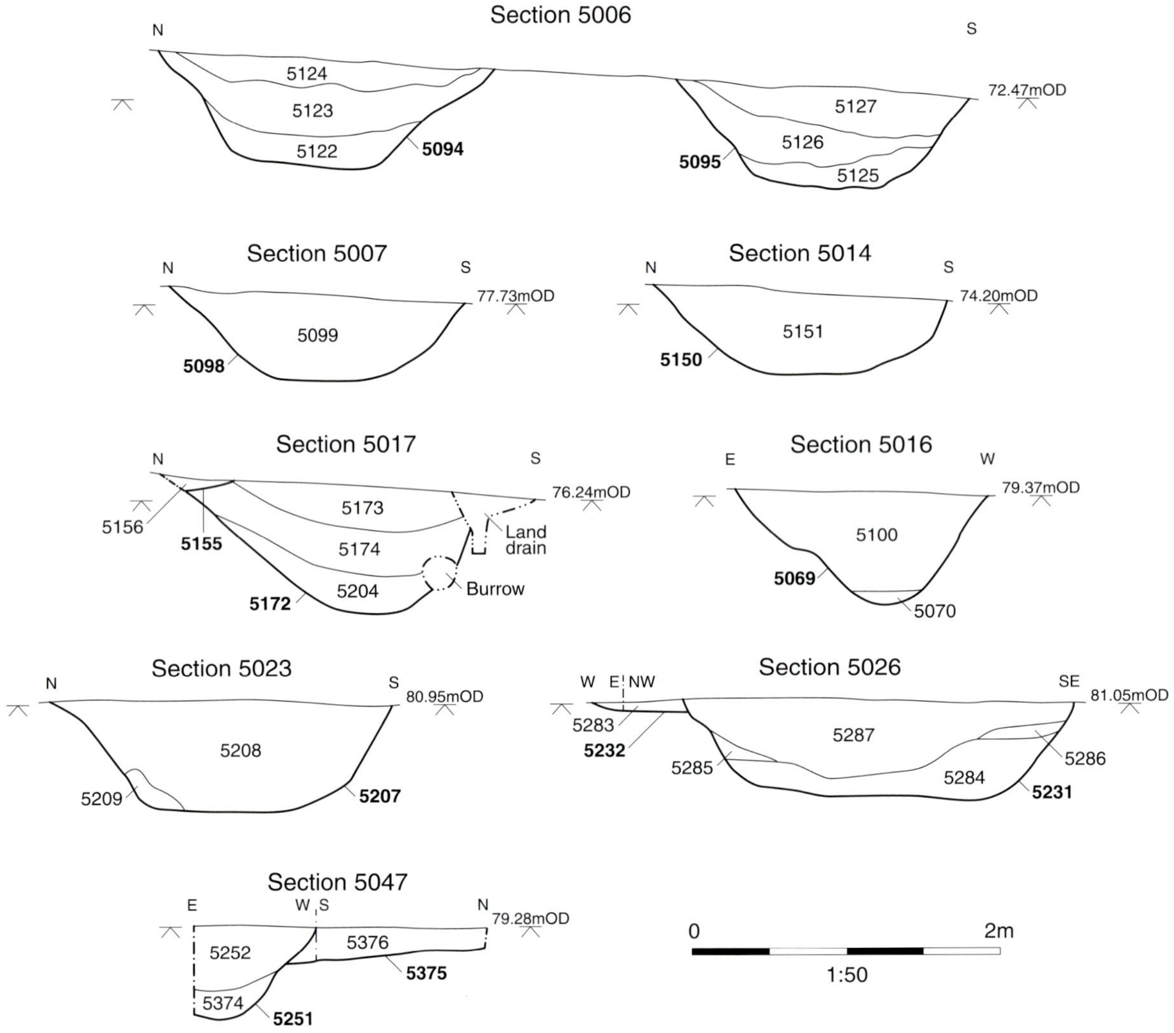

Section 5006

Section 5007

Section 5014

Section 5017

Section 5016

Section 5023

Section 5026

Section 5047

0   2m
1:50

Fig. 2.10 Pit alignment – sections through selected pits

Areas 2 and 4, suggesting that the pit alignment was earlier than the settlement. Pottery in shell-tempered fabric that could only be ascribed to a broad period spanning the middle Iron Age to the early Roman period was recovered from the middle or upper fills of several pits: a single body sherd was recovered from fill 5100 of pit 5069 (Fig. 2.10, section 5016), seven body sherds were recovered from fill 5252 of pit 5251 (Fig. 2.10, section 5047), and three sherds of pottery were collected from the middle fill (5123) of pit 5094; the top fill (5124) of the latter pit contained a sherd of grog-tempered ware (E80) dating to the late Iron Age or early Roman period. Four body sherds in the same shell-tempered fabric were also recovered from the surface of unexcavated pit 5257. Pottery recovered during the evaluation was limited to a few sherds of late Iron Age/early Roman pottery from the main fill of a pit beneath the late Iron Age/early Roman ditch that was not seen during the excavation, and one sherd of late 1st-century Roman pottery from the only fill of a feature that equates to pit 5269. Taken together, this evidence suggests that the alignment was probably constructed

during the early Iron Age or the early part of the middle Iron Age, before the settlement in Area 4 was established, and silted up over the course of the following centuries, during which a handful of sherds were deposited. It was evidently still visible and significant as a boundary during the late Iron

Fig. 2.11 Pit 5107, view to south-east, scale 1m

Fig. 2.12 Pits 5094 and 5095, view to east, scale 1m

Age, when the northern part was replaced by a ditch that defined the western limit of the newly constructed settlement (see below).

In three locations (5232, 5392 and 5563; Fig. 2.9; Fig. 2.10, sections 5026 and 5047) shallow gullies were recorded that lay on the same alignment as, and were cut by, the pits. The gullies may be the remains of an earlier form of the boundary, or may have been associated with the marking out of the intended line on which the pits were to be dug. The gullies were nowhere more than 0.25m deep, and usually considerably shallower, and contained no artefactual material. Near the northern limit of the alignment was a similar gully (5551) that cut pits 5247 and 5249. It was unclear whether this represented a further version of the boundary or whether the stratigraphic relationships with the pits were wrongly recorded.

Fig. 2.13 Pit 5150, view to east, scale 1m

PHASE 3: LATE IRON AGE TO EARLY ROMAN

Settlement in Areas 1 and 5 (Fig. 2.14)

The boundary defined by the middle Iron Age pit alignment in Area 5 continued to be significant into the later part of the Iron Age, when the northern part was recut as a ditch that defined the western limit of a ditched complex. Three subphases (3a–3c) were defined on the basis of stratigraphic evidence and ceramic dating, all falling within the period between 50 BC and AD 100. Post-conquest pottery forms first appeared in small quantities during the second of these subphases (3b) and increased in number in subphase 3c, indicating that the settlement was established during the late Iron Age and continued in use into the early part of the Roman period. There appears to have been a hiatus in activity before the landscape was reorganised shortly after the middle of the 2nd century, and no elements of the complex were incorporated into the new arrangement.

Subphase 3a

The earliest late Iron Age activity was situated at the north end of Area 5 and comprised a curvilinear gully (5536) and an L-shaped ditch (5540) that may have formed part of a rectilinear enclosure. Both ends of gully 5536 had been truncated by later features, but it may have been the surviving part of the penannular gully of a roundhouse. If this were the case, then only the northern perimeter survived, as a gully up to 0.25m deep with a projected diameter of *c* 17m. A single sherd provided evidence

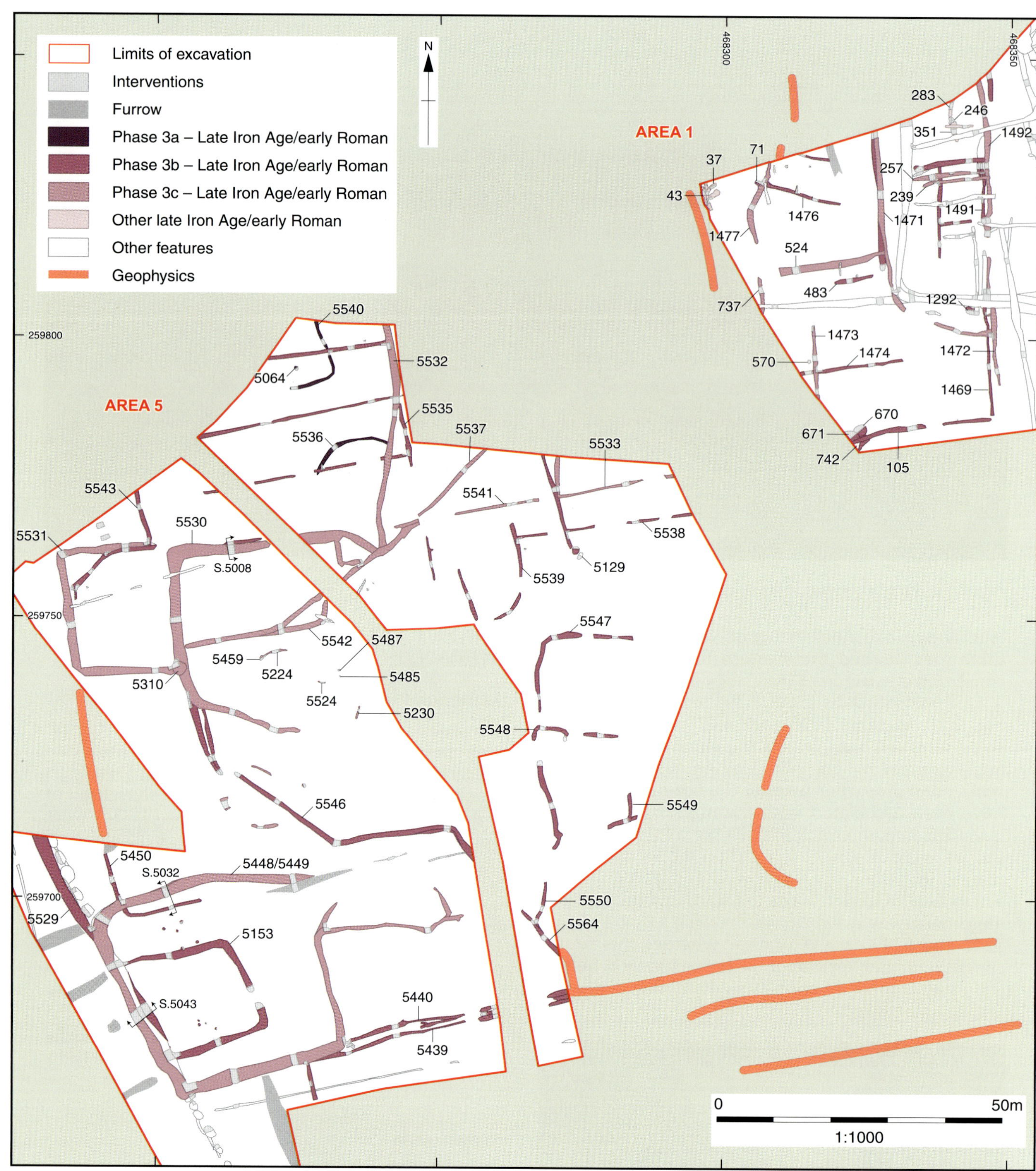

Fig. 2.14 Late Iron Age/early Roman settlement in Areas 1 and 5

for its date. Ditch 5540 was also 0.25m deep and enclosed an area that measured 8.5m E–W and at least 10.2m N–S, continuing beyond the excavation area to the north and apparently open to the west. The only artefactual material comprised two sherds of pottery from the western terminal. Within the area thus enclosed was a single undated pit (5064), which

was only 0.1m deep and had a charcoal-rich fill that mostly comprised oak and ash.

Subphase 3b

The features of subphase 3a were cut by the ditches that were established in subphase 3b. The complex

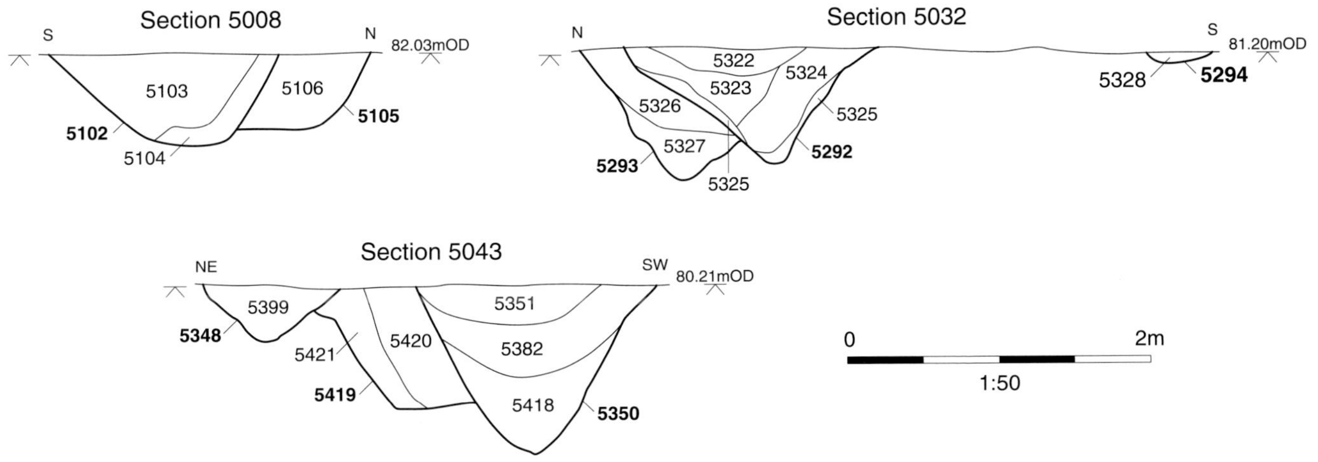

Fig. 2.15 Sections through late Iron Age/early Roman features

was clearly delineated by perimeter ditches that were significantly larger than the ditches that defined the internal divisions. The western boundary was represented by ditch 5529 (Fig. 2.15, section 5043, cut 5348), which followed the line of the middle Iron Age pit alignment and was 0.68m deep in the only intervention in which it was fully excavated. To the south, the limit was defined by ditches 5439 and 5440, which are likely to have represented successive iterations of the boundary, in addition to an intermittent third ditch, although their sequence could not be established. Ditch 5439 was 0.17–0.42m deep and ditch 5440, 0.32–0.64m deep. The ditches in Area 1 were typically a little shallower than those in Area 5, presumably indicating greater truncation in this field by more recent ploughing, and the eastern boundary of the settlement (1469/1491) was 0.11–0.30m deep. The ditches of the internal divisions, in contrast, were rarely more than 0.25m deep, and the majority were much shallower. The total area thus enclosed appears to have been trapezoidal and encompassed an area that measured *c* 165m E–W and more than 185m N–S, the northern limit lying somewhere beyond the northern edge of the excavation area. These limits were consistent with the results of the geophysical survey and evaluation, which identified no features to the west or south of the excavated areas. The southern boundary was detected by the geophysical survey as an anomaly that extended for a further 75m east of Area 5 before being obscured by a modern pipe trench. No evaluation trenches were excavated north of Area 5, and the northern edge of Area 1 corresponded with the limit of the development on the frontage of the A4500, so the arrangement here is unknown.

Southern and central parts of the settlement, Area 5

The only exception to the general pattern of there being only shallow ditches within the interior of the complex was enclosure 5153, which had ditches 0.49–0.68m deep. The enclosure was situated at the south-western corner of the complex and its ditch was integral to perimeter ditch 5529. It was roughly square in plan, measuring 16–17m across, and an entrance 2m wide, off-centre on the east side, provided access from the rest of the complex. The only internal features were a cluster of four postholes near the southern side of the enclosure, but the greater size of the ditches clearly marked this enclosure out as having a function distinct from the rest of the complex and it may have been the location of a domestic structure that has not survived. The only other possible structural evidence within the complex comprised a group of five postholes immediately north of enclosure 5153, one of which may have cut the edge of the enclosure ditch, although this relationship was not certain. Further north again lay an L-shaped ditch (5450) that probably formed an enclosure with an alignment parallel to enclosure 5153.

Enclosure 5153 and the associated features in the south-western part of the complex were divided from features in the central area by a dog-legged ditch (5546/5564) that extended across the complex on a NW–SE alignment. Ditch 5550 branched off this boundary and linked it to a possible pair of conjoined enclosures (5547 and 5549) in the eastern part of the excavation area. Interpretation of the precise arrangement is difficult, since the ditches were very slight, typically less than 0.2m deep, and were intermittent due to truncation by later ploughing. Enclosure 5549 appeared, however, to be roughly rectilinear, measuring 18m by 13m, while L-shaped ditch 5547 defined an enclosure that adjoined its north side and measured 16m N–S and at least 15m E–W. Ditch 5548, which was U-shaped in plan, may have formed part of a small subenclosure situated at the junction of enclosures 5547 and 5549.

The northern part of the complex in Area 5 had a more regular rectilinear arrangement, typified by a series of ditches that defined rectilinear enclosures adjoining the west side of N–S ditch 5535, possibly delimited to the west by ditch 5543. Ditch 5538 only survived intermittently but lay on a similar E–W alignment. At the west end of this ditch was a D-shaped enclosure (5539) that measured *c* 16m by 15m.

Eastern part of the settlement, Area 1

The part of the complex exposed within the western end of Area 1 included the eastern boundary (1469/1491), with an arrangement of N–S and E–W aligned ditches that defined rectilinear divisions within. A small rectangular enclosure measuring 10m by 7m adjoined perimeter ditch 1491, with a continuation of the ditch which defined the west side of the enclosure, suggesting there may have been a second such enclosure adjacent to the south. Also in this area was a 4.5m-wide break between ditches 1469 and 1491, representing the only possible evidence for an entrance into the complex, but the ditches in this location were too shallow to be certain that the break was deliberate. West of this, N–S ditch 1471 and E–W ditches 105, 483 and 1474 were evidently the remains of a system of rectilinear divisions, while ditch 1476 and an unexcavated ditch that lay parallel to it 6.5m to the north extended on a more oblique alignment.

Waterhole 351 was situated near the northern limit of the excavation area and had been truncated by a later ditch. The surviving lower part of the shaft was 0.56m in diameter and extended to a depth of 0.98m. The basal fill comprised a black silty clay characteristic of deposition in standing water and had accumulated to a depth of 0.3m, from which a single sherd of pottery was recovered. The surviving fills above this probably represented deliberate backfill.

At the south-western corner of the excavation area, ditch 105 cut large intercutting pits 670, 671 and 742, each of which was more than 2m across. Pits 670 and 671 were excavated, pit 670 proving to be the earlier and 0.55m deep, filled largely with redeposited natural clay. Pit 671 was more substantial, measuring 4.1m across and 1.1m deep. It, too, had a substantial deposit of redeposited material (712) at the base, which filled the lower 0.4m of the feature. Above this was a thin layer that appeared to be a dump of charred plant material (711) that included seeds of wheat, barley and flax as well as grasses and weeds. The backfill deposits that filled the bulk of the pit similarly contained a high proportion of charred plant material, although not as great a concentration as layer 711, and included a

discrete deposit of reddish clay that had been discoloured by heat (713) against the north-east side of the pit. The overlying backfill was also distinctly grey from the inclusion of further charred material.

Two discrete pits in somewhat disparate locations contained interesting groups of pottery. Pit 71, which lay near the north-western limit of the excavation area and had been truncated by the junction of ditches 1476 and 1477, contained a substantial part of a globular jar, and pit 1292, which was located close to eastern boundary ditch 1469, contained a single large sherd from a storage vessel.

Subphase 3c

Some elements of the settlement were subsequently altered or redefined. It is likely that some of the ditches from subphase 3b that were not affected by the rearrangement continued in use alongside the new boundaries, particularly those in the south-western part of Area 5.

Southern and central parts of the settlement, Area 5

The location of subphase 3b enclosure 5153 appears to have retained its special character, as the enclosure was replaced by larger enclosure 5448/5449. The enclosure was roughly square, *c* 32m across, with an out-turned entrance 8m wide at the north-east corner. The enclosing ditch was a substantial, V-shaped feature that was up to 1.15m deep and had been recut on one occasion (Fig. 2.15, sections 5032 and 5043; Figs 2.16–2.17). On the west and south sides it was dug along the alignments of earlier ditches 5529 and 5439/5440, and to the north it slighted the enclosure hitherto defined by ditch 5450. The south side of the entrance continued eastward as a boundary ditch that extended for 26m. No internal features were identified, unless the posthole groups near to enclosure 5153 belonged to this subphase.

A pair of conjoined enclosures (5530 and 5531) was constructed to the north of enclosure 5448/5449, in the west-central part of the complex. The ditches that defined these enclosures were notably deeper than those of the boundaries of

Fig. 2.16 *Late Iron Age/early Roman enclosure ditch 5448/5449 (middle and right) cutting boundary ditch 5529, view to north-west, scale 2m*

Fig. 2.17 *Section through north side of late Iron Age/early Roman enclosure ditch 5448/5449, view to north-east, scale 1m*

subphase 3b, typically measuring 0.5–0.65m deep, except for the southern part of enclosure 5530, which became progressively shallower and eventually petered out. Enclosure 5530 was the larger of the two and was subdivided by ditch 5542, which enclosed a rectangular subenclosure within the northern half that measured 28m by 15m. The subenclosure was accessed via an entrance at the east end and lacked any internal features. The southern half of enclosure 5530 was less regular in shape and had no definable eastern boundary. A few discrete features may have been associated with the enclosure, including a pair of undated postholes (5485 and 5487), two short linear gullies (5230 and 5524), and curving gully 5224, which was 4.4m long and ended in a pit or posthole (5459). Finds from this group of features were few, but gully 5524 contained articulating metacarpals from a pig. Enclosure 5531 adjoined the western side of enclosure 5530 and formed a quite regular rectangle in plan, measuring 20m by 17m with an entrance 3.5m wide at the north-eastern corner. Large circular pit 5310 had been dug into the junction where the enclosure ditches met. The pit was 2m across and 0.75m deep and yielded a few sherds of pottery and a ceramic spindle whorl made from a piece of early Roman pottery (SF 200; Fig. 4.12, no. 10).

To the east of this arrangement, ditches 5533 and 5541 formed a linear boundary that continued the alignment of the northern sides of enclosures 5530 and 5531 and extended beyond the excavation area. The only feature in the northern part of the excavation area that was attributed to this subphase was ditch 5532, which appeared to be partly a replacement for the earlier N–S boundary 5535.

The stratigraphically latest feature within the complex was ditch 5537, which lay on a NE–SW alignment that cut obliquely across ditches 5532, 5541 and 5542. The reason for its disparate orientation in relation to the rest of the boundaries is unknown.

Eastern part of the settlement, Area 1

The eastern boundary of the settlement was redefined by the digging of ditches 1472 and 1492, which replaced subphase 3b ditches 1469 and 1491. Within the complex, ditch 1471 was dug as a curving boundary for a large D-shaped enclosure, within which ditches 239, 246, 257 and 283 formed recti-

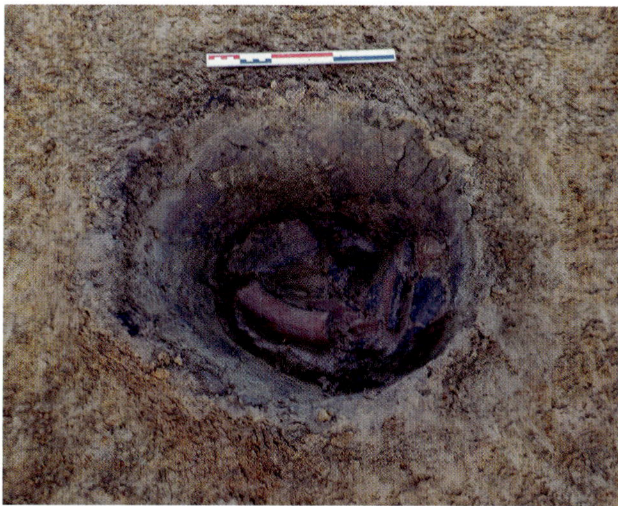

Fig. 2.18 Pot 571 in pit 570, view to north, scale 0.3m

linear subdivisions in the area where a small rectangular enclosure had previously been located. West of the D-shaped enclosure, ditches 737 and 1477 may have defined a boundary roughly parallel to ditch 1471, with ditches 524 and 1473 forming a rectilinear arrangement in the intervening area. A small concentration of intercutting features was situated at the north-west corner of the excavation area, but too little was exposed to allow any meaningful interpretation. One of these features, a shallow curving ditch (43) that was cut by a second similar ditch (37), yielded the end of a firebar, probably from a pottery kiln, although no wasters or other evidence for pottery production were found.

The only discrete feature in this area that was attributed to this subphase was pit 570, which appeared to have been dug specifically to hold an extremely large storage jar (571; Fig. 2.18). The pit was only 0.24m deep but the surviving pottery amounted to some 7.4kg of sherds, comprising the lower part of the vessel *in situ* on the base of the pit and the upper part which had evidently been pushed in when the feature was backfilled. It is possible that the vessel was used to store grain, since barley and oat grains, albeit few in number and poorly preserved, were recovered from an environmental sample taken from inside the vessel, although these may have been introduced with the backfill.

Chapter 3

The villa landscape, *c* AD 150–400

PHASE 4: MIDDLE ROMAN

Sometime shortly after the middle of the 2nd century the Panattoni Park landscape was completely reorganised, perhaps indicating that this was the date when the villa was established. It is difficult to be certain whether this followed a hiatus in activity or whether the late Iron Age/early Roman settlement continued in use until this time; certainly, deposition in the field ditches did not continue beyond the 1st century but this could indicate either than the fields had been abandoned or that they continued to be divided by above-ground boundaries, with the ditches by this time fully silted. Whatever the case, the eastern part of the former settlement was now slighted by the construction of a new enclosure system.

The newly designed landscape was composed of four distinct elements, defined by their location and function, each of which was further developed over time. These comprised a complex of enclosures in Area 1 adjacent to the villa; a possible temple or mausoleum (Building 1320) at the eastern edge of Area 1 beside a spring channel; a group of enclosures and crop-processing area south of this in Area 2; and a field system to the east of the channel in Areas 2 and 3 and the intervening Watching Brief Area (Fig. 3.1).

Enclosure complex adjacent to the villa (Fig. 3.2)

A group of predominantly rectilinear enclosures was constructed in the central part of Area 1, immediately south of the main villa complex. The full northern extent of the features was not established, as the intervening area, between the edge of the development area and the villa, lay beneath the modern road. Ditch 1385/1475/1495 formed the southern boundary, and the enclosures encompassed a clearly defined, broadly rectangular area that measured *c* 75m north–south and 70m east–west, with no contemporary features to the west and a similarly blank area *c* 30–40m wide to the east that separated them from the area of activity associated with Building 1320. The latter buffer was further emphasised by the substantial boundary represented by ditch 339 and its smaller companion ditch 1499 (see below). The function of the enclosures was not certain, although the artefactual assemblage was quite limited compared to the late Roman features in the same area, comprising *c* 17.5kg of pottery (a total inflated by four large localised deposits in ditches 342, 404, 717 and 1489,

which amounted to more than 7.5kg between them) and 41kg of ceramic building material with very little other material, and this, combined with the absence of any structures or domestic features may indicate an agricultural rather than domestic function, or perhaps a mixed agricultural/storage/working area associated with low status domestic activity. Ditch 342 defined a boundary that extended eastward from the complex, running along the northern edge of the excavation area, and was exposed for a length of 65m. The east end was cut by ditch 339 and the west end continued beyond the excavated area, as a result of which its relationship with the enclosures was not seen, being located in the area beneath the modern road. A pottery deposit recovered from a lower fill (333) near the east end of the ditch comprised six large sherds from a substantial storage jar in pink grogged ware, amounting to more than 2.5kg.

Ditch 1385/1475/1495 was traced for a distance of 140m, extending beyond the enclosures in both directions. To the west it continued beyond the excavation area and to the east it ended 8m from the north–south boundary represented by ditch 1499. It was notably more substantial than the ditches of the enclosures within, measuring 0.5–0.6m deep whereas the enclosure ditches were rarely much more than 0.3m deep. In contrast to either end of the ditch, the central part, where it bounded the enclosures, had been recut several times, creating a sequence of at least four phases that extended on parallel alignments with only slight intercutting (Fig. 3.3). The attention that was evidently taken in maintaining this part of the ditch is likely to reflect its significance as the boundary of the enclosure complex, and perhaps indicates that it had greater longevity than the parts to the east and west. The upper fill (1088) of the second ditch in this sequence (1089) contained the remains of a butchered cattle carcass and a horse scapula (Fig. 3.4). A pair of articulating cattle phalanges were recovered from the eastern part of the ditch (1495). The only features south of ditch 1385/1475/1495 were curving boundary ditch 1386 and the shallow ditch 1389 which branched off it. Both features extended beyond the southern limit of the excavation area, and unfortunately their arrangement could not be traced in the geophysical data, which in this area was obscured by furrows.

The most northerly enclosure was defined by N–S ditch 604 and angular ditch 404, which enclosed a roughly trapezoidal area measuring 18m from north

27

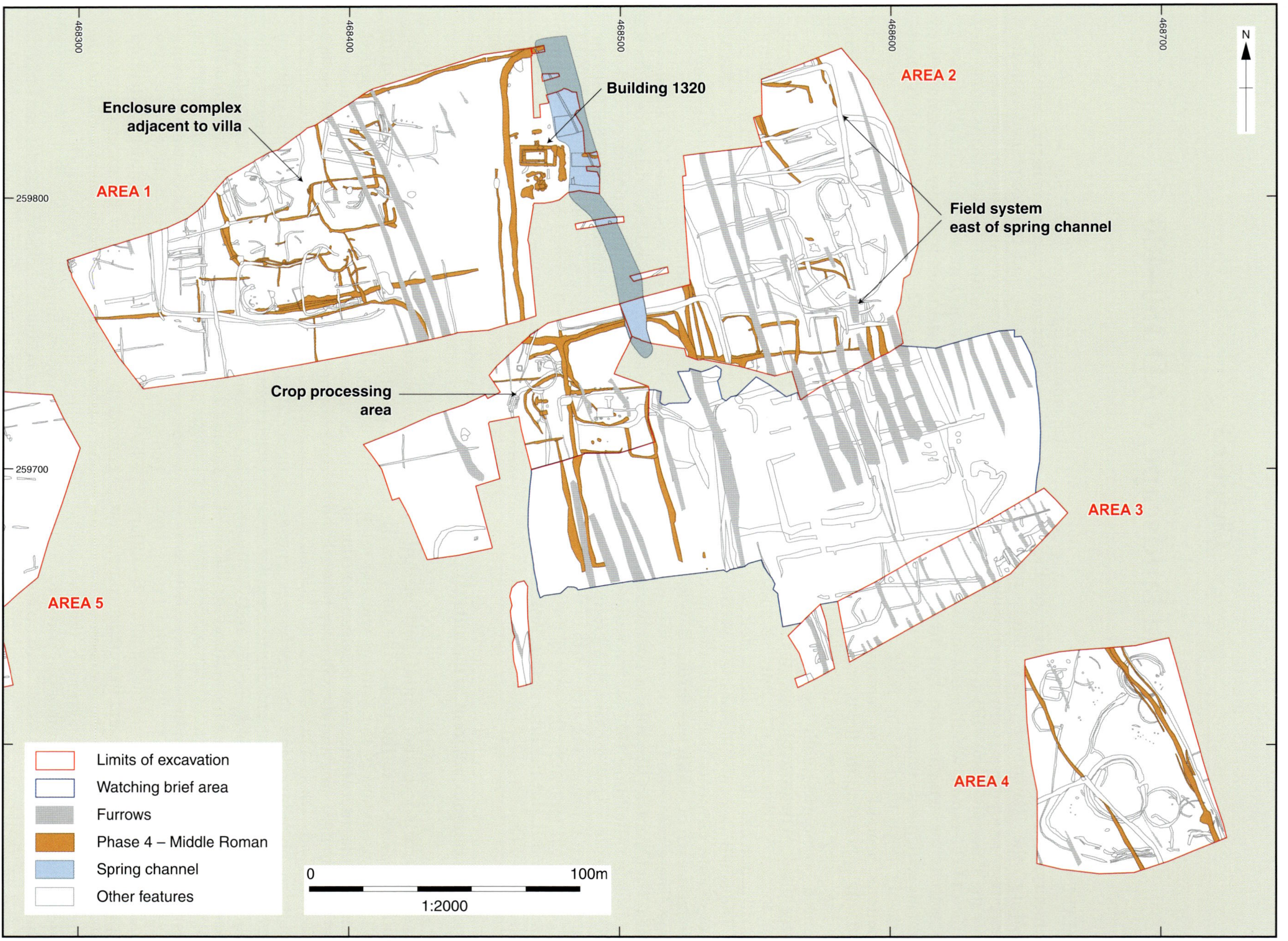

Fig. 3.1 Plan of all middle Roman (Phase 4) features

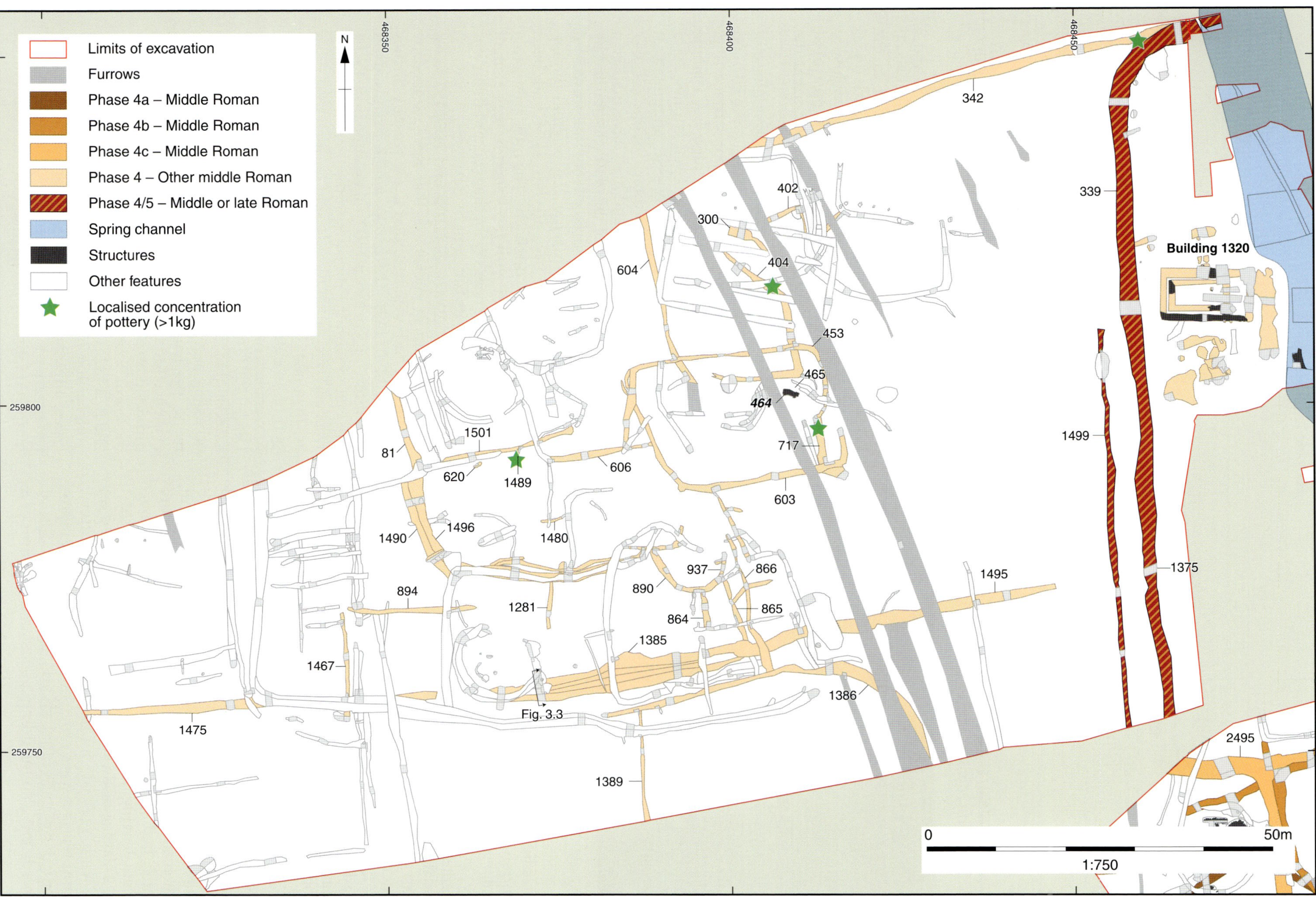

Fig. 3.2 The enclosure complex adjacent to the villa, Phase 4

29

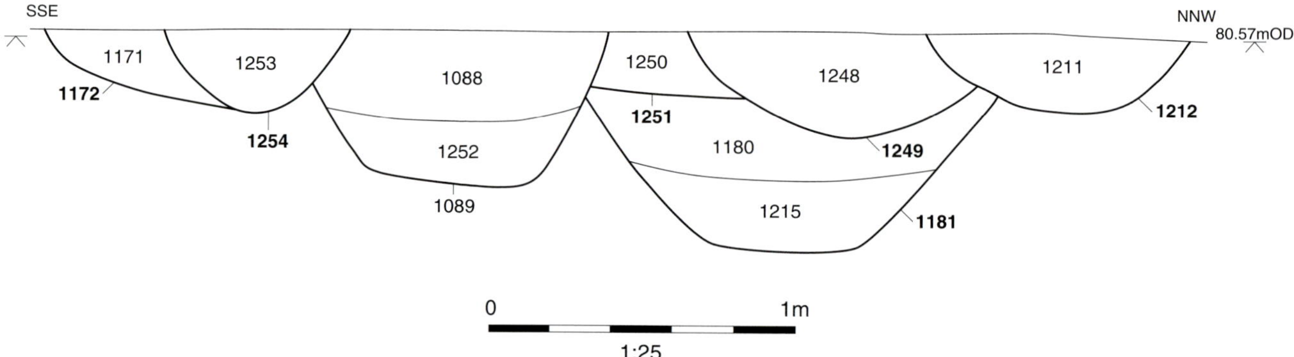

Fig. 3.3 Section through middle Roman boundary ditch 1385 and late Roman enclosure ditches 1245 and 1246, in the enclosure complex adjacent to the villa

Fig. 3.4 Butchered cattle carcass in fill 1088 of ditch 1385

to south and 16m wide. There was probably an entrance at the north end, although this area was somewhat obscured by late Roman Building 3 and by later furrows. Ditch 404 was notable for a deposit of more than 2kg of mixed pottery near the north-east corner of the enclosure. Adjacent, to the east of this enclosure, ditch 300, possible L-shaped ditch 402 and some other short lengths of ditch hint at the presence of related enclosures, but this area had been similarly affected by later features and consequently it was not possible to establish a coherent arrangement. The southern side of enclosure 404/604 formed the northern boundary of a large subrectangular enclosure that was enclosed to the west, south and east by ditch 603. The enclosure measured 26m by 14m and may have been accessed via entrances at the north-west corner, where there was a gap of *c* 8m between ditch 604 and the end of ditch 603, and on the east side, where the enclosure ditch had two phases, each of which was incomplete, leaving the enclosure partly open on this side. The earlier of these two phases (717) produced an assemblage of more than 1.8kg of pottery, comprising a wide range of vessels generally represented by individual sherds or small groups of sherds but also including a substantial portion of a

folded beaker in a reduced coarse ware fabric and a single large sherd from a pink grogged ware vessel. Enclosure 603 was subsequently extended to the north by the construction of a new ditch (453) which slighted the southern end of enclosure 404/604. The new layout of the enclosure measured 27m by 17m and no longer had an entrance at the north-west corner.

The only structure associated with this phase of the complex was situated within enclosure 603 and comprised a possible wall and floor surface (Fig. 3.5). The wall (464) was represented by a single course of blocky, roughly shaped stones, and extended for 2.2m on a NNW–SSE alignment. It included a complete lower rotary quern (SF 64), which had been placed flat and may have marked a threshold. The north side of the wall was abutted by an amorphous cobbled surface (465) that measured 2.6m NW–SE and 2.1m wide, the original dimensions of which did not survive as it had been truncated by Phase 5 ditch 716. The only artefactual evidence associated with the structure was a small group of pottery sherds from the wall and there was no evidence for its function or form.

West of enclosures 404/604 and 603/453 lay a pair of rectilinear enclosures that were divided by ditch 1501 and were bounded to the west by ditches 81 and 1490/1496. Ditch 606, which branched off the ditch of enclosure 603, also appeared to be associated with the division of these enclosures; its west end oversailed the east end of ditch 1501 in an arrangement that may have been designed to form part of an entrance arrangement for controlling the movement of livestock between the enclosures. Ditch 1490/1496, which defined the southern enclosure of this pair, had been recut on at least one occasion and followed a rather circuitous alignment, particularly on the southern side. Possible evidence for subdivisions within the enclosure was provided by a spur ditch (1489) that projected from the north boundary and a central short gully (1480). Ditch 1489 yielded an assemblage of 1.3kg of pottery that included a number of different vessel types, although much of the weight was accounted for by sherds from a large storage jar in a shell-tempered fabric from Harrold, Bedfordshire. Within

Fig. 3.5 Wall 464 and surface 465, view to east, scale 1m

this enclosure lay elongated oval pit 620, situated close to the north edge, which measured 1.3m by 0.5m and was interpreted as an oven due to the associated ceramic building material. Excavation of a single quadrant produced 11.4kg of material, comprising mainly large pieces of tegula and brick (Fig. 4.14, nos 17 and 21), together with a small fragment of flat tile and imbrex. One of the tegulae was burnt along its flange and adjacent surfaces, which is typical of pieces built into a flue wall where the flange is exposed in the face of the flue. Another had patches of burning on the upper and lower surfaces, suggesting possible use as floor or lining in an oven. A shattered brick had possibly been overfired or refired during use in the oven. The absence of associated evidence for occupation suggests that the oven was used for drying crops rather than in a domestic context. A spearhead of possible Iron Age date was also recovered from the feature (Fig. 4.11, no. 1).

There were evidently further enclosures between these and ditch 1385/1475/1495, although their boundaries were somewhat intermittent. Ditches 894 and 1467 defined the north and west sides of a rectangular enclosure that abutted ditch 1385/1475/1495. The enclosure was 12m wide and may have extended as far east as ditch 1281, beyond which was a similar enclosure that was bounded to the east by one of three parallel N–S ditches (864, 865 and 866). The same area of the complex included the only curvilinear enclosure in this phase, an asymmetrical semicircular feature

measuring 9m by 5m with no internal features, which had been constructed in two phases, the later of which (890) recut all but the east end of the earlier (937).

Building 1320 and the spring channel
(Figs 3.6 and 3.7)

East of the enclosure complex associated with the villa lay a strip of land some 30–40m wide that was devoid of archaeological features, that clearly separated the enclosures from activity associated with the spring channel at the eastern edge of Area 1, including Building 1320. The division of the two areas was further emphasised by a substantial V-shaped ditch (339) that ran north–south between the blank area and the channel-side complex. The ditch was exposed for some 95m, with no indication of a break to provide access between the two areas. At the north end it curved westward, joining the alignment of ditch 342, which it cut. To the south it extended into Area 2, where it similarly turned eastward as ditch 2495 (below). It was 3.14m wide and up to 0.93m deep at the north end but became less substantial to the south, where it was only 1.8m wide and 0.65m deep. It was largely devoid of artefactual material, but a small group of pottery was recovered from the upper fill near the south end (1375) and included a tiny sherd from a 4th-century Oxfordshire colour-coated ware necked bowl. Smaller ditch 1499, which was up to 0.26m deep, extended parallel to the southern part of ditch

Fig. 3.6 Building 1320 during excavation, viewed across the spring channel. The spoil heaps to the rear show the location of the enclosure complex adjacent to the villa. View to west

339, 4m to the west, and may have been part of the same boundary.

Building 1320

Building 1320 was situated, presumably deliberately, in close proximity to the west bank of the spring channel, from which it was separated by a distance of only *c* 5m. The building was oriented toward the channel and, if the extension at the eastern end of the building is correctly interpreted as a porch, then this was evidently the building's frontage. The concentric plan of the building, as well as indirect artefactual and palaeo-environmental evidence from the associated features and layers, has led to an interpretation as a temple or mausoleum (see Chapter 6).

The building had been comprehensively robbed, with very little of the original structural material left in place, and consequently its plan was reconstructed largely from the arrangement of robber trenches that fortunately appeared to have followed the wall lines quite accurately (Figs 3.7-8). This seems to indicate systematic demolition in antiquity, since the fill of the robber trenches was similar to the fills of other contemporary features in the vicinity. Stonework remained only at the north-east corner, along the south wall and in a few localised patches elsewhere. The few surviving areas of the footings were sufficient to demonstrate that the building was stone-founded, but the construction of the superstructure cannot be established except that it was evidently roofed with ceramic tiles, 46.4kg of which was recovered from the surrounding area and presumably derived from this building since no

other structure that might have been the source of this material was situated closer than Building 3, 50m away to the west. Fourteen fragments of stone tile were also recovered.

The building consisted of two concentric rectangular wall circuits, the outer circuit subsequently having been extended to the east. Before the extension, the building measured 10m by 7.5m, the stone footings of the outer circuit surviving along the entire length of the south wall (55) and in two closely spaced localised patches of the north wall (990 and 991), and the remainder of the footprint being indicated by a robber trench. The remains of the footings in each instance comprised a single course of pitched stones representing a wall 0.74–0.94m wide. Fortuitously, a key relationship was preserved at the south-east corner, where a stub of stonework that projected northward and evidently represented the remains of the southern end of the original east wall was clearly butted by the foundation of the eastern extension (Fig. 3.9). The inner circuit appears to have abutted the east wall and enclosed a single cell measuring 7m by 3m internally. Foundations, again of pitched stones, survived only in two locations, 0.7m wide in the west wall and 1.2m wide at the east end of the south wall. The only feature within the building was a single shallow pit filled with stone (898) that may have been a post setting.

The addition of the eastern extension increased the total length of the building to 13.5m. It was represented by a short length of pitched-stone foundation (1448) that projected from the south-west corner of the original building and a more substantial section at the north-east corner (1071)

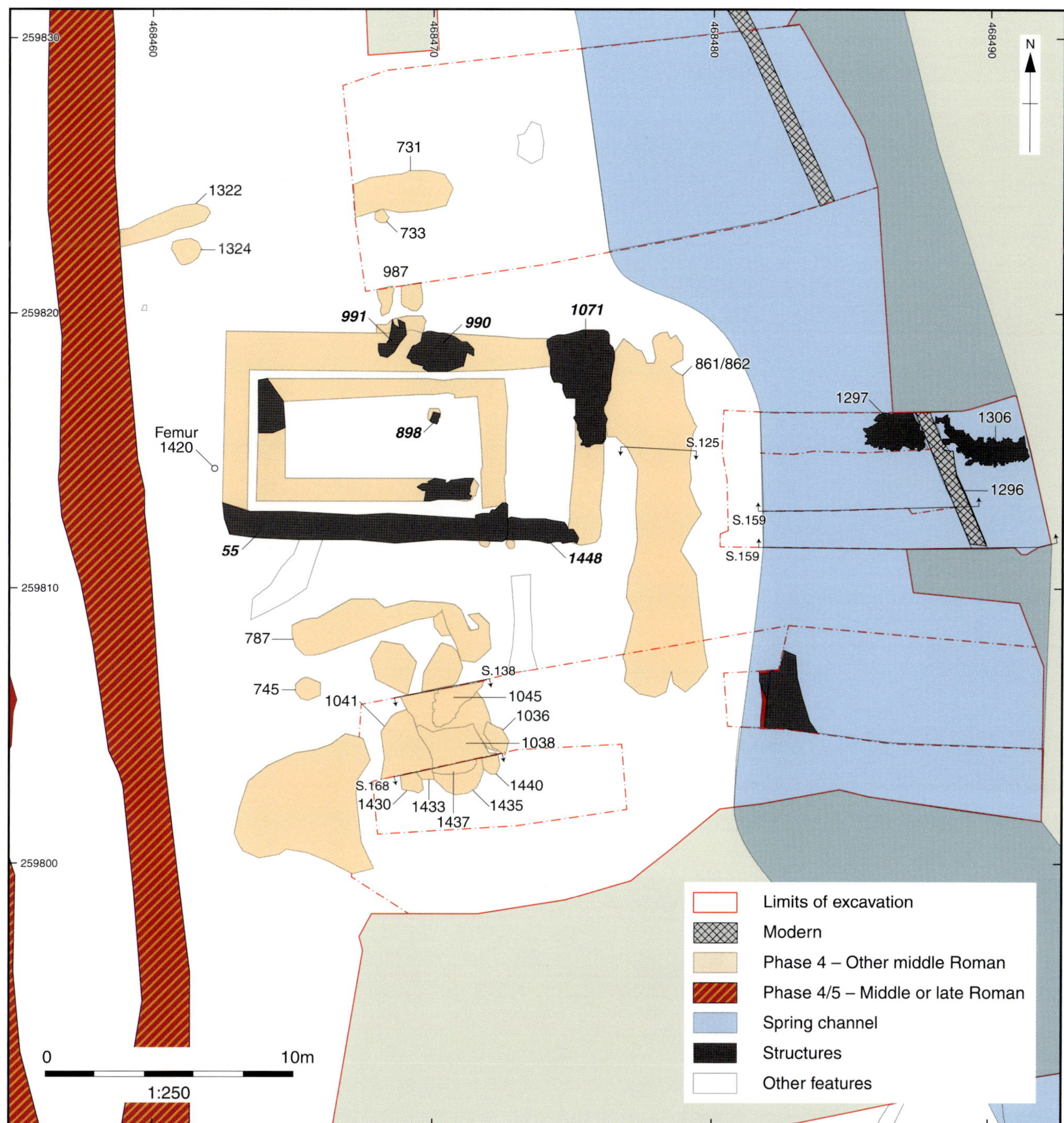

Fig. 3.7 Building 1320 and associated features

that constituted the best preserved section of stonework in the entire building (Fig. 3.10). Here the foundation trench (1071) achieved a maximum depth of 0.38m and three distinct courses of stonework were identified which presented some evidence of the care with which the building had been constructed. The lower course (1072) comprised a basal layer of rubble composed of large cobbles, on which a layer of pitched stone foundations (1073) had been constructed using flatter pieces evidently selected preferentially for this task. Along the outer, east face of the wall, and in one location on the inner face, a series of large, flat stones (1074), measuring up to 0.48 x 0.40 x 0.10m, had been laid flat, representing either the first course of the wall proper or a levelling course on which the actual wall was constructed. The greater depth of the foundation in this location than elsewhere in the building, and the additional basal layer of stone rubble, may indicate that greater precautions were considered necessary due to this part of the building being constructed on the softer sediments associated with the adjacent spring channel.

No artefactual material was recovered from stratified deposits associated with the building, but an

Fig. 3.8 Building 1320 during excavation, view to west

Fig. 3.9 Building 1320, the junction of the south wall and the cross wall, view to north

Fig. 3.10 The north-east part of Building 1320 during excavation, with surface 860 to the right and foundation 990 at extreme left, view to north-east

assemblage of 755g of pottery was recovered during surface cleaning (558). This was a chronologically mixed group that included parts of several 2nd-century samian bowls including a Dragendorff 79 dish with a name stamp of Beliniccus III (160–200), with later material represented by a sherd from an Oxfordshire white ware mortarium and a rim sherd from a 4th-century Nene Valley ware colour-coated necked jar/bowl. Given the small size of the group and the context of the sherds it is of course not possible to be certain how they relate to the use and demolition of the building, but the pottery may represent activity spanning the late 2nd to early 4th centuries, particularly given the similar chronological focus of the pottery from the surrounding features. The dating of the ceramic building material is similarly ambiguous, including both middle and late Roman tiles (see Poole, Chapter 4). The layer also contained some fragments of animal bone, some of which were burnt.

Outside the east end of the building were successive surfaces of gravel (862) and sandstone fragments (861), 1.1–1.2m wide, that extended for *c* 13m N–S, parallel to the frontage of the building and along the edge of the adjacent spring channel, partly overlying the edge of an infilled former channel (Fig. 3.15, section 125). A localised overlying layer of limestone rubble (860) may derive from demolition of the building.

The only evidence for human skeletal remains in the vicinity of the building was a femur (1420) that was recovered from immediately outside the south-west corner (Fig. 3.7). The bone lay within a poorly defined, extremely shallow feature but insufficient survived to be certain whether this was a deliberately dug grave.

Features north of the building

Two small areas of gravel (987) outside the north wall of the building, each a little under 1m across and no more than 0.03m thick, may be the remnants of a surface on this side of the building comparable to surface 861/862 to the east. Roughly 3m north of the building were two pits (733 and 1324), 0.47m and 0.24m deep, and two short sections of ditch (731 and 1322) on a similar ENE–WSW alignment that may represent a single boundary.

Features south of the building

South of the building was a complex of intercutting pits, which was bounded to the north by a short length of ditch (787) 6.5m long and 0.21m deep. The main part of the pit group was investigated by means of two sondages (Fig. 3.11). In the central part of the group the earliest feature was pit 1041 (Fig. 3.12, section 139). This was 0.60m deep and had been largely cut away by later pits, but the surviving part of the east side was straight, and it is possible that the feature originally comprised a linear, trough-like feature, although this is far from certain. The only finds comprised a small quantity of pottery from the lower fill (1042) including a body sherd from a Nene Valley white ware flagon and several sherds from a South Spanish Dressel 20 amphora, indicating a date after *c* 170. Pits 1038 and 1045, which were of a similar depth, had been dug respectively through the eastern and middle parts of pit 1041. The lower fill (1039) of pit 1038 was a mixture of dark soil and redeposited clay and was overlain by a grey upper fill flecked with charred remains (1040); soil

Fig. 3.11 Intercutting pits south of Building 1320, view to north, scale 2m

samples from both deposits contained burnt bone of mammals and birds, mostly unidentifiable, although a possible chicken tarsometatarsus and a vertebra from a possible cattle neonate were identified. The pit was cut by the very shallow pit 1036, which contained a few fragments of unidentified burnt animal bone. Pit 1045 contained a particularly noteworthy sequence of deposits comprising the burial of a calf (Fig. 3.13) in the lower fill (1046), complete except for the absence of the skull, overlain by a middle fill (1047) of burnt material including bone that may represent the cremated remains of a piglet as well as at least one burnt chicken bone. The upper part of the pit had been backfilled with redeposited clay (1048) and was artefactually sterile. The pits were overlain by a localised layer of dark, charcoal-rich

soil (1001) that included burnt bone similar to the material in pits 1036, 1038 and 1045, much of it unidentifiable but including cattle and bird, with at least one certain chicken bone. The layer contained an assemblage of artefactual material including a denarius of Hadrian minted in AD 134–8 (SF 79), 17kg of ceramic roof tile, a small sherd from a colourless glass vessel, and a pottery assemblage that amounted to more than 3kg and included two flagons, two beakers, four bowls, six jars and one storage jar as well as the spout of a lamp and part of a vessel that may come from the cup of a triple vase. Above this lay a layer of stone rubble that may have derived from the demolition of Building 1320 but which contained no artefactual material save two small pieces of melted lead waste (SF 76 and 78). Pit 745, a discrete feature set apart slightly to the west of the main group of intercutting pits, had a distinctly charcoal-rich fill but produced no finds.

The pits at the southern end of the group were similar, with depths of 0.3–0.5m (Fig. 3.12, section 168). Pit 1435 contained the articulating rear limb bones of a neonatal calf, and this may have been a complete animal when deposited, since the pit was substantially truncated by pit 1437. The fill also contained fragments of burnt bone, none of which could be identified to species although both bird and mammal were represented. Further such deposits of burnt bone were recovered from soil samples from pits 1430, 1433 and 1440. The

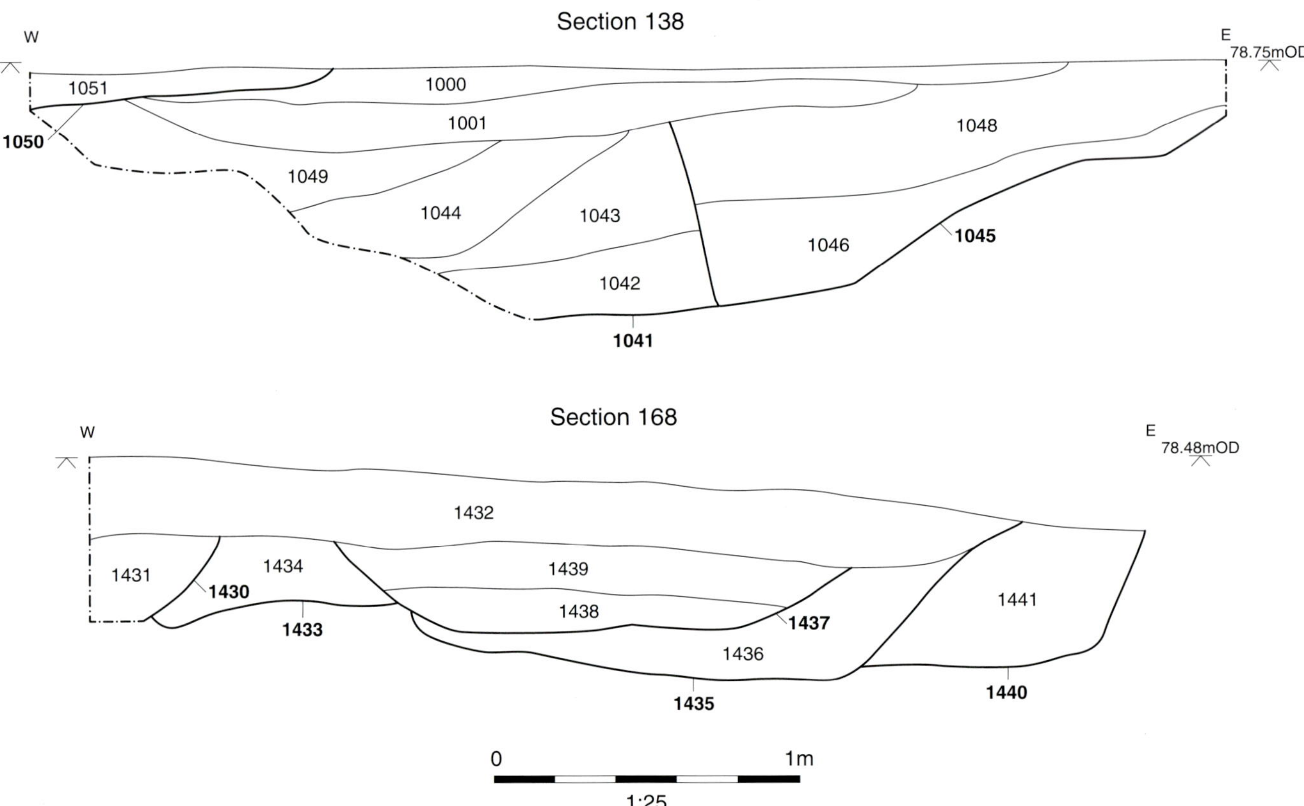

Fig. 3.12 Sections through the intercutting pits south of Building 1320

Fig. 3.13 Animal burial in pit 1045, view to south-west, scale 0.3m

lower fill (1438) of pit 1437 contained only a few fragments of bone, despite the presence of charred material, which included a scale from a stone pine.

The spring channel

The spring channel extended from north to south along the east edge of Area 1 and passed through Area 2 and the Watching Brief Area to the south (Figs 3.1 and 3.7), and the proximity of Building 1320 suggests that the building was deliberately located close to it. Before excavation the channel was apparent on the ground surface as an amorphous break in the otherwise ubiquitous ridge and furrow earthworks, and it would appear therefore that water flow from the spring has been a perennial feature of this location, from the Roman period until the modern day. The channel was recorded and sampled in a sondage east of the building and was also exposed in plan in two machine-dug trenches to the south (Fig. 3.14). In Area 2 it was not excavated and may have been obscured by associated post-Roman alluvium. Further south in the Watching Brief Area no Roman-period channel could be defined and it is likely that the flow here was channelled into the drainage ditches that extended through this area.

The full width of the Roman-period channel was not exposed and was partly truncated by a modern stone-built culvert (1296/1299) but was only *c* 0.35m deep (Fig. 3.15). It was filled by a sequence of three layers, most of which were deposited during the late Roman period and which are described in the corresponding section below.

Field system and crop-processing area west of the spring channel

Three phases of middle Roman activity were identified in this area (Fig. 3.16), but correlations with features in the adjacent areas were limited. The earliest feature (Phase 4a) was a single isolated enclosure (2488), which was slighted when a rectilinear system of field or enclosure boundaries was constructed that continued to be maintained and reorganised into Phase 5 (below). The spring channel appeared to be a post-Roman phenomenon in this area, and it is likely that any flow during the Roman period was channelled into the boundary ditches, some of which exhibited fills characteristic of water-lain deposition. Indeed, one of the enclosures extended into the area to the east and was cut by the channel. Activity here appeared to be entirely agricultural in character and included the initiation of crop-processing, which was to become

Fig. 3.14 The spring channel during excavation, with Building 1320 in the background: a) view to south-west; b) view to north-west

a principle focus of this location during the late Roman period.

Subphase 4a

Enclosure 2488 comprised a ditch that enclosed three sides of a subrectangular area measuring 20m wide and at least 15m long; it may have been longer if ditch 2518 was also part of it, but the relationship was truncated by later features. The enclosure lay on a NW–SE alignment that was distinctly divergent from the alignments of the boundaries of subsequent phases. The ditch was up to 0.56m deep and contained very little artefactual material, amounting to only a few sherds of pottery, a fragment of Roman brick and two pieces of tegula. The less extensive ditch 2097 followed a parallel alignment within the west side of the main enclosure ditch and may represent another iteration of the same enclosure or an internal feature.

Subphase 4b

The earlier enclosure was superseded by a more rectilinear arrangement, in which N–S ditch 2511 and E–W ditch 2494 appeared to form the west and north sides of an enclosure that measured 44m by 22m. The east end of the enclosure extended beyond the spring channel, and the south side had been completely cut away by later features that followed the same alignment. Ditch 2494 continued for at least 11m beyond the north-west corner of the enclosure, and ditch 2511 may similarly have extended further to the north. The ditches were typically 0.5–0.6m deep, although ditch 2511 was up to 0.9m deep, and the lower fills were characterised by gleyed clay deposits indicative of deposition in standing or slow-flowing water (Fig. 3.17). A soil sample from basal fill 2501 contained frequent waterlogged seeds including aquatic taxa indicative of plants growing in the base of a water-containing ditch, scrubbier vegetation presumably growing on the slopes of the ditch, as well as plants characteristic of more open ground that perhaps reflects wider vegetation in the area around the ditch. The fills above this comprised backfill of redeposited clay, and one such fill from ditch 2511 contained a copper alloy key handle with a broken iron shaft (SF 52, Fig. 4.12, no. 17). Artefacts were extremely scarce, but a complete pedestal base from a Lower Nene Valley grey ware jar from the bottom fill of ditch 2511 indicated that the ditches began to silt up sometime after AD 150, and the few sherds recovered from the upper fills were of similar date.

Subphase 4c

The boundaries established in subphase 4b were recut and additional enclosures were constructed to the south and west, one of which contained a corndrying oven and a stone-lined pit. Ditch 2494 was recut as ditch 2495, which continued west to

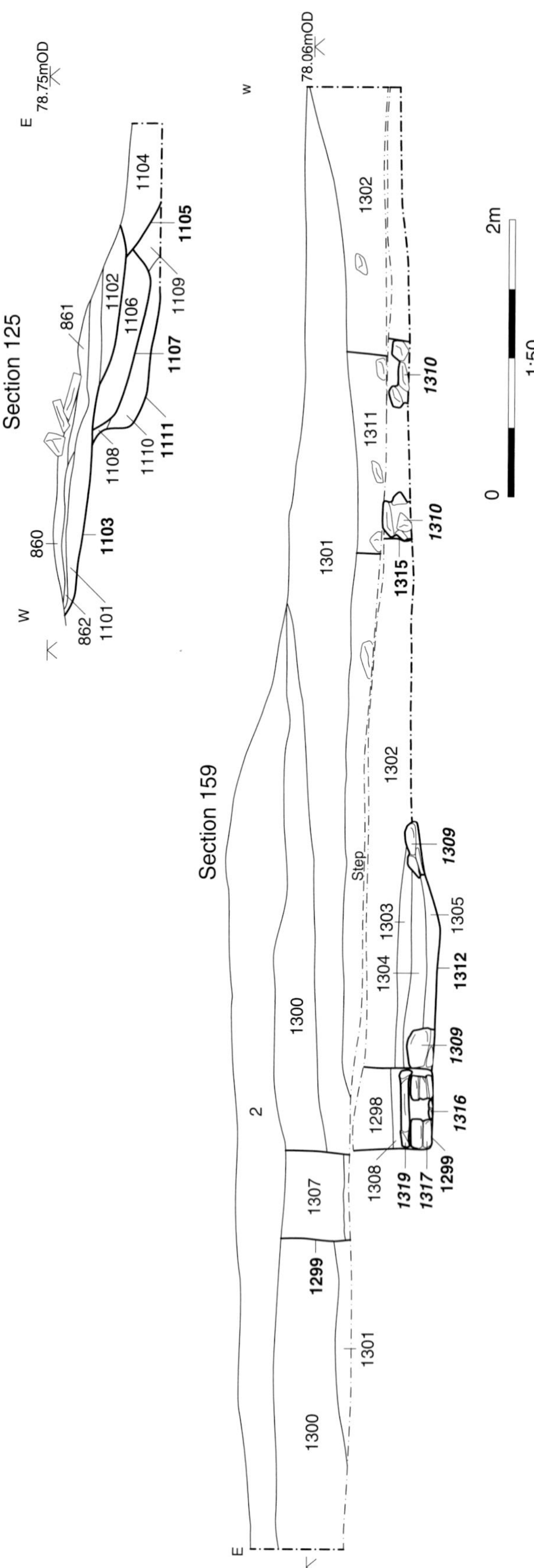

Fig. 3.15 Section through the spring channel

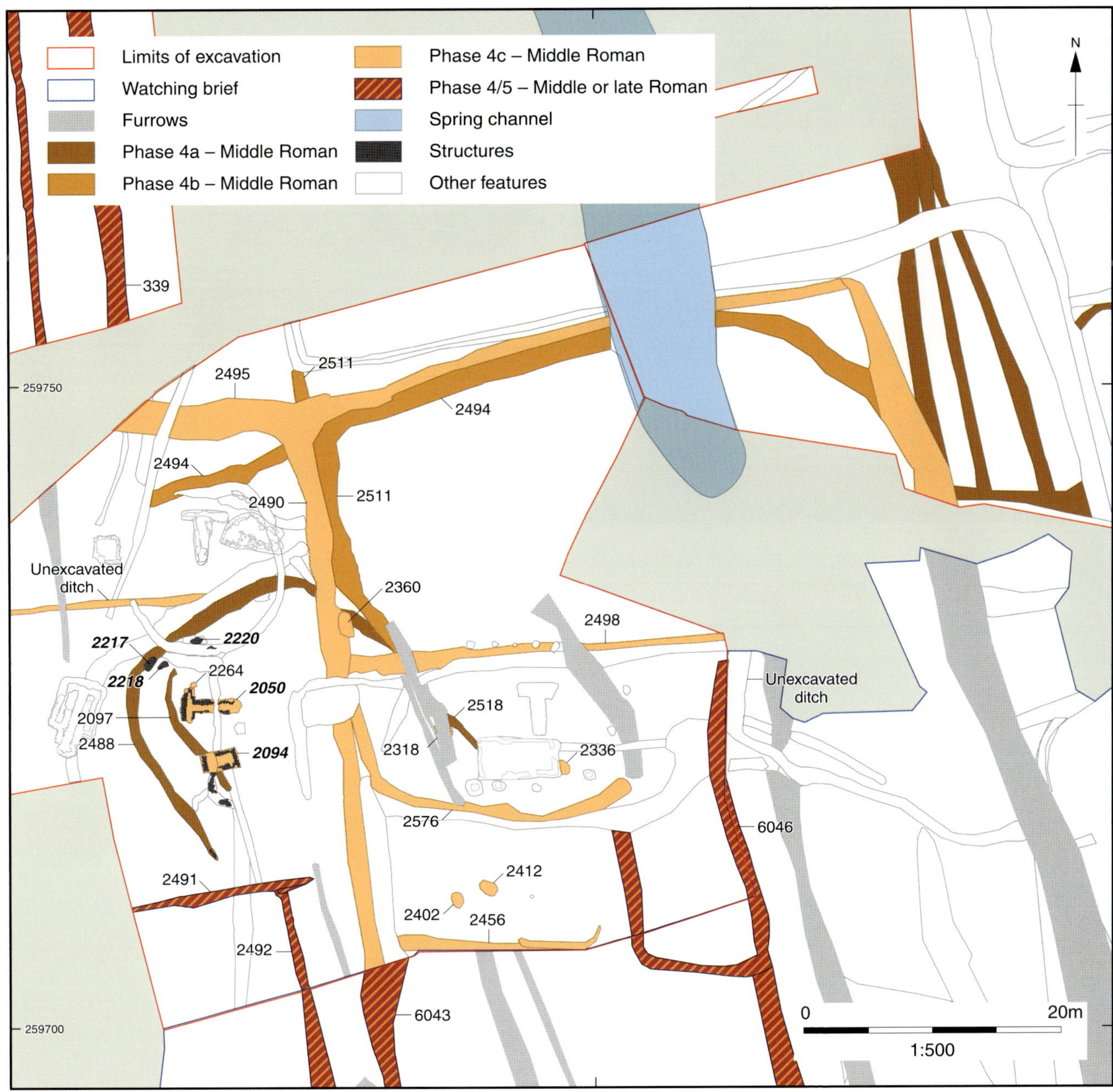

Fig. 3.16 Field system and crop-processing area west of the spring channel, Phase 4

the edge of the excavation area, beyond which it may have turned northward to extend across Area 1 as ditch 339. This ditch appeared to define the northern limit of the enclosures in this area, with ditch 2490 branching off it and extending to the south, dividing two groups of enclosures to east and west and continuing into the Watching Brief Area to the south as ditch 6043.

The enclosure that had been constructed in subphase 4b formed the north-eastern element of this arrangement and was now redesigned to a more strictly rectangular shape (2498). As in the preceding subphase there were no features within the enclosure, but the western boundary was cut by pit 2360, a steep-sided feature 0.5m deep that contained 22 sherds of pottery weighing 547g,

which accounted for more than half the pottery by weight from this subphase.

To the south were two smaller enclosures, defined by ditches 2576 and 2456 and possibly delimited to the east by an unexcavated ditch at the edge of the excavation area that continued south into the Watching Brief Area as ditch 6046. The first of these enclosures was slightly D-shaped in form and may have been open to the east, measuring 19m by 13m. Two shallow pits were situated within it: pit 2336 was backfilled with charcoal-rich soil and stones and had been cut by Phase 5 stone-lined pit 2129, and pit 2318 had been largely destroyed by furrows. The enclosure bounded by ditch 2456 measured 17m by 10m and similarly may have been open to the east. The only features within it were

Fig. 3.17 Main N–S boundary in the crop-processing area, showing the gleyed lower fill of ditch 2511 cut by dark-filled ditch 2490, view to north-east

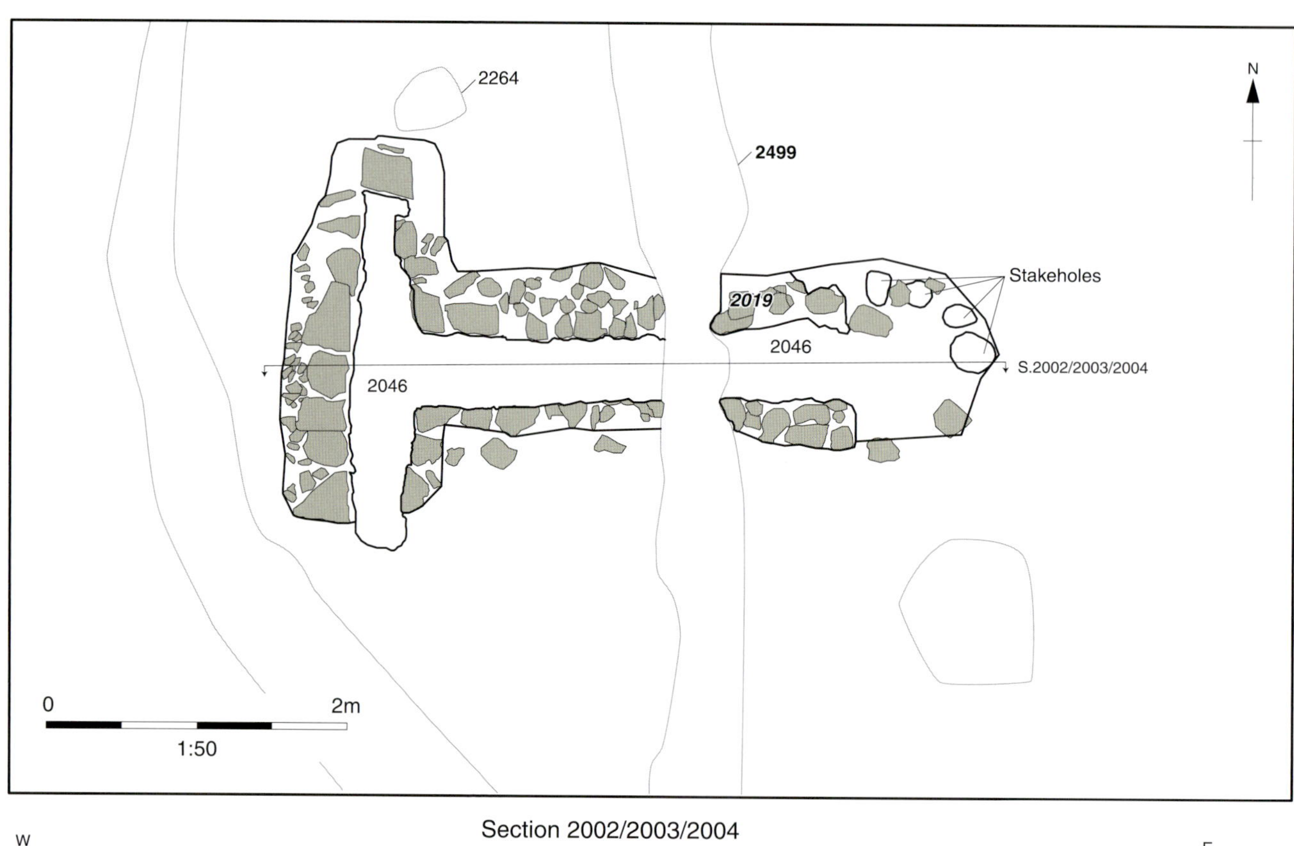

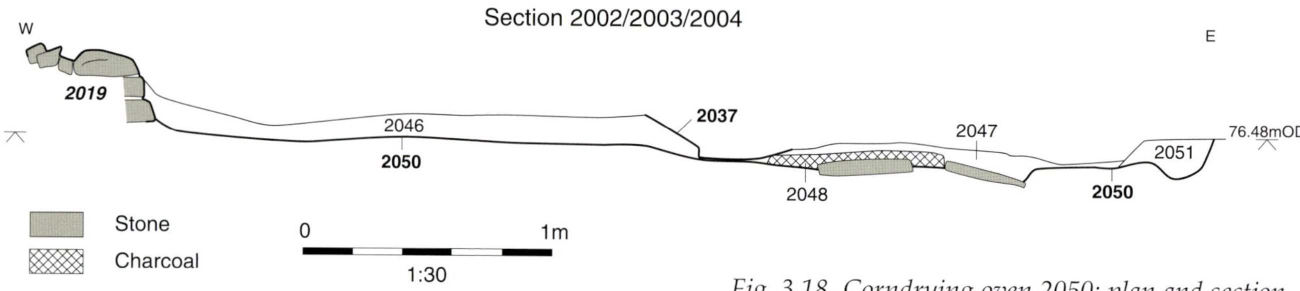

Fig. 3.18 Corndrying oven 2050: plan and section

Fig. 3.19 Corndrying oven 2050 with stone-lined pit 2094 to the rear, view to south, scale 2m

pits 2402 and 2412, which were 0.2m and 0.32m deep respectively and were backfilled with dark soil but lacked artefactual material.

On the west side of ditch 2490, an unexcavated ditch divided two enclosures whose western boundaries were not located, and further south ditches 2491 and 2492 formed the north and east sides of a third enclosure that extended into the Watching Brief Area to the south and could have dated from this phase or Phase 5, since they produced no dating evidence. The only features in this area were corndrying oven 2050, stone-lined pit 2094 and pit 2264 in the middle enclosure, and possible corndrying oven 2219.

Corndrying oven 2050

The corndrying oven (Figs 3.18-19) was a T-shaped structure 4.75m long and oriented E–W parallel to the nearby boundary ditches. The stokehole at the east end was surrounded by a loose arrangement of stones, and excavation of the north half revealed a group of four stakeholes around its edge (Fig. 3.20). The main flue was 2.75m long and 0.36m deep and was constructed from stonework, up to four courses of which survived, creating a vertical inner face (2019). The pattern of burning on some of the stones appeared random and may indicate that they had been reused from some previous structure. The cross-flue was slightly deeper than the main flue, at 0.45m, and was 2.65m wide. A black, charcoal-rich layer (2048) that extended along the base from 0.5m to 1.2m from the stokehole indicated the location of the fire. This layer produced an extremely large quantity of charred plant remains that indicated that the oven was used

Fig. 3.20 East end of corndrying oven 2050, showing stakeholes around the edge of the stokehole, view to south, scale 2m

for drying grain as part of the malting process, and the presence of a large quantity of chaff suggests that crop-processing debris was being used as fuel. The deposit additionally contained nine small sherds of pottery, including a sherd of Lower Nene Valley grey ware that indicates a date after AD 150, but none were burnt, so they were presumably introduced incidentally during backfilling. It was overlain by a main backfill (2046) that included a smaller amount of redeposited charred grain.

Pit 2264

Pit 2264 lay adjacent to the north end of the cross-flue of oven 2050 and comprised a small pit that had apparently been dug specifically in order to bury a pair of piglets (2265).

Stone-lined pit 2094

Stone-lined pit 2094 (Fig. 3.21) was situated a little under 3m south of the corndrying oven. Much of

Fig. 3.21 Stone-lined pit 2094, cut by Phase 5 ditch 2450/2515, view to south, scale 2m

the western half had been destroyed by the digging of Phase 5 ditch 2499. The pit was rectangular, measuring 2.65m by 1.65m and 0.37m deep, with vertical sides and a flat base. All four sides had been lined with a stone wall that comprised a bedding layer of pitched stone supporting up to four surviving courses of roughly squared stones measuring 0.15–0.30m long. A tumble of stones in the south-west corner may have been associated with the collapse or demolition of the structure, and the backfill contained further rubble as well as three nail fragments, a tapered iron spike and six sherds of pottery.

Corndrying oven 2219

A second corndrying oven may have been represented by some stonework a short distance north of oven 2050 that had been substantially truncated by later ditches. A pair of parallel walls (2217 and 2218), of which only about 1m survived, appeared to form the south-west end of a flue, and a patch of similar material (2220) some 2.4m to the north-east may also have been part of the structure. No associated deposits of charred plant remains were observed and the identification as a corndryer is not certain.

Field system east of the spring channel

The features in this area produced very little artefactual material and were evidently agricultural in function (Fig 3.22). They consisted of a group of enclosure boundaries at the northern end, which had been substantially truncated and obscured by later features, and a more regular arrangement of rectilinear enclosures adjoining a boundary ditch at the southern end. The latest ditches in the southern sequence formed the east end of subphase 4b/4c enclosure 2494/2495 in the crop-processing area west of the spring channel.

Subphase 4a

Enclosures at the north end of Area 2

The evidently partial survival of the ditches at the north end of the excavation area hampered any attempt at understanding their arrangement, although there was sufficient evidence to indicate that they represented more than a single phase of boundaries. Ditches 20355 and 20398 may have formed successive phases of the west side of an enclosure whose east side was enclosed by ditches 20127 and 20357. Ditch 20355, which extended into the excavation area from the north before curving towards the south-east, was the earlier of the western ditches, and extended for a total length of 30m, the south-east end being truncated by Phase 5 ditch 20581. The north part of this ditch was recut as L-shaped ditch 20398, which was likewise truncated by a Phase 5 ditch. The sequence of the eastern ditches could not be established since they did not intersect. Ditch 20127 extended on a slightly irregular N–S alignment for at least 19.5m, broken by a single interval 1.2m wide that might represent an entrance, whereas ditch 20357 had an L-shaped form and petered out to the south. Ditch 20127 contained by far the largest pottery assemblage from the Phase 4 features east of the spring channel, but this still amounted to only 1.3kg of mixed sherds.

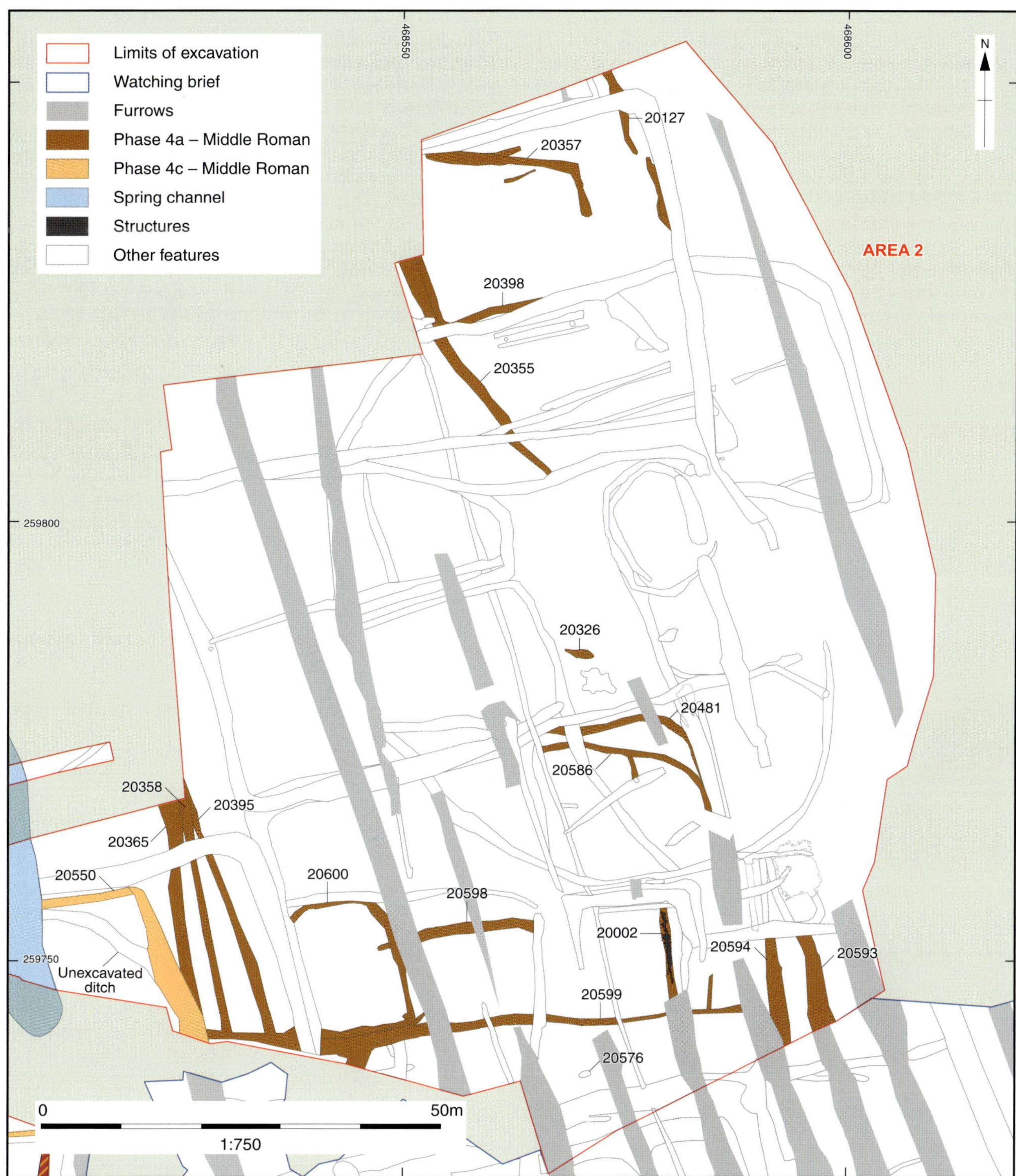

Fig. 3.22 Field system east of the spring channel, Phase 4

Enclosures at the southern end of Area 2

The arrangement at the southern end of the excavation area comprised a series of enclosures that adjoined the north side of the E–W boundary defined by ditch 20599. The ditch was 0.25–0.46m deep and extended for at least 60m, the east end obscured by a medieval furrow but apparently respecting N–S ditch 20594, which must therefore have been a contemporary boundary and perhaps marked the eastern limit of the field system. A second ditch which lay parallel to this boundary (20593) yielded some fragments of lava stone that, though of undiagnostic shape, are likely to have been part of a quern or millstone. Only six sherds of pottery were recovered from ditch 20599, but the presence of a handle from a large fish dish in Dorset black-burnished ware indicated that deposition continued into the 3rd century. A sequence of three ditches (20358, 20365 and 20395) that extended from the northern edge of the excavation area had dark grey, gleyed lower fills indicative of deposition in water (Fig. 3.23) and it is possible that they channelled the flow from the spring channel into ditch 20599, although the fills of 20599 were not so obviously water-lain. Further east, part of a stone-built culvert (20002) was uncovered, which probably also ran into ditch 20599, although the relationship had been truncated by another medieval furrow. The culvert (Fig. 3.24) was exposed for a total length of 10m, and its point of origin could not be established since the northern end was truncated by Phase 5 ditches. It was constructed in a ditch up to 0.86m wide and 0.28m deep and had sides that each comprised two or three courses of stones with a larger, flat capstone across the top. It was unsurprisingly devoid of artefacts save two tiny fragments of pottery recovered from a soil sample, one of which was a sherd of pink grogged ware that indicates a date after AD 160.

Between these drainage features that flowed into it from the north, ditch 20599 was adjoined by

Fig. 3.23 Drainage ditches 20358, 20365 and 20395, view to north, scale 2m

Fig. 3.24 Stone culvert 20002, view to north, scale 1m

enclosures 20600 and 20598. The former measured 14m by 10m, while the latter was identified only from the presence of a ditch defining its northern side – it probably adjoined enclosure 20600, but the intersection had been truncated by a medieval furrow. Neither enclosure contained internal features and the only finds were a very small group of sherds from ditch 20600 and a single sherd from ditch 20598. This group of features may have been adjoined to the north by a further enclosure whose north-east corner was defined in successive iterations by curving ditches 20481 and 20586. Further north again lay an irregularly shaped pit (20326) – the only discrete feature attributed to this phase – which contained a few sherds of middle Roman pottery.

Subphase 4b

The western end of boundary ditch 20599 and drainage ditch 20365 were observed in plan to be cut by an unexcavated ditch that formed the east end of enclosure 2494 in the crop-processing area west of the spring channel (see Fig. 3.16).

Subphase 4c

The enclosure that was constructed during subphase 4b was recut in subphase 4c with a more regular, rectangular shape (20550). This corresponded with enclosure ditch 2495 in the crop-processing area (see Fig. 3.16).

Burial associated with the field system

Grave 20576 was situated near the southern limit of the excavation area, 5m south of ditch 20599. It had no stratigraphic relationships that would enable it to be attributed to any of the subphases described above, but the recovery of three sherds of pottery from the fill that included a fragment of Lower Nene Valley grey ware dated to AD 150–300 allowed it to be assigned broadly to Phase 4. It comprised the inhumation of an adult of indeterminate sex (20575) who had been buried with the torso supine, arms by the sides, and the legs flexed and turned to the left. No grave goods were present.

Area 4

The complex of rectilinear enclosures recorded to the north in Areas 2 and 3 and the Watching Brief Area did not continue into Area 4, but instead a pair of ditched boundaries were exposed, the western of which (4379) may have been a continuation of the eastern boundary of the enclosures (Fig. 2.1). The boundaries extended across the excavation area on roughly parallel, slightly curving alignments, 27–35m apart. The western boundary was represented by a single ditch (4379), 0.5m deep, but the eastern boundary comprised a similar ditch (4386) with two shallower ditches (4385 and 4388) that presumably indicate successive redefinitions of the boundary. Artefactual material was very sparse, limited to scraps of animal bone and pottery, some of which was residual from the middle Iron Age settlement in this area.

PHASE 5: LATE ROMAN

The villa landscape that had been established during the 2nd century continued in use uninterrupted during the 3rd and 4th centuries (Fig. 3.25). The different elements of the landscape that were identified in Phase 4 maintained their distinctive characters and each underwent a continuing process of development. The enclosures in Area 1 were reorganised twice during this period, and exhibited increasing evidence for occupation, culminating in the construction of an aisled building (Building 3). There was insufficient dating evidence to establish the longevity of Building 1320, but the recovery of a few sherds of 4th-century pottery suggest that it may have continued in use this late, and it was during this period that the spring channel silted up. Activity in the crop-processing area appears to have intensified, with three corndrying ovens, three steeping tanks and a threshing/malting floor attributed to this phase. East of the spring channel, the disparate enclosures of the middle Roman period were replaced first by a large circular enclosure (20350) and then by a series of rectilinear field enclosures.

Enclosure complex adjacent to the villa

During this phase, the enclosure complex occupied approximately the same area as it had during Phase 4, except that the western boundary was extended slightly to increase the overall width to 85m from west to east (Fig. 3.26). It was enclosed to the west and south by a continuous L-shaped ditch (1387/1390/1486), and although no such boundary was identified on the east side, the enclosures did not extend beyond the limit established during Phase 4, perhaps indicating that there was a boundary here that was marked above ground but was not visible archaeologically. As in Phase 4, there was a large area devoid of archaeological features between this side of the complex and the closest feature to the east, boundary ditch 339. The northern extent of the complex again lay beyond the edge of the development. Boundary ditch 1387/1390/1486 was considerably more substantial than the boundaries within the complex, typically measuring more than 0.5m deep with a maximum depth of 0.97m at the north edge of the excavation area. The internal boundaries, by contrast, were mostly less than 0.3m deep, and the only ditches deeper than 0.5m were enclosure 398/399, at the north-east limit of the exposed part of the complex, and ditch 960, which enclosed an area in the southern part of the complex and may indicate that the area had a distinct function. The west end of

ditch 1387/1390, which defined the southern boundary, extended along the line of the corresponding boundary in Phase 4, ditch 1475/1385/1495, but further east the later boundary diverged somewhat to the south. It exhibited evidence for two phases, the earlier of which (1390) only survived along the south side of the complex, having been completely dug away by the later cut (1387/1486). Artefactual evidence from both iterations was extremely limited, comprising a small quantity of pottery and tile and a few scraps of animal bone, but dating evidence from ditch 1390 comprised the base sherd from an Oxfordshire colour-coated ware bowl, possibly of Young form C45, dated after AD 240, and a coin (SF 17) issued between AD 268 and 270.

Subphase 5a

Enclosure in the west, central and north parts of the complex

Most of the complex comprised a rectilinear arrangement of enclosures. The area west of ditch 960 was divided into three such enclosures by E–W ditches 393 and 1464, the latter of which produced a fragment cut from a 1st-century armilla (SF 33). The fragment may have been residual, derived from activity associated with the late Iron Age/early Roman settlement in this area, or may represent contemporary reuse and disposal of an object that was by this time of some antiquity. The enclosures measured *c* 26m long from east to west, although no eastern limit to the middle enclosure was identified, and the middle and south enclosures were 10m and 15m wide respectively. None contained any contemporary features.

East of this, a further pair of enclosures were divided by ditch 1502, which was an extension of ditch 1464. The northern enclosure, defined by ditches 1462/1463 and 1483, lay on a N–S alignment and was 11m wide with an unknown length. It had no internal features and finds from the ditches were generally sparse, although ditches 1483 and 1502 each contained a poorly preserved radiate dated to AD 260–96 (SF 8) and AD 268–70 (SF 30) respectively, and hand-cleaning of the junction of ditch 1483 and Phase 4 ditch 1501 resulted in the recovery of 1.1kg of pottery that could have originated from either ditch. An entrance 1.6m wide at the south-west corner allowed access between this enclosure and its western neighbour, while a break 4.9m wide at the south-east corner communicated with the enclosure to the south. The latter was approximately square and measured 15m across, constructed against ditch 960 and bounded to the east by ditch 1482. Curving gully 827 enclosed an area *c* 7m across in the south-west corner of the enclosure. The gully was no more than 0.18m deep and it is unclear whether it was a subdivision within the enclosure or constituted the surviving part of a penannular ditch of a roundhouse. A

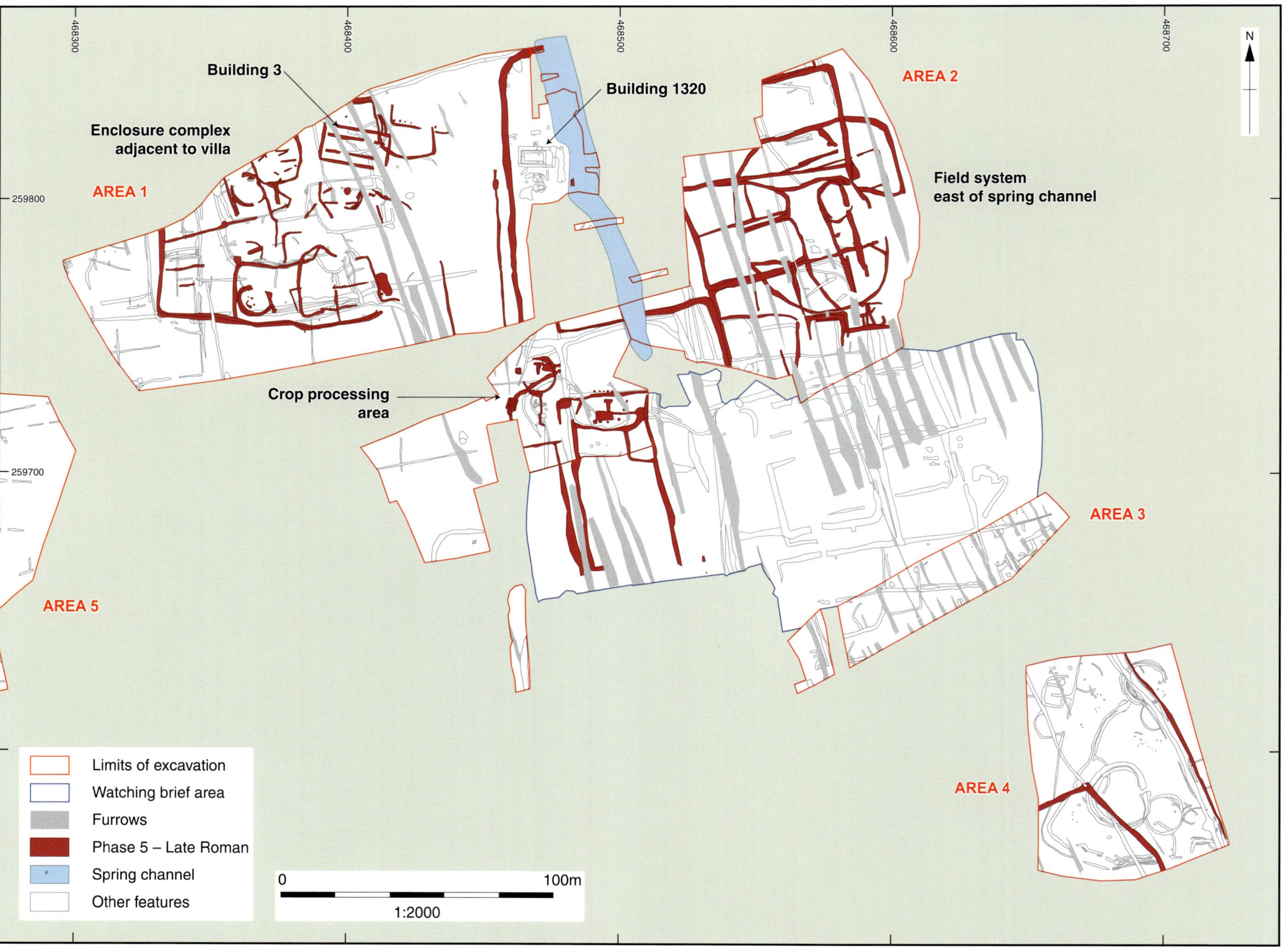

Fig. 3.25 Plan of all late Roman (Phase 4) features

Fig. 3.26 The enclosure complex adjacent to the villa, Phase 5

pottery assemblage of 1.1kg was recovered from the gully, more than half of which was accounted for by sherds from a shell-tempered 'cooking pot type' jar, possibly from Harrold, Bedfordshire, as well as small sherds from several other vessels. A large pit (582) up to 0.7m deep had been dug at the south-west corner of the enclosure, possibly within the area enclosed by gully 827, but there was no indication as to its function.

Ditch 1096, which branched off the east side of ditch 1483, may have divided a similar pair of enclosures, perhaps delimited to the east by ditch 454, although the evidence in this area was not particularly coherent. The latter ditch contained the mandible and right forelimb of a small dog. To the north lay a group of shallow, narrow gullies on varying, broadly E–W alignments, the function of which was unclear. Gully 261 yielded a radiate issued between AD 260 and 296 (SF 3) and gully 259 an incomplete coin of similar date (SF 2).

Two successive enclosures were constructed at the north-east limit of the complex. Enclosure 401 was subrectangular in plan, 20m wide, and had sides of differing lengths, the east side ending in a definite terminus after only 9m whereas the west side extended for at least 16m before being obscured by later features. It appeared to be open to the north. The west side of this enclosure was slighted by the construction of an enclosure defined successively by ditches 398 and 399. Ditch 399 formed the initial boundary and was quite slight, measuring no more than 0.3m deep, but the recut ditch 398 was the most substantial ditch within the complex, with a depth that ranged from 0.46m on the south side to 0.9m on the north. The enclosure measured 17m N–S and must have been open on the west side, as no corresponding ditch was identified there and it is unlikely that so substantial a feature could have been completely truncated, although this area was somewhat obscured by the later Building 3 and medieval furrows. There were two small pits within the enclosure. One was undated, but the other (145) contained three near-complete imbrices (Fig. 4.14, no. 26).

The features in the area south of enclosure 398/399 were difficult to interpret and appear to have represented more than a single phase of activity. The linear character of N–S ditches 454 and 607 and E–W ditch 455/559 suggests that they may have been the surviving elements of further enclosures of broadly rectilinear form, and the proximity of the east end of ditch 559 to curvilinear gullies 560 and 561 suggests that they were not contemporary. The latter gullies were concentric and may have represented successive phases of a roundhouse or curvilinear enclosure with a diameter of *c* 8m. An articulating cattle forelimb had been deposited in gully 561. Also in this area, and within the area encompassed by gullies 560 and 561 if they did indeed represent a circular structure, was pit 227. It was *c* 2.5m in diameter and 0.64m deep, with vertical sides and a flat base. Its original function was uncertain, but it had been backfilled with

material that included nearly 1kg of assorted, mostly quite small pottery sherds and 5.5kg of brick and tile. Unusually, the small bone assemblage included specimens of duck and woodcock. West of this, short ditch 504 yielded a coin of AD 364–78 (SF 14), and to the east, ditch 716 extended on a circuitous, somewhat divergent NW–SE alignment that was unexplained.

Features enclosed by ditch 960

Ditch 960 enclosed an area in the south-eastern part of the complex. The ditch was more substantial than the other boundary ditches in the complex, with a depth of 0.4–0.6m, suggesting that it may have defined an area with a distinct function, and the character of the features within suggested that it may have contained an area of domestic occupation. Ditch 821 may have formed the eastern limit, enclosing an area that measured *c* 50m by 20m. A probable entrance 3.5m wide at the south-east corner was associated with the out-turned southern end of this ditch, possibly designed to assist in the management of livestock passing into and out of the enclosure. The outward curve of the eastern end of ditch 960 may similarly have been associated with an entrance on the north side of the enclosure, but the break between this and ditch 822 on the opposite side was 18m wide, too large to represent an entrance; it is likely that part of the perimeter here was bounded by an above-ground feature such as a fence or hedge line for which no direct evidence has survived.

Within the south-west corner of the area lay curvilinear enclosure 1245/1246. The enclosure comprised a slightly irregular oval in form, measuring *c* 12m by 7m internally, with a north-west-facing opening *c* 6.7m wide in one of the long sides. It was defined initially by ditch 1245 and subsequently by ditch 1246, which was dug along the inner edge of the earlier ditch (see Fig. 3.3, cuts 1249 and 1212 respectively). Both ditches attained a maximum depth of 0.48m but petered out toward the terminals, and it was not certain whether feature 1064, at the eastern terminus, was a discrete feature or the end of ditch 1246. Similarly, pit 957, which contained a fragment from an upper rotary quern (SF 86), may have been the end of ditch 1245. Otherwise, the ditches produced only *c* 1.1kg of pottery, a single coin dated AD 202–3 (SF 29), some brick and tile and a few scraps of animal bone. The enclosure contained an oven (1247) and four pits/postholes. The oven (Fig. 3.27) comprised a shallow hollow 0.12m deep, beneath which the natural clay had been discoloured by heat, producing a reddish hue. A curving flue projected from the north-west side for 1.5m before turning towards the north-east and extending for a similar distance. A hollow on the south-east side of the oven may have been a stokehole, the fill of which (1134) yielded three sherds of pottery including part of a rim from an Oxfordshire red colour-coated ware mortaria. Samples taken from the oven and flue were not particularly rich in charred plant remains, although both include grain, with both wheat and

Fig. 3.27 Excavation in progress in enclosure 1245/1246, with oven 1247 in the foreground, view to south-west

barley present, and the charcoal was mostly black-thorn/cherry, with only a minor oak component, suggesting that it would not have achieved a sufficient temperature for an industrial function and is more likely to have been a domestic feature. The pits and postholes were all shallow and contained no artefactual material. The only features in the eastern part of the enclosure were shallow ditches 964 and 1388, which appeared to form part of a rectilinear arrangement of internal subdivisions.

Outside the east end of enclosure 960/821 were small pit 1409 and large, shallow hollow 970. The hollow was 8m long and 4m wide but only 0.28m deep and there was no indication of its function. It may have been a waterhole or quarry hollow. Further east again, pit 931 lay in a decidedly isolated location and was cut through ditch 1499. It measured 3.7m in diameter and 0.72m deep, and the mottled character of the fills might represent the gleyed deposits of a waterhole. Between these pits, the relationship of N–S ditch 1487 to the enclosure was uncertain, but a late Roman date for it was indicated by a single coin dated 260–96 (SF 28).

Subphase 5b

In contrast to the fairly regular arrangement of rectilinear enclosures that characterised the complex during subphase 5a, the structures that were inserted during subphase 5b comprised more irregular or curvilinear enclosures, as well as Building 3. Nevertheless, the limits of the complex that were established previously continued to be respected. It is possible that the recutting of the boundary to the west and south represented by ditch 1387/1486 in fact belonged to this phase, although the artefactual dating evidence from the ditch was insufficient to be certain; at the very least, the recutting provides

evidence for the longevity of the boundary, whereas most of the enclosures within the complex exhibited evidence for only a single phase. Whereas the dating evidence for subphase 5a was essentially open-ended and would allow this activity to date anytime from the middle of the 3rd century until the end of Roman occupation, the coins from the enclosures of subphase 5b were predominantly 4th century; indeed, five of the eleven pieces certainly dated from the second half of the century. The extent to which the earlier enclosures were retained is uncertain: in the eastern part of the complex, the new enclosures certainly slighted the earlier ones, but the western-most enclosures may have continued, since no new structures were constructed here and a minim issued in AD 350–64 (SF 34) was recovered from ditch 1468, which also yielded a glass counter (SF 35).

Curvilinear enclosure 241 and adjacent enclosure 1208 were constructed in the central part of the complex. Enclosure 241 measured *c* 11m by 9m and was oval in form. The defining ditches were very shallow, with depths of less than 0.3m, and consequently breaks at the north-west and south-east ends appeared to be the result of plough truncation rather than representing original entrances. A 4m-wide break on the east side, however, may have been an entrance. Two phases of ditch were identified on the south-west side, where the later ditch was dug along the outer edge of its predecessor. Despite their shallow depth, the ditches contained a large assemblage of artefacts including 2.9kg of pottery and two coins issued in AD 364–75 (SF 23) and AD 268–70 (SF 32) as well as no less than 33kg of brick and tile and parts of some naturally flat stones that may also have been used as roofing. Most of the pottery came from a localised deposit of more than 2.1kg of sherds on the south-west side of the enclosure that included a 4th-century flanged bowl in shelly ware (C11;

Marney 1989, fig. 26, no. 41), the base of a beaker in Oxford red colour-coated ware (F51) that is likely to date from the late 3rd century onwards (Young 1977), and a fragment of a mortarium in Mancetter-Hartshill white ware (M23), a fabric generally produced up to the mid-4th century. Together, the group was deposited no earlier than *c* AD 300–50. Shallow pit 151 was situated in the middle of the entrance and contained a well-used whetstone (SF 53) as well as some pottery and tile, while similar neighbouring pit 152 contained only a single sherd and a smaller assemblage of tile. The function of the enclosure was uncertain, but the artefactual evidence would be consistent with some degree of domestic occupation and in the absence of evidently structural features it is possible that the enclosure surrounded a building of mass-wall construction. The relationship between the enclosure and ditch 1208 was unclear. They may have been contemporary, with ditch 1208 adjoining the enclosure ditch immediately north of the eastern entrance, but alternatively it is possible that short ditch segment 280, within the enclosure, was the end of ditch 1208, and that 1208 was the earlier feature. Ditch 1208 enclosed an area some 17m across, and although there were no contemporary features within it, the ditch itself contained a large assemblage of tile, amounting to 16.6kg, as well as a coin of Constantine I issued in AD 330–5 (SF 4).

Ditches 1095 and 1097 branched off the south side of ditch 1208, the former being dog-legged and the latter linear, and indicate the presence of at least two phases of subdivisions in this area. Both were shallow and contained a single fill. Ditch 1097 was the earlier and yielded a coin issued in AD 350–64 (SF 87) and, from a different intervention, a coin of Victorinus dated AD 268–70 (SF 6) as well as a rim sherd from a 4th-century curving-sided dish probably from Harrold. A coin of probable 3rd- or 4th-century date (SF 5), completely encrusted with an iron nail fragment corroded to one face, was recovered from ditch 1095. Further evidence for enclosures in this part of the complex was provided by L-shaped ditch 1481, which is likely to have formed the north and west sides of a rectilinear enclosure measuring 11m by 7m and produced two adjoining fragments from the upper stone of a rotary quern (SF 83) as well as a small pottery assemblage that included a rim sherd from an Oxfordshire colour-coated ware dish with white-painted decoration on the flange, dated to after *c* AD 325.

The southernmost enclosure during this subphase was the large curvilinear enclosure 1007, which measured 25m by 15m. The enclosure appeared to be open on the east side, although ditch 1494 may have partly enclosed this side, in addition to forming a rectilinear arrangement with ditch 863. Two shelly ware jars had been placed in the north-west terminal of the enclosure ditch (Fig. 3.28). The vessels were found side-by-side in the feature, albeit not placed upright, and appear to have been deliberately deposited together. The jars were sooted

Fig. 3.28 Two shelly ware jars placed in the north-west terminal of enclosure ditch 1007

externally, having been used as cooking pots, and typologically date to the second half of the 2nd or early 3rd century. Elsewhere the ditch yielded a coin issued in AD 364–78 (SF 10) and a pair of radiates dated to AD 260–96 (SF 26 and 27) that were apparently deposited together. In addition to this, ditch 863 contained the skeleton of a small dog.

To the west of enclosure 1007, a group of pits were dug in the vicinity of subphase 5a enclosure 1245/1246. Pit 1034, 0.8m wide and 0.36m deep, was dug into the fill of the enclosure ditch on its south-west side but contained only four sherds of pottery, while the other pits formed an approximate N–S alignment adjacent to the east end of the enclosure. Most contained no artefacts, but pit 1176 yielded a small assemblage of pottery that included two large rim sherds from hammerhead mortaria; one sherd was blackened by burning across the exterior surface but the other was not, indicating that they came from different vessels. The upper fill of pit 1224 contained a large assemblage of some 165 sherds of pottery. The group was relatively well-preserved, comprising many large fragments, and may represent a deliberate dump of household waste. The assemblage contained a variety of locally made pottery and wares from further afield, including material from Derbyshire, the Nene Valley, Mancetter-Hartshill, Oxfordshire and Dorset. The presence of typically late Roman forms, such as black-burnished ware bowls with dropped-flange rims, in association with 2nd-3rd-century pottery, such as grey ware from the Nene Valley and a mortarium with a hammerhead-shaped rim, suggests that the group was deposited after *c* AD 270, but probably not much later than *c* AD 300. The deposit also included a coin minted in AD 388–402

(SF 90), a fragment from a millstone (SF 88) and more than 22kg of brick and tile.

Building 3

The building was stratigraphically the latest element of the enclosure complex, built over the ditches of enclosures 398/399 and 401. It was of aisled construction and was represented only by the surviving parts of its rubble foundations, which defined the outer walls and two inner walls that divided the aisles, with no floor surfaces or other internal features present (Fig. 3.29). The slope of the local topography dropped by *c* 1m over the length of the building. The remaining foundations had been seriously affected by medieval ploughing, surviving to a maximum depth of 0.2m where they were preserved beneath ridges but being truncated or completely absent where cut by furrows.

The structure measured 25.2m by 13.8m, with each aisle 2.6m wide and the central nave 4.7m wide. A notable feature of the construction of the building was the stone used in the foundations, which comprised pitched limestone pieces in the outer walls, of which two courses survived in the parts beneath ridges, and sandstone cobbles in the aisle walls. The walls that defined the aisles did not extend for the entire length of the building, ending 0.9–1.25m short of the end walls. The absence of rubble associated with the building indicated that it had been systematically demolished, and the resulting debris carefully removed for reuse or disposal. Consequently, only a small assemblage of 8.2kg of ceramic building material was recovered,

mostly comprising well-preserved fragments of tegula and imbrex but also including two pieces of brick and a single flue tile. While this may represent material from the roof, much of the tile exhibited evidence of burning and may therefore derive from ovens or hearths. The few pieces of tile that can be dated typologically were made during the mid-2nd to mid-3rd century. Despite the late date indicated by its relationship to the earlier ditches, the small assemblage of pottery, mostly from cleaning, was all of middle Roman date. Also recovered were a bone hairpin with a decorative head (SF 18; Fig. 4.12, no. 18) and a small (5g) sherd from the neck of a blue glass vessel of uncertain form.

Ditches 403 and 519, immediately east of the building, were the only features that lay on the same alignment and were likely to have been contemporary. They were shallow, less than 0.25m deep, and formed an L-shaped boundary 22m long that may have been part of a rectilinear enclosure. An alignment of five postholes extended along the inner edge of the ditch, each of which contained probable packing stones, albeit disturbed. It is not impossible that the postholes represent the surviving elements of a building.

Building 1320 and the spring channel

Building 1320

There was insufficient dating evidence to establish the longevity of Building 1320, but the recovery of a sherd from an Oxfordshire white ware mortarium

Fig. 3.29 Building 3, view to north-west

and a rim sherd from a 4th-century Nene Valley ware colour-coated necked jar/bowl from the cleaning of the building, and a tiny sherd from a 4th-century Oxfordshire colour-coated ware necked bowl from the upper fill of ditch 339 suggest that it may have continued in use into the 4th century. At the very least, this evidence indicates that some form of activity continued in this area.

Spring channel

The late Roman period witnessed the main phase of silting of the spring channel (see Fig. 3.15, section 159). The basal layer (1305) was a dark, organic silt, 0.09m thick, from which an ash twig preserved by waterlogging produced a radiocarbon date range of 260–540 (Table 5.18). The insects and waterlogged plant remains from this deposit were consistent with shallow water, which the presence of watercress and buttercups suggests was particularly clear and mineral rich (see Chapter 5). A particularly unusual feature was the predominance of walnut pollen, indicating the presence of a grove nearby. Overlying this was layer 1304, a brownish silty clay, 0.14m thick. This was the earliest deposit in the sequence to contain artefactual material, in the form of the base from an Oxfordshire colour-coated ware bowl dated after AD 240 and a rim sherd from a 4th-century shell-tempered dish probably made in Harrold, Bedfordshire. Environmental material was less well preserved than in the underlying layer due to reduced waterlogging, and no pollen was

Fig. 3.30 *Field system and crop-processing area west of the spring channel, Phase 5*

preserved, but generally the waterlogged plant remains pointed to a reduction in vegetation indicative of wet grassland and an increase in plants associated with disturbance, suggesting that the land around the channel was becoming increasingly overgrown and had the character of wasteland. It was the first deposit in this sequence to produce evidence for arable cultivation, in the form of charred spelt chaff. The final fill of the channel (1303) was a soft grey alluvial silty clay, which again produced walnut pollen. Above this was a more extensive layer of mottled bluish grey and brownish grey alluvium (1302), 0.66m thick, that sealed the channel cut and extended throughout the 7.5m width of the sondage. A rough stone surface (1297/1306) had been constructed on the surface of this layer and yielded a small assemblage of pottery including a large sherd from a 4th-century narrow-necked jar, a copper alloy finger ring (SF 94) and a small sherd from a blue glass bottle (SF 98). The

Roman part of the sequence was overlain by alluvial layers 1300 and 1301, with a combined thickness of 0.95m, which contained no artefactual material but were evidently more recent in date.

Field system and crop-processing area west of the spring channel

The use of this area that had been established during Phase 4, as agricultural enclosures and for crop processing, continued. The latter activity appears to have intensified, with three corndrying ovens, three stone-lined pits and a threshing/malting floor attributed to this phase. Two subphases (5a and 5b; Fig. 3.30) were identified on stratigraphic grounds, although they need not correspond with the subphases in the enclosure complex associated with the villa or the field system east of the spring channel. Where there was no stratigraphic relationship, it is possible that features

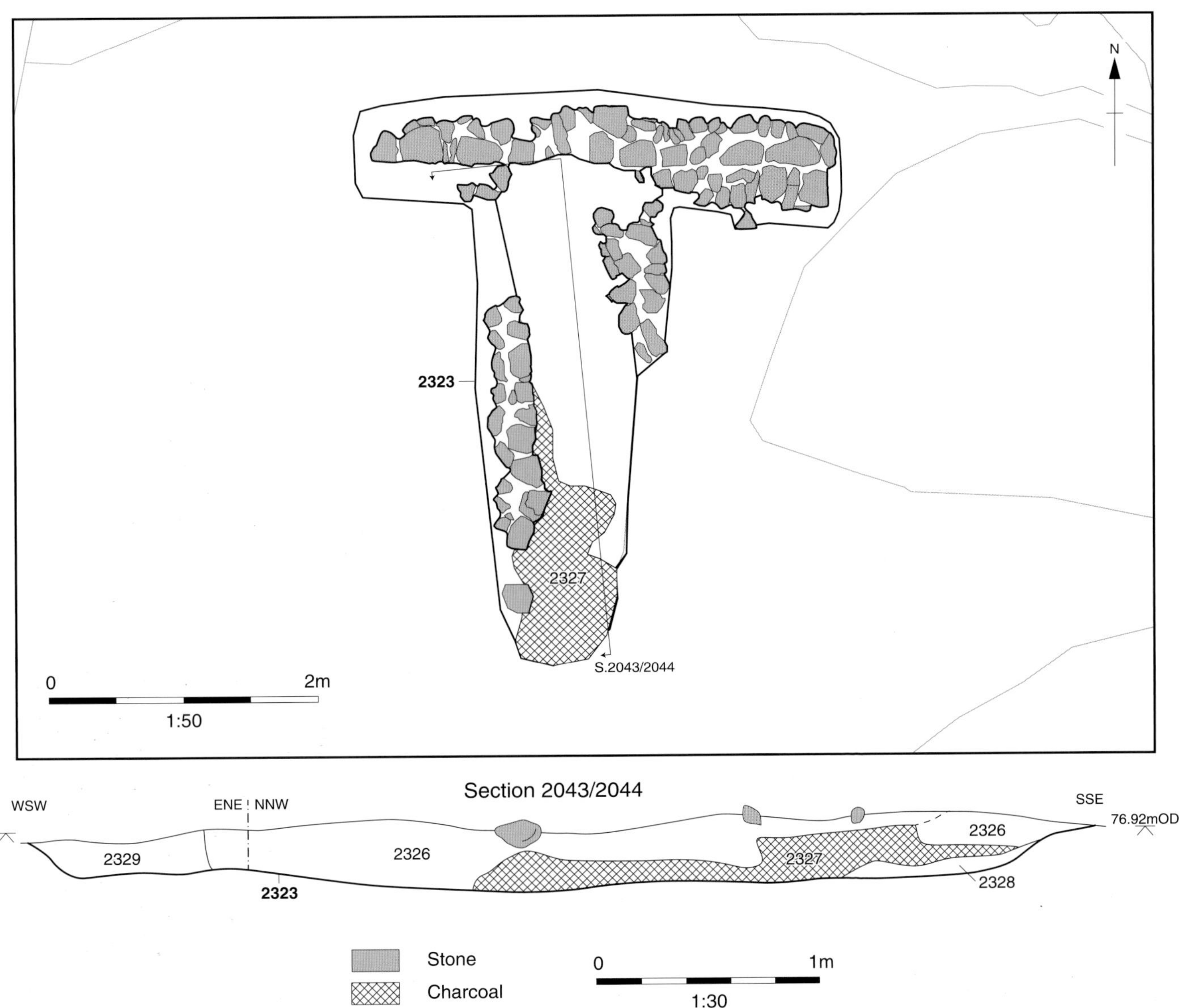

Fig. 3.31 Corndrying oven 2323: plan and section

of subphase 5a continued in use alongside those of subphase 5b (eg the complex including corndrying oven 2130 and pits 2129 and 2135).

The alignments of some of the Phase 4 boundaries were retained, and the modifications made during Phase 5 evidently comprised systematic development of the existing arrangement rather than its replacement. Ditch 2495, for example, which had defined the northern limit of the field system during Phase 4, was replaced by ditch 2493/2519, which extended on a similar alignment slightly further north and continued into the excavation area to the east as ditch 20601. The boundary defined in Phase 4 by axial ditch 2490 similarly appears to have continued in use, at least until it was slighted by the construction of ditch 2188 and pit 2135.

Subphase 5a

Features west of ditch 2490

Ditches 2489 and 2512 were constructed branching off the west side of ditch 2490 and extending on decidedly diverging alignments, the former partly following the north-west side of Phase 4 enclosure 2488 (see Fig. 3.16). They were unusually deep ditches, both measuring up to 0.8m deep, and two postholes identified in the base of ditch 2512 may indicate that it originally held a palisade. South of these features, ditch 2499 formed a boundary parallel to ditch 2490. Corndrying oven 2323, stone-lined pit 2018 and threshing/malting floor 2146 were situated within the triangular area between

ditches 2489 and 2512, their close spatial association suggesting that they represent a functionally related complex.

Corndrying oven 2323 (Figs 3.31–32)

The oven was a T-shaped structure 4.8m long and 0.32m deep, with a cross-flue 3.6m wide at the north end. The stone lining was rather intermittent: it survived best on the north side of the cross-flue, where there were three courses of roughly shaped stones that presented a flush inner face, but only two courses were present on the west side of the main flue and one in the northern part of the east side. Stonework was completely absent for much of the east side and from the north end of the west side, and it is possible that a 19th-century horseshoe recovered from the surface of the oven may have been deposited during an episode of stone-robbing that resulted in the removal of the masonry in these areas. Above a patch of heat-discoloured natural clay (2328), the stokehole was almost completely filled by charcoal-rich layer 2327, which continued into the southern half of the flue as a thin layer. Almost all the charcoal from this layer was oak, and the charred plant remains mostly comprised grains and chaff of spelt. The oven was particularly poor in artefacts, the backfill (2326 and 2329) producing only four small sherds of pottery.

Stone-lined pit 2018 (Fig. 3.33)

Pit 2018 was 5.5m west of the corndrying oven and was approximately square, measuring 2.3m by 2.1m. The south-west corner had been removed by a medieval furrow, and the structure survived best

Fig. 3.32 Corndrying oven 2323 before excavation with part of threshing floor 2146 to right, view to north, scales 1m

Fig. 3.33 Stone-lined pit 2018, view to east, scale 1m

on the north and east sides, where the lining had three courses of stonework surviving, with the fourth course represented by a single stone at the north-east corner. The base of the pit was provided with a floor composed of flat stones up to 0.4m across. No fills survived that were associated with the use of the pit, which had been backfilled with rubble that probably derived from the upper parts of the walls. The rubble contained just two sherds of pottery, one of which came from a bowl in Oxfordshire colour-coated ware and provided a *terminus post quem* after *c* AD 240 for the demolition of the structure.

Threshing/malting floor 2146 (Fig. 3.34)

The floor lay immediately east of corndrying oven 2323 and comprised a semicircular flagstone surface measuring 4.5m by 2.3m, set into a purpose-dug hollow up to 0.27m deep. On the surface was a localised deposit of burnt material (2148), some 1.5m by 1.0m across, a sample (2022) from which contained detached coleoptiles suggestive of waste from the removal of glumes and sprouts from part-processed malt. The deposit may have built up on this surface, although it may be a dump rather than an *in situ* accumulation on a primary working surface. The remainder of the feature had been backfilled with stone rubble, much of it burnt, which was clearly distinct from the flat stones forming the surface, and therefore probably derived from one of the other structures nearby. The small pottery assemblage recovered from the rubble included a rim sherd and sooted body sherd from an Oxfordshire colour-coated ware bowl dated after *c* AD 240, and there were also a socketed object or rolled strip (SF 105), a small group of poorly preserved binding fragments (SF 106) and a small piece of colourless window glass.

Features east of ditch 2490

The enclosure that was bounded during Phase 4 by ditches 2498 and 2576 (see Fig. 3.16) was redefined by their replacement on the same alignments by ditches 2513 and 2056 (Fig. 3.30). Corndrying oven 2130 and stone-lined pit 2129 were constructed centrally within it, and when the enclosure was subsequently extended to the west by the construction of ditch 2188, large pit 2135, which may have had a stone floor, was dug in the north-west corner. This group of features appears to have represented a coherent set similar to the structures west of ditch

Fig. 3.34 Threshing floor 2146, with the corner of corndrying oven 2323 in the foreground, view to east, scales 2m

Fig. 3.35 Stone-lined pit 2129 and corndrying oven 2130 before excavation, view to north

2490, forming a second focus of crop-processing activity (Figs 3.35-36).

An unusual element of the arrangement in this enclosure was the presence of a U-shaped arrangement of 11 postholes that encircled corndrying oven 2130 and pit 2129. The postholes were substantial features, measuring up to 0.7m across and 0.4m deep, and all but three contained packing stones, although the stones were clearly disturbed, most likely as a result of the removal of the posts. The similarity of the postholes indicates that they formed part of a single structure around the pit and oven, measuring 11m by 11m. This would be rather wide for a single span roof but there was no

evidence for internal supports, so it is uncertain whether the structure was a building over the pit and oven or a palisade around them.

Corndrying oven 2130 (Fig. 3.37)

This was a T-shaped structure, aligned N–S, with the stokehole at the south end very close to the adjacent edge of pit 2129. It was in fact difficult to distinguish between the stokehole and the flue, since the stonework of the latter was incomplete, particularly at the south end, and the fill was identical throughout. The entire structure was 4.2m long and the cross-flue was 2.8m across. Stone lining was present only on either side of the

Fig. 3.36 Corndrying oven 2130 with stone-lined pit 2129 to the rear, filled with groundwater, view to south, scales 1m and 2m

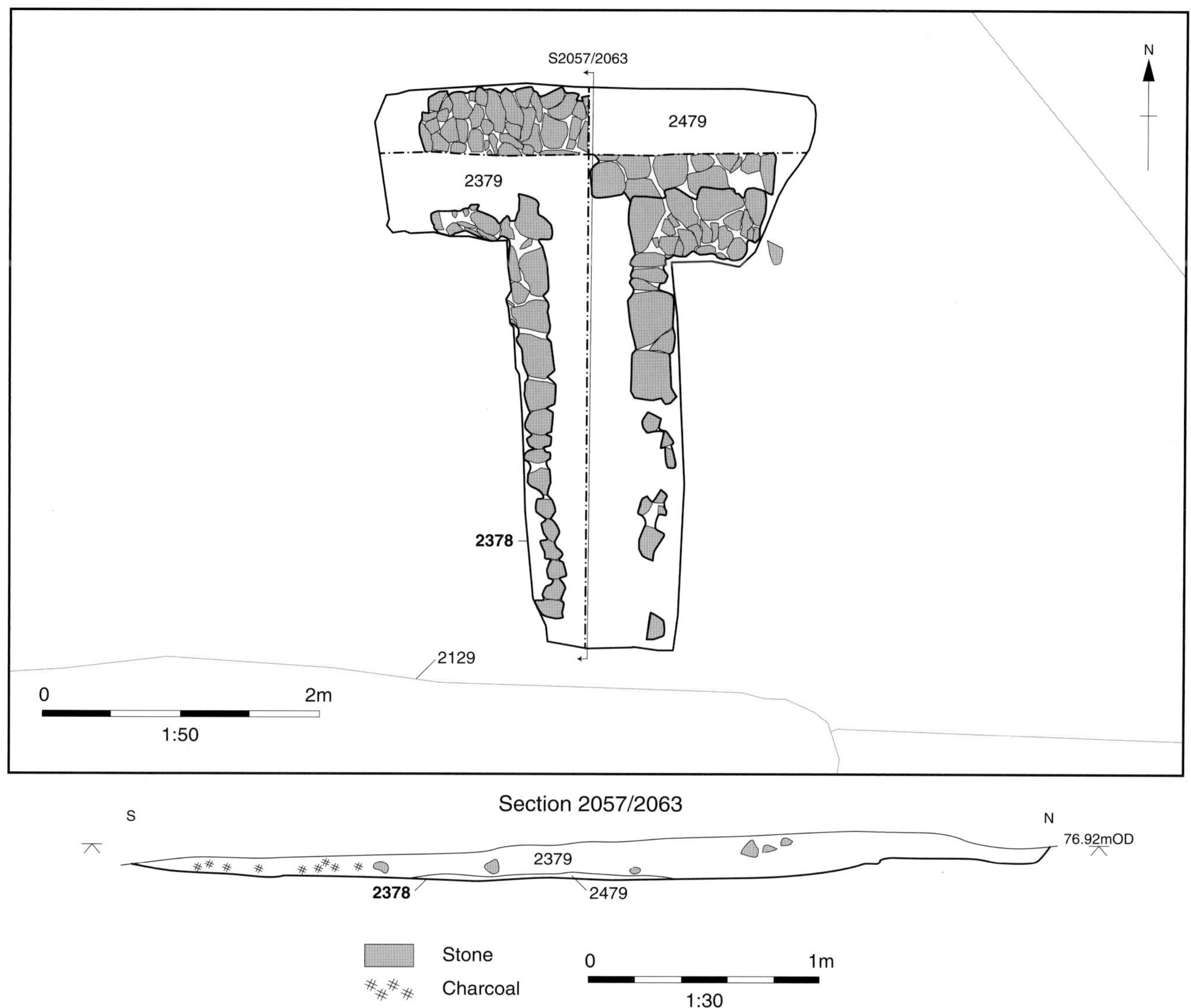

Fig. 3.37 Corndrying oven 2130: plan and section

northern part of the flue and on the south side of the cross-flue, and nowhere survived as more than a single course. Unusually, the cross-flue was provided with a floor of flat stones. The fill (2379/2479) was sampled spatially (samples 2044, 2045 and 2046; Chapter 5), the results indicating that spelt chaff was predominant in the cross-flue and grain in the main flue (albeit in smaller quantities), while the stokehole produced an assemblage of charcoal that was almost all oak. The fill also contained some rubble and a fragment of oven plate.

Stone-lined pit 2129 (Figs 3.38-40)

Pit 2129 was a large rectangular feature that measured 5.9m by 3.5m and 0.8m deep, and had a flat base and stone-lined sides. The stonework appeared to have been constructed in two stages (Fig. 3.39): the lower part, amounting to almost the entire surviving height of the wall on the north and east sides but only a little over half the height on the

south and west, comprised thin stones that had evidently been carefully laid in fairly regular courses, whereas the upper part utilised larger stones of more varied shapes and had a more irregular, rubbly appearance. The reason for this difference is uncertain, and there was no evidence to indicate whether the two types of coursing were part of the original construction or result from subsequent repair or replacement of the upper courses.

There were no deposits within the pit that were associated with its use, the fills all being the result of demolition and backfilling (Fig. 3.40). Collapse or deliberate demolition of the walls was evident in two localised locations at the east end and south side, resulting in spreads of rubble on the corresponding part of the base (2172). Initial backfilling comprised a deposit of yellow clay (2174–5, 2250–2) that extended throughout the base of the feature but was particularly thick in the eastern half, where it was 0.5m thick and originated as a distinct mound (2250) in the central part of the pit, having perhaps

Fig. 3.38 Recording stone-lined pit 2129, view to south-east

been shovelled into it from the adjacent ground surface. A few sherds of pottery were recovered from these deposits, including part of the base from a Nene Valley colour-coated ware dish dated after *c* AD 270. The upper part of the pit was filled with very different material (2176=2254): a deposit of charred material dominated by spelt glume bases, perhaps representing a dump of waste from the removal of glumes and sprouts from part-processed malt

Pit 2135 (Figs 3.41-42)

The pit was located at the north-west corner of the enclosure and intersected with the surrounding ditch 2188, although it was not possible to discern the relationship between the two since they were

Fig. 3.39 Stonework in the south-west quadrant of stone-lined pit 2129, view to south, scale 2m

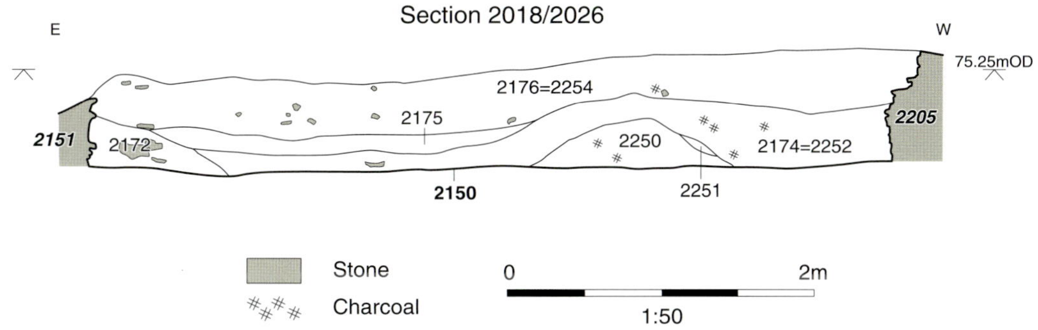

Fig. 3.40 Section through stone-lined pit 2129

filled with identical material. It was subrectangular in plan and measured 4.0m by 2.9m, with a flat base at a depth of 0.58m. A rough floor of unshaped but generally flat stones (2134) of rather random form with frequent gaps between the stones, was laid across the base. Once again, the fills derived from backfilling and provided no evidence for the function of the pit, comprising a layer of yellow clay (2074/2137) and a dark main fill (2075/2138) that contained 38 sherds of pottery, weighing 1368g, that

appeared to be largely 2nd-century in date based on the presence of a flanged bowl in black-burnished ware, a wall-sided mortarium in Colchester white ware and some pink-grogged ware.

Subphase 5b

To this subphase were attributed features associated with the final episode of activity at the crop-processing area west of ditch 2490. The existing

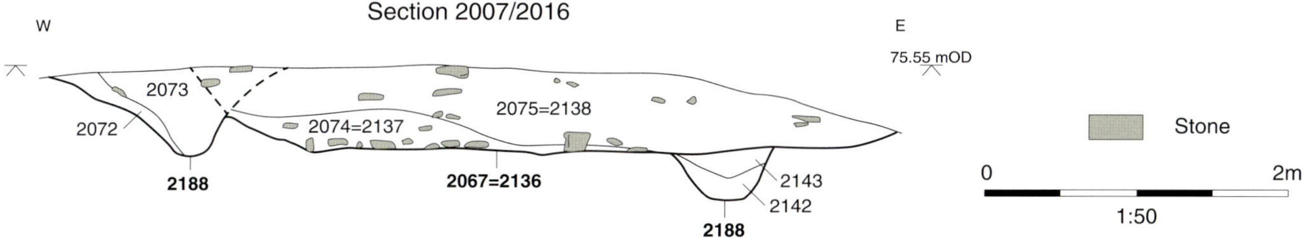

Fig. 3.41 Section through pit 2135 and ditch 2188

Fig. 3.42 Stone floor in the north-east quadrant of pit 2135, view to west, scale 1m

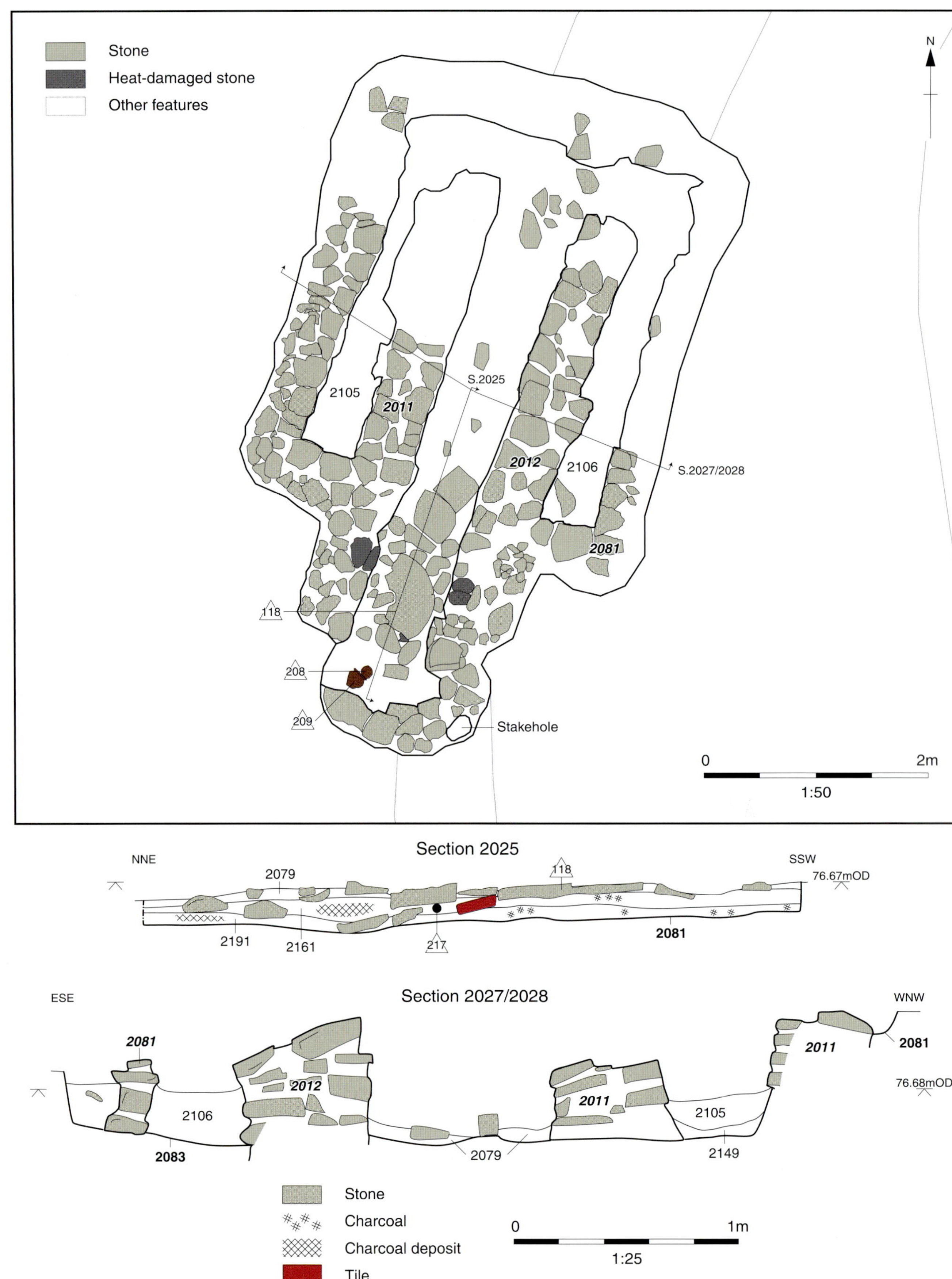

Fig. 3.43 *Corndryer 2039: plan and sections*

features appear to have gone out of use, and a new corndrying oven (2039) was constructed, as well as a circular ditched enclosure (2487). The southern part of main N–S boundary ditch 2490 was recut as ditch 2514 at this time; dating evidence was limited to two sherds of pottery but included a rim sherd from a lid-seated jar in a shelly fabric, probably from Harrold and of 4th-century date. The dating evidence from the small artefactual assemblage was insufficient to demonstrate whether the eastern processing area also continued into this subphase.

Corndrying oven 2039 (Figs 3.43–46)

This was the only corndrying oven at Panattoni Park that was not of T-shaped form, instead comprising a reversed-tuning-fork type. It also differed from the earlier ovens in being aligned NE–SW rather than N–S or E–W. The stonework of the north-eastern half had been comprehensively robbed, but the south-western half was well preserved and survived to a height of 0.5m. Some of the stonework leaned inward as a result of subsidence caused by the oven having been constructed over infilled ditch 2489, but since it had evidently been successfully used, this damage may not have occurred until after the structure was abandoned.

The stokehole was situated at the south-west end and comprised an oval measuring 1.0m by 0.6m, enclosed by a stone lining except for a break on the west side although it was uncertain whether this was to allow access or resulted from later damage.

From the stokehole, the main flue extended for 4.5m and was flanked by the returns of the cross-flue, the footprint of which was clearly evident from the remains of the fill that survived *in situ*, although its stonework only survived at the ends of the returns. Where stonework was preserved, amounting to up to five courses, it was carefully constructed, with a straight inner face except where affected by subsidence. Heat damage to the stones on either side of the main flue indicated that the fire was typically located a little under 1m from the entrance. Heat-damaged stones elsewhere in the structure, where exposure to fire resulting from use of the oven was unlikely, were probably reused from one of the earlier ovens, and a few roof-tiles were also incorporated into the flues. A piece of fired clay with tile impressions, recovered from the backfill, is likely to have derived from a drying floor constructed from tiles bonded with clay.

A thin layer of dirty clay with charcoal inclusions (2149/2191) extended along the base of the main flue (Fig. 3.12, section 2025), which may represent debris from the initial use of the oven but could alternatively be trample from its construction. More certainly derived from use of the kiln was a layer of charcoal-rich material (2161) that produced a soil sample (2019) rich in spelt wheat glume bases with a smaller proportion of weed seeds; the paucity of cereal grains in the layer implies the material is burnt fuel rather than derived from the accidental burning of grain during kilning. The layer contained a coin dated

Fig. 3.44 Corndrying oven 2039, view to north

Fig. 3.45 Shelly ware jars SF 108 and 109 in the stokehole of corndrying oven 2039, view to north-east, scale 0.3m

Fig. 3.46 Corndrying oven 2039, showing millstone SF 118, view to north-east, scale 1m

AD 364–78 (SF 117). Above this, the oven was backfilled with a mixture of soil and rubble (2079). Two groups of artefacts at the base of this layer appeared to have been placed deliberately before the main episode of backfilling. These comprised a pair of shelly ware jars, one standing upright and somewhat damaged (SF 108) and the other nearly complete and lying on its side (SF 109), which had been placed against the side of the stokehole (Fig. 3.45), and two adjoining fragments (one of which broke into three on lifting) of a large upper millstone (SF 118) that had been placed flat within the main flue (Fig. 3.46).

Enclosure 2487

The enclosure was defined by a penannular ditch, open to the north-west, which cut through threshing/malting floor 2146. There was no stratigraphic relationship with corndrying oven 2323, which lay within the enclosure, or with stone-lined pit 2018, which lay outside to the west, and it is possible that they continued in use. The ditch was 11m in diameter and up to 0.65m deep and yielded a small assemblage of pottery and tile and a small fragment of window glass.

Field system east of the channel

The geophysical survey had recorded a field system that was exposed, from north to south, in the eastern part of Area 2, the Watching Brief Area and Area 3, with further associated boundaries in Area 4 (see Figs 1.2-3). The level of stratigraphic detail obtained for each area varied depending on the size of the area and whether it was subject to full excavation or watching brief level recording. Consequently, while three subphases were identified in the large Area 2, it was not possible to achieve such definition in the Watching Brief Area, and although a clear sequence was established in Area 3 it could not be related to the sequence in Area 2. The earliest late Roman activity in Area 2 (subphase 5a) comprised an

unusual arrangement of two concentric oval enclosures and a possible stone structure, the function of which is uncertain, which appear to represent a localised episode with no contemporary features in the areas to the south. The subsequent rectilinear field system comprised subphases 5b and 5c in Area 2 and the only Phase 5 features in the Watching Brief Area and Area 3.

Area 2

Three subphases were defined in this area (Fig. 3.47). The first (subphase 5a) comprised an unusual arrangement of two concentric oval enclosures and a possible stone structure, the function of which is uncertain, which were completely removed when they were replaced by a rectilinear field system (subphase 5b) which was subsequently recut and slightly reordered (subphase 5c). The detailed chronology of this sequence was problematic and is discussed in detail in Chapter 6.

Subphase 5a

The Phase 4 enclosures in this area were replaced by an unusual arrangement comprising large oval enclosure 20350, with a roughly central smaller enclosure (20348/20351), perhaps for a domestic structure, and other subdivisions. A second focus of activity, immediately adjacent to the larger enclosure, was represented by possible stone structure 20035. The composition of the pottery assemblage suggests that domestic occupation may have formed an element of the activities in this subphase (see Biddulph, Chapter 4), although the quantity of pottery from most of the features was not notably larger than those from other areas or phases.

Main enclosure 20350

The outer, main enclosure was defined by a steep-

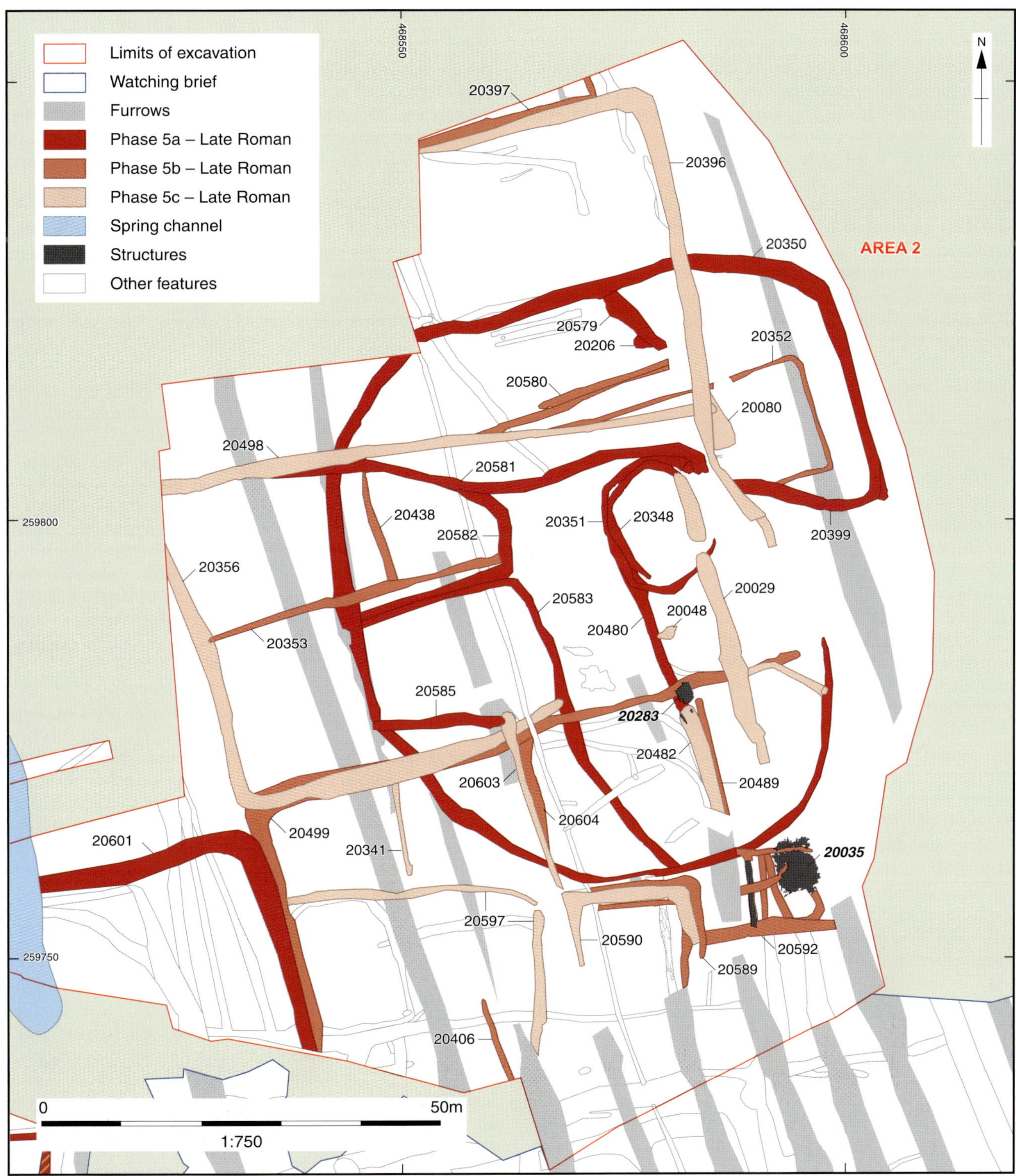

Fig. 3.47 Field system east of the spring channel, Phase 5

sided V-shaped ditch that was up to 2m wide and 0.85m deep, although it appeared more truncated to the south, where it was only 0.4m deep. In most interventions it had only one single fill, perhaps indicating a single episode of deliberate backfilling. There were few artefacts, but the pottery assemblage included sherds of Nene Valley colour-coated ware dated after AD 270. It enclosed an area that measured 65m by 60m, with access provided by a break of 15m on the east side, between an in-turn of the enclosure ditch (20399) and a terminus to the south. Ditch 20399 yielded a single coin dated AD 335–41 (SF 44). A possible earlier terminus on the north side, preceding the in-turned ditch, represented the only evidence that the enclosure may have been of more than a single phase.

Enclosure 20348/20351

Set slightly east of the centre of the main enclosure, and facing the entrance, was a smaller oval enclosure defined by a ditch with two phases (20348 and 20351). The earlier phase (20348) was up to 0.42m deep on the west side but petered out to the east and south, and so the full circuit did not survive. Ditch 20351, however, was more complete, and defined an area of 13.5m by 11m with an east-facing entrance. The entrance was 8m wide, but was probably originally smaller, since the south terminus appeared to peter out due to plough-truncation. The enclosure would have been of a size appropriate to enclose a domestic structure such as a roundhouse, but there were no internal features, and the finds assemblage from the ditch was small.

Other subdivisions within enclosure 20350

A series of ditched boundaries, each 0.4–0.5m deep, created internal subdivisions within the main enclosure. The northern part was divided from the rest by a slightly circuitous boundary formed by ditches 20399 and 20581, the latter producing a coin of AD 335–41 (SF 40). This area was accessed via an entrance adjacent to central enclosure 20348/20351, although the east side of the entrance was truncated by a later ditch. A further subdivision within the northern area was represented by ditch 20579, which branched off the main enclosure ditch and extended for 9m, cutting pit 20206, which was the only discrete feature within the northern area. The pit was 0.5m deep and contained a substantially complete funnel-necked beaker, as well as a few other sherds and pieces from both ceramic and stone roof tiles.

The western side of the main enclosure was divided into three enclosures of differing size (20582, 20583 and 20585), constructed against the perimeter ditch. None contained internal features and the finds assemblages from the ditches were negligible, but ditch 20583 contained a coin dated AD 388–402 (SF 45) and a less well preserved coin of probable 4th-century date (SF 120). A further subdivision (20480) extended south from central enclosure 20348/20351 and may originally have continued to the perimeter ditch, although its southern end had been destroyed by the digging of later ditches. The upper fill of this ditch also contained a coin dated AD 388–402 (SF 46).

Stone structure 20035 (Figs 3.48-49)

South of enclosure 20350, immediately adjacent to the enclosure ditch, lay structure 20035, which comprised wall foundation 20045 and stone surface 20042. The close proximity of the two elements suggests that they were parts of a single structure, although the precise form was less certain. The foundation was aligned N–S, roughly perpendicular to the adjacent enclosure ditch, and extended for *c* 7.5m, although neither original end survived: to the north it was cut by ditch 20032 and to the south by

ditch 20592. It was 1.2m wide and more than 0.3m deep, constructed from at least two courses of pitched stone. A possible robber trench at the north end of the wall contained an iron knife (SF 187).

Surface 20042 was a little less than 3m from the wall. It comprised a single layer of stones and was roughly rectangular, measuring 6m by 4.5m, although the edges were somewhat irregular and poorly defined. No stratified finds were recovered, but cleaning of the surface (20436) resulted in the recovery of 58 sherds, weighing 1499g, that were deposited during the late 3rd century or later, as suggested by the presence of bead-and-flanged bowl in black-burnished ware, Hadham oxidised ware, Oxford red-colour-coated ware and Nene Valley grey ware, as well as a coin dated AD 364–78 (SF 66) and a radiate of AD 271–4 (SF 57). Also recovered was part of an articulating cattle leg, comprising the humerus, radius and part of the ulna.

It was unclear whether the wall and surface formed part of a building or represented external features, not least because they had been substantially disturbed by a series of shallow ditches: ditch 20043 ran adjacent and parallel to the wall foundation, while ditch 20040 extended along (or cut) the western edge of the stone surface, and ditches 20032 and 20052 both began within the surface and followed curving alignments to the west, cutting through the wall foundation. A small part of a curving ditch (20031) was also recorded at the south-east edge of the surface, but the relationship between them was not established. This represents an unusual concentration of such features, but their purpose remains obscure; one possibility is that they were drains associated with the surface, but if this were the case, the relationship between ditches 20032 and 20052 and the wall foundation would require the wall and surface to be unrelated, since they could not have been contemporary.

Subphase 5b

The arrangement of rectilinear fields that was subsequently constructed across the area completely disregarded the oval enclosure that preceded it. The boundary ditches of the original layout were typically 0.3–0.5m deep and in some locations were substantially truncated by recutting in subphase 5c, when the ditches were slightly deeper, but sufficient survived to indicate the original form of the complex. L-shaped ditch 20499, which was the most substantial of these boundaries, with a depth up to 1.0m, evidently formed a significant boundary that marked the western limit of the complex as well as dividing the northern part from the south, where the different form of the enclosures may indicate a different function. The results of the geophysical survey suggested that ditch 20397 was probably the northern limit of the complex. Between these boundaries, neither the western nor the eastern limits of the field system survived, but it is likely that they were defined by ditches that lay in

Fig. 3.48 Plan of structure 20035

Fig. 3.49 Structure 20035, with surface 20042 in the foreground and wall 20045 to the left, view to north-west

the same locations as ditches 20356 and 20396 in subphase 5c and had been completely destroyed when they were recut. The complex was thus *c* 65m wide and the part north of ditch 20499 was divided laterally into three large rectangular enclosures by E–W ditches 20353 and 20580, with N–S ditch 20438 representing a further subdivision within the middle enclosure. Within the eastern part of this area, ditch 20352, which was one of the shallower features, defined a discrete rectangular enclosure 12.5m wide and at least 28m long.

The arrangement south of ditch 20499 was less clear, but ditch 20604, which branched off 20499, and ditch 20489 probably defined a square enclosure 18–20m across, with an entrance provided by a break 1.2m wide between the north end of ditch 20489 and the adjacent edge of ditch 20499. This enclosure was abutted to the south by an enclosure whose north and east sides survived as L-shaped ditch 20589, with ditch 20406 perhaps forming the west side. A further boundary was defined by ditch 20592, which branched off the east side of ditch 20589.

Finds assemblages from this subphase were rather meagre and most of the pottery groups were assigned quite broad date ranges, the only certainly 4th-century sherds being a small, burnt rim sherd from an Oxfordshire mortarium of Young's type C100 from ditch 20580 and two sherds in a shelly fabric probably from Harrold, from a straight-sided bowl in ditch 20589 and a curving-sided dish in ditch 20604. The latter ditch also yielded an articulating cattle skull and mandible and an articulating naviculo-cuboid and metatarsal from successive fills, one of which also included four fragments of fallow deer antler, representing evidence for a species that is rare in Roman contexts in Britain.

Subphase 5c

The arrangement of the field system in subphase 5c was very similar to that in subphase 5b, most of the boundary ditches being recut with only a few alterations to the existing disposition. The ditches of this subphase were larger than the previous ones, rarely measuring less than 0.4–0.5m deep, and ditches 20396 and 20601 were particularly deep at 0.9–1.0m. The northern part of the field system was bounded by ditches 20356 and 20396, which may have been a single ditch, meeting beyond the north-western limit of the excavation area. Ditch 20029 also formed part of the eastern limit of the field system, and a complex entrance between the northern end of this ditch and the southern end of ditch 20396 may have been designed to facilitate processing of livestock entering or leaving the complex; the end of ditch 20396 curved outward to create a funnel-shaped passage 11m long that was 3.2m wide at the mouth and increased to 6.5m at the southern end, while a 1.2m-wide break in the adjacent part of ditch 20029 provided an alternative access point. Immediately north of the entrance, ditch 20396 was overlain by a rubble layer (20080) that extended for some 7m by 4m. It was uncertain whether the layer was associated with the entrance, perhaps representing the remains of a hardcore surface laid down after the arrangement of ditches went out of use, or rubble from demolition of an associated structure. The only notable find from the layer was copper alloy bracelet (SF 36). Ditch 20029 was particularly productive of artefactual material, an intervention in the central part being the only location in this subphase that produced more than 1kg of pottery, and also yielded two coins dated AD 350–64 (SF 100 and 101) from the upper fill. The tripartite division of this area during subphase 5b may have been replaced by a division into two halves since ditch 20580 was replaced by ditch 20498 but ditch 20353 was not recut. The southern end of ditch 20356 turned eastward to replace ditch 20499 as the boundary between this area and the features to the south; unlike the earlier ditch, it did not extend all the way across the complex, leaving access between the areas to the north and south. A copper alloy finger ring (SF 143) was recovered from the surface of the ditch terminus. The only discrete feature within this part of the field system was irregularly

shaped pit 20048, which was 0.32m deep and produced a small group of pottery.

South of ditch 20356, the enclosure formerly defined by ditches 20489 and 20604 was recut as ditches 20482 and 20603. The upper fill of the former contained one of the latest-dated sherds from the excavation, a rouletted Oxfordshire colour-coated ware dish of Young type C46 dated after *c* AD 340, and the northern terminal of ditch 20603 yielded a curving blade probably from a scythe or sickle (SF 48). The terminal was associated with a localised spread of stone rubble (20283) that had been laid down over the fills of subphase 5b ditch 20499, perhaps as hardstanding at a busy entrance to the enclosure. A coin of 2nd- or 3rd-century date (SF 119) was recovered from the layer. The enclosure adjacent to the south, formed in subphase 5b by ditch 20589, was recut as ditch 20590, and the two enclosures that were formerly located to the west of this were replaced by a single larger enclosure with a possible corner entrance (20597). The area west of these enclosures was subject to more subdivision than had previously been the case; L-shaped ditch 20597 formed two sides of an enclosure that measured *c* 25m across and continued beyond the southern limit of the excavation area, and to the north ditch 20341 divided a pair of smaller enclosures that each measured *c* 15m by 10m. In this subphase the field system may have been integrated into the smaller block of enclosures associated with the crop-processing area by the westward extension of ditch 20601, the alignment of which suggested that it continued into that area as ditch 2493/2519 (see Fig 3.30), although admittedly there was a large discrepancy in their dimensions: both comprised two phases of ditch, but the earlier phase of ditch 20601 was 0.85m deep, whereas its later phase and both phases of ditch 2493/2519 measured only 0.2–0.3m deep. The uppermost fill of the earlier phase of ditch 20601 yielded a coin dated AD 341–8 (SF 59).

Watching Brief Area and Area 3 (Fig. 3.50)

The dates of the features in the Watching Brief Area could only be obtained from pottery recovered from their upper surface, which did not allow for detailed elaboration of the chronological sequence. The pottery indicated that activity here did not begin until after *c* AD 160, but the small quantity of sherds and the broad (and in many cases effectively open-ended) associated date ranges were of limited utility in this respect. It should be noted, however, that although only a small number of features produced sherds of definitely late Roman (Phase 5) date, very few pottery groups precluded so late a date, and this, as well as the alignment and arrangement of the ditched boundaries, suggested that most of the features were probably late Roman.

A possible exception to the late Roman date was provided by ditches 6043, 6046 and 6052, in the western part of the area, which were continuations of boundary ditches in Area 2 that could equally

Fig. 3.50 Watching Brief Area and Area 3

have been middle or late Roman from the excavated evidence. They appeared to define an enclosure some 40m long that adjoined the south side of the crop-processing area. The possibility of a middle Roman date in this instance is increased by the proximity of inhumation burial 6005 and cremation burial 6007, which were the only features in the Watching Brief Area that were excavated, the latter grave including a vessel of this date. The inhumation grave was only 0.18m deep and contained the remains of an adult male (6004) who had been interred supine with the hands crossed over the pelvis, without evidence for coffin or grave goods. The cremation, in contrast, had been placed within a shell-tempered urn (Fig. 4.9, no. 24) and was accompanied by a near-complete flagon or bottle in Lower Nene Valley white ware, probably made between AD 120 and 230 (Fig. 4.9, no. 23). The urn contained the remains of an adult of unknown sex (6006).

The main part of the field system was *c* 80m wide, delimited by ditches 6021 and 6032. Ditch 6023/6038/20561 appeared to be a significant boundary, dividing the enclosures in Area 2 from those in the Watching Brief Area and Area 3. The central part of the ditch extended through the southern limit of Area 2, where excavation of a small intervention resulted in the recovery of a mixed assemblage of animal bone that included a large skull fragment from a red deer with the antler base attached, as well as two further fragments of red deer antler. South of this boundary, ditches 6022 and 6018/6033 defined a pair of conjoined enclosures each measuring *c* 35m by 20m, with ditches 6013 and 6032 forming an enclosure adjacent to the east. A lump of Roman concrete measuring *c* 210mm by 110mm was recovered from ditch 6018 during the evaluation (MOLA 2015c, 52), but in the absence of other evidence for a building here it may have been transported from the main complex of villa buildings. Ditches 6031 and 6040 may represent further subdivisions or a separate phase in the development of the field system. The northern part of ditch 6032 produced a particularly large concentration of pottery amounting to 75 sherds (2.2kg) including a bead-and-flanged bowl in Nene Valley grey ware, a funnel-necked beaker in Oxford red colour-coated ware and a dish in a fine oxidised ware copying an Oxford red colour-coated ware prototype, together indicating a date no earlier than *c* AD 270–300, and short ditch segment 6024, which may have been associated with an entrance between this enclosure and enclosure 6018/6033, yielded the only certainly 4th-century sherd: a large part of a straight-sided bowl from Harrold. Enclosure 6013/6032 contained the only discrete feature from which any material was recovered, oval pit 6015, which yielded the base of a beaker or flagon with a dark slip, probably from the Nene Valley. At the eastern end of this arrangement, two pits (6010), 1m apart and each 1.75–1.85m across, were exposed in an area where an L-shaped arrangement of discrete

anomalies in the geophysical survey results had indicated a possible building (C2; MOLA 2015a, 15). Neither pit yielded any artefactual material, and immediately to the south, where the geophysics suggested a possible associated penannular feature, the watching brief identified only an amorphous spread (6008) and a linear feature on an anomalous NE–SW orientation (6051).

The southern limit of the field system comprised a pair of rectangular enclosures that each measured 35m by 15m and extended into Area 3. The earliest boundary in Area 3 was E–W ditch 3078, which had two phases and was cut by the eastern enclosure of the conjoined pair at the southern end of the field system (3075/3076/3077), perhaps indicating that these were a later addition and that this ditch marked the southern limit of the complex in its original form. The eastern half of this enclosure was defined by two successive ditches, each 0.3–0.4m deep, but in the western part only a single ditch could be discerned, which was up to 0.8m deep. Its relationship with the adjoining enclosure 6026/6036 had been truncated by a combination of a medieval furrow and a more recent field drain, but the upper fill of ditch 3076 yielded a remarkable hoard of three agricultural tools, comprising a spud (SF 189), a field or mower's anvil (SF 190) and the head of cross-pane hand hammer (SF 191), as well as a base sherd from an Oxfordshire colour-coated ware beaker or jar dated after *c* AD 240. The enclosure was cut by L-shaped ditch 3074. A few irregular curvilinear features were identified but could not be investigated due to flooding of the trench, and it is uncertain whether they were associated with the field system, or indeed whether they were archaeological in origin.

Shallow grave 3004 was situated at the western end of the excavation area and lay on an E–W alignment similar to that of the field system. Ploughing had truncated all but the bottom 0.1m of the grave and had removed the skull. The individual interred was a prime adult male (3006), who was placed supine with the arms extended by the sides. Three sherds of pottery recovered from the fill included a fragment of Lower Nene Valley grey ware dated to AD 150–300.

Area 4

The two ditched boundaries that extended across this area in Phase 4 continued in use in Phase 5, with minor modifications (see Fig. 2.1). The southern half of the western boundary (4379) was recut on a slightly different alignment as a more substantial feature than its predecessor, 0.5–0.94m deep, with a return to the west that continued beyond the edge of the excavation area (4384). The ditch had been recorded in evaluation Trench 70, and the geophysical survey indicated that it may have continued to the west of the excavation area for a further 100m. There was no evidence for a corresponding replacement for the northern part of the Phase 4 boundary. The eastern boundary (4387) was recut on an alignment slightly to the east of its Phase 4 iteration. Artefactual material in this area was again sparse, but a pair of coins of Constantine I (SF 112 and 113) minted between 330–5 were recovered from the upper fill of ditch 4384 and a single incomplete issue (SF 56), dated 320–1, came from ditch 4387.

Chapter 4

Artefactual evidence

WORKED FLINT *by Tom Lawrence*

The excavation produced 243 struck and 40 burnt unworked flints weighing 417g (Table 4.2). For the most part, the flints dated from the Neolithic to Bronze Age but derived from later features. However, a small scatter in Area 4 provides *in situ* evidence for early Mesolithic activity, a rarity for Northamptonshire.

Methodology

The artefacts were catalogued according to OA South's standard system of broad artefact/debitage types (Anderson-Whymark 2013; Bradley 1999). During the analysis, additional information on the condition (rolled, abraded, fresh and degree of cortication) and state of the artefacts (burnt, broken, or visibly utilised) was also recorded. Retouched pieces were classified according to standard morphological descriptions (eg Bamford 1985, 72–7; Healy 1988, 48–9; Bradley 1999). Technological attribute analysis was undertaken and included the recording of butt and termination type (Inizan *et al.* 1999), flake type (Harding 1990), hammer mode (Ohnuma and Bergman 1982), and the presence of platform edge abrasion. The length, width and breadth of all complete debitage greater than 10mm and all tools were measured according to Saville (1980), as was the platform width and depth where present.

Flint scatter 4235

The assemblage

A scatter of 71 flints (4235; Table 4.2) lay on a gravel spur on the southern edge of Area 4 and had been truncated by several ditches. Three flints, including a microlith, lay to the north-east of this. Scatter 4235 has a high blade index of 52% and its curated pieces consist of opposed platform blade cores (Fig. 4.2, no. 1), single partial crested pieces, a core tablet, a rejuvenation flake and a mishit microburin. The tool count is very high at 12%. This may either be due to disruption of the scatter by the ditches, or reflect the fact that the scatter represented a task-specific occupation area (see below). The tools consist of piercers (Fig. 4.2, no. 2), scrapers and a denticulate. Although no microliths were present, an obliquely blunted point found to the north-east of the scatter could represent stray hunting activity associated with the scatter. The microburin and the high blade count clearly show that the scatter is Mesolithic and that microlith production took place. This is further supported by the opposed platform cores (which have evidence of tableting) and crested pieces. Generally, opposed platform cores are more common in the early Mesolithic than the late Mesolithic. The nearby obliquely blunted point (Fig. 4.2, no. 3) may be early Mesolithic but its small length (19.4mm) might also suggest a late Mesolithic date (eg Saville 1990). A comparison of

Table 4.1 Quantification of the artefactual assemblage by phase

| | Phase 1 | | Phase 2 | | Phase 3 | | Phase 4 | | Phase 5 | | Other Roman | | Unstratified | |
	No.	Wt (g)	No.	Wt (g)	No.	Wt (g)	No.	Wt (g)	No.	Wt (g)	No.	Wt (g)	No.	Wt (g)
Bone object									1	-				
Building material (ceramic)					9	860	800	120365	1471	274246	48	5826	16	469
Building material (stone)					2	172	34	10753	42	16344				
Coins					1	-	1	-	35	-			4	-
Fired clay			5	112	135	1098	56	421	362	4700	3	7	13	79
Flint	243	-												
Glass (vessel and objects)							1	-	6	-			2	-
Glass (window)									2	-				
Metal objects					3	-	31	-	92	-			15	-
Pottery			666	4408	1906	25339	1550	30428	2909	59006	43	836	245	3160
Querns and millstones							1	-	5	-				

the debitage size and blade index of scatter 4235 with sites across England (Tables 4.3-4) suggests an early Mesolithic date is appropriate.

Condition

The condition of the flintwork from scatter 4235 suggests that it was *in situ* (Table 4.5). Many of the flints remained in fresh condition (72%) with only 7% of pieces being moderately damaged. This may be due to interference from the ditches or abrasion from the stony natural on which the flints lay. The majority of flints also had little or no patina.

Table 4.2 The lithic assemblage

Category type	Scatters	Features	Total
Flake	16	86	102
Blade	12	15	27
Bladelet	4	13	17
Blade index	16/32 (50%)	28/114 (24.56%)	44/146 (30.14%)
Chip	21	4	25
Irregular waste	3	11	14
Microburin	1		1
Crested piece	3	1	4
Core tablet	1		1
Core rejuvenation flake	1	2	3
Core single platform blades		1	1
Core opposed platform blades	2	2	4
Core multi-platform flakes		4	4
Core on a flake		1	1
Core fragment	1	6	7
Scraper side and end	1	1	2
Scraper side	1	1	2
Microlith	1		1
Leaf arrowhead		3	3
Barb and tang		1	1
End truncation		3	3
Piercer	2	3	5
Microdenticulate		3	3
Denticulate	1	1	2
Notch		1	1
Knife		1	1
Flake retouched		5	5
Blade retouched		1	1
Burin		1	1
Total	71	171	242
Burnt un-worked no./weight (g)		40/417	40/417
No. burnt (%)	7/71 (9.86%)	9/171 (5.26%)	16/242 (6.61%)
No. broken (%) (not including waste)	33/50 (70.21%)	63/167 (37.72%)	93/217 (42.86%)
No. retouched (%) (not including waste)	6/50 (12%)	26/167 (15.57%)	32/217 (14.75%)

Table 4.3 Comparison of length/width ratios with selected Mesolithic and Neolithic sites in southern Britain

	Scatter 4235	Dagenham, Essex, early Mesolithic (Champness et al. 2015)	Great Western Park, Didcot, early Mesolithic (Hayden et al. in prep.)	Street Lane, East Sussex, early and late Mesolithic (Butler 2007)	Dagenham, Essex, late Mesolithic (Champness et al. 2015)	Gill Mill, late Mesolithic (Booth and Simmonds 2018)	A2, early Neolithic (Allen et al. 2012)
Broad	11.1%	24.72%	23.84%	18%	18.52%	8.77%	27.11%
Medium	55.6%	44.57%	51.96%	40%	48.15%	37.72%	61.01%
Narrow	33.3%	30.71%	23.64%	42%	33.33%	53.51%	11.88%

<table>
<tr><td colspan="2">

Table 4.4 Comparison of blade index to dated scatters at Bexhill, East Sussex

Site	Blade index (average)
Scatter 4235	51.6
Bexhill (Upper Palaeolithic)	48.9
Bexhill (Early Mesolithic)	51.1
Bexhill (Middle Mesolithic)	33.3
Bexhill (Late Mesolithic)	32.6

</td><td colspan="4">

Table 4.5 Condition of flints in lithic scatter 4235

	Condition			Cortication	
	Total	Percentage		Total	Percentage
Fresh	31	72.0	None	6	14.0
Light	9	20.9	Light	23	53.5
Moderate	3	7.1	Moderate	13	30.2
Heavy			Heavy	1	2.3
Total	43	100		43	100

</td></tr>
</table>

Chaîne opératoire *and zones of activity*

The assemblage from scatter 4235 represents the complete *chaîne opératoire*. Although refitting was not attempted due to disturbance from the nearby ditches, a rough sequence of events can be assumed from the types of debitage present:

1. The raw material probably derived from cobbles in the direct vicinity of the scatter. Towards the northern end of the scatter, platforms were created on the nodules by the removal of preparation flakes. From there, cortex was removed length-ways and side-trimming pieces were discarded.

2. Cresting was attempted but only as a correction of ridges gone awry towards the proximal end of the dorsal face. The remnant of single partial

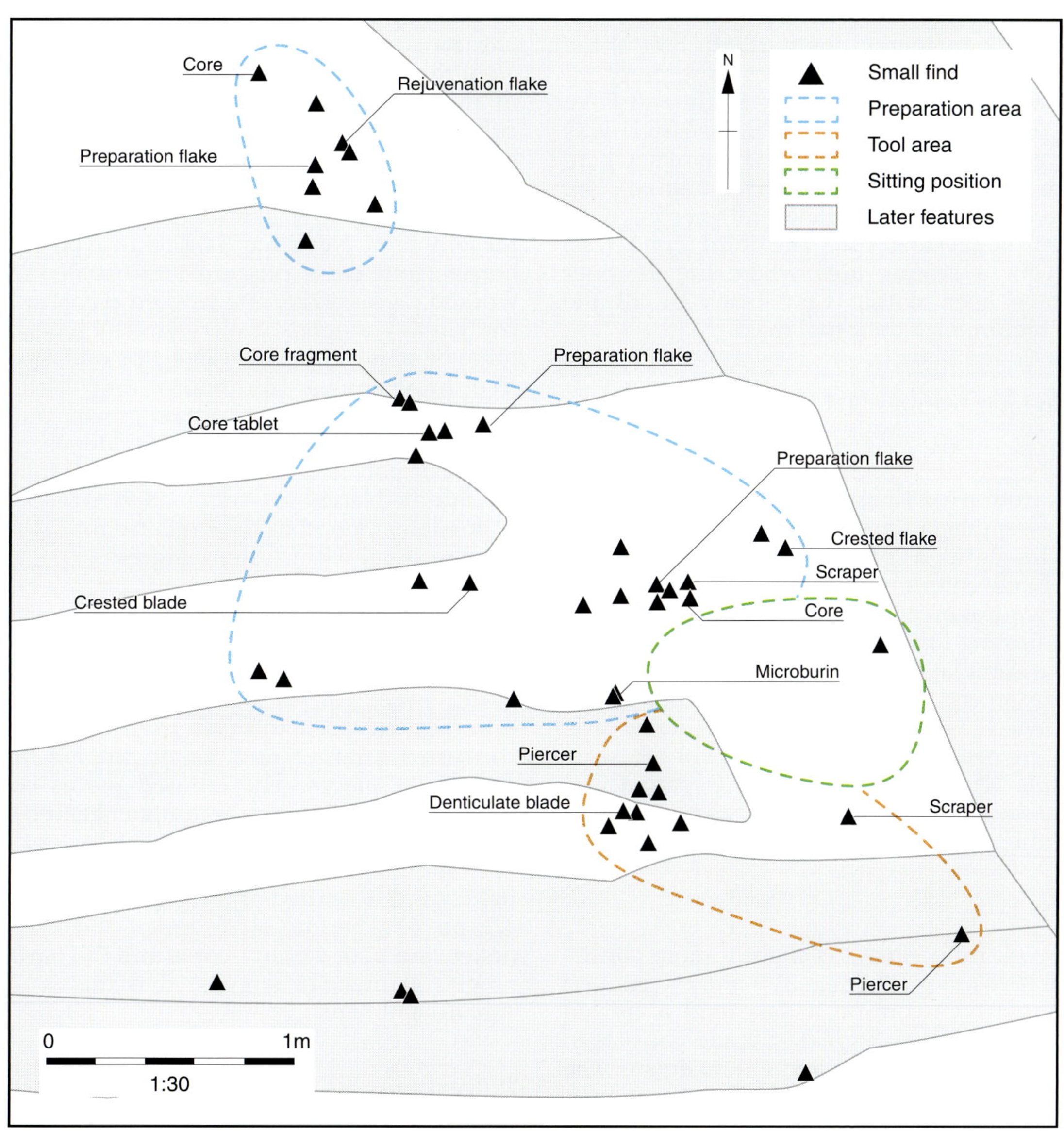

Fig. 4.1 Plan of lithic scatter 4235 showing possible zones of activity

cresting is present on several flakes. This is demonstrated by opposed flaking patterns towards the proximal end and cross-flaking towards the distal.

3. An opposed platform technique was used to produce blades and bladelets. Core tablets were used to modify the platform edge.

4. Tools were produced from the blanks and used at the south end of the scatter. Piercers and scrapers may have been used for hide-working, including the creation and maintenance of clothing. Microliths, evidenced by the poor quality microburin, were created, but were probably carried away for hunting activities. Some may have gone astray and missed their target, like the obliquely blunted point found to the north-east of the scatter. The point of this microlith is broken suggesting impact damage (eg Cooper *et al.* 2017).

We might be able to suggest three activity zones from this *chaîne opératoire* schema (Fig. 4.1). The first was a preparation zone in the northern half of the scatter (shown in blue) where cores were prepared and used to produce good quality blade and flake blanks. The southern half of the scatter was reserved exclusively for tools and blanks where tools were created and used (shown in orange). The tools, especially the denticulate and piercer, were well worn, suggesting use. The third zone was, speculatively, a seating area where the knapper would have been within easy reach of all the elements required for their tool making.

Flint from later features (Table 4.2)

Area 1

The flints from Area 1 have a mixed signature. The debitage assemblage consists of one bladelet and 13 flakes. The curated pieces consist of a single platform blade core, a multiplatform flake core and a single core fragment. The tool count is very high at 26% indicating little *in situ* knapping in this area. The tool assemblage comprises piercers, a microdenticulate, an end truncation and a leaf arrowhead (Fig. 4.2, no. 4) which, along with the blade core, suggests an early Neolithic component. A scale flaked knife with retouch through its patina and several *ad hoc* retouched flakes suggest a smaller late Neolithic or early Bronze Age component.

Area 2

The flintwork from Area 2 is slightly more consistent. The blade index is high at 21% and the curated pieces consist of a core on a flake and a crested piece. The tool count is high at 13% and consists of an end truncation, a piercer and a denticulate. The tools, blade index and mixed flaking patterns may tentatively suggest an early Neolithic date for this assemblage.

Area 3

The flint assemblage from Area 3 is very small and consists of a microdenticulate, a leaf arrowhead, a side-and-end scraper and a single bladelet. The tools again suggest an early Neolithic date.

Area 4

Area 4 contains the largest assemblage of flints from features at 68 worked pieces. The blade index is high at 37% and the curated pieces consist of two opposed platform blade cores, two cubic cores and two core fragments, as well as a rejuvenation flake. The tool count is high at 12% and consists of an end truncation, a burin and a leaf arrowhead of kite type (Fig. 4.2, no. 5). Given the proximity to early Mesolithic scatter 4235, this may again represent a mixed assemblage. The blade assemblage may either relate to Mesolithic or Neolithic occupation and the opposed platform cores are very similar to those found in the scatter. The crested pieces may be either Mesolithic or early Neolithic but again are very similar to those found in the scatter, being of single partial type. The cubic cores are typically of early Neolithic date, as is the leaf arrowhead.

The only material culture found in pits 4224 and 4226 in Area 4 was flint, perhaps suggesting a Mesolithic or Neolithic date. However, the assemblages from these pits are very small (4224: four worked pieces, 4226: one worked piece) and do not contain any diagnostic elements. In general, Mesolithic pits are very varied in shape and often utilise tree-throw holes (Blinkhorn and Little 2018). Neolithic pits normally contain greater numbers of flints and often contain special deposits of tool caches or polished axe fragments, especially during the middle Neolithic (Anderson-Whymark 2008). It is possible, then, that the flints from 4224 and 4226 were residual within later features.

Area 5

Area 5 contained 46 worked pieces with a low blade index of 11%. This assemblage has a different character to those from other areas, and contained a larger number of preparation flakes and squat pieces. The curated pieces consist of three poor quality core fragments geared towards flakes and a rejuvenation flake. The tool count is very high at 7% and consists of *ad hoc* retouched flakes and a barbed-and-tanged arrowhead (Fig. 4.2, no. 6). The low blade index, the shape of the flakes, the poor-quality cores and the barbed-and-tanged arrowhead suggest that this is a Bronze Age assemblage.

Provenance

The flintwork from features were mostly residual, with the possible exception of pits 4224 and 4226.

Table 4.6 Condition of lithics from features

	Condition			Cortication	
	Total	Percentage		Total	Percentage
Fresh	65	42.8	None	44	29.0
Light	58	38.1	Light	88	57.9
Moderate	28	18.4	Moderate	18	11.8
Heavy	1	0.7	Rolled	2	1.3
Total	152	100		152	100

The majority of the assemblage derived from ditches (68%) and pits/postholes (12%). The rest derived from structures such as corndryers or was from topsoil and subsoil layers. Despite this, many of the flints remained in fresh (42%) condition with only 16% of pieces being moderately or badly damaged (Table 4.6). Likewise, most of the flints from features had little or no patina. The good overall condition of the assemblage suggests that, though the majority of flints were not *in situ*, they probably derived from the immediate vicinity of the features in which they were found.

Discussion

The flint assemblage covers a range of periods. Bronze Age activity was almost completely restricted to Areas 1 and 5, occupying the area of higher ground. In the more southerly and downhill reaches of the site there was a larger proportion of early Neolithic and Mesolithic finds. The *in situ* early Mesolithic scatter 4235 occupied the low ground on the southern edge of Area 4.

The early Mesolithic flintwork is the most significant part of this assemblage due to the rarity of *in situ* early Mesolithic scatters in Northamptonshire and its neighbouring counties. The majority of finds from this region are derived from fieldwalking collections or were residual within later features (Wessex Archaeology and Jacobi 2014). In a few cases Mesolithic finds have been washed into geological features (Williams and Shaw 1981). With the exception of the Honey Hill type-site assemblage (Saville 1981), few of these finds have been studied in detail. This has led to a dearth of knowledge about the Mesolithic of Northamptonshire (Deegan and Foard 2008). Aside from scatter 4235, the only other *in situ* activity in the region can be found under the long barrow at Raunds (Harding and Healy 2008). This was dated to the final stages of the late Mesolithic, bearing little comparison to scatter 4235.

Though little *in situ* Mesolithic evidence has been found in Northamptonshire, regional patterns of activity can be teased out. Through the use of large-scale fieldwalking techniques in the county, Hall and Martin were able to identify a link between Mesolithic activity areas and permeable geologies (Martin and Hall 1980; Hall 1985). This is a pattern observed in both the south and north of England (Simmonds *et al.* 2019; Waddington 2000). Valleys and waterways were favoured, perhaps as travelling networks or hunting grounds. Findspots cluster around the permeable geologies of the Nene, Welland and Ise Valleys (Philips 2000). The close proximity of scatter 4235 to the Nene demonstrates that Mesolithic activity at Panattoni Park follows regional patterns.

It is the finer resolution of early Mesolithic life that has been lacking in Northamptonshire archaeology until now. Scatter 4235 suggests small-scale but highly organised activity on a gravel spur close to the River Nene. Tool manufacture and domestic tasks were probably performed at the site, perhaps by only one or two people. This may have related to nearby hunting activity evidenced by the stray microlith. It is likely that this small group would have been part of a much larger social network of communities that used the river systems of Northamptonshire to move, meet and exchange information, a model ascribed to the Mesolithic in other parts of the country (Champness *et al.* 2015).

Catalogue of illustrated flint (Fig. 4.2)

1   Opposed platform blade core, SF 154, scatter 4235
2   Piercer, SF 129, scatter 4235

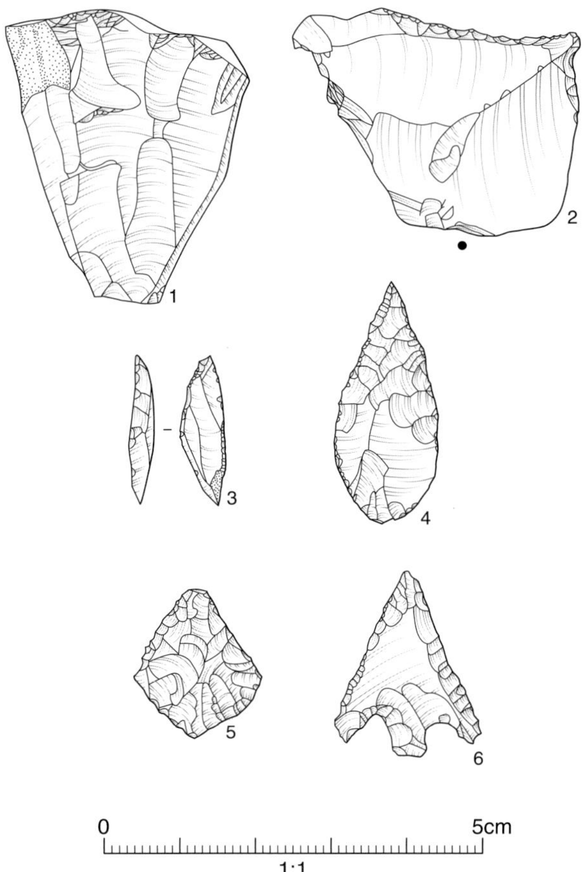

Fig. 4.2 Worked flint

3 Obliquely blunted point, broken (impact damage?), SF 136, layer 4236
4 Leaf-shaped arrowhead, ogival, SF 99, context 1323, ditch 1322 (Middle Roman), Area 1,
5 Leaf-shaped arrowhead, kite type, SF 179, context 4264, ditch 4384 (Late Roman), Area 4
6 Barbed-and-tanged arrowhead, SF 201, context 5254, pit 5253 (Middle Iron Age?), pit alignment 5552, Area 5

PREHISTORIC POTTERY *by Alex Davies*

The excavations produced 645 sherds (4341g) of prehistoric pottery from 93 contexts, representing a maximum of 164 vessels. The vast majority of the material is middle Iron Age, although sherds from two late Bronze Age vessels from a single context in Area 5 and four early Iron Age vessels from the pit alignment were also found, as well as a residual early Iron Age sherd from Area 5. All the material from Areas 3 and 4 was middle Iron Age. Ten fabrics were defined. The assemblage is summarised in Table 4.7.

Methodology

The pottery was recorded broadly following the recommendations of the Prehistoric Ceramics Research Group (PCRG 2010; PCRG *et al.* 2016). Sherds from each context were separated into vessels and details of each vessel were recorded.

No cross-context refitting was attempted, and vessel quantities in this report are maximum figures as it is very likely that sherds from the same vessels were found in multiple contexts. The following data were recorded: fabric (including inclusion type, grade, frequency and how well sorted the inclusions are), level of abrasion, vessel form, rim form, number of body sherds, number of rim sherds, number of base sherds, weight, decoration, surface treatment, rim diameter, estimated vessel equivalent (EVE, or percentage of rim surviving; Orton and Hughes 2013, 210–13), features (eg handles or modifications) and presence of carbonised residue. Further details of the fabrics and vessel forms are given in Table 4.8.

Late Bronze Age

A single feature, pit 5129 in Area 5, produced sherds from two late Bronze Age vessels. Both are in coarse vesicular fabric Vo3, and no Iron Age material is made in the same fabric. Some of the voids have indications that shell was formerly present. The fabric compares well to late Bronze Age material from Apex Park, Daventry (Davies 2020), and the description of late Bronze Age pottery at Harlestone Quarry, Northampton (Chapman *et al.* 2017, 55).

One of the vessels has an in-curving rim (Fig. 4.4, no. 1), and another is from a probable shouldered jar with an out-turned rim (Fig. 4.4, no. 2).

Table 4.7 Prehistoric pottery fabrics and quantities

Fabric	Sherds	Weight (g)	Vessels	Description	Phase
Late Bronze Age					
Vo3	28	106	2	Voids, usually irregular but some striations suggesting at least some shell. Abundant, very coarse.	Late Bronze Age
Iron Age					
Vo1	177	1182	48	Voids, usually irregular, and occasional pieces of possible limestone surviving. Medium grade, sparse-moderate frequency.	Early and middle Iron Age
Vo2	253	1898	42	Voids, unusually irregular but some certain leached shell. Occasional shell present. Coarse, very common frequency.	Early and middle Iron Age
Qs1	5	62	3	Quartz sand. Rare, very fine grade.	Middle Iron Age
Qs2	80	329	35	Quartz sand. Sparse to moderate frequency, fine grade. Can be micaceous. Occasional ironstone.	Middle Iron Age
VoQs	16	98	8	Voids, irregular. Some probable limestone surviving. Moderate frequency, medium grade.	Middle Iron Age
Gr	30	253	11	Grog. Can contain quartz sand and mica. Sparse, fine grade.	Middle Iron Age
GrVo	28	191	7	Grog and voids, usually irregular. Medium grade, moderate to abundant frequency	Middle Iron Age
VeQs	23	214	6	Voids from vegetal, organic and/or grass inclusions, and quartz sand. Medium grade, moderate frequency.	Middle Iron Age
Io	4	7	2	Iron oxides. Fine grade, rare.	Middle Iron Age
None	1	1	1	-	Middle Iron Age
Total Iron Age	617	4235	163		

Table 4.8 Correlations between fabric and form, and estimated vessel equivalent (EVE)

	Vo3	Vo2	Vo1	Gr	Qs2	Total	EVE
Vessel with incurving rim (LBA) Fig. 4.4, no. 1 (eg Jackson 2001, fig. 5.27)	•					1	0.10
Shouldered jar with out-turned neck (LBA) Fig. 4.4, no. 2 (eg Morris 1994, fig. 11.21)	O					(1?)	0.04
Shouldered jar with upright neck (EIA) Fig. 4.4, no. 3 (eg Hancocks and Woodward 2015, fig. CER1.7)			O			(1?)	0.02
Slack-shouldered vessel (MIA) Fig. 4.4, no. 5 (eg Hancocks *et al.* 2006, fig. 53.34)			•••		•	4	0.74
Globular vessel without neck (MIA) Fig. 4.4, no. 4 (eg Hancocks and Woodward 2015, fig. CER4.39)		O	•★			2(1?)	0.14
Globular vessel with upright neck (MIA) (eg Timby 2007, fig. 4.2. 25)				•	•☆	2(1?)	0.09

• = One vessel   O = Possible vessel   ★ = Carbonised residue

Incurving or 'hooked-rim' jars are common in late Bronze Age assemblages (eg Barclay 2001, fig. 14 nos 8–9 and 19–26; Jackson 2001, fig. 5.2, 9, 14, 27; Morris 1994, fig. 11.7–14; 2006, 386). These are often attributed to the earlier part of the period (*c* 1150–900 cal BC; Davies 2018, 279), but associations in Northamptonshire at Thrapston (Hull 2001) and Harlestone Quarry (Chapman *et al.* 2017) suggest that the form continued later in this region, up to at least *c* 800 cal BC. The vessel with an incurving rim has an estimated diameter of 24cm. The shouldered jar is a form that continues into the early Iron Age, although its association here with the incurving rim vessel suggests a late Bronze Age date.

Early Iron Age

Diagnostic early Iron Age material was limited to three vessels. These were from fill 5125 of pit 5095 and fill 5208 of pit 5207, both parts of pit alignment 5552 in Area 5, and fill 5413 of late Iron Age/early Roman ditch 5449, which cut the pit alignment. Identification was not absolutely certain and includes a possible shouldered jar with an upright neck (Fig. 4.4, no. 3) with an estimated dimeter of 24cm and a vessel with a neck that was slightly flaring that has an estimated diameter of 26cm. This latter vessel has external carbonised residue. The pots were both in fabric Vo1. Two undiagnostic vessels were also found in context 5125, one in fabric Vo1 and the other in Vo2. The residual sherd from ditch 5449 is a rim probably from a shouldered jar.

Two vessels in Area 4 have early Iron Age characteristics. These are both represented by small sherds and include one vessel with a fingertipped rim (Roman ditch 4379) and another decorated with incised parallel lines (middle Iron Age gully 4389). It is likely that the vessels are middle Iron Age in date but retain earlier characteristics. These vessels are in fabric Qs2.

Middle Iron Age

The vast majority of the material dated to the middle Iron Age – some 598 sherds (4122g) from a maximum of 154 vessels. Three forms were defined, and these include globular vessels without (Fig. 4.4, no. 4) and with necks, and slack-shouldered vessels (Fig. 4.4, no. 5). Rims are typically plain (11; 65% of total rims), although bead rims are present (5; 29%) and there is a single (6%) in-curving example. Decoration is limited to the two vessels with probable early Iron Age ancestry described above, and a vessel with a single incised horizontal line. There were no examples of Scored Ware decoration.

The majority of the material is in medium–coarse vesicular fabrics most likely originally tempered with shell and/or limestone. Occasional sherds have surviving pieces of shell or impressions of shell, and in others probable limestone is still present, demonstrating the use of both these materials. The voids were generally rather irregular and suggest that pieces of limestone may have originally been the dominant temper. The differentiation between shell and limestone might only be of minor significance as both may have derived from similar fossiliferous limestone sources. Quartz sand and grog were the only other inclusion types of significance. There were no instances of granitic or other igneous rocks.

Iron Age fabrics in Northamptonshire can be very locally diverse with few very clear regional patterns. The most common inclusion types in the middle Iron Age are shell, grog and sand, although not all of these are found at every site and the relative quantities differ considerably (eg Crick Covert Farm: Hancocks and Woodward 2015, table CER3; Long Dole: Blinkhorn *et al.* 2015, table 2.2; Swan Valley Business Park: Jackson 2005, 35; Grange Park: Woodward and Hancocks 2006, table 8; Borough Hill: Jackson 1994, 64-6; and Silverstone Fields Farm and Silverstone 2 and 3: Timby 2007, 95, 98, 102). Fossiliferous limestone was specifically noted in Iron Age pottery at Nortofts Lane (McSloy 2015a, 102) and probably Crick Hotel (McSloy 2015b, 76–8).

One chronological change noted at Crick Covert Farm (Hancocks and Woodward 2015, 208) and Grange Park (Woodward and Hancocks 2006, 75) was an increase in the use of sand in the later middle Iron Age compared to earlier in the period, with a parallel decline in grog and shell. There was no very clear change in fabrics between middle Iron Age subphases 2a and 2b at Panattoni Park. The proportion of sand was stable, at 8% in subphase 2a and 11% in subphase 2b. Grog increased from 4% in subphase 2a to 14% in subphase 2b with a parallel decrease in shell/limestone from 88% to 75%.

The outer surface of nine (6%) of the vessels has been smoothed, and a single vessel was burnished. This was one of the few vessels in very fine fabric Qs1. One of the smoothed vessels was in medium–coarse fabric Vo2, but otherwise there appeared to be a tendency to smooth vessels in finer fabrics Vo1 and Qs2.

Rim dimeters could be estimated on 14 middle Iron Age vessels (Fig. 4.3). There is a clear peak at 16–18cm, with five falling outside of this range. There is no clear relationship between typology and size, as the largest and smallest middle Iron Age vessels were in the slack-shouldered form. As a group, the middle Iron Age pots are smaller than the late Bronze Age and Iron Age examples, although the latter sample is very limited.

Carbonised residue from cooking was noted on nine (6%) vessels. All except one were on the external side of the pots, with one instance of

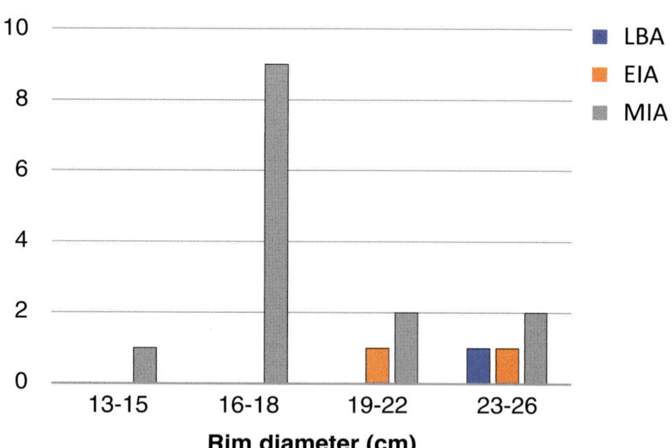

Fig. 4.3 Prehistoric pottery rim diameters (no. vessels)

charred internal residue. Residue was present on all three middle Iron Age forms.

Few comments can be made about differences in the assemblage between the different areas of the site as only the settlement in Area 4 produced a middle Iron Age assemblage of any size. Almost all the sherds in fabric VeQs were found in Area 2, and no sherds in the Qs fabrics were found in Area 3. It is uncertain if either of these observations are significant.

Catalogue of illustrated sherds (Fig. 4.4)

1 Vessel with incurving rim. Area 5, pit 5129. Vo3. Late Bronze Age.
2 Biconical or shouldered jar. Area 5, pit 5129. Vo3. Late Bronze Age.

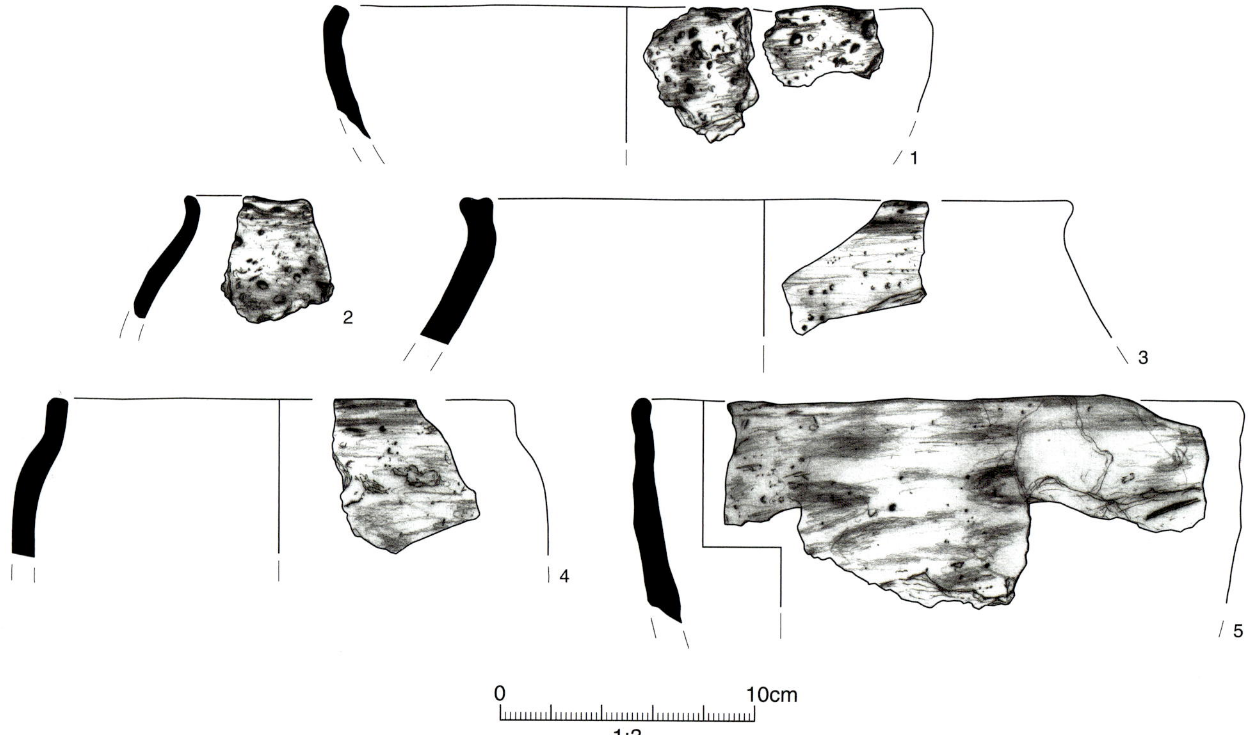

Fig. 4.4 Prehistoric pottery

3 Shouldered jar with upright neck. Area 5, pit 5207, pit alignment 5552. Vol. Early Iron Age.
4 Globular vessel without neck. Area 4, penannular gully 4032. Vol. Middle Iron Age.
5 Slack-shouldered vessel. Area 4, ditch 4379. Vol. Middle Iron Age.

LATE IRON AGE AND ROMAN POTTERY
by Edward Biddulph

Introduction and methods

A large pottery assemblage of some 6600 sherds weighing almost 120kg was recovered. The pottery was quantified by sherd count and weight, with forms identified by rim additionally quantified by minimum number of vessels (MV) and estimated vessel equivalents (EVE), the latter measuring the surviving percentage of the rim circumference (a complete rim equalling 100% or 1 EVE). Forms and fabrics were assigned codes from OA's standard recording system for late Iron Age and Roman pottery (Booth nd). Fabrics were correlated with the fabric series for Northampton developed by P Aird and E MacRobert (Perrin 2006) and, where possible, the National Roman Fabric Reference Collection (NRFRC; Tomber and Dore 1998). A list of the fabrics encountered, with quantification, is presented in Table 4.9. Forms were cross-referenced where possible to regional or industry corpora (eg Marney 1989; Perrin 1999; Webster 1996; Young 1977), and are listed in Table 4.10. Forms were additionally given rim codes to describe the shape of the rim. These will only occasionally be mentioned below, mainly in reference to bowls and dishes in, or deriving from, black-burnished ware prototypes (eg JB 210, curving-sided dish with bead-rim).

Assemblage composition and pattern of pottery supply

Phase 3

Pottery recovered from contexts assigned to Phase 3 (late Iron Age/early Roman period) accounted for 14% of the assemblage by EVE (Table 4.11). Pottery of this date was dominated by grog-tempered wares (E80, E810 and E820). These were available mainly as jars and bowls. Among the jars were barrel-shaped (CB), narrow-mouthed (CC), high-shouldered and necked (CE), globular (CG), bead-rimmed (CH), lid-seated or channel-rimmed (CJ) and large storage (CN) types. The pottery was mainly dark-surfaced; vessels with red or orange-brown surfaces (Northants fabric A4) included CC and CE types. Fabrics of lid-seated types invariably included shell (Northants fabric AB). Bowls were restricted to deep carinated vessels (HA). These were red-surfaced, cordoned, and decorated with finely incised lines or lattices between cordons (Marney 1989, fig. 36, nos 71–3) and may be products of the kiln site at Hunsbury, some 6km to the east, or Bozeat Quarry, some 20km to the east, where such vessels were made (PKRB nd, Hardingstone 4; Perrin 2018, 86–7, fig. 3.6a, no. 58). Drinking vessels included butt-beakers (EA), a globular beaker (ED) and a cup (FC; ?Cam 56) recalling Gallo-Belgic prototypes. All were red-surfaced or orange-brown in colour, a finish that in grog-tempered wares generally appears to have been reserved for vessels intended for presentation or social functions, such as dining. Much of the grog-tempered pottery could have derived from several production sites attested in the region, Hunsbury and Bozeat among them.

Shelly wares (E40 and C10) were also well-represented. These were available exclusively as jars, of which type CJ was the most common; several examples had scored or notched rims. Other jars included types CB, CG, CH and CN. Vessels were generally dark-surfaced. Sandy fabrics of Iron Age tradition (E20 and E30) made a smaller contribution. Forms included bucket-shaped (CA) and CJ-type jars and butt-beakers (EA), the last in a fine reduced fabric. Jars (C), a bowl or jar (D) and a platter (JC) were recorded in sandy fabrics (R20 and R30) that are certain to have been deposited after *c* AD 43. Another platter, as well as a necked jar or bowl (DC) and jar (C), were present in sandy oxidised ware O20; a CE-type jar was recorded in fine oxidised ware (O10). All had been deposited after *c* AD 43.

Other pottery of note included Verulamium-region white ware (R21), North Gaulish white ware (W39) and the substantial portion of a pedestal base of a large globular beaker or flagon in an unsourced colour-coated ware (F60).

Many of the context-groups attributed to Phase 3, the settlement in Areas 1 and 5, were broadly dated by the pottery to *c* 50 BC/AD 1–100, and generally it has not been possible to place groups that contain pottery of late Iron Age or 'Belgic' tradition exclusively (essentially the 'E' wares) on either side of the conquest period (*c* AD 43) with confidence. However, it can be noted that groups that contained Roman-period pottery (F, O, R and W categories, except W39, which may have arrived before AD 43) contained no E wares. This does not necessarily indicate that most groups were deposited before the conquest, but the use of E wares does not appear to have survived for very long afterwards, and a terminal date for their deposition up to *c* AD 50/70 seems a reasonable one. By way of comparison, it is notable that, in groups from Milton Keynes sites, the proportion of grog-tempered ware, dominant in the early/mid-1st century AD, had declined sharply by the late 1st century (Marney 1989, 7–16).

Phase 4

Some 25% of the overall assemblage by EVE was recovered from contexts assigned to Phase 4 (middle Roman). For the purpose of gaining a

Table 4.9 Quantification of late Iron Age and Roman fabrics, and fabric concordance

Fabric (OA)	Fabric (Northants)	Fabric (NRFRC)	Description	No. sherds	Weight (g)	MV	EVE
S Samian wares							
S	D40	-	Unsourced samian wares	5	17	-	-
S20	D40	LGF SA	South Gaulish samian ware	2	4	-	-
S30	D40	LEZ SA 2	Central Gaulish samian ware	51	887	18	1.97
S40	D40	-	East Gaulish samian ware	15	172	3	0.26
F Fine wares							
F20	D	-	Unsourced glazed ware	1	3	-	-
F30	D25	ROB MD	Unsourced mica-dusted ware	1	33	1	0.03
F43	D14	CNG BS	Central Gaulish 'Rhenish' ware	2	2	-	-
F51	D4	OXF RS	Oxford red/brown colour-coated ware	88	1639	25	1.99
F52	D1	LNV CC	Nene Valley colour-coated ware (cream/pink fabric)	189	3829	36	4.81
	D22		Nene Valley colour-coated ware (grey fabric)	9	131	2	0.15
	D24		Nene Valley colour-coated ware (orange fabric)	20	257	3	0.26
F56	D5	HAD OX	Much Hadham red colour-coated ware	1	10	-	-
F60	D	-	Unsourced colour-coated wares	17	378	-	-
A Amphorae							
A11	D50	BAT AM 1/2	South Spanish amphora fabric	8	312	-	-
M Mortaria							
M22	D27	OXF WH	Oxford white ware mortaria	14	805	2	0.39
M23	D28	MAH WH	Mancetter-Hartshill white ware mortaria	26	1974	11	1.21
M24	D21	LNV WH	Nene Valley white ware mortaria	5	152	-	-
M29	D29	COL WH	Colchester white ware mortaria	1	80	1	0.18
M31	D	OXF WS	Oxford white-slipped oxidised ware mortaria	4	115	2	0.13
M41	D4	OXF RS	Oxford red/brown colour-coated ware mortaria	12	212	3	0.26
W White wares							
W10	D	-	Unsourced fine white wares	11	320	2	0.17
W14	D21	LNV WH	Nene Valley white ware	121	1110	8	1.57
W20	D	-	Unsourced sandy white wares	22	348	7	0.58
W21	D6/D9	VER WH	Verulamium-region white ware	2	10	-	-
W30	D	-	Fine white ware, ?imported	1	6	-	-
W39	D10	NOG WH 3	North Gaulish fine sandy white ware	2	6	-	-
W50	D	-	White ware with glauconitic inclusions	1	36	-	-
Q White-slipped wares							
Q20	D	-	Unsourced white-slipped oxidised wares	1	12	-	-
Q21	D	OXF WS	Oxford white-slipped oxidised ware	1	37	1	0.07
E Iron Age/early Roman wares							
E20	C	-	Iron Age/early Roman fine sandy fabrics, dark surfaces	5	23	1	0.15
E30	C	-	Iron Age/early Roman coarse sandy fabrics, dark surfaces	30	340	3	0.4
	D	-	Iron Age/early Roman coarse sandy fabrics, orange/yellow-brown surfaces	39	824	1	0.16
E40	B	-	Iron Age/early Roman shelly fabrics	346	2750	30	3.18
E60	C	-	Iron Age/early Roman flint-tempered fabric, dark surfaces	1	13	-	-
E80	A	SOB GT	Grog-tempered ware, dark surfaces	437	8343	33	4.59
	A4		Grog-tempered ware, red-surfaced	177	3547	13	2.41
E810	A	-	Grog-and-sand-tempered fabrics, dark surfaces	55	859	4	0.51
	A4	-	Grog-and-sand-tempered fabrics, red-surfaced	2	56	1	0.17
E820	AB	-	Grog-and-shell-tempered fabrics	937	9859	8	2.71
O Oxidised wares							
O	D	-	Indeterminate oxidised fabrics	6	11	-	-
O10	D	-	Unsourced fine oxidised wares	79	681	9	0.74

Table 4.9 continued

Fabric (OA)	Fabric (Northants)	Fabric (NRFRC)	Description	No. sherds	Weight (g)	MV	EVE
O20	D	-	Unsourced sandy oxidised wares	90	1062	12	0.96
O210	D	-	Oxidised ware with quartz and black (glauconitic) sand	13	456	-	-
O57	D5	HAD OX	Much Hadham oxidised ware	12	158	3	0.36
O60	D	-	Calcareous oxidised wares	3	22	-	-
O80	D	-	Coarse-tempered oxidised wares	47	1625	3	0.57
O81	A2	PNK GT	Pink grogged ware	246	12612	24	2.83
R Reduced wares							
R	C	-	Indeterminate reduced fabrics	5	9	-	-
R10	C	-	Unsourced fine reduced wares	28	167	4	0.58
R10	C7	-	Micaceous fine reduced ware	13	118	2	0.24
R20	C	-	Unsourced sandy reduced wares	286	5785	43	4.99
	C10	-	Sandy reduced ware; coarse, hard grey fabric	6	82	-	-
R201	C	-	Coarse sandy storage jar fabric	8	680	6	0.8
R211	D	DER CO	Derbyshire coarse ware	4	40	-	-
R26	C	HOR RE	?Horningsea reduced ware	1	21	-	-
R30	C	-	Unsourced medium sandy reduced wares	1055	18944	162	20.34
R46	C1	-	Nene Valley grey ware, grey slipped	297	6666	65	8.97
	C2	-	Nene Valley grey ware, 'fumed'	9	193	3	0.34
R50	C	-	Unsourced dark-surfaced wares	410	6932	49	6.87
R70	BC	-	Unsourced shelly reduced wares	18	493	3	0.72
R90	C	-	Coarse-tempered reduced wares	49	1044	5	0.49
R911	C	PNK GT	?Reduced pink grogged ware (cf Marney 1989, fabric 2d)	12	404	1	0.14
B Black-burnished wares							
B11	C8	DOR BB 1	Dorset black-burnished ware	103	1304	23	1.44
B22	C22	COL BB 2	Black-burnished ware, category 2 (Colchester)	6	46	2	0.16
B30	C21	-	Imitation black-burnished wares	81	1418	28	2.38
C Calcareous/shelly wares							
C	B	-	General shelly fabrics	3	5	-	-
C10	B	-	Unsourced shell-tempered wares	78	629	4	0.59
	BC	-	Unsourced sand- and shell-tempered wares	1	8	-	-
C11	B	HAR SH/ ROB SH	Shelly ware, general	314	3746	35	4.11
	B1		Shelly ware, oxidised	380	9633	28	4.1
	B2		Shelly ware, reduced	334	4217	70	7.48
	B4		Shelly ware, hard buff/yellow/grey	2	13	-	-
Z Indeterminate fabrics							
Z	Z	-	Indeterminate fabrics	9	30	-	-
			Total	6670	118765	803	98.51

robust picture of pottery supply, it is useful to restrict analysis of the Phase 4 pottery to context-groups with group-dates (spot-dates) confined to the middle Roman period, thus removing residual or very broadly dated groups. This gives us two Phase 4 assemblages, one encompassing groups dated within the period *c* AD 120–200, the other dated within the period *c* AD 200–240/50.

Turning to the mid/late 2nd-century group (Table 4.12), medium sandy reduced wares (R30) made the single largest contribution. This was mainly available as jars – narrow-mouthed (CC), medium-mouthed (CD), lid-seated (CJ) and wide-mouthed (CM) jars among them – but a bead-rimmed dish (JB 210), poppyhead beaker (EF) and necked jar or bowl were also recorded. Jar types CD, CJ and CM were seen in dark-surfaced wares (R50), while a necked jar (CE) was recorded in sandy reduced ware R20. A dish or bowl (I) was present in a fine micaceous fabric (R10; Northants fabric C7). None of these vessels in reduced wares are readily attributable to source, but many of them are likely to have been made locally, and indeed several kilns are known in the

Table 4.10 Quantification of forms

Type	Description	MV	EVE
BA	Small flagon	3	1.33
BC	Larger flagon	1	0.18
C	Jar	115	9.25
CA	Bucket-shaped jar	1	0.17
CB	Barrel-shaped jar	4	0.59
CC	Narrow-mouthed jar	16	3.16
CD	Medium-mouthed jar	28	4.94
CE	Squat, high-shouldered necked jar	6	1.25
CG	Globular jar	4	1.18
CH	Bead-rimmed jar	5	0.4
CJ	Lid-seated jar	51	6.56
CK	'Cooking-pot'-type jar	91	12.32
CM	Wide-mouthed jar	89	15.05
CN	Storage jar	47	5.78
D	Jar/bowl	23	2.33
DB	Wide-mouthed jar/bowl	7	0.73
DC	Necked jar/bowl	15	1.24
E	Beaker	12	1.41
EA	Butt-beaker	5	0.91
EC	Bag-shaped beaker	3	0.18
ED	Globular beaker	5	0.88
EE	Indented beaker	2	0.35
EF	Poppyhead beaker	1	0.24
FC	Conical cup	7	0.73
H	Bowl	12	0.84
HA	Carinated bowl	10	1.68

Table 4.10 continued

Type	Description	MV	EVE
HB	Straight-sided, flat-bottomed bowl with flanged or bead rim	51	7.7
HC	Curving-sided bowl	15	1.53
HD	Necked bowl	6	0.74
HG	Globular bowl	1	0.16
I	Bowl/dish	12	0.65
IA	Straight-sided bowl/dish with bead or flanged rim	5	0.47
IB	Curving-sided bowl/dish with plain, bead or flanged rim	5	0.49
J	Dish	5	0.78
JA	Straight-sided dish with plain, bead or flanged rim	39	3.57
JB	Curving-sided dish with plain, bead or flanged rim	73	6.13
JC	Platter	2	0.17
K	Mortarium	1	0.01
KC	Hammerhead mortarium	11	1.21
KD	Wall-sided mortarium	2	0.26
KE	Mortarium with tall bead and stubby flange	5	0.69
L	Lid	1	0.17
MC	Lamp	-	-
MM	Costrel	-	-
Z	Indeterminate	6	0.1
	Total	803	98.51

Table 4.11 Pottery from late Iron Age/early Roman settlement in Areas 1 and 5 (Phase 3)

Fabric	C Jar	D Jar/bowl	E Beaker	F Cup	H Bowl	J Dish	Z Indet.	Total EVE	% EVE
C10	0.38							0.38	2.8
C11								*	-
E20			0.15					0.15	1.1
E30	0.38	0.18						0.56	4.2
E40	3.12						0.01	3.13	23.4
E60								*	-
E80	1.85	0.95	0.63		1.66			5.09	38.1
E810	0.2	0.17	0.2	0.11				0.68	5.1
E820	2.55							2.55	19.1
F60								*	-
O10	0.13							0.13	1
O20	0.08	0.05				0.12		0.25	1.9
O80	0.14							0.14	1
R10								*	-
R20		0.06						0.06	0.4
R201								*	-
R30	0.18					0.05		0.23	1.7
R50								*	-
R70								*	-
W21								*	-
W39								*	-
Z								*	-
Total EVE	9.01	1.41	0.98	0.11	1.66	0.17	0.01	13.35	-
% EVE	67.5	10.6	7.3	0.8	12.4	1.3	0.1	-	-

* Fabric attested but not represented by rim

Northampton area (PKRB nd). Some of the forms (types CJ and CM in fabric R30) resemble products of the Delapré Roman kiln field site, *c* 8km east of the site (Woodfield 2010, figs 8 and 15), although production there was dated to the late 1st/early 2nd century. Some reduced ware was supplied by the Nene Valley industry (R46). Forms included a wide-mouthed bowl (CM; Marney 1989, fig. 46, no. 2), a bead-rimmed dish (JA 210) and a flanged bowl (HB).

More jars were available in shelly ware (C11). Forms were largely restricted to two types: 'cooking-pot' jars with everted rims (CK) and lid-seated jars (CJ). Black-burnished wares arrived from Dorset (B11) – a plain-rimmed dish (JB 110) was recorded in the fabric – and were imitated locally; a flanged bowl or dish (I 400) was recorded in fabric B30. Dishes and bowls were also supplied in oxidised wares (O10 and O20), as was a flagon (BA) with a triangular rim. Pink grogged ware (O81) from the Stowe area near Buckingham arrived after *c* AD 150.

Fine wares were dominated by products from two sources: the Nene Valley (F52) and Lezoux in Central Gaul (S30). Beakers (E) and a plain-rimmed dish (JB 110) were seen in the former, while cups (Drag. 33) and dishes (Drag. 18/31 or 31, Drag. 31, and Drag. 36) were recorded in the latter. Samian ware also arrived from East Gaul. These were joined by a bead-rimmed dish (JA 210) in a mica-dusted fine ware (F30). Other pottery of note included mortaria from the Mancetter-Hartshill industry (M23) and white ware from the Nene Valley (W14). Some sandy white ware (W20) may have been manufactured locally at Upton, *c* 4km to the east of the site (Walker and Maull 2010, 50), but if so, quantities were low.

The context-groups reported on here belong to Phase 4 and date to the period *c* AD 120-200, but it is likely that most of the groups were deposited after *c* AD 150. None of the groups were certain to date to the second quarter of the 2nd century, and over 70% of the pottery belonged to groups dating between AD 150 and 200. Additionally, it is telling that the principal samian ware dish is Drag. 31, which was introduced after AD 150; earlier Central Gaulish forms, such as cup Drag. 27 and dish Drag. 18/31, were absent. Given the chronological emphases apparent in Phases 3 and 4, it is possible that there was a hiatus or reduction in activity across the site, or at least in the level of pottery deposition, between the late 1st/early 2nd century and the third quarter of the second 2nd century.

Table 4.12 Pottery from ceramic groups dated to c *AD 120–200 (Phase 4)*

Fabric	B Flagon	C Jar	D Jar/bowl	E Beaker	F Cup	H Bowl	I Bowl/dish	J Dish	Total EVE	% EVE
B11								0.03	0.03	0.7
B30							0.01		0.01	0.2
C10									*	-
C11		0.59							0.59	13.4
E810									*	-
F30								0.03	0.03	0.7
F52				0.3				0.11	0.41	9.3
M23									*	-
O									*	-
O10							0.06		0.06	1.4
O20	0.13					0.03			0.16	3.6
O81									*	-
R									*	-
R10							0.09		0.09	2
R20		0.24							0.24	5.4
R30		0.84	0.05	0.24				0.09	1.22	26.7
R46		0.2				0.06		0.01	0.27	6.1
R50		0.55							0.55	12.5
R90		0.15							0.15	3.4
S									*	-
S20									*	-
S30					0.32			0.28	0.6	13.6
S40									*	-
W10									*	-
W14									*	-
W20									*	-
Total EVE	0.13	2.57	0.05	0.54	0.32	0.09	0.16	0.55	4.41	-
% EVE	2.9	58.3	1.1	12.2	7.3	2	3.6	12.5	-	-

* Fabric attested but not represented by rim

The supply of Nene Valley grey ware (R46) increased during the first half of the 3rd century (Table 4.13), becoming the principal reduced ware (although the proportion may be somewhat inflated, given the relatively small size of the phased assemblage). Forms included bead-rimmed and flanged bowls (HB, rims 210 and 410) and wide-mouthed jars (CM). More CM-type jars, as well as medium-mouthed jar CD, were available in unsourced reduced wares (R30). The proportion of shelly wares (C11) increased. Forms included a CK-type jar and bowls (HB and HC) with flanged rims. A lid-seated jar (CJ) was recorded in a sandy grey ware that contained occasional shell and grog (R70).

Fine wares were again dominated by Nene Valley colour-coated ware (F52); a bag-shaped beaker (EC) and a dish (JB) copying samian form Drag. 36 (Perrin 1999, fig. 63, no. 242) were recorded in the ware. Other fine wares comprised Central Gaulish 'Rhenish' ware (R43), a glazed ware (F20) and Oxford red/brown colour-coated ware (F51), the last arriving after c AD 240. Samian ware was confined to East Gaulish fabrics. No forms were identified by rim, but a body sherd from a decorated bowl, possibly from Trier (Tomber and Dore 1998, TRI SA) was recorded. Mortaria from the Mancetter-Hartshill industry (M23) made a more significant contribution during this time, compared with the later 2nd century; hammerhead mortaria (KC) were present.

Phase 5

Pottery from groups assigned to Phase 5 (late Roman period) took a 58% share of the assemblage by EVE. Groups dated to the second half of the 3rd century (Table 4.14) were dominated by reduced wares. Forms in unsourced wares (R10, R20, R30 and R50) included narrow-mouthed (CC), medium-mouthed (CD), lid-seated (CJ) and wide-mouthed (CM) jars, and dishes or bowls with incipient bead-and-flanged rims (IA 430), dropped flanges (HB 440) and bead rims (JA 210), the last probably being residual. Storage jars (CN) and a large bowl (HC) were seen in coarse sandy fabric R201. Nene Valley grey ware (R46) continued to make an important contribution. Forms included CM-type jars, and dishes and bowls (HB, IA and JA/JB) with plain, bead and flanged rims. This period also marked the appearance of Derbyshire coarse ware (R211), though no forms were recognised.

The proportion of shelly wares (C11) declined in the later 3rd century and were almost exclusively available as 'cooking-pots' (CK). Black-burnished ware (B11) from Dorset arrived in the form of bowls with dropped-flange rims (HB 440) and plain-rimmed dishes (HB 110), and dishes were also present in imitation fabrics (B30). Of the oxidised wares, pink grogged ware (O81) was the most conspicuous, having increased its share of the assemblage from the middle Roman period. A storage jar (CN), a large narrow-mouthed jar (CC)

Table 4.13 Pottery from ceramic groups dated to c AD 200–240/50 (Phase 4)

Fabric	C Jar	E Beaker	H Bowl	J Dish	K Mortarium	Total EVE	% EVE
B30						*	-
C11	0.3		0.28			0.58	15.5
F20						*	-
F43						*	-
F51						*	-
F52		0.13		0.17		0.3	8
M23					0.29	0.29	7.8
O10						*	-
O81						*	-
R20			0.04			0.04	1.1
R201						*	-
R30	0.91					0.91	24.4
R46	0.28		0.95			1.23	33
R50						*	-
R70	0.38					0.38	10.2
R90						*	-
S40						*	-
W10						*	-
W14						*	-
W20						*	-
Total EVE	1.87	0.13	1.27	0.17	0.29	3.73	-
% EVE	50.1	3.5	34	4.6	7.8	-	-

* Fabric attested but not represented by rim

and a wide-mouthed jar (CM; Marney 1989, fig. 27, no. 13) were present. What appeared to be a reduced version of the ware (R911) was also recorded. A small amount of fine oxidised ware reached the site from the Much Hadham workshops in Hertfordshire (O57).

Fine wares were restricted to Oxford red/brown colour-coated ware (F51) and Nene Valley colour-coated ware (F52), the latter being better represented. Fabric F52 was available mainly as globular, funnel-necked beakers (ED) and plain-rimmed dishes (JB 110), and a flagon (BA; Perrin 1999, fig. 62, no. 190) was also present. Bowls (HC) and dishes (JB) copying samian prototypes (Young 1977, types C45 and C51) were recorded in fabric F51. More Oxford products arrived in the form of mortaria in fabrics M22, M31 and M41. A vessel with a tall bead and stubby flange (KE; Young type WC7) was seen in fabric M31. Hammerhead mortaria (HC) were recorded in Mancetter-Hartshill white ware (M23). White wares were also available as flanged dishes (fabric W14, type JB; Perrin 1999, fig. 63, no. 244), a wide-mouthed jar (fabric W20, type CM) and jar or bowl (fabric W10, type D).

The 4th-century assemblage (Table 4.15) is dominated by shelly ware (C11) and unsourced reduced wares (R30). Nene Valley grey ware had all but disappeared by this time. Fabric R30 was available mainly as wide-mouthed jars (CM; eg Marney 1989, fig. 46, no. 2), bowls (HB 440) and dishes (JB 110). Narrow-necked jars with a 'frilled' cordon below an almond-shaped rim, a product characteristic of East Midland and Lincolnshire kiln sites (Perrin 1999, 114, fig. 68, nos 380–1), were also recorded. The repertoire in fabric C11 was more diverse than in the later 3rd century, reflecting the

Table 4.14 Pottery from ceramic groups dated to c AD 240/50–300 (Phase 5)

Fabric	B Flagon	C Jar	D Jar/bowl	E Beaker	H Bowl	I Bowl/dish	J Dish	K Mortarium	Total EVE	% EVE
B11					0.55		0.12		0.67	4.5
B30					0.03		0.15		0.18	1.2
C10		0.1							0.1	0.7
C11		1.33	0.1						1.43	9.7
E80									*	-
E810									*	-
F51					0.19	0.04	0.56		0.79	5.3
F52	0.2			0.57		0.06	0.43		1.26	8.5
M22									*	-
M23								0.51	0.51	3.5
M24									*	-
M31								0.12	0.12	0.8
M41									*	-
O10			0.14				0.06		0.2	1.4
O20									*	-
O57		0.1							0.1	0.7
O80									*	-
O81		0.58							0.58	3.9
Q20									*	-
R10		0.14							0.14	0.9
R20		1.65							1.65	11.2
R201		0.2			0.1				0.3	2
R211									*	-
R30		1.56	0.14		0.37	0.17	0.11		2.35	15.9
R46		0.77			1.01	0.08	0.25		2.11	14.3
R50		1.76							1.76	11.9
R70									*	-
R90									*	-
R911									*	-
S30									*	-
S40									*	-
W10			0.07			0.1			0.17	1.2
W14								0.28	0.28	1.9
W20		0.07							0.07	0.5
Z									*	-
Total EVE	0.2	8.26	0.45	0.57	2.25	0.45	1.96	0.63	14.77	-
% EVE	1.4	55.9	3	3.9	15.2	3	13.3	4.3	-	-

* Fabric attested but not represented by rim

apparent increase in the level of supply, and comprised everted rim 'cooking-pot'-type jars (CK), plain-rimmed dishes (JB 110) and bowls (HB and HC) with flanged or triangular rims. A medium-mouthed jar (CD) was available in a sand-and-shell-tempered fabric (R70). A plain-rimmed dish was also recorded in fabric B11, and a dropped-flange dish or bowl in fabric B30 (the latter decorated with unusual fingertip impressions on the tip of the flange). Oxidised wares, including pink grogged ware (O81), were recorded as body sherds only, suggesting that the level of supply had declined.

The level of fine-ware supply, specifically from Oxford (F51) and the Nene Valley (F52), was virtually unchanged. In the former, plain dishes (JB; Young 1977, type C45) were joined by rouletted (Young 1977, type C46) and white-painted (Young 1977, type C50) variants, and a necked bowl (HD; Young 1977, type C79) was recorded. These additional forms are characteristic of the 4th century; the dishes were among the latest products, arriving after *c* AD 325/40. The Nene Valley industry also supplied dishes and bowls, including a dropped-flange (HB 440) bowl and a dish with a hammerhead rim (JA; Perrin 1999, fig. 63, no. 237). Interestingly, the painted or barbotine decoration usually found on examples of the latter

had in this case been replaced by fine notching. A narrow-necked jar (CC; Perrin 1999, fig. 65, no. 273) and a handle from a flagon were also recorded. Mortaria arrived from Mancetter-Hartshill (M23), the Nene Valley (M24) and Oxford (M41). Only Oxford vessels were identified by rim, these being confined to mortaria with tall beads and stubby flanges (KE; Young 1977, type C100) dating to the 4th century.

Chronological summary

The main chronological trends that emerge from the description of the pottery assemblage by phase are an intense period of settlement activity during the late Iron Age/earliest Roman period (up to *c* AD 50/70); a decline, perhaps even a hiatus, in activity during the late 1st and first half of the 2nd century AD; resumption or resurgence of settlement activity after *c* AD 150, reaching a peak during the second half of the 3rd century; and decline in the level of pottery deposition during the 4th century. Pottery deposition continued at least to the mid-4th century and may have continued beyond this time, but this cannot be demonstrated by the pottery itself.

The chronological pattern is reflected in the composition of the samian assemblage (Table 4.16).

Table 4.15 Pottery from ceramic groups dated to c AD 300–400/10 (Phase 5)

Fabric	C Jar	D Jar/bowl	H Bowl	I Bowl/dish	J Dish	K Mortarium	Z Indet.	Total EVE	% EVE
B11					0.04			0.04	0.6
B30				0.05				0.05	0.7
C11	2.58		0.56		0.26		0.03	3.43	51
F51			0.04		0.33			0.37	5.5
F52	0.15		0.19		0.21			0.55	8.2
F60								*	-
M23								*	-
M24								*	-
M41						0.18		0.18	2.7
O10								*	-
O20								*	-
O80								*	-
O81								*	-
Q21			0.07					0.07	1
R								*	-
R20								*	-
R30	1.71	0.07	0.06		0.04			1.88	28
R46								*	-
R50								*	-
R70	0.1							0.1	1.5
R90								*	-
S30								*	-
S40			0.05					0.05	0.7
W14								*	-
Total EVE	4.54	0.07	0.97	0.05	0.88	0.18	0.03	6.72	-
% EVE	67.6	1	14.4	0.7	13.1	2.7	0.4	-	-

* Fabric attested but not represented by rim

Table 4.16 Samian forms by fabric. Quantification by number of vessels identified to form based on all sherds

Form	Class	S20 South	S30 Central	S40 East	S Indet.	Total no. vessels
Drag 18/31 or 31	Dish		5			5
Drag 30	Decorated bowl		1	1		2
Drag 30 or 37	Decorated bowl		1			1
Drag 37	Decorated bowl		1	1		2
Drag 31	Dish		7			7
Drag 31 or 31R	Dish		2	1		3
Drag 33	Cup		5	1		6
Drag 36	Dish		2			2
Drag 38	Bowl		1	1		2
Drag 79	Dish		1			1
Beaker/jar	Beaker/jar		1			1
Bowl/dish	Bowl/dish		8	3	1	12
Cup	Cup	1				1
Total no. vessels		1	35	8	1	45

South Gaulish samian ware (S20) from La Graufesenque, which typically dates to *c* AD 43–110, was poorly represented, with just a single vessel (a cup) identified. Central Gaulish samian, arriving probably exclusively from Lezoux after *c* AD 120, was much more common, but, as noted above, an emphasis on the later 2nd century is evident, with the absence of forms typically dated in the ware to the second quarter of the 2nd century, such as Drag. 18/31 dishes and Drag. 27 cups. This is supported by the potters' stamps, of which two clear examples were recorded. One, on a Drag. 79 dish, is the stamp of Beliniccus iii, a Lezoux potter working *c* AD 140–70 (Hartley and Dickinson 2008, 49), while the other, on the base of a Drag. 31 dish, is that of Martinus iii, who worked at Lezoux during the period AD 170–200 (Hartley and Dickinson 2009, 320). East Gaulish samian, whose date range spans *c* AD 140–240, was relatively well-represented. Rheinzabern and Trier appear to be the main sources, with Trier being the more important supplier in this case.

Pottery use

We can gain information on pottery use, at least in broad terms, through several means. The functions of some vessels are self-evident, at least in a general sense, from their forms – mortaria (K), flagons (B), cups (F), storage jars (CN), and beakers (E), as well as a lamp (MC) and cheese-press (MF). The function of jars, bowls and dishes, in contrast, is not straight-forward, and we must look to other evidence.

Surface colour provides one indication. As was noted in relation to grog-tempered wares (E80 etc), what may be termed dining or other forms of vessels used in a more social setting (beakers, bowls and some types of jars, such as CC and CE) tended to be oxidised (red- or orange-brown surfaced). Other types of jars tended to have dark

surfaces and appear to be more closely associated with cooking. A similar pattern can be seen in shelly wares (C11). Most vessels with dark surfaces were necked, everted rim 'cooking-pot'-type jars (CK). The few other vessels included bowls or dishes with plain rims (IB/JB 110). Vessels with oxidised surfaces, typically yellow-brown, included CK-type jars, but these were less common, with bowls and dishes with heavy or triangular flanges (eg Marney 1989, fig. 26, nos 41-2; Perrin 1999, fig. 72, no. 476) being almost as well represented. Excluding storage jars in pink grogged wares, oxidised wares (O wares) were dominated by bowls and dishes.

It can be suggested, then, that not all jars were necessarily associated with cooking and that, conversely, not all dishes and bowls were necessarily associated with dining or other social functions. This is supported by evidence of 'sooting' or carbonised deposits on the external surfaces of vessels, caused by the vessel being in close proximity to fire, typically having been placed over the hearth. Most vessels showing such evidence were in reduced, shelly or black-burnished fabrics (Table 4.17), and two-thirds were jars, mainly CK-type, as well as dishes and bowls with plain or dropped-flange rims.

Wear patterns also offer an insight into vessel use, although the evidence was limited, being confined to just six vessels. Two carinated bowls (HA) in grog-tempered ware (E80) had deep scoring on their interior surfaces, which could relate to cleaning, removal of stubborn contents or some other use. That two separate vessels had identical marks suggests a degree of consistency in their use. Interior use-wear was also recorded on vessels in samian wares (S30 and S40) and Oxford red/brown colour-coated ware (F51). These comprised two Drag. 38 flanged bowls and a Drag. 18/31 dish and their copies in fabric F51. The wear was typical for the forms (cf Biddulph 2008) and suggests that such

Table 4.17 Incidence of 'sooting' by form and fabric. Quantification by number of vessels based on all sherds

Form	B11	B30	C11	E80	E810	E820	F52	R10	R20	R50	R70	R90	Total no. vessels
C									1				1
CJ					1	1				1	2		5
CK		1	10				1					2	14
HB (dropped flange; plain-rim)	1		1										2
HC										1			1
IB (plain rim)			1										1
J	2							1					3
Z			1	1						1			3
Total no. vessels	3	1	13	1	1	1	1	1	1	3	2	2	30

vessels were used for food preparation (eg mixing ingredients), as well as dining or other ostentatious functions.

A drainage function is suggested by perforations made after firing through the bases of five vessels, probably jars, in fabrics E80, F51, O81, R20, and R46. A body sherd in fabric C11 had been trimmed to create a roundel, possibly a counter or a blank for a spindle whorl. A perforated roundel, identified with certainty as a spindle whorl, was collected from pit 5310 in Area 5 (see Scott, below). The object was in fabric E80 and dated to the late Iron Age/early Roman period.

Two examples of graffiti, cut after firing and presumably owners' marks, were recorded. One was a cross or X that had been cut into the wall of a jar in fabric R30 from context 1026, a fill of Phase 5 ditch 1097 from the enclosure complex adjacent to the villa (Area 1). The second was another X-graffito that had been cut into the exterior surface of a cup (FC) in fabric E810 copying a prototype in terra rubra from context 5076, a fill of Phase 3 ditch 5463 in Area 5.

Complete or near-complete vessels

A near-complete vessel – a storage jar (CN) with a thick, everted rim in fabric E820 – was collected from pit 570 in the late Iron Age/early Roman settlement in Area 1. On excavation, the lower part of the jar was found to be intact and *in situ*, the vessel appearing to have been deliberately inserted whole into what was a close-fitting pit. Most of the remains of the upper part of the vessel were recovered from the fill of the pit, having collapsed or been pushed into it in antiquity. The jar was very large; the total weight of the remains was some 7.2kg, while the rim, of which 85% survived, had a diameter of more than 400mm. Given its type and position, it is almost certain that the vessel had been used to line a storage pit. Quite what was being stored is unknown. It is possible that the vessel held grain, and indeed barley and oat grains, albeit few in number and poorly preserved, were recovered from an environmental sample taken

from inside the vessel. Organic residue analysis on Bronze Age pots used to line small pits at a site in Somerset found that the vessels contained lipid residues, suggesting that they had stored foodstuffs such as meat or dairy products (Davies *et al.* 2022). The closeness of the parallel should not be overstated, but it does remind us that in any settlement, storage of various food products would have been an important concern.

Several other complete or near-complete vessels were recovered from the site. One of them, a flagon (or, less likely, a bottle) in Nene Valley white ware (W14), was an accessory vessel that accompanied a cremation urn – a jar in shelly ware C11 – in Phase 4 grave 6007. Other vessels came mainly from the late Iron Age/early Roman settlement and the middle/late Roman field system east of the spring channel. Pottery from the former comprised two lid-seated jars (CJ), a storage jar (CN) and a carinated bowl (HA), the last, as noted above, having deep interior scoring suggestive of scraping or cleaning. The vessels from the latter area comprised a dropped-flange bowl (HB 440), a wide-mouthed jar (CM) and a funnel-necked, globular beaker (ED). The pottery is likely to have been deposited close to areas of use, and given the general domestic character of the pottery, may represent casual discard of household pots. Two near-complete, heavily sooted cooking-pot-type jars (CK) in shelly ware (C11) were recovered from ditch 1007 in the enclosure complex adjacent to the villa. The vessels were found side-by-side, appearing to have been deliberately deposited together (see Fig. 3.28).

Intra-site comparison

We can use the broad functions assigned to the pottery vessels based on the criteria outlined above to compare different parts of the site. Did all areas receive the same sort of pottery? What do differences, if any, reveal about the status or functions of those areas?

For the purpose of this analysis, all jars (C), with the exception of storage jars (CN), finer narrow-necked jars (CC) and necked, high-shouldered squat jars (CE) have been assigned to 'cooking' (representing all forms of food preparation), as have wide-mouthed jars or bowls (DB), plain-rimmed dishes (J 110), dropped-flange bowls (HB 440), Drag. 38-type curving-sided flanged bowls (HC) and mortaria. Narrow-necked jars (CC) in storage jar fabrics and storage jars themselves (CN) have been assigned to the category of 'storage'. Type CE, necked jars or bowls (DC) and all other dishes (J) and bowls (H) and bowls or dishes (I) are categorised as 'eating/social' vessels. Flagons (B), finer narrow-necked jars (CC), beakers (E) and cups (F) are 'drinking' vessels. All remaining D-class vessels were divided equally between 'cooking' and 'eating/social.' This categorisation is more nuanced than has been seen in previous analyses of vessel function (eg Evans 2001a; Allison *et al.* 2018), eschewing the standard division between utilitarian vessels (essentially jars) and table wares (bowls, dishes and drinking forms), but takes clear evidence of use (eg sooting) into account.

The results are shown in Figure 4.5a. Pottery with eating/social and drinking functions is best represented in the area defined as 'Building 1320 and the spring channel', accounting for 50% of the pottery from that area by EVE. Cooking vessels, in contrast, are best represented in the area of the field system east of the spring channel, taking a share of almost 70% of pottery from that area by EVE. This area has, in addition, a relatively high proportion of storage vessels. An emphasis on cooking and storage vessels in the enclosure complex adjacent to the villa can be noted. The field system and crop-processing area west of the spring channel has a similar profile, though a relatively high proportion of eating/social and drinking vessels is also evident. In the late Iron Age and early Roman settlement in Areas 1 and 5, cooking and storage are well-represented – the proportion of storage jars is the highest here out of all areas – but the proportion of eating/social and drinking vessels is not insignificant.

These trends show differences in pottery use between the landscape areas. Most notably, Building 1320 appears to be an area of diverse pottery use and social activities such as dining and feasting. Pottery may also have derived from the villa on the opposite side of the A4500, just *c* 100m to the north, where Continental dining habits are likely to have prevailed, but the area is the site of a temple/mausoleum, where people may have gathered for festivals, religious ceremonies or other commemorative events requiring food and drink, and the spring itself may have been a focus of communal activities. One of the largest pottery groups from the area is from dark layer 1001, to the south of the building; taking all sherds (body and base, as well as rim) into account, the group is weighted towards eating, drinking or other social functions, with two flagons, including the substantial part of one, two beakers, four bowls (assigned

by type to 'eating/social'), six jars and one storage jar. In addition, there is a vessel with a curiously small, rounded base (possibly part of a cup from a triple vase), and the spout of a lamp. The lamp is especially interesting, since such vessels are very rare in Romano-British pottery assemblages and have a very narrow distribution, being limited largely to major military sites and urban centres (Eckardt 2002). The presence of a lamp at the current site is therefore noteworthy and suggestive of specific and restricted use. Eckardt reminds us that, as a source of light, lamps would have had a role in ritual contexts (Eckardt 2011, 191), a role suggested not least by the recovery of lamps from temple sites, among them London's Temple of Mithras (Shepherd 1998, 159), an octagonal Romano-Celtic temple at Chelmsford (Wickenden 1992, 18), and a property next to a temple at the roadside settlement and religious centre at Springhead, Kent (Seager Smith *et al.* 2011, 51). Such associations potentially link the vessel from context 1001 with ritual or religious activity connected to the temple or mausoleum. The jars themselves were not necessarily utilitarian cooking pots. One was sooted (CJ), but the others assigned to a type were a little more unusual, one being a neckless medium-mouthed jar (CD), and two others being almost identical versions of

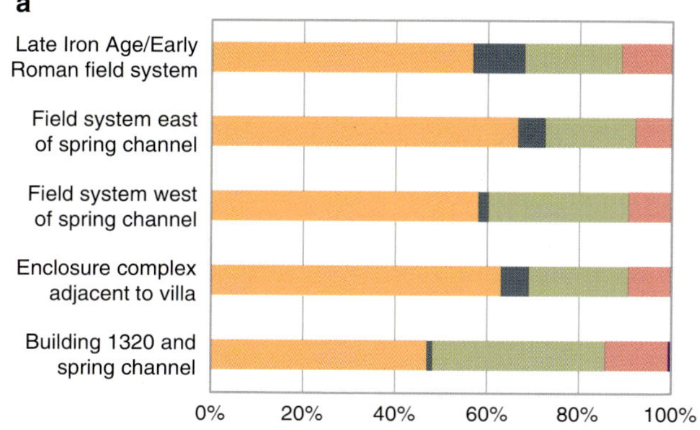

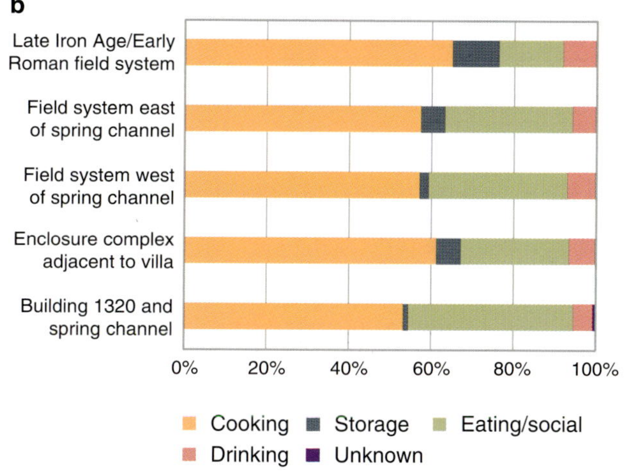

Fig. 4.5 Roman pottery: comparison of vessel function by landscape area, based on quantification by EVE

wide-mouthed jars (CM) with slightly bifid rims. The CM-type jars could have been supplied and used as a pair. Together, the group is unusual and suggestive of feasting and other activities, including activities of a ritual nature, associated with the temple/mausoleum.

In contrast, the pottery from two areas – the enclosure complex adjacent to the villa and the field system east of the spring channel – has an emphasis on cooking and storage vessels, a signature consistent with Iron Age or basic Roman rural sites (cf. Evans 2001a, 28). This tallies with the agricultural, 'lower status' character of the areas, and indeed an aisled building was recorded in Area 1. The variety of pottery forms suggests that the areas saw habitation, but the relatively high proportion of storage jars hints too at agricultural use, with storage jars, say, being used for the storage of grain and other produce. The picture, however, is a complex one. The pottery from the Phase 5a circular enclosure 20350 has a profile that points to less basic pottery use, with a higher proportion of drinking vessels and lower proportion of cooking vessels compared with the landscape assemblage overall.

The assemblages from the remaining two areas – the late Iron Age/early Roman settlement and the crop-processing area and field system – were more diverse, suggesting that there was a varied range of activities – domestic, as well as agricultural or industrial – carried out in these areas. This involved Continental-style food consumption, as well as storage and more basic food preparation.

For the purpose of comparison, Figure 4.5b again shows the relative proportions of vessel functions by landscape area, but in this case, vessels have been assigned more traditional functions. Thus, all jars (other than storage jars), lids and mortaria are cooking-related vessels, while all bowls and dishes are eating-related vessels. All D-class vessels are divided equally between cooking and eating. Storage jars have been assigned to the storage category, while flagons, cups and beakers are labelled as drinking vessels. As a result, differences between the landscape areas are flatter than they are in Figure 4.5a, particularly in relation to jars and drinking vessels. It can also be noted that the proportion of eating/social vessels in the field system east of the spring channel is larger than it is in Figure 4.5a, although this reflects the middle/late Roman emphasis of the assemblage, when dishes and bowls of the type assigned to cooking in Figure 4.5a were largely current. However, the strong representation of eating/social and drinking vessels associated with Building 1320 is more-or-less retained, supporting the view that this area was different from the other areas in terms of pottery use.

Pattern of pottery deposition

Information about deposition patterns can be gained not only from the quantities of pottery recovered from different parts of the site, but also from the condition of the pottery. Two measures are particularly useful: mean sherd weight (MSW, weight divided by sherd count) and the average EVE value or mean EVE (EVE divided by MV). High values generally point to the presence of large fragments and large proportions of rims and suggest that the pottery was deposited fairly soon after initial breakage and close to areas of use. Conversely, low values indicate high fragmentation and suggest multiple episodes of redeposition, with final burial potentially occurring some distance from areas of use.

Looking first at site area, the largest amounts of pottery were recovered from Areas 1, 2 and 5. The pottery from these areas was also the best preserved, having high overall mean sherd weights and mean EVE values. Among the landscape divisions of Area 1, the enclosure complex adjacent to the villa contained the most pottery. Less pottery was collected from Building 1320 and the spring channel and the late Iron Age/early Roman settlement, but the pottery from both landscape groups was as well preserved as that from the enclosure complex. All three landscapes may have seen domestic and, in the case of Building 1320 (see above), ritual and religious activity. In Area 2, the majority of the pottery was recovered from the field system east of the spring channel. A smaller amount was recovered from the field system and crop-processing area west of the spring channel, but this was marginally better preserved, as measured by MSW and mean EVE, than the pottery from the field system east of the spring channel, and it is possible that both were areas of pottery use.

Turning to feature type, most of the pottery was recovered from ditches (65% by sherd count), with a smaller, though not inconsiderable, quantity (21%) collected from pits (Table 4.18). The mean number of sherds per context was 7.7 sherds and 19 sherds respectively, indicating that, on average, larger groups were deposited in pits. The pottery from both feature types was similar in terms of condition; the MSW for pottery from ditches was 18.7g, while that for pits was 15.5g. These values indicate that pits and ditches provided a focus for deposition, with inhabitants looking to such features to discard broken pottery or clear household waste. The condition of the pottery suggests that generally the pottery had not been subjected to prolonged periods of exposure, disturbance and redeposition before final burial. The difference in group size may simply reflect the nature of the features, with pottery being spread along the length of ditches but necessarily concentrated in the more limited space of a pit.

Data relating to the position of the pottery deposits within the sequence of filling in the pit or ditch add to the picture. Some 83% of the pottery from pits and 89% from ditches by sherd count were recovered from single or top fills, suggesting that pottery was generally deposited, along with other waste, in order to fill up features and take them out

Table 4.18 Roman pottery, quantities and condition of the pottery by feature type

Feature type	No. sherds	Weight (g)	MSW	MV	EVE	Mean EVE
Ditch	4329	80901	18.7	627	74.51	0.1
Pit	1388	21573	15.5	82	10.77	0.1
Layer	182	5273	29	26	3.94	0.2
Cleaning	157	3405	21.7	21	2.45	0.2
Furrow	123	1631	13.3	7	1.65	0.2
Cremation	92	442	4.8			
Corndryer	87	986	11.3	6	1.74	0.3
Robber trench	64	716	11.2	8	0.54	0.1
Threshing floor	53	525	9.9	3	0.31	0.1
Void	43	569	13.2	5	0.47	0.1
Aisled building	37	388	10.5	3	0.76	0.3
Tree-throw hole	31	652	21	2	0.13	0.1
Foundation	24	626	26.1	5	0.29	0.1
Ditch/pit	14	242	17.3	2	0.17	0.1
Posthole	9	26	2.9	1	0.03	0.03
Waterhole	9	58	6.4	1	0.05	0.1
Trackway surface	7	465	66.4	1	0.5	0.5
Grave	6	32	5.3			
Culvert l	4	80	20	1	0.06	0.1
Kiln/hearth stokehole	4	68	17	2	0.14	0.07
Buried soil	3	31	10.3			
Channel	3	113	37.7			
Rectilinear enclosure	3	28	9.3			
Hollow	2	6	3			

MSW = mean sherd weight (weight/no. sherds); Mean EVE = EVE/MV

Table 4.19 Quantity and condition of pottery from pits and ditches by fill position

| | Pits | | | | Ditches | | | |
Position	No. sherds	Weight (g)	MSW	Mean EVE	No. sherds	Weight (g)	MSW	Mean EVE
Top	356	8048	22.6	0.12	777	11839	15.2	0.1
Middle	53	882	16.6	0.1	160	3033	19	0.11
Primary	65	1176	18.1	0.16	274	6926	25.3	0.12
Single	234	3457	14.8	0.13	2810	52247	18.6	0.12

of use. The condition of the pottery was reasonably uniform across all fill positions, however, generally pointing to similar taphonomic histories for all the pottery before deposition, regardless of fill position (Table 4.19).

Other feature types did not routinely receive pottery in the form of household waste, with the pottery recovered from those features instead resulting from more casual, opportunistic or incidental deposition. This pottery was generally in relatively poor condition, reflecting multiple episodes of redeposition and prolonged weathering, but there were exceptions. Pottery collected from corndryer fills, deposits associated with the aisled building, layers, and pottery from Area 5 furrow 5565 was relatively well-preserved, having some of the highest MSW and mean-EVE values. The high values obtained from corndryer fills, from the field system and crop-processing area west of

the spring channel, derive to a large extent from the presence of two shelly ware jars (fabric C11, type CK) in corndryer 2039, one near-complete, the other substantially complete (see Fig. 3.45). That the values obtained from layers were so high was almost entirely owing to the well-preserved character of the pottery from context 1001, the dark layer south of Building 1320. Similarly well preserved pottery was collected from the aisled building in the enclosure complex adjacent to the villa. That is not to say that the pottery from these three landscape areas was put to identical use. The potentially ritual or religious use of the pottery from the layer south of Building 1320 has been discussed above. The pottery from the aisled building included dishes and bowls in samian ware and a beaker, as well as jars, suggesting domestic activity. In contrast, the pottery from the corndryers was less diverse. With the exception of a single beaker, all vessels identified by rim were coarseware jars or vessels that were either jars or bowls. This is a more utilitarian profile, with the pottery perhaps having a use related to the corndryers.

An interesting phenomenon observed during recording was the presence of 'pairs' of more unusual or distinctive vessels in individual groups. One pair, the two near-identical wide-mouthed jars (CM) with bifid rims in fabric R30 from layer 1001, has already been noted, as has the pair of shelly ware jars (fabric C11, type CK) in corndryer 2039, but other pairs were evident. Another pair of CM-type vessels, this time in fabric R50, was recovered from context 6032, a deposit from an (unexcavated) enclosure ditch in the field system east of the spring channel. A pair of hammerhead mortaria (KC) in fabric M23 was found in the fill of pit 1176 in Area 1 in the enclosure complex adjacent to the villa. How such pairs came together is uncertain, but potentially they can be regarded as an indicator of groups from single households (or the temple/mausoleum in the case of context 1001). Each pair may have been acquired together for use in the same household and consequently experienced similar 'life histories' (or degree, length and type of use). On breakage, the pairs may have retained their association, having been disposed of onto the same household midden before being cleared together, along with the other waste, into pits or ditches. On this basis, the pairs hint at the location of nearby structures, while the composition of each group gives us a snapshot of what may have been seen in a household if it had been preserved *in situ*. In the case of ditch 6032, at a particular time during the late 3rd century AD, the

household was equipped with a cooking jar, two wide-mouthed jars (perhaps for food presentation, if not cooking), a dropped-flange bowl and plain-rim dish (perhaps used together as cooking vessels), another couple of dishes (possibly dining vessels) and a beaker. The interpretation of the pairs is speculative, and more research involving other assemblages is required to establish the principle, but it is useful to note that the landscape divisions from which the pairs were recovered were those from which large amounts of well-preserved pottery were collected, pointing to foci of pottery use nearby.

One aspect that remains to be addressed is the distribution of pottery in the late Iron Age and early Roman complex in Areas 1 and 5. Can we identify areas of domestic occupation and refuse disposal from the distribution? No part of the landscape appears to have been an area of very concentrated pottery deposition; pottery was recovered in fairly small quantities across the landscape. Nevertheless, relatively large quantities (as measured by sherd count) were collected from ditch 5541 in the north-eastern part of Area 5, ditch 5439 the southern part, and in Area 1 pits 570 and 671, and it may be in or close to these parts of the site that domestic activity was focused. As discussed above, the buried storage vessel in pit 570 may have been used to store foodstuffs, possibly belonging to a single household.

Analysis of the condition of the assemblage from this landscape area offers further insight. Figure 4.6 presents the relationship between MSW and mean EVE by ditch group and pit. Groups with the 'best preserved' pottery have relatively

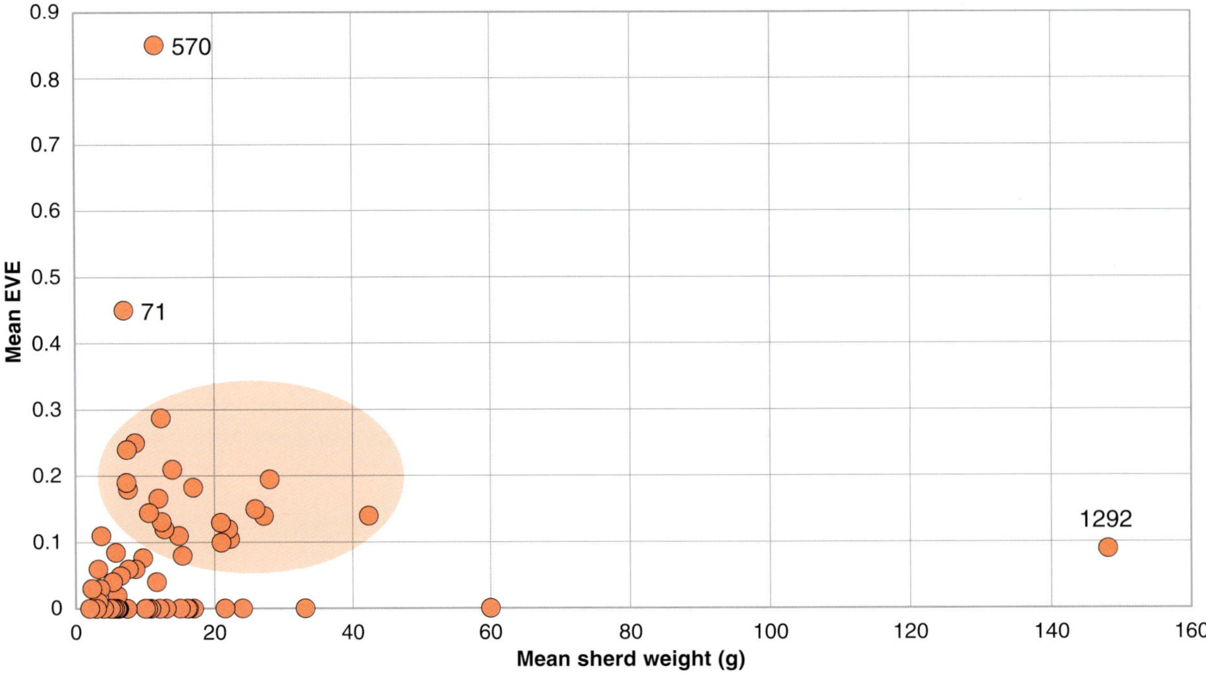

Fig. 4.6 Roman pottery: plot of assemblages from ditches and pits in the late Iron Age and early Roman settlement in Areas 1 and 5, showing the relationship between mean sherd weight and mean EVE

high MSW and mean EVE values and represent vessels that have retained a good level of integrity, plausibly having been deposited reasonably rapidly after discard and close to areas of use. A group of pottery from pit 71, largely comprising the substantial part of a globular jar, would appear to fall into this category. The special character of the pottery from pit 570 is shown by its isolated position on the scattergram, but the pottery from pit 1292 is a clear outlier, comprising a single storage jar sherd whose deposition may have been incidental. The remaining groups are not so clearly differentiated, but of these it is possible to detect a loose cluster of groups (circled on the scattergram), which contain relatively well-preserved pottery. These include ditches 5439 and 5541, which are joined by ditches 5530, 5537, 5546, and 5566 in the central part of Area 5, ditches 5449 and 5529 in the south-western part, ditch 5532 in the north-eastern part, ditch 5549 in the eastern part, and ditch 5531 to the north-west. The analysis points to occupation across the landscape area, but with a greater focus of domestic activity in the central part of Area 5.

Site status and inter-site comparison

While analysis of the pottery by function has highlighted differences between areas in pottery use and, by extension, the sorts of activities carried out in those areas, comparison of the assemblage with others in the region suggests that the site was of relatively low status.

Samian ware provides a useful indicator. The ware accounted for just 0.9% of the entire assemblage by weight, which is well within the range obtained for rural sites across Roman Britain (Willis 2004, table 24). At Upton, a site whose pottery suggested 'a fairly well-appointed household in the immediate vicinity' (Timby 2010, 40), a value of 3.4% was recorded (ibid., table 4). At Bozeat Quarry, a farming and industrial settlement, samian accounted for 0.1% of the assemblage (Perrin 2018, table 3.3). The relatively low percentage of samian at Panattoni Park may in part be due to the apparent early Roman hiatus in activity, considerably reducing supply of South and Central Gaulish samian between *c* AD 50/70 and 150. However, turning to decorated samian as a percentage of the samian assemblage, another value linked to site type (Willis 2004, section 7.3.10), Panattoni Park appears to have been somewhat lacking in samian even during the well-attested 'Antonine peak' in supply (Willis 2004, table 10). Some 7.6% of the samian assemblage by EVE, or 11% by vessel count, was decorated. These values are consistent with lower-order rural sites (ibid., table 35), including those relatively close to the Panattoni Park site. The latter value is identical to that obtained from Site H on the M1, Junction 12 improvement scheme (Monteil 2020, table 6.29) and only a little higher than the value (8.3% by vessel count) from the

samian assemblage from the rural settlement at Crick Covert Farm near Rugby (Hancocks and Willis 2015, 104).

The relative proportions of vessel classes also suggest a lower-status rural signature. In her report on the pottery from Upton, Timby (2010, table 5) presents percentages of vessel classes, separated into 'tablewares' – essentially drinking-related forms in any fabric and all forms in fine wares – and 'coarsewares', comprising forms except drinking forms in reduced, shelly and other coarse fabrics. It can be noted that the chronology of both sites is similar, except that the early Roman period is better represented at Upton. Generating comparative values for Panattoni Park (Table 4.20), we see that the Panattoni Park assemblage has consistently lower proportions of tablewares, although a higher proportion of dishes can be noted. Among the coarsewares, dishes and bowls are less well represented at Panattoni Park, but the site has a higher proportion of jars. Interestingly, the proportion of mortaria is identical, suggesting a similar level of supply to both sites.

While the apparent early Roman hiatus at Panattoni Park and the resulting pattern of samian supply (and that of other finewares) are likely to have had an impact on the representation of dining forms, especially cups, the low proportions of coarseware dining forms (ie dishes and bowls; cf. Evans 2001a, 28) suggest that these forms were relatively unimportant to the inhabitants of Panattoni Park. That is not to say that the inhabi-

Table 4.20 Roman pottery, comparative proportions of vessel classes

| | Vessel class | % EVE | |
		Panattoni Park	Upton
Tableware	B flagon	1.5	3.2
	C jar	1.5	0.1
	D jar/bowl	0.1	-
	E beaker	4	7.1
	F cup	0.7	4.2
	H bowl	1.5	2.9
	I bowl/dish	0.3	-
	J dish	4.8	3.5
	L 'box' lid	-	0.9
Coarseware	C jar	60	52.1
	D jar/bowl	4.3	-
	H bowl	11.3	13.8
	I bowl/dish	1.3	-
	J dish	6	9.7
	K mortarium	2.2	2.2
	L lid	0.2	0.7
	Z indeterminate	0.1	-
		100	100
	Total EVE	98.51	54.23

tants were not aware of Continental dining practices, and as we have seen, consideration of factors in addition to vessel class – surface colour, burning, wear and so on – points to a more complex picture of vessel use, with individual classes serving multiple functions, but in general, pottery supply was focused on more utilitarian forms.

As Evans (2001a) has shown, the ratio of jars to dishes/bowls is another useful measure of status, with the relationship correlating well with site types, basic rural sites tending to have jar-dominated assemblages reflecting the continuation of Iron Age patterns of pottery use. The ratio tends to change through time, with dishes and bowls generally becoming more important in the middle and late Roman periods, but this is relative to site type. Based on values in Table 4.20, Panattoni Park sits comfortably among the mass of rural sites in southern Britain presented by Evans (2001a, fig. 5). However, setting the site against other rural sites in the region and, for the purpose of comparison, the extramural nucleated settlement at Alchester (Fig. 4.7), the assemblage generally ranks higher than the agricultural settlements of Bozeat Quarry and Monksmoor Farm, Daventry, but lower than Upton and, as expected, Alchester, although not by a particularly large margin until the late Roman period.

Drawing on these observations, it is clear that while the assemblage has a rural signature, it is by no means a very basic one. Indeed, as discussed above, the pottery from the area of Building 1320 and the spring channel has relatively high-status elements, including a ratio of jars to bowls/dishes that allies the assemblage more closely with Alchester, and, of course, a lamp. Overall, the assemblage would appear to be consistent with a settlement within the estate of the villa on the opposite side of the A4500, but one that was typically used by, and catered towards, the villa's workforce and associated community rather than the villa's occupants. Cooking and dining practices largely followed pre-Roman Iron Age traditions, although Continental practices were by no means eschewed. Some of the pottery, notably the material

associated with Building 1320, may well have derived from the villa itself and have been used by the inhabitants of the villa.

Of the pottery from the villa itself, we know very little. The site was discovered in 1846 and uncovered again in 1849. Further investigations prior to the construction of the A45 (now the A4500) were carried out in the 1960s. A mosaic pavement, stone cistern, and robbed-out walls were among the discoveries. There is little precise information about the pottery, but systematic fieldwalking across the site of the villa, undertaken by the Community Landscape Archaeology Survey Project (CLASP), recovered a large assemblage of some 5000 sherds, which was subsequently recorded using the Northamptonshire fabric series (CLASP, nd b). Several observations can be made when we compare that assemblage (known as 'Harpole 1') with Panattoni Park. Curiously, the Harpole 1 assemblage appears to be 'lower status' than the pottery from Panattoni Park. The proportion of samian wares in the Harpole 1 assemblage (0.3% by sherd count) is lower than Panattoni Park (1.1%). While the proportion of amphorae is similar, the proportion of oxidised wares overall (ware category D), which includes samian, amphorae and fine wares, is noticeably lower in the Harpole 1 assemblage: 6.3% by sherd count, compared with 13.9% at Panattoni Park.

The differences between the assemblages, based on sherd count, are clearly seen on a scattergram displaying the results of correspondence analysis (Fig. 4.8). This multivariate technique is a useful way of demonstrating differences and similarities between variables, in this case sites (and landscape divisions) and ware types. Sites and landscapes that are similar to each other in terms of the composition of their assemblages will plot close to each other on the scattergram. The axial intersection represents the average point of the entire dataset (cf. Shennan 1997). We can see, then, that Harpole 1 is set apart from any single landscape area and the overall Panattoni Park assemblage, being plotted in the upper part of the top left quadrant. Indeed,

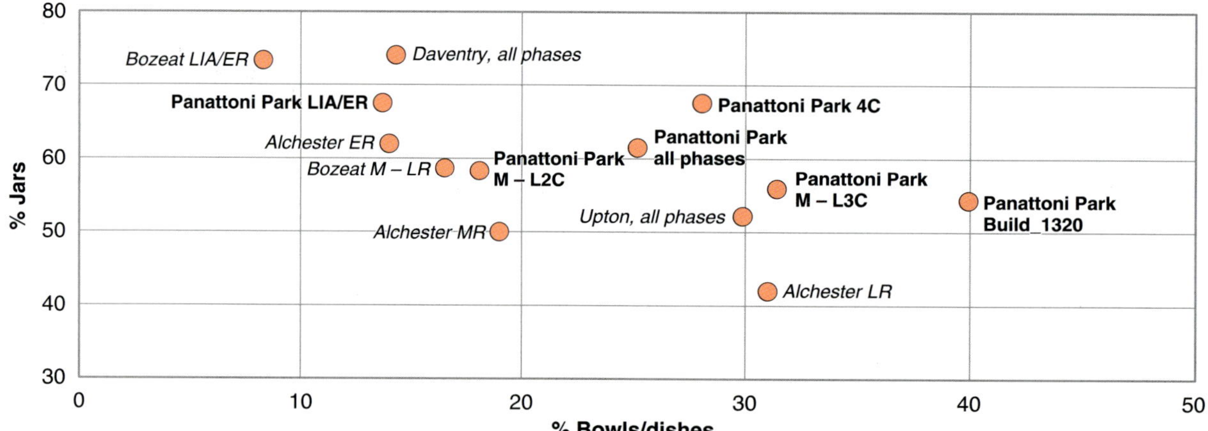

Fig. 4.7 Roman pottery: scattergram showing the proportions of jars and bowls/dishes

Table 4.21 Roman pottery: correspondence analysis data, showing the number of sherds by ware type and site or landscape area

Site/landscape name	A Grogged	B Shelly	C Reduced	D Oxidised	Total no. sherds
CLASP	1094	669	2911	314	4988
Late Iron Age/early Roman settlement in Areas 1 and 5	1425	352	48	80	1905
Enclosure complex adjacent to the villa	175	564	1060	344	2143
Building 1320 and the spring channel	4	101	153	77	335
Field system and crop processing area west of the spring channel	25	86	259	89	459
Field system east of the spring channel (including Phase 5a circular enclosure)	74	326	831	316	1547
Phase 5a circular enclosure within the field system east of the spring channel	19	58	128	101	306
Panattoni Park – all pottery	1854	1476	2405	926	6661

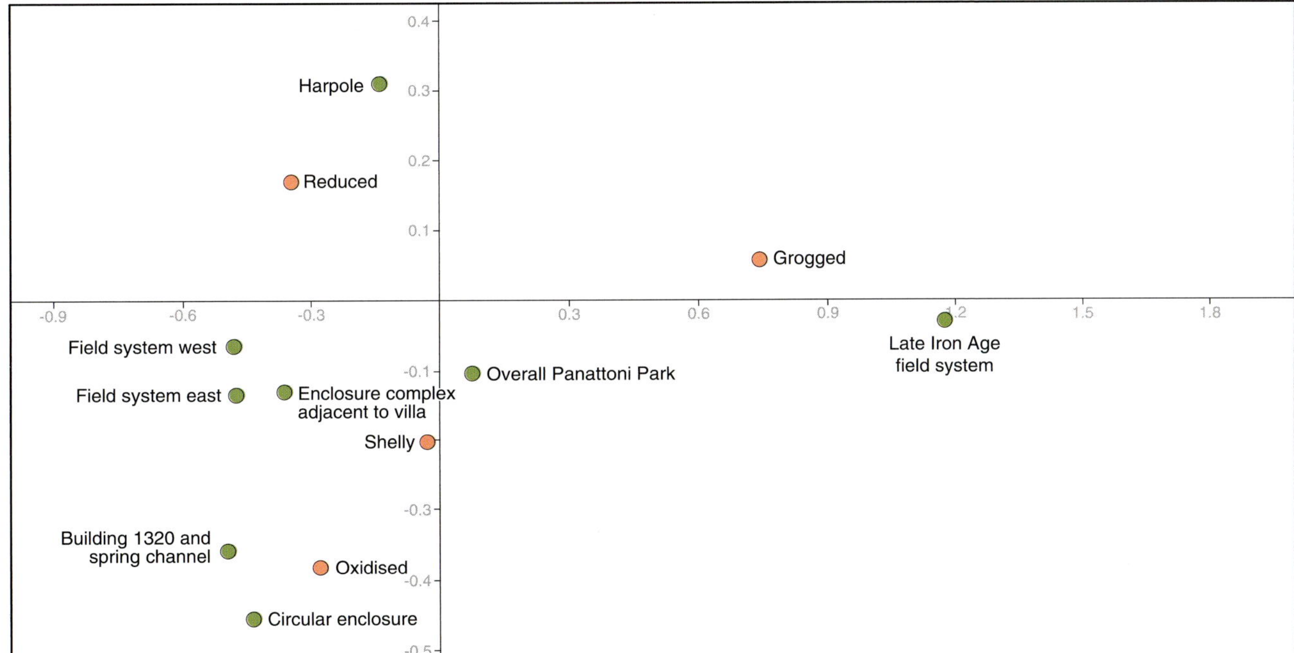

Fig. 4.8 Roman pottery: correspondence analysis plot showing relationship between sites and landscape areas

Harpole 1 is associated most strongly with reduced wares (ware type C), which dominates the assemblage by sherd count (Table 4.21). As discussed above, there is also variation within the Panattoni Park assemblage. The late Iron Age and early Roman settlement in Areas 1 and 5 is isolated in the right-hand-side of the scattergram and, unsurprisingly, is most strongly associated with grogged wares (ware type A). Another area that is relatively isolated is Building 1320 and the spring channel, which is plotted towards the bottom edge of the scattergram. It is not quite on its own, however, more-or-less occupying the same space as the Phase 5a circular enclosure 20350. Both areas are associated strongly with oxidised wares, with the analysis supporting the view that the areas are set apart from the others in terms of their pottery use and by the fact that their assemblages have a more specialised and diverse character; however, it should be noted that the groups are smaller than those of the other areas (Table 4.21). The remaining areas – the enclosure complex adjacent to the villa, the field system and crop-processing area west of the spring channel and the field system east of the spring channel – are in a loose cluster relatively close to the axial intersection and are therefore have assemblages that are similar to each other and are closest to the 'site average', as their position next to 'overall Panattoni Park' suggests.

Conclusion

The pottery analysis has drawn on a large and diverse assemblage to gain insights into pottery supply and use, the character of the settlement, and the nature of occupation and land-use. The analysis has demonstrated that while occupation spanned the late Iron Age to the late Roman period, there were fluctuations in the level of activity. The pottery was primarily put to household use – cooking, dining, storage and the like – but examination of surface colour and evidence of use, such as wear and burning, highlighted the fact that there is no simple correlation between vessel shape and use; some jars, for example, appeared to have been used for food presentation and dining, rather than cooking. Such observations allowed different areas of the site to be differentiated. For example, Building 1320 and the spring channel were potentially identified as an area where people gathered for communal events involving food and drink, while the field system east of the spring channel saw a more basic, domestic level of pottery use. Measures of fragmentation provided a means of identifying core and more peripheral areas of occupation across the site. A comparison with assemblages from other sites in the region and beyond helped characterise the sort of site that was represented by the pottery. While the site is associated with a villa, the pottery pointed to a lower-status, rural site, perhaps one that was occupied and worked by the villa's workforce and associated community. Overall, the analysis has shown how pottery can be used to go beyond issues of date and typology to address questions about life in rural settlements.

Catalogue of illustrated pottery (Figs 4.9-10)

The selection of pottery shown here illustrates the chronological range of the assemblage and presents unusual or intrinsically interesting pieces.

Context 5359, fill of ditch 5440, phase 3, late Iron Age/early Roman field system in Areas 1 and 5

1. Fabric E820, lid-seated jar (CJ) with a notched rim
2. Fabric E80, storage jar (CN)
3. Fabric E80, jar or bowl (D)
4. Fabric E80, carinated bowl (HA). Substantially complete vessel (SF203); scratches on interior surface made after firing
   Ceramic date: Early/mid-1st century AD

Context 5395, fill of furrow 5394

5. Fabric E80, narrow-necked jar (CC)
6. Fabric E80, high-shouldered necked jar (CE)
7. Fabric E80, globular jar (CG) with cordoned shoulder. Smooth, orange-brown, fine fabric
8. Fabric E80, lid-seated jar (CJ)
9. Fabric E80, storage jar (CN)
   Ceramic date: 1st century AD (residual)

Context 572, fill of pit 570, phase 3, late Iron Age/early Roman field system in Areas 1 and 5

10. Fabric E820, complete or near-complete storage jar (CN), inserted as lining of storage pit. (Rim and shoulder shown only)
    Ceramic date: 1st century AD

Context 5076, fill of ditch 5463, Phase 3, late Iron Age/early Roman field system in Areas 1 and 5

11. Fabric E810 with dark red surfaces; cup (cf. Hawkes and Hull 1947, type Cam 56), copying Gallo-Belgic prototype. Possible 'X' graffito incised after firing on exterior surface of vessel
    Ceramic date: early/mid-1st century AD

Context 5090, fill of ditch 5541, Phase 3, late Iron Age/early Roman field system in Areas 1 and 5

12. Fabric E80, oxidised surfaces, dark grey core; cordoned carinated bowl, with fine lattice between cordons (as Marney 1989, fig. 36, nos 71–3). Deep scoring on interior surface after firing.
    Ceramic date: 1st century AD

Context 2138, fill pit 2135, phase 5, field system and crop processing area west of the spring channel

13. Fabric R30, wide-mouthed jar (CM; cf. Perrin 1999, fig. 57, nos 38–40)
14. Fabric C11, jar (C)
15. Fabric R30, straight-sided bowl (HB) with flanged rim
16. Fabric R30, straight-sided bowl (HB) with flanged rim
17. Fabric R30, straight-sided bowl (HB) with squared, bifid rim
18. Fabric B11, straight-sided bowl (HB) with incipient bead-and-flanged rim
19. Fabric B11, curving-sided dish (JB) with plain rim
20. Fabric R46, straight-sided dish (JA) with squared rim, projecting base and rilled body
21. Fabric M29, wall-sided mortarium (KD; as Hawkes and Hull 1947, Cam 501)
22. Fabric R30, base of beaker, overfired and with diagonal scratches on interior surface made after firing
    Ceramic date: Late 2nd-early/mid-3rd century AD

Cremation grave 6007, phase 4, field system east of the spring channel

23. Fabric W14, near-complete flagon or bottle, very fragmented (ancillary vessel)
24. Fabric C11, base and body sherds of jar (urn)
    Ceramic date: Mid-2nd to early/mid-3rd century AD

Context 1183, fill of ditch 606, phase 4, enclosure complex adjacent to villa

25. Fabric R30, pedestal base with pre-firing circles impressed on interior base, as if perforations intended but none actually piercing base
    Ceramic date: 2nd to 4th century AD

Context 1184, layer, phase 5, enclosure complex adjacent to villa

26. Fabric S30, curving-sided bowl (HC; Drag. 38), worn through use extensively across interior surface

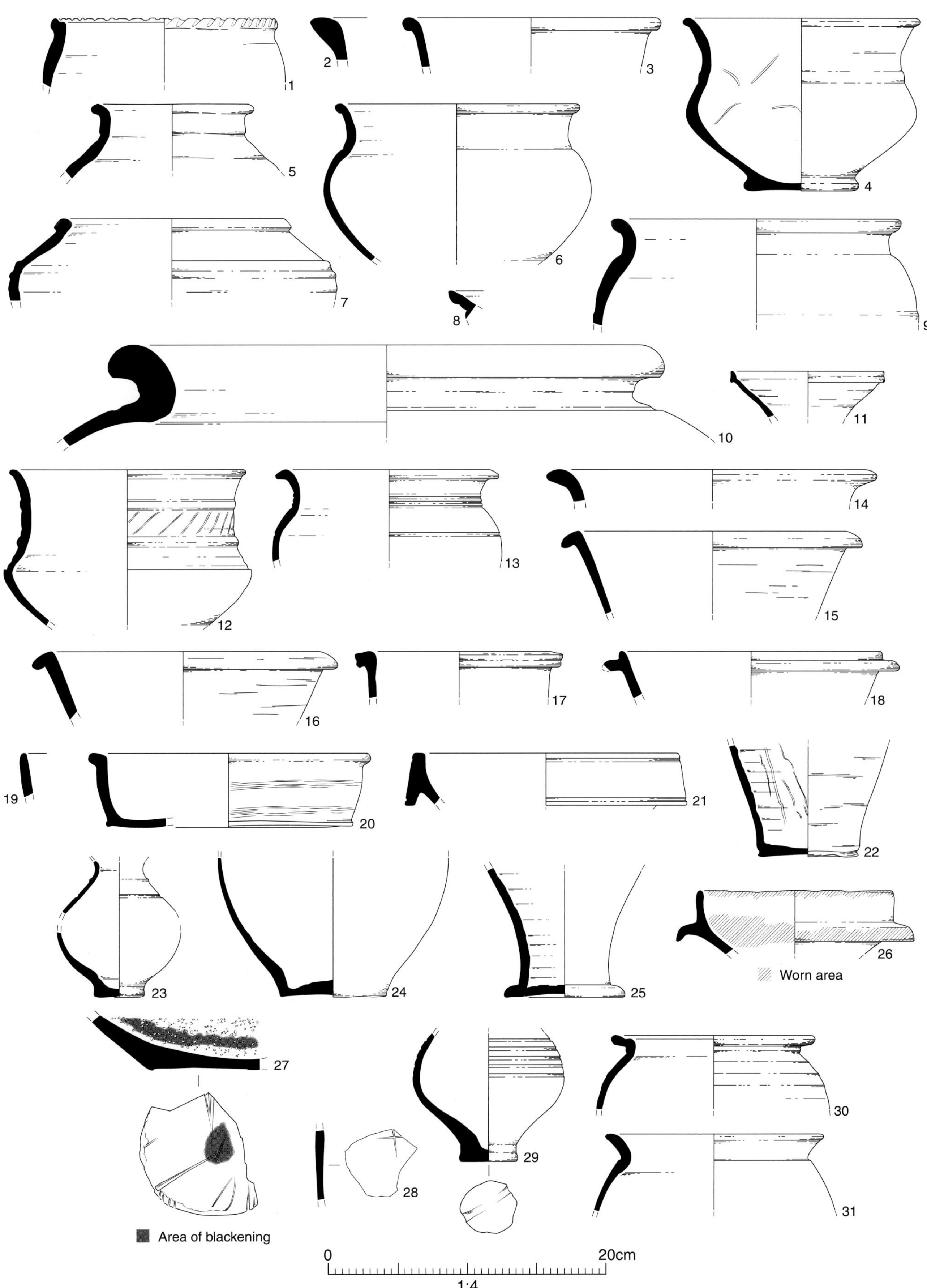

Fig. 4.9 Roman pottery, nos 1–31

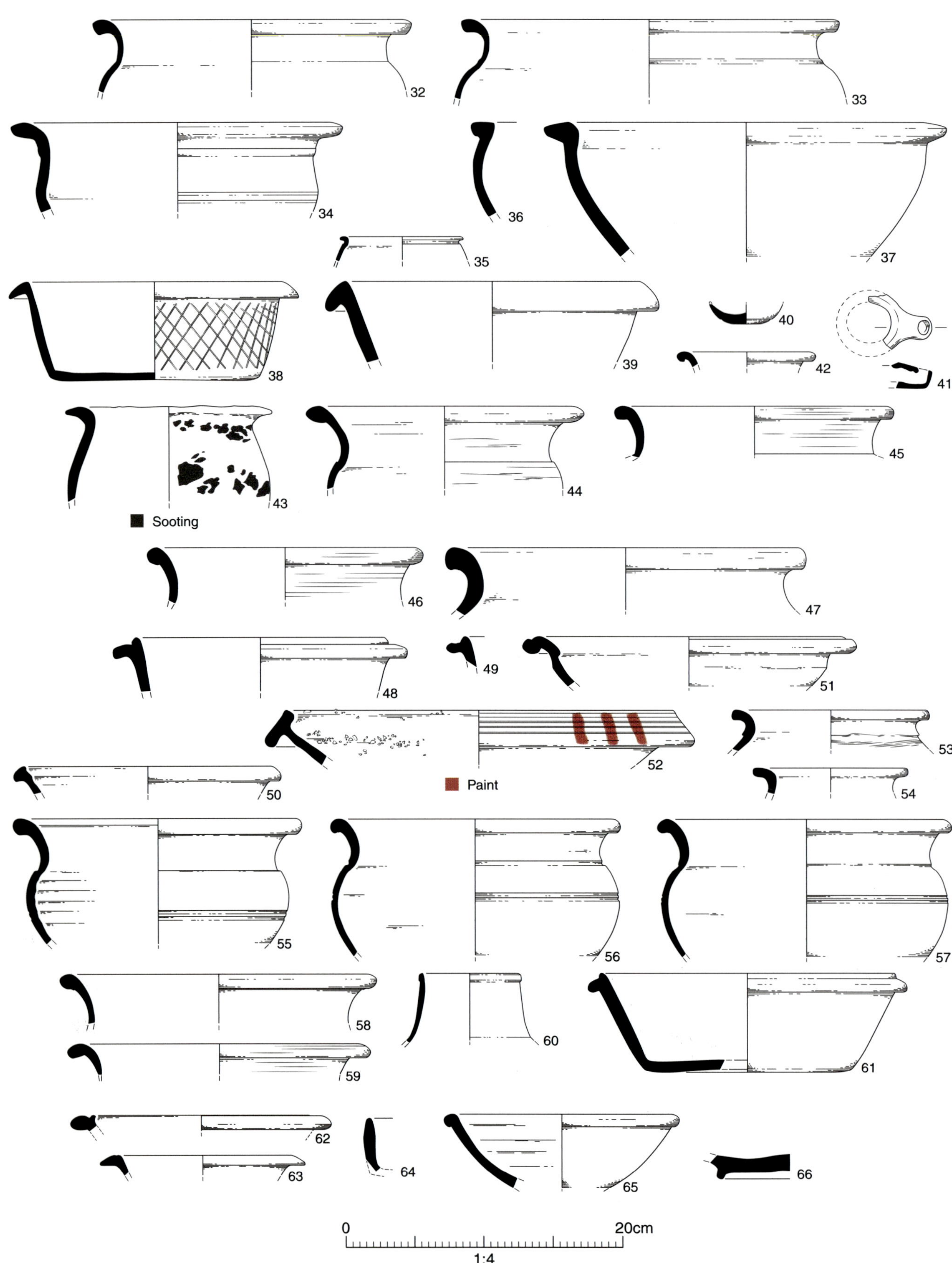

Fig. 4.10 Roman pottery, nos 32–66

Ceramic date: Mid/late 2nd century AD

Context 1431, fill of pit 1430, phase 4, Building 1320 and spring channel

27. Fabric M23, mortarium base, blackened on interior and exterior surfaces; potter's tool marks on exterior surface
    Ceramic date: Mid-2nd to mid-3rd century AD

Context 1026, fill of ditch 1097, phase 5, enclosure complex adjacent to villa

28. Fabric R30, 'X' graffito, incised after firing on wall of vessel
    Ceramic date: Late 2nd to mid-4th century

Context 1001, layer, phase 4, Building 1320 and spring channel

29. Fabric W10, substantial portion of flagon. Two linear impressions in base, made before firing
30. Fabric R70, lid-seated jar (CJ), sooted on exterior surface
31. Fabric R30, cooking pot (CK)
32. Fabric R30, wide-mouthed jar (CM), slight bifid rim
33. Fabric R30, wide-mouthed jar (CM), slight bifid rim
34. Fabric R46, wide-mouthed jar (CM), similar to Perrin 1999, fig. 57, no. 40
35. Fabric F52, bag-shaped beaker (EC)
36. Fabric R20, curving-sided bowl (HC)
37. Fabric C11, curving-sided bowl (HC)
38. Fabric R46, straight-sided bowl (HB) with flanged rim
39. Fabric R46, straight-sided bowl (HB) with flanged rim
40. Fabric R30, vessel with curiously small, rounded base
41. Fabric O10, nozzle of lamp (MC)
    Ceramic date: Late 2nd to early 3rd century AD

Context 1090, fill of pit 1224, phase 5, enclosure complex adjacent to villa

42. Fabric R10, narrow-mouthed jar (CC)
43. Fabric C11, cooking-pot (CK), heavily sooted on exterior surface
44. Fabric 46, wide-mouthed jar (CM), as Marney 1989, fig. 30, no. 4
45. Fabric R30, wide-mouthed jar (CM), as Marney 1989, fig. 30, no. 4
46. Fabric R50, wide-mouthed jar (CM), as Marney 1989, fig. 30, no. 4
47. Fabric C11, storage jar (CN)
48. Fabric B11, straight-sided bowl (HB) with dropped flange rim
49. Fabric B11, straight-sided bowl (HB) with dropped flange rim
50. Fabric R30, straight-sided dish (JA) with bead rim
51. Fabric W14, curving-sided dish (JB), with trace of red paint on flange (cf. Perrin 1999, fig. 63, no. 244)
52. Fabric M23, hammerhead mortarium (KC);

burnt patches or blackening on rim
Ceramic date: Late 3rd century AD

Context 6032, fill of unexcavated ditch, phase 5, field system east of the spring channel

53. Fabric C10, medium-mouthed jar (CD)
54. Fabric C11, cooking-pot (CK)
55. Fabric R50 , wide-mouthed jar (CM), as Marney 1989, fig. 46, no. 2
56. Fabric R50, wide-mouthed jar (CM)
57. Fabric R20 , wide-mouthed jar (CM)
58. Fabric R20, wide-mouthed jar (CM)
59. Fabric W10, jar or bowl (D). Fine sandy white ware with yellow-brown paint; parchment ware, possibly Oxford or Nene Valley
60. Fabric F52, globular beaker with funnel neck (ED)
61. Fabric R46, straight-sided bowl (HB) with dropped flange
62. Fabric R30, straight-sided bowl (HB) with dropped flange
63. Fabric R30, straight-sided bowl or dish (IA), with incipient bead and flange
64. Fabric B11, curving-sided dish (JB) with plain rim
65. Fabric O10, curving-sided dish (JB) with bead rim, copying samian form Drag. 31
    Ceramic date: Late 3rd century AD

Layer 20436, group 20035, phase 5, field system east of the spring channel

66. Fabric F51. Base of bowl; no slip remaining on interior surface; centre of exterior surface of base is 'pock-marked' with 15+ circular impressions, made after firing
    Ceramic date: Late 3rd century AD

COINS *by Paul Booth*

Introduction

Forty-one Roman coins were recovered during the excavation. Most date to the later 3rd and 4th centuries. The coins are generally in poor condition in terms of surface encrustation and corrosion. A number of pieces are very eroded, and a significant number have damaged edges which severely limited identification. The coins were scanned rapidly at the post-excavation assessment stage and some hand-cleaning to facilitate identification was undertaken by the writer; five coins were subject to subsequent specialist cleaning, but with minimal consequent refinement of identification. An indication of the poor condition of the assemblage is the fact that only four coins could be assigned a specific reference in the standard catalogues. Nevertheless, many of the coins could be assigned to one of the issue periods in the scheme devised by Richard Reece (eg 1991), albeit with varying degrees of certainty, and are presented in relation to these periods in Table 4.22, with further totals relating to broader phases of

Table 4.22 Quantification of Roman coins by issue period and phase

Date	Reece period	Total coins	Phase total	% of coins assigned to phase
Before AD 41	1			
41–54	2			
54–68	3			
69–96	4			
96–117	5			
117–138	6	1		
138–61	7			
161–180	8			
180–192	9			
193–222	10	1		
222–238	11			
238–260	12			
Phase A	Uncertain	2	4	10.8
260–275	13	7		
275–296	14			
Phase B	Uncertain	6	13	35.1
296–317	15			
317–330	16	1		
Phase C			1	2.7
330–348	17	7		
348–364	18	3?		
364–378	19	6		
378–388	20			
388–402	21	3		
Phase D	Uncertain		19	51.4
3–4C/unassigned		4		
Total		41	37	

issue (ibid.). Details of the individual coins are given in Table 4.23, with further comments contained in the archive record. Wear is recorded using the stages defined by Brickstock (2004).

The assemblage

The earliest identifiable coin is a denarius of Hadrian dated AD 134-8 and only fairly lightly worn. Two further denarii, both plated, are of later date, one of Julia Mamaea and the other uncertain. A single heavily worn sestertius is also probably of broad 1st to 2nd-century date. The later 3rd century is well represented. The Period 13 coins included four certainly or probably of Victorinus, two probably of Claudius II and a single issue of Tetricus I. The condition of many of the Phase B coins makes it impossible to be certain if they were regular or irregular issues. Examples of the latter are likely to have been present and would be assigned to Period 14 if identified. One coin of this phase had been pierced.

A single (incomplete) coin of AD 320-1 was of Reece's Phase C. In the following phase Periods 17-19 were fairly consistently represented. The Period 18 identifications, however, are tentative, based on the general character of coins (two of them very small) which are most likely to have been imitations of the common FEL TEMP REPARATIO fallen horseman type. All of these coins were heavily eroded. An earlier (eg late 3rd-century) date for some of them cannot be ruled out completely, but is considered unlikely. The presence of two certain and one possible coin of the last issue period regularly represented in Roman Britain (Period 21) is notable in an assemblage of this size.

Distribution and phasing

The coins are divided evenly between component contexts of the enclosures associated with the villa (Area 1, 21 coins) and the rest: the field systems east of the spring (Area 2, 14 coins) and Areas 3 and 4 (3 coins each). In Area 1 a single small coin perhaps of the mid-4th century was clearly intrusive in a Phase 3b ditch fill (context 356), while the denarius of Hadrian came from layer 1001 south of Building 1320 and assigned to Phase 4. The remaining coins were from Phases 5a (6) and 5b (12) and one unphased. In Area 2, seven coins were of Phase 5a, one of Phase 5b, four of Phase 5c and two unphased. The three coins in Area 3 were all from topsoil/subsoil and the three in Area 4 were assigned to generic Phase 5.

The Area 1 coins included two of the early pieces, ten of the later 3rd-century (Phase B) radiates and a possible Period 21 coin. By contrast the Area 2 coins included only two radiates and the two confidently identified Period 21 pieces. The unstratified coins in Area 3 were of mixed dates, while the three coins from Area 4 were all of the earlier 4th century.

The chronological breakdown of the coins in relation to the site phases reveals no clear patterns. The six Phase 5a coins in Area 1 were all of the later 3rd century. One coin from Phase 5a contexts in Area 2 was of the later 3rd century with the remaining six spanning the 4th century and including two Period 21 coins. Another 13 coins came from Phase 5b contexts, all but one in Area 1, and included more radiates, but also four coins of the House of Valentinian and a possible Period 21 issue. The four coins from contexts assigned to Phase 5c in Area 2 are a mixed group and shed no light on the absolute chronology of that phase.

The assemblage is too small for the significance of the relative quantities and spatial distribution of coins of different issue periods and broader phases to be completely clear, but overall the high proportion of coins of Reece's Phase B is striking, as is the concentration of this material in Area 1, and is unusual in a rural site, where assemblages tend to be more heavily dominated by issues of Phase D. As noted above, the relatively high proportion of coins of Period 21 may also be significant.

Local comparison

Two late Roman coins were recovered from the evaluation, the only identifiable one being an issue of the House of Constantine dated *c* AD 330 (MOLA 2015c, 53). Extensive comparison based on such a small assemblage is not warranted, but there are data from nearby sites recorded by CLASP (Community Landscape Archaeology Project). Some 32 coins are recorded from the immediately adjacent villa, directly associated with the present site. These comprise a single issue of Antoninus Pius, seven of later 3rd-century and 24 of 4th-century date. The balance of this list is therefore rather different from that at Panattoni Park, with its stronger late 3rd-century representation. The CLASP list terminates with three issues of the House of Valentinian, so Period 21 coins are absent, though this may be a function of the small size of the group. The villa north of Road Hill Farm, also in Harpole parish, has a much longer coin list of 174 coins, of which 21 are illegible 3rd-4th or 4th-century pieces. The list ranges from three late Iron Age coins to a single issue of the House of Theodosius. The 2nd-early 3rd centuries are relatively well represented (11 coins) and 64 coins are of the later 3rd century and 22 of Reece's Phase C (early 4th century). Here the proportion of radiates, even higher than that on the present site, is again notable.

METAL, CERAMIC, WORKED BONE AND GLASS ARTEFACTS *by Ian R Scott*

Introduction and methodology

The small finds assemblage is quite small and comprises 103 iron objects, 18 copper alloy objects, an object made of iron and copper alloy, 19 pieces of lead, a glass bead, a glass gaming counter, one bone hairpin and one ceramic spindle whorl. There were also seven sherds of vessel glass (two post-medieval or later) and two of window glass. The largest single category of find is nails, followed by unidentified fragments and miscellaneous pieces as well as a number of pieces of waste. Nails are quantified by head count and fragment count to give minimum and maximum numbers. Most nails were recovered from Phase 4 and particularly Phase 5 contexts (Table 4.24). The bulk of the waste consists of lead offcuts and pieces of melted lead.

Provenance and phasing

Phase 3 was the earliest phase from which small finds were recovered. Most finds were recovered from Phase 5, including all the Roman glass. Spatially, the majority of the small finds were found in the enclosure complex adjacent to the villa

and the field system east of the spring channel (Table 4.25).

Late Iron Age/early Roman field system in Areas 1 and 5

From the eastern part of the settlement, in Area 1, came a simple bow brooch (Fig. 4.12, no. 11) from waterhole 351. The part of the complex in Area 5 produced perhaps ten poorly preserved iron fragments from ditch 5463 which might be parts of a blade. The form of the blade is far from certain. Pit 5310 contained a ceramic spindle whorl made from a piece of early Roman pottery (Fig. 4.12, no. 10).

Enclosure complex adjacent to villa

The enclosure complex yielded 50 objects, including 23 nails. The only significant find from Phase 4 (middle Roman) is potentially very interesting: from oven 620 came a socketed object which could be a somewhat eroded socketed spearhead with a small leaf-shaped head and lozenge-section stem (Fig. 4.11, no. 1). This could potentially be of Iron Age date.

The finds from Phase 5 (late Roman) include a cluster of objects from ditch 607. At the north terminus, a narrow, pierced iron strip with regularly spaced sub-square holes (Fig. 4.11, no. 8) was recovered from the upper fill, and a fragment of a possible whittle-tang knife and another possible blade fragment with a number of the unidentified iron fragments from the lower fill. Another possible knife blade fragment (Fig. 4.11, no. 7) was found in the middle part of the same ditch.

Amongst the other finds are a small fragment of a broad 1st-century armlet (Fig. 4.12, no. 12) from ditch 1464, a glass counter or gaming piece (Fig. 4.12, no. 20) from ditch 1465 and a fragment of a ribbon-twist bracelet (Fig. 4.12, no. 13) from ditch 1478, as well as a bone hairpin (Fig. 4.12, no. 18) from a Building 3 robber trench and an iron split spike loop from pit 145. The robber trench also produced a small undiagnostic sherd from a glass vessel, and a second came from ditch 401.

A plain octagonal finger ring (Fig. 4.12, no. 15) from the subsoil is of a form that is undoubtedly late Roman.

Building 1320 and spring channel

The metal objects from this area were limited to nails, two pieces of melted lead waste and a copper alloy washer. The neck of a glass bottle and a small undiagnostic vessel sherd were recovered from layer 1297 in the spring channel.

Field system and crop-processing area west of the spring channel

Phase 4 (middle Roman) contexts produced eight finds, all but two of which were nails. One of the finds was a cast copper alloy lobate handle

Table 4.23 List of coins

SF	Cxt	Est date	Reece period	Denomination	Obv
79	1001	134–138	6	denarius	HADRIANVS AVG COS III PP
29	1190	202–203?	10	denarius 16mm	?IVLI[A AVGVSTA, Julia Domna
74	3001	1–2C		sestertius	head r
119	20283	2–3C		?plated denarius 17–18mm	laureate head r IMP A[ ]C
6	1086	268–270	13	radiate 18mm	IMP C VICTORI[NVS …
32	127	268–270	13	radiate 18mm	…VICTO]RINVS PF AVG
73	3001	268–270	13	radiate 18mm	?] VICTORINVS [
194	20015	268–270?	13	radiate 20mm	]?ICT[ ]VS PF AVG ?Victorinus
17	1271	268–270	13	radiate 17–18mm	]S AVG radiate head r, ?Claudius II
30	623	268–270?	13	radiate 17mm	? IMP [ ]S AVG, ?Claudius II
57	20436	271–274	13	radiate 18–20mm	IMP C TETRICVS [
3	262	260–296?		radiate 20mm	radiate head r?
8	1236	260–296?		radiate 15–20mm	radiate head r
26	1264	260–296?		radiate 19mm	?
27	1264	260–296?		?radiate 15–16mm	?
28	1368	260–296?		radiate 15–17mm	radiate head r
2	260	260–296?		?radiate 16mm+	head r
56	4055	320–321	16	AE2? 17mm+	DN CRISPO NOB CAES[helmeted head r
15	2	333–334	17	AE3 17mm	CONSTANTINOPOLIS
4	184	330–335	17	AE3 17mm	VRBS ROMA
112	4221	330–335	17	AE3 12mm+	head r
113	4221	330–335	17	AE3 13mm	head r
40	20437	335–341	17	AE3 15mm	head r
44	20236	335–341	17	AE3 14mm	CONST[ANS PF AVG]
59	20567	341–348	17	AE3 15mm	head r
34	356	350–364?	18	AE4 11mm	head r
87	1026	350–364?	18	AE4 6–7mm	??
101	20000	350–364??	18	AE4 6–7mm	
23	127	364–375	19	AE3 17mm	DN VALENTINI] ANVS PF AVG
10	857	364–378	19	AE3 17mm	head r
14	503	364–378	19	AE3 17mm	head r
58	20015	364–378	19	AE3 16–17mm	DN VA]LEN S PF AVG
66	20436	364–378	19	AE3 15mm	head r
117	2161	364–378	19	AE3 14mm	head r
46	20049	388–402	21	AE4 12–13mm	head r
45	20471	388–402	21	AE4 12–13mm	head r
90	1090	388–402??	21	AE4? 12–13mm	
100	20000	350+	18 or 21?	AE4 11–12mm	
120	20325	4C??		AE4 12–13mm	
72	3001	3–4C		AE3 13–14mm	head r, possibly radiate?
5	1084	3–4C?		? 21mm	head r??

mounted on an iron shank from ditch 2511 (Fig. 4.12, no. 17). Similar handles have been identified on keys. The only other non-nail find was a piece of melted copper alloy from ditch 2500.

Finds from Phase 5 (late Roman) include ten nails. Other finds include unidentified fragments, but also a more recent horseshoe fragment (layer 2021 over corndryer 2323) and a cast-iron ploughshare (ditch 2493). There is also a length of slightly tapered, square-sectioned rod with barley sugar twist through much its length (Fig. 4.11, no. 9) from a ditch in the south-eastern part of Area 1, *c* 120m south of Building 1320. This may have been the handle of a spatula or spoon probe. Both sherds of window glass from the excavation came from this area. One sherd in greyish-tinged colourless glass is a piece of probable Roman cast matt/glossy glass and came from threshing floor 2146. The second sherd in very pale green glass came from ring ditch 2487.

Field system east of the channel

The earliest stratified small finds come from Phase 4 (middle Roman) contexts and comprise two nails and two pieces of lead. One lead object is a plug or rivet used as a ceramic repair; the other is a small lead block (22mm x 15mm x 10mm) with holes; both came from ditch 20127.

Finds from Phase 5 (late Roman) contexts include 18 nails. There is a curved blade fragment possibly

Rev	Ref/mint	Condition
FELICI TAS AVG	RIC II 3, 2038	SW/SW
PIE]TAS PV[BLI]CA Pietas l with altar at feet[	cf RIC IVi Severus, 643	W/W
standing figure		VW/VW
?		SW/W
?		SW/rev encrusted
Figure advancing l, r hand raised		SW/
CO [AV]G victory l		SW/SW
figure l		W/W
IOVI VI[CTORI, stg l holding thunderbolt and spear		W/W
] AD[, figure l		W/W
VIRTVS [AV] G		W/W
standing figure, eta in field		W/W, pierced
figure		W/W
figure stg l		EW/EW
figure stg l		VW/VW
		VW/VW
		EW/EW
VIRTVS [EXERCIT] standard and 2 captives, VOT XX on standard	Lyons?	SW/SW
victory on prow	RIC VII Lyons 266	W/W
wolf and twins		W/W
Gloria Exercitus 2 standards		SW/SW
Gloria Exercitus 2 standards		SW/SW
Gloria Exercitus 1 standard		VW/VW
Gloria Exercitus 1 standard		VW/W
Victoriae Dd Augg Q Nn		VW/VW
?Fel Temp Reparatio fh		VW/VW
??		EW/EW?
		EW/EW?
SECVRITAS] REIPVBLICAE		W/W
Securitas Reipublicae		VW/VW
Securitas Reipublicae		W/W
SECVRITAS REIPVBLICAE	Arles	SW/SW
Gloria Romanorum		VW/VW
GLORIA R[OMANORVM	Lyons	SW/SW
V]ICTOR [IA AVGGG		W/W
victory		VW/VW
victory?		VW/VW
		EW/EW?
		EW/EW
figure??		EW/EW
		W/W??

from a scythe (Fig. 4.11, no. 5), possibly reworked to make a short, curved knife. This was recovered from ditch 20264. Another interesting find was a tiny glass bead (Fig. 4.12, no. 19) from ditch 20399.

Other finds from this area include a fragment of late Roman strip bracelet (Fig. 4.12, no. 14) and a finger ring formed from a cut-down fragment of another strip bracelet (Fig. 4.12, no. 16). There is also a more or less complete whittle-tang knife blade (Fig. 4.11, no. 6) from robber cut 20083, and a probable medical/cosmetic instrument, with a twisted shank, a probe at one end and the opposite end missing, was recovered during the evaluation (MOLA 2015c, 54). There are just four finds from the southern part of the field system in Area 3. One is a recent horseshoe, probably 19th-century or later in date. However, the other three finds were recovered from ditch 3076 and comprise a group of agricultural tools of Roman date: a spud (Fig. 4.11, no. 3), a field or mower's anvil (Fig. 4.11, no. 2) and the head of a cross-pane hand hammer (Fig. 4.11, no. 4). The spud would have been for weeding, for breaking up clods or for cleaning mud from a plough. The field anvil and hammer would have been used for running repairs to scythes and sickles in the field.

Conclusions

The finds are of limited number and are concentrated in Areas 1 and 2, with most finds from middle

Table 4.24 Quantification of metal, glass and worked bone objects by function and phase

Function	Phase				
	3 Late Iron Age/ early Roman	4 Middle Roman	5 Late Roman	Modern	Total
Binding			2		2
Counter/gaming piece	1				1
Footwear		2	4		6
Glass, vessel		1	3	3	7
Glass, window			2		2
Hairpin			1		1
Household		2	4	2	8
Key handle		1			1
Nails		20	44		64
Personal	1		5	1	7
Structural		1	2		3
Spearhead		1			1
Tools	1		5	1	7
Transport			1	1	2
Waste		4	4	5	13
Other	1	2	23	5	31
Total	4	34	100	18	156

Table 4.25 Quantification of metal, glass and worked bone objects by location

Area	Phase				
	3	4	5	Med/modern/un-strat metal-detector finds	Total
Late Iron Age/early Roman settlement in Areas 1 and 5	4			1	5
Enclosure complex adjacent to villa		12	35	3	50
Building 1320 and spring channel		10	2		12
Field system and crop-processing area west of the spring channel		8	20	2	30
Field system east of the spring channel		4	43	8	55
Unlocated				4	4
Total	4	34	100	18	156

and especially late Roman contexts. The range of finds is much as might be expected from a rural settlement. Particularly interesting are the possible Iron Age spearhead (Fig. 4.11, no. 1) from oven 620 and the small group of agricultural tools (Fig. 4.11, nos 2–4) from late Roman ditch 3076.

Catalogue of illustrated artefacts (Figs 4.11-12)

1 **Socketed spearhead**, with incomplete possibly closed socket, lozenge sectioned stem ending in a small blade possibly leaf-shaped with central mid-rib. Fe. L: 260mm. Area 1, oven 620. Ph. 4.
Probably Iron Age. The object is poorly preserved, with both head and socket damaged. It is unclear whether the socket was closed with a welded seam or left with unwelded split seam. The head is eroded but there is clear evidence of a mid-rib. The head may have been leaf-shaped rather than triangular. Inall's study of Iron Age spearheads identified a spear form (Type 1.7) with a small head attached to a long stem and socket which is 'approximately three times the length of the blade, or longer' (Inall 2015, 79). She illustrates two examples, one from the South Cave weapon cache from East Yorkshire and the other from Hunsbury (ibid., fig. 4.18). There are examples of similar spearheads from Danebury (Cunliffe and Poole 1991, 352, fig. 7.18, no. 2.283, and microfiche 28: C12) and from South Cadbury (Macdonald 2000, 127–9). The Danebury spearhead has a circular-sectioned stem and a split socket and measures overall 258mm long, and the two examples from South Cadbury comprise one with a narrow triangular head and square

cross-sectioned stem, measuring 289mm long overall (ibid., fig. 61.35), and the second with a small triangular blade and circular-sectioned stem and split socket measuring 220mm long (ibid., fig. 62.41).

2   **Mower's or field anvil**, comprising a tapered spike with slightly domed head. A strip passes through the spike and is coiled on either side. Fe. L: 245mm; W: 93mm. Area 3, ditch 3076.

Ph. 5. SF 190.

See Manning (1985), 59, pl. 25, F62 for parallels. Found with nos 3 and 4.

3   **Spud**, socketed with worn edge. Fe. L extant: *c* 190mm; W blade: 47mm; socket D: *c* 33mm. Area 3, ditch 3076. Ph. 5. SF 189. Found with nos 2 and 4.

4   **Cross-pane (or -peen) hammer head** with circular eye in a wide expansion. Has

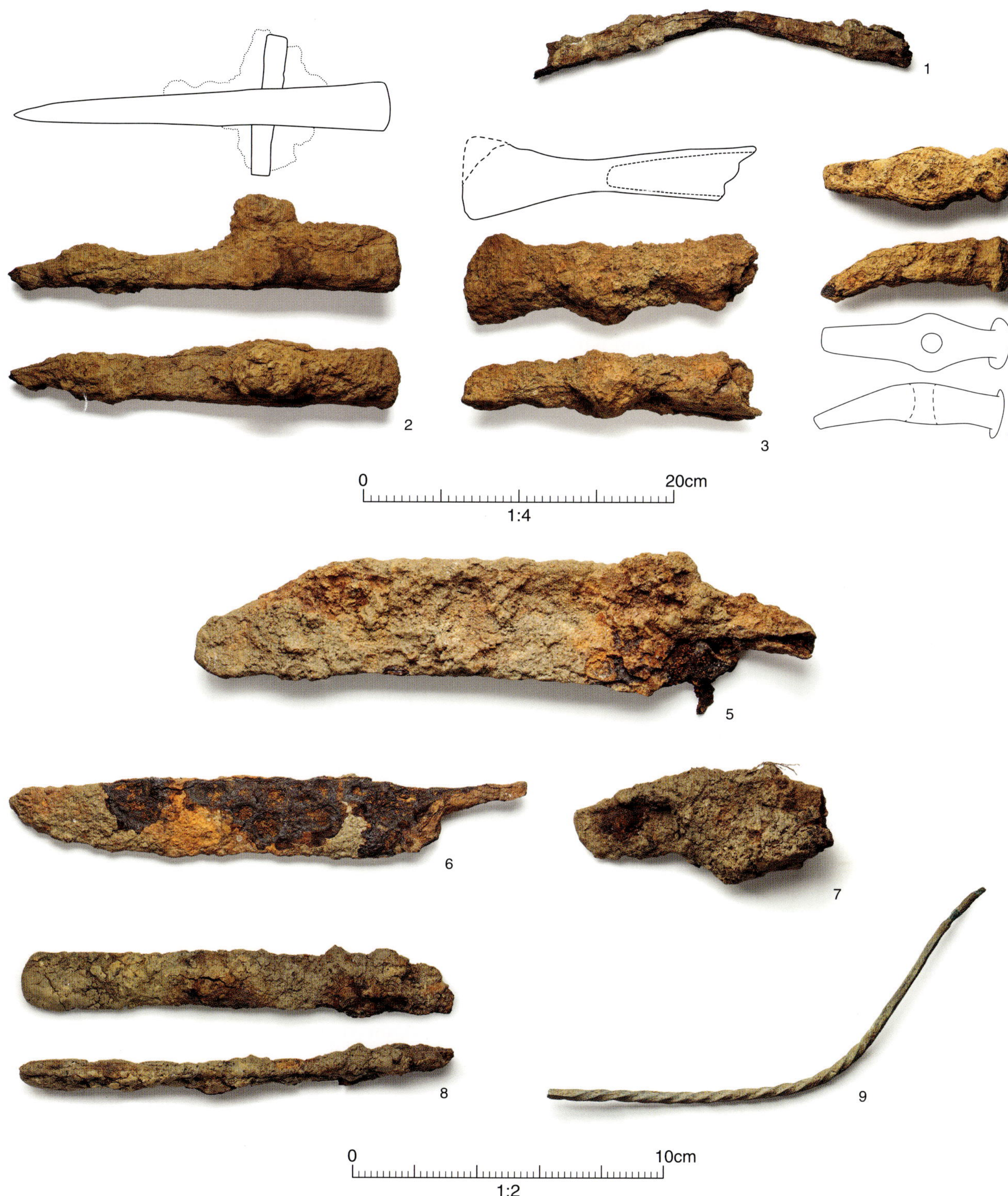

Fig. 4.11 Iron and copper alloy artefacts, nos 1–9

expanded striking face. The cross pane (or peen) is slightly curved back. Fe. L: 125mm; W: 40mm. Area 3, ditch 3076. Ph. 5. SF 191.
A smith's hand-hammer. Found with nos 2 and 3.

5   **Tanged curved blade fragment**, possibly a complete knife or more probably a sickle or scythe blade fragment. Cutting edge on the inside curve. Fe. L: 195mm; Blade W: 40mm. Area 2, ditch 20482. Ph. 5. SF 48.
The curvature of the blade and the width suggest that it could have been part of a scythe blade, which may have been cut down and reused as knife.

6   **Knife** with whittle tang on the line of the straight back of the blade. The back angles slightly down towards the tip. The dropped cutting edge is curved or bellied. Fe. L: 165mm; W: 25mm. Area 2, robber cut 20083. Ph. 5. SF 187.

7   **Possible blade fragment.** Fe. L: 80mm; W: 34mm. Area 1, ditch 607. Ph. 5.

8   **Pierced strip or binding** with four evenly spaced subsquare holes. Fe. L: 137m; W: 14mm. Area 1, ditch 607. Ph. 5.

9   **Thin bar or rod** of square cross-section with a barley sugar twist through much of its extant length. It tapers to one end and is possibly the stem of spatula probe? Cu alloy. L: 157mm. Area 1, ditch 339. Ph. 5. SF 22.
A spatula probe from Wanborough, Wilts, although shorter, has a stem with a similar barley-sugar twist tapering to a point at the outer end (Hooley, 2001, 109, fig.46, no. 220). Also from Wanborough is a long object identified as pin with a barley sugar twist stem (ibid., 102, fig. 41, no. 159).

10   **Spindle whorl** made from fragment of pottery (fabric E80). D: 42mm; Th: 9mm. Area 5, pit 5310. Ph. 3. SF 200.

11   **Bow brooch fragment** comprising narrow plain bow tapering to the catch-plate. The upper portion of the brooch is lost, but probably had a four-coil spring with internal chord. Catch-plate with single circular piercing. Cu alloy. L extant: 50mm. Area 1, waterhole 351. Ph. 3. SF 62.
A simple bow brooch, or 'Nauheim derivative', with sprung pin, dating to the first century AD but more common after the Roman conquest than before.

12   **Armlet.** Small fragment of a broad 1st-century armlet, possibly of military origin. Two parallel bands of cable pattern. L extant: 15mm; W: 15mm. Area 1, ditch 1464. Ph. 5. SF 33.
This small fragment was clearly cut from a 1st-century broad bracelet or armlet of the type that Crummy (2005) has argued may have been a military decoration or award. This idea is supported by the distribution, concentrated mainly south-east of the line of the Fosse Way, and particularly in Essex and East Anglia, and the early post-conquest dating. One aspect that Crummy did not directly address is the fact that of the 57 examples that she listed, some comprised small more-or-less square pieces similar to the current example (ibid., fig. 3, nos 6, 7, 13, 17, 22), and eleven comprised longer rectangular pieces usually including a terminal (ibid., fig. 3 nos 11, 12, 15, 16, 18, 19, 21, 24, 30).

13   **Ribbon-twist bracelet fragment**, curved. Cu alloy. L: extant: 56mm. Area 1, ditch 1478. Ph. 5. SF 77.
Like the more common cable-twist bracelets this form was probably used largely throughout the Roman period in Britain.

14   **Strip bracelet.** Fragment of a late Roman bracelet with two surviving decorative elements: a panel of ring-and-dot and a tapering section central groove and edge nicks. The bracelet would have had a hook-and-eye closure. Cu alloy. L extant: 72mm; W: 7mm. Area 2, rubble layer 20080. Ph. 5. SF 36.
A late Roman bracelet fragment of Cool Group XXXI (Cool 1983, 181, fig. 5.8: 2; Swift (2000), 145, fig. 192).

15   **Finger ring**, plain octagonal. Cu alloy. D: 18 x 19mm. subsoil. SF 11.
This form of ring is found in later 3rd- and 4th-century contexts both in Britain and on the Continent (Cool 1983, 264–6, table 6.9).

16   **Finger ring.** Finger ring fashioned from a piece of cut-down bracelet. Cu alloy. D: 29mm. Area 2, metal-detector find from surface of ditch 20356. Ph. 5. SF 143.
Finger rings formed from cut-down late Roman bracelets occur quite widely in late Roman contexts, particularly on rural sites and occasionally in Anglo-Saxon cemeteries. The phenomenon has been discussed at length by Swift (2012). Swift's conclusion was that most of the finger rings reworked from bracelets have been found on rural sites and were intended as jewellery rather than as votive objects (ibid., 186) and may reflect a breakdown in the supply of craft products.

17   **Handle for key**, cast Cu alloy, attached to iron shank, incomplete, with possible rivet hole visible on x-ray. L: 50mm; W: 30mm. Area 2, ditch 2511. Ph. 4. SF 52.
Similar items have been published as handles for keys (eg Verulamium: Goodburn 1984, 49, fig. 18, no. 166; Richborough: Henderson 1949, 125, pl. xxxiv, no. 86; Wanborough: Hooley 2001, 97, fig. 38, no. 125), Unlike the examples cited, the current object has two lobes rather than three.

18   **Hairpin** with conical head and grooves below. Incomplete stem. Bone. L:59mm. Area 1, robber trench 5, Building 3. Ph. 5. SF 18.
Crummy's Type 2 (Crummy 1979, 160–1, fig.1:2)

19   **Bead.** Tiny blue-green wound bead (wt 1g). D: 6mm Area 2, ditch 20399. Ph. 5. SF 110.
Tiny glass beads such as this are generally

Fig. 4.12 Copper alloy, ceramic, worked bone and glass artefacts, nos 10–20

found in late Roman contexts and often as grave goods in female burials.

20 **Counter or gaming piece**, dark blue (green) glass (wt 3g). D: 17mm. Area 1, ditch 1468. Ph. 5. SF 35.

CERAMIC AND STONE BUILDING MATERIALS AND FIRED CLAY
by Cynthia Poole, with a contribution by Ruth Shaffrey

Introduction

A large assemblage of ceramic building material (CBM) amounting to 2344 fragments weighing nearly 402kg was recovered (Table 4.26). The bulk of this came from Areas 1 and 2 (east and west) associated with the villa complex and no doubt originated from the villa itself immediately north of the site, whilst only a handful of fragments were found in Areas 3, 4 and 6. The tile recovered was exclusively of Roman date and included all the standard forms of tegula, imbrex, brick and flue tile. Those examples that could be more closely dated are predominantly of mid-2nd to mid-3rd century types together with a small number of 3rd/4th-century types. Much of the tile was in a good, fresh condition, with abrasion low or absent and a fairly high mean fragment weight of 162g, but few complete or near-complete tiles were recovered, and few complete dimensions, apart from thickness, survived.

Ceramic building material

Fabrics

The fabrics divide into two broad groups. One is a shelly fabric (Sh), which equates with the Harrold production site, and the second is sandy, which can be divided into several subtypes and is probably of local or regional production (Table 4.26).

Harrold shelly fabric

This is typically light brown or buff on the exterior with a grey core, or sometimes has a reddish-brown colour on the outer surfaces. It contains a high density of crushed shell fragments, mostly less than 5mm in size but usually with a scatter of larger fragments up to 8–12mm. In some fragments the shell had been heavily leached. Moulding sand was absent from the tile and it is possible that crushed shell or some organic material was used as a separator and did not adhere or leave any trace on the tile.

Sandy fabric group

This group is characterised by the presence of medium-coarse quartz sand, ironstone or weathered iron oxide/haematite grits and flint grits in a micaceous clay, and was usually fired to an orange-red colour, though a more pinkish-red colour was particularly common in type B. Moulding sand, usually medium or coarse quartz sand, was identified on a proportion of the tile, but it was also clear that a large quantity had no moulding sand adhering, and it is again possible that some form of organic material was used. The group was divided into six subtypes during recording, based on the dominant inclusions and characteristics:

Type A contained small chalk/limestone grits up to 15mm in size but usually less than 5mm and usually occurring as a sparse scatter, though some have a higher density.

Type B was dominated by red and maroon ironstone/haematite grits and was more commonly noted as micaceous.

Type C was characterised by a high density of medium-coarse quartz sand, usually well sorted and evenly distributed.

Type D was a smooth, hard, fine clay with sparse inclusions and frequently had a grey core.

Type E was characterised by cream laminations through the clay matrix and contained frequent quartz sand, ironstone grits and angular flint grits. Most grits were less than 15mm in size but ironstone and flints up to 30mm were not uncommon.

Fired clay fabric: variable mottled colouring including brown, black, reddish and pinkish brown, orange, red, pink, cerise, fine sandy micaceous clay containing in variable density, medium and coarse quartz sand and ironstone or red iron oxide grits up to 5mm.

A substantial number of pieces were recorded as a combination of subtypes, indicating that these formed a continuum, and it is questionable whether the subdivisions recorded for the sandy group have any great significance.

The site lies in an area of mixed geology with superficial Quaternary glaciofluvial deposits of clay, sand and gravel overlying the Jurassic bedrock geology of siltstones and mudstones of the Dyrham, Marlstone Rock and Whitby Mudstone Formations of the Lias Group. The Dyrham Formation on which the site lies provides the closest parallels for the sandy fabric based on the lithological description: 'pale to dark grey and greenish grey, silty and sandy mudstone, with interbeds of silt or very fine-grained sand (locally muddy or silty), weathering yellow. Variably micaceous. Impersistent beds or doggers of ferruginous limestone (some ooidal) and sandstone, which tend to occur at the top of sedimentary cycles' (BGS nd). The Northampton Sand Formation, which contains ironstone, also outcrops relatively close to the site. It is possible that the various components of these bedrock formations were combined through erosion in the Quaternary glaciofluvial deposits, which may have been easier to exploit and could account

Table 4.26 Quantification of ceramic building material by form and fabric groups

| | Sandy | | Shelly | | Total | | | |
Form	No.	Wt (g)	No.	Wt (g)	No.	% No.	Wt (g)	% Wt
Brick	234	99376	8	11801	242	10	111177	27.7
Flat	631	65024	160	11651	791	34	76675	19.1
Tegula	432	117960	127	26859	559	24	144819	36.0
Imbrex	335	31273	177	26104	512	22	57377	14.3
Flue	25	3571	59	6193	84	3.6	9764	2.4
Misc	149	1937	7	17	156	6.7	1954	0.5
Total	1806	319,141	538	82,625	2344		401,766	

for the variations observed in the sandy fabric group.

Forms

Brick

Brick accounted for 242 fragments (111.2kg), forming 10% (27.7% by weight) of the assemblage. The brick was made in both the sandy and shelly fabrics, but the latter accounts for only 10% (3% by count). A minimum of ten bricks in the sandy fabric is indicated by the number of corners (37) and one (4 corners) in the shelly fabric (though it is clear from other characteristics thar at least four or five different bricks are represented).

No complete bricks were recovered, though substantial parts of five bricks were found (Fig. 4.13, no. 1). These included two complete widths of 300mm and 315mm by 46mm and 50mm thick, and though both surviving lengths were under 300mm, it is likely that these were both *lydion* bricks (rectangular bricks measuring 1 x 1.5 Roman feet). Part of a *bessalis* brick, the smallest variety, measured 193mm wide and 36–9mm thick and when complete would have been two thirds of a Roman foot square (Fig. 4.13, no. 2). Whilst the thicker bricks may be indicative of larger types such as *sesquipedales* or *bipedales* being present in the assemblage, this need not necessarily be the case, as *bessalis* bricks used in *pilae* can also be of such thickness (Brodribb 1987, 34).

One unusual piece (ditch 2494) was a brick 42mm thick and over 120mm long/wide, made in the Harrold shelly fabric, which had four cylindrical perforations, each of 6mm diameter, stabbed into the base of the brick (Fig. 4.13, no. 3). A few examples of similar bricks were noted at Harrold, found in kiln 5 (Brown 1994, 86–7), though no reason for the holes was proffered, and similar holes, described as air holes, were noted in the bases of most of the bricks in Harrold fabric at Redlands Farm (Pringle 1997). Holes such as these are most characteristic of malting floor bricks, better known from medieval sites such as Southampton (Poole 2009a, 152) and early modern contexts (Crew 2004).

Flue tile (tubulus *and* tubulus cuneatus)

Flue tile, accounting for 84 fragments (9.8kg), formed the smallest proportion of the assemblage at 3.6% (2.4% by weight). Only one example was identified as a voussoir (*tubulus cuneatus*). Two thirds of the flue tile were made in Harrold shelly fabric and one third in sandy local fabrics. Keying was the major feature used to identify the flue tile, though corners enabled a small number of plain fragments to be identified; it is likely that most plain faces of flue tile remained unrecognised amongst the flat tile. The low numbers of flue tiles may reflect the overall quantities needed in the construction of any building, but also that it was less amenable to reuse, both in terms of the limited subsequent uses for this form and the difficulty in extracting them where they were mortared into a solid structure.

Only three fragments had evidence of rectangular vents cut into the plain face of the *tubuli*, one in the sandy fabric and two in the shelly. The vents were cut after the tile had been keyed, as in one case the tip of the narrow blade used to cut the vent had lightly slipped across the keyed face (Fig. 4.13, no. 4).

All keying was in the form of combing, and no scored or roller-stamped keying indicative of 1st- and 2nd-century production was present. A variety of keying patterns are present (Table 4.27), with the widest variety occurring in the shelly fabrics (Fig. 4.13, nos 5, 8, 10, 12–14). The more limited range of designs found in the sandy fabric are also present in the shelly examples. The keyed faces exhibited three basic combing patterns: type

Table 4.27 Flue tile combing designs

Combing type	Shelly fabric	Sandy fabric	Description
1	4	1	Straight vertical band
3	15	7	Alternating straight and wavy vertical bands
4	4	2	Two straight bands running diagonally from corners to form an X
5	1	-	Saltire: Three straight bands: two diagonal forming an X and a third either
5a	2	-	horizontal (5a) or vertical (5b) bisecting them
5b	1	-	
14/15/16	2	1	Straight bands forming a frame around the edges enclosing diagonals forming an X, or saltire, or line of Xs
16/24	6	-	Two or more Xs running vertically
20 or 21	4	-	Two intersecting curving bands forming two or more 'onion' patterns vertically
25	1	-	Straight band of combing running parallel to side turning back on itself to form a tight U
Straight	3	1	Straight band or uncertain orientation
Curved	1	1	Curved band or uncertain orientation or pattern
Diagonal	2	-	Curved or straight band diagonal

1 (Fig. 4.13, no. 5), comprising straight vertical bands, type 3, a mix of vertical and wavy vertical bands, and types 4 or 16, a cross or series of crosses. Most common is type 3 (Fig. 4.13, no. 4), which comprises a combination of vertical straight and wavy bands adjacent; the most common arrangement seems to be straight bands down either edge with one or two wavy bands in the centre, with or without gaps between the bands. Diagonal bands in a variety of patterns were also a common feature, forming an X (type 4; Fig. 4.13, no. 9), either alone or within a rectangular frame, as saltires (type 5; Fig. 4.13, nos 10 and 11) or as lines of two or more crosses vertically (type 16) or possibly cross-hatch (type 24; Fig. 4.13, no. 12). Less common and occurring only on the shelly fabric were intersecting curving bands (type 20/21) forming figures of 8 or a vertical line of 'onion' patterns (Fig. 4.13, no. 13). A similar pattern has been found at Northchurch and Boxmoor villas, Hertfordshire (Neal 1977, 26 and 86). There was also a single example where a straight vertical band turned back itself as it reached the edge to form a tight U pattern (Fig. 4.13, no. 14).

Circular discs had been deliberately chipped from three flue tiles, and it would seem that these were deliberately chosen for the decorative effect of the keying (Fig. 4.13, nos 5, 7 and 11). They measure 60mm by 72mm, 70mm diameter and 88mm by 94mm, and were 14mm, 20mm and 24mm thick respectively. One had a very neat curving edge around one half and two straight facets around the other, suggesting it may have broken during manufacture, though still possibly utilised. Discs of this size were probably used as lids for large storage jars or amphoras.

At Harrold only roller-stamped tile was associated with 2nd-century production, and combed flue tile was found only in 3rd/4th-century contexts. However, it is clear from this site that combed flue tile in the shelly fabric must have been produced earlier. Similar combed flue tile was identified in late 2nd-century features at Redlands Farm (Pringle 1997), also raising the issue that combed flue tile was being produced earlier at Harrold than has been found at the production site, perhaps in an area of the industry not yet investigated.

Tegulae

Tegulae amounted to 559 fragments (144.8kg), forming 24% (36% by weight) of the assemblage. The minimum number of tiles in the shelly fabric represented by number of corners (38) is ten, though when separated into corner position it is 18 (number of lower left-hand corners). By contrast, in terms of weight (26.9/3.5kg) the minimum number is only eight (the estimate for the weight of a complete tegula in shelly fabric is based on the example from Redlands Farm; Pringle 1997). In the sandy fabric there is a minimum number of 31 based on corners (124), or 34 taking lower right-hand corners, and 20 using weight (117.8/6kg using Brodribb's average weight for tegulae).

A fifth of the tegulae were made in the Harrold shelly fabric. Smooth surfaces in all areas are characteristic of the tegulae made in this fabric (Fig. 4.13, no. 16). They measure 15–24mm thick, with the majority concentrated at 18–21mm. One is estimated to have a width of *c* 300mm at its upper edge on the assumption that the nail hole lay equidistant from both sides; this is consistent with the sizes found at Harrold (Brown 1994, 83). No complete lengths were present, but the longest surviving piece was over 300mm. The flanges cover a range of rectangular and curved forms closely paralleled in the phase 3 tegulae at Harrold (ibid., fig. 41), but the most common is type A3, a rectangular profile with the upper surface sloping inwards (Fig. 4.13, no. 16). The upper cutaways are all rectangular recesses neatly made with a mould insert and not subsequently knife-trimmed. This suggests they were made face down in an inverted five-sided mould form equivalent to type F as described by Warry (2006, 8–9 and fig. 2.1). The lower cutaways are all of Warry's type C4, except for a single example of D16.

The tegulae in the sandy fabrics exhibited a greater range of thickness, from 15mm to 41mm but with a peak at 23–25mm. No other dimensions survive complete, though one tile had an estimated width of *c* 315mm and another *c* 300mm. The widest surviving fragment was over 270mm wide and the two longest over 290mm long. The general impression is that the tiles would tend to fall within the smaller size range of tegulae as defined by Brodribb (1987, 12). Flange profiles in the sandy fabric include the same range as the shelly, but with the inclusion of two additional types. One, classified as A3/B, is a combination of these two types, having both inclined top and inner edge. Type C has a triangular profile. These two, together with type B, dominate the sandy fabric group, accounting for nearly three quarters of the flanges in distinct contrast to the shelly fabric, where they are all but absent. Upper cutaways in sandy fabrics were all cut and were of types A2 and A2a, where the base of the rectangular cutaway was cut sloping outwards. Lower cutaways included a wider variety of types than the shelly fabric. It is probable that all are of Warry's groups C and D, but a number have been assigned to group B6 as only the lower part of the cutaway survives and insufficient evidence survives to allocate them with certainty to type C. Nail holes occurred in ten of the sandy tegulae (Fig. 4.14, no. 24), and two tiles (one with a lower cutaway of AD 240–380 date) appeared to have the remains of red paint on the upper surface (Fig. 4.14, no. 15).

Imbrex and ridge tile

Imbrex and ridge tile was represented by 512 fragments (57.3kg), forming 22% (14.3% by weight) of the assemblage. Examples made in the shelly fabric (177 fragments, 26.1kg) accounted for a third of the imbrex (nearly half by weight). The number of corners represent a minimum of 10 tiles and the weight is equivalent to about 12, based on an average weight of 2.2kg at Redlands Farm (Pringle 1997). The sandy fabric (335 fragments, 31.2kg) produced the same minimum numbers of 10 based on corners and 12 by weight (using Brodribb's average weight of 2.55kg). One near-complete imbrex survived (Fig. 4.15, no. 26), together with some complete cross-sections. In the shelly fabric the most complete tile had a length of 385mm, a breadth of 120–50mm and a height of 72–95mm, and in the sandy fabric only one complete lower half survived, which measured 140–170mm wide and 70mm high.

One very fragmentary piece of curved tile from late Roman ditch 339 appeared to have part of a flat end at right angles. This has been tentatively identified as an eaves imbrex with a closed end or a plain integral antefix. On the end is an arc of circular depressions made with the fingers, which appear to be deliberate impressions not handling marks. Examples of such tiles are few, but one was found at Higham Ferrers (Poole 2009b, 266) and another from a villa at Northchurch, Hertfordshire (Neal 1977, 27).

In addition to the standard imbrex, two curved tiles (one near-complete and one half-tile) with a semicircular profile without any taper made in the shelly fabric have been identified as ridge tiles (Fig. 4.15, no. 27). The half-tile had been split along its apex and has the unusual feature of very faint combing or rilling on the surface (Fig. 4.15, no. 28). This feature was observed on 14 fragments of imbrex. Clearer examples of fine rilling running longitudinally over the whole surface of the imbrex were best preserved on those made in the sandy fabric. This is identical to that found on the pottery from Harrold in shelly fabric. Rilling, described as 'fine combing similar to that seen on some shelly pottery', was also observed on imbrices made in both shelly and sandy fabrics at Redlands Farm (Pringle 1997).

Flat tile

Flat tile, which encompasses all plain flat fragments that cannot be assigned to a definite form, accounted for 791 fragments (76.7kg), forming 34% (19.1% by weight) of the assemblage. Harrold shelly fabric formed about a fifth of the flat tile and had a similar finish to the tegulae.

Miscellaneous

A small quantity of indeterminate tile (156 fragments, 2.0kg) represented 6.7% (0.5% by weight) of the assemblage. This was mostly broken, largely amorphous scraps with little or no surface surviving and no complete dimensions. A single tessera (29g) was recovered from the late Roman circular enclosure 20350. It is trapezoidal in shape and was made from a flat tile in red fabric E. It measures 32mm by 25–35mm and 20mm thick.

Fired clay

Fired clay from Roman deposits amounted to 434 fragments (5.2kg) of structural debris and portable furniture. Portable or integral furniture (25 fragments, 2.1kg) comprised predominantly pieces of flat plates or discs, mostly 40–42mm thick, of both circular and rectangular forms. Surface finish was variable, including smooth, finger-ridged and rough. One had a flat surface formed by tile impressions with clay squeezed between the tiles, suggesting this was an integral surface or part of the drying floor within late Roman corndrying oven 2039, in which it was found. Another piece with roughly moulded surfaces formed a perforated plate with evidence of two cylindrical holes 25 and 35mm in diameter piercing it (Fig. 4.16, no. 29). Perforated plates most commonly formed the suspended floor in pottery kilns, and this piece was found in middle Roman pit 2336. Two smaller circular discs measuring 20–23mm and 28mm thick are more certainly portable items. One measured 300mm in diameter and was well finished with smooth surfaces burnt and blackened (Fig. 4.16, no. 30). The second, thicker example had been burnt grey along its edge.

Fragments from a firebar provide further evidence for pottery kilns. This formed the end of the rectangular fire bar with straight flat side edges with even moulded surfaces and a rougher flat end (Fig. 4.16, no. 31). It measures 23–36mm thick by 93mm wide and over 90mm long; it appears to taper to the end, which is a common characteristic of firebars used to form the suspended floor of a pottery kiln.

Structural material formed the remainder of the fired clay. Most of this (362 fragments, 2.8kg) comes from ovens, hearths or corndryers, and nearly all was concentrated in the crop-processing area. Much of this consisted of fragments of wall lining and drying floor from corndrying ovens 2039, 2130 and 2050. There were also thin flat fragments with evidence of wattle, split wattle, and lath impressions on the underside. The impressions were poorly preserved, and few complete dimensions could be measured. Industrial activity was represented by two fragments (18g) of furnace lining and five fragments (67g) of a metal casting mould (Fig. 4.16, no. 32). The furnace lining is characterised by a vitrified slaggy or cindered vesicular surface. One piece came from middle Roman ditch 2490 and the second from late Roman ditch 607. The mould fragments came from the same late Roman context and formed one or more circular or possibly oval discs, which measure 7.7–16.9mm thick and 72mm in diameter.

Markings

In addition to the keying described in relation to flue tile and the rilling on imbrex, a variety of other markings were found on the tile, all occurring at the manufacturing stage, including signature marks, imprints, and a graffito.

Signatures (including tally/signature)

Signature marks were found on 93 tile fragments of tegulae, flat tile and brick (Table 4.28) and all but one occurred on tile made in the sandy fabrics. The majority occurred in late Roman contexts, with only 15 from middle Roman and two from middle/late

Roman. A total of eight different signature types were defined and there were also examples which could not be assigned with certainty to a specific design. The most common type was the standard form of a hoop, semicircle or arc made with one, two or three finger marks (types 1.1–1.3; Fig. 4.14, nos 18 and 19; Fig. 4.17, no. 33). Single examples of a very small arc (type 1.1a), a horseshoe design (type 2) and a tall U-shaped arc (type 21; Fig. 4.17,

Table 4.28 Signature types

Type	No.	Fabrics	Form	Phase	Width (mm)	Height (mm)	Description
1.1	23	B, C, D, E	Tegula (10), flat tile (7), brick (6)	4 (4); 5 (19)	55, 85, *c* 160–210, 250	55, 70, 75–100, 115	Single arc or hoop
1.1a	1	E/B	Flat	5		41	Small hoop/arc
1.2	3	C, D, E	Flat	5	*c* 200	*c* 65	Double arc/hoop
1.3	2	E	Tegula, flat tile	5	*c* 200–210	95, >120	Triple arc/hoop
2.1	1	E	Brick	4	*c* 160	70	Horseshoe
5.1	1	C/B	Flat	5	40	80	Loop
12.1, 14.1 or 5.1	2	C	Brick, flat tile	4; 5			Incomplete finger grooves forming an X, diagonal line or crossing tails of loop
12	1	B	Tegula	4	>50	>55	Straight diagonal
21	1	A	Tegula	4		>90	Tall arc/hoop
22	1	B	Brick	5	>90	>45mm	Arc with vertical finger groove within
24	22	E, B, C, D	Tegula (6), flat tile (11), brick (5)	4 (2); 5 (20)	*c* 170	75–102	Loop in form of p on right with top ending in long curving arc to left. On one example another finger groove intersecting on left – possibly a pair of loops.
24b	1	C	Flat	5	Loop 35mm wide	>50	Mirror image of 24 or a pair of loops
1 or 24	4	E, B, C	Tegula (2), flat tile, brick	4 (1); 5 (3)			Curved arc
24 or 5	4	E, B, C	Flat tile	4 (1); 5 (2); 4/5 (1)			Fragmentary marks most likely parts of tails or loops of type 5 or 24.
25	10	E, C, B	Tegula (6), flat tile (3), brick	4 (3); 5 (7)	>40, >100, >70, >80	42, 80, 90, 60	Two or three overlapping or converging arcs
X (scored)	7	E, C	Brick (4), Flat (3)	4 (2); 5 (5)	140, 40	130, 65	Large X formed by two scored lines ranging in size from 51mm long up to 175mm starting close to tile edge.
Curved	5	E, C, Sh	Tegula, flat tile (2), imbrex	4 (1); 5 (4)			Very fragmentary arcs – could be parts of a variety of types (eg 1, 5, 24, 25 etc). Uncertain that the example on the imbrex is anything but accidental
Indet.	4	E, B	Brick (3), tegula	4; 5 (3)			Very short lengths; one possibly forming a V

no. 34) represent variations on this basic form. A single example of an arc enclosing a separate vertical groove (type 22) also represents a further variant on the theme (Fig. 4.17, no. 35). A more unusual variant was a pattern of two or three overlapping arcs (type 25), often fading out towards one end without forming a complete semicircle (Fig. 4.17, nos 38-9).

The loop is another common form found on many sites, usually made with one, less often two, finger grooves in the pattern of a bow with crossing tails (type 5), which here was represented by a single certain example (Fig. 4.17, no. 41).

An unusual signature (type 24) accounted for one of the largest groups, with at least 22 examples. It took the form of a steep vertical upstroke from the tile edge usually starting at the right-hand side, with a tight loop formed at the top, which continued as a long shallow arc to the left (Fig. 4.14, no. 23; Fig. 4.17, no. 36). Two very fragmentary examples appear to have the loop on the left or may have ended in a second loop on the left (Fig. 4.17, no. 37). No parallels have been traced from other sites for this signature, suggesting it may have been unique to production for this villa.

A second unusual marking took the form of a large X scored with a stick or tool, not the fingers (Fig. 4.13, no. 1). Whilst not especially common, signatures in the form of a cross (type 14) made with the fingers are certainly known from other sites, but it is uncertain whether this scored type was in fact a signature rather than a tally mark. Scored crosses occurred on tiles at Northfleet, where they certainly formed part of a series of tally marks made on the upper surfaces rather than the edges (Poole 2011, 335). However, there are no other varieties that would point to a series of tally marks, and signatures are occasionally made with other objects, such as combed marks at Winchester (Poole and Shaffrey 2011, 291) and Silchester (Timby 2000, fig. 94).

Imprints and impressions

A variety of imprints and impressions occurred during the manufacturing process, some directly related to manufacture and others purely incidental. The most common marks related to manufacture were handling marks, noted on 47 pieces, in the form of finger depressions or grooves on surfaces and edges. The better preserved comprised an arc of all four fingertips on one side and a thumb print on the other from grasping the tile. Others had linear grooves running from a finger depression suggestive of a tile slipping from the grasp. In a couple of cases the impressions look more like the clay being deliberately smoothed with the fingers, possibly removing a blemish in the surface. Impressions on the base of one tegula look like the ends of a flat blade with a rounded end, like a palette knife, which might be the tool used to trim the tile edges and base. An indented border occurred along the edge of one brick and probably resulted from another brick being stacked on it before the clay had hardened sufficiently; this is not a common feature of Roman tile, though a sufficient number were found at Maylands, Hemel Hempstead (Poole 2020, 46) to suggest that the bricks were stacked for drying.

Very fragmentary hobnail impressions occurred on two tiles, and incidental plant impressions occurred in the form of occasional grass or straw stem and chaff impressions on both lower and upper surface. Straw is very likely to have been used to protect tiles from rain whilst drying if this took place in the open. More common than plant impressions are the imprints of animal tracks, which occurred on 35 tiles. Dog paw prints in a variety of sizes were the most frequent, on 17 tiles, in addition to claw marks on three (Fig. 4.17, no. 42). Cat paw prints (Fig. 4.17, no. 45) were found on nine tiles, whilst very partial hoof prints of ovicaprid, deer or pig occurred on three tiles. Three possible human heel prints were also observed.

Graffiti

One tegula in shelly fabric, from Building 3, produced a graffito in the form of a series of parallel scored lines in two directions forming a grid on the upper surface (Fig. 4.17, no. 43). Four lines have been scored lengthways, with a further four at right angles. The lines appear to have been scored pre-firing and may represent a short-lived gaming board used by the tile-makers. An imbrex tile also had some lines scratched on it, but they formed no discernible pattern (Fig. 4.17, no. 44).

Miscellaneous marks

Other marks included scratches or score lines post-firing which may be crude keying of the surface prior to reuse, some sort of graffiti or purely accidental damage (Fig. 4.14, no. 25). On a tegula fragment, a short length of pecked groove may have been initial marking out prior to chipping into a disc that was not completed.

Stone roofing *by Ruth Shaffrey*

A total of 76 fragments (27kg) are likely to have been used as stone roofing. Most of this material was recovered from the complex of enclosures directly associated with the villa and may derive from the villa buildings, but 14 fragments came from the area around Building 1320. All but one are probably from flat roofing slabs; the exception was a tufa block. Many of the fragments are too small to be identified with certainty and have been identified only as possible roofing, but four fragments from the area around Building 1320, two from pit 2029 in the crop-processing area and one from ditch 20594 are large enough for identification as roofing or retain the diagnostic perforations associated with stone roofing. The most complete example, roughly oval in shape, measures >230mm long by >190mm

Table 4.29 Quantification of stone roofing material

Location	Lithology	Phase 3	4	5	Total
Area 1	Sandstone	2	26	23	51
	Limestone		4	6	10
	Tufa			1	1
Area 2 east	Sandstone			10	10
	Limestone		2	0	2
Area 2 west	Limestone			2	2
Total			34	42	76

wide and 21mm thick. Another had a length of over 270mm. Nine pieces had been burnt and blackened, suggesting reuse in hearths or ovens.

Most of the stone roofing by count (61 fragments) was found in Area 1, and of these, about half (30) are from Phase 4 features (Table 4.29). Two fragments from Phase 3 ditch 37 are not diagnostic and may not be roofing. All 16 fragments from Area 2 east and west were recovered from Phase 4 or 5 contexts.

The complete tufa block was roughly rectangular, measuring 290 x 149 x 79mm and weighed 3.5kg. Such blocks were commonly used as roof vaulting in bathhouses because of their light weight compared to other materials, but have also been observed built into walls, possibly providing evidence of reuse or use of surplus material.

The stone roofing is made from a pale yellow or pale brown, non-shelly limestone or a fine-grained pale brown sandstone, neither of which are particularly distinctive, but which are comparable in appearance to Collyweston slate. Collyweston slate is one of the more common stone roofing materials in the wider region, as seen at Godmanchester (Clifton-Taylor 1987). No Roman quarries for this stone have been identified, but during more recent times Collyweston stone for roofing was quarried near Stamford to the west of Collyweston and some 50km north-east of the site. Historic records also note workings slightly closer, around Corby (Stone Roofing Association 2014), *c* 30–35km from the site. Stone roofing is occasionally recovered from 2nd-century contexts, as at Higham Ferrers (Shaffrey 2009), but it is mainly recovered from features of 3rd-century or later date.

Discussion

Production and sources

The tile is very consistent in character, comprising two groups in sandy and shelly fabrics, which have a variety of features in common resulting from the production process. The shelly fabric has sufficient features typical of tile from the kilns at Harrold, Bedfordshire, to suggest it was produced there and

transported some 26km to the site. In contrast to the CBM, the stone roofing may have been transported a significantly greater distance if it was quarried in the area of Collyweston.

The sandy fabrics are a local or regional product, on the evidence of the inclusions in the clay, which closely reflect the constituents of the geological deposits of the area. A significant number of pieces (61 fragments, 17.2kg) were overfired, as is evidenced by distortion, vitrification, cindering and the blown character of the fabric and the purple, maroon, and blue-grey colouring of the pieces. This suggests the tile was produced close to the site, possibly specifically for the villa. No potential site of a tile kiln was located by the geophysics survey within the development area (MOLA 2015b), and no evidence of quarry pits for clay extraction has been identified. A location to the north of the villa may be deduced if production took place specifically for the villa. Examples of tile kilns set up close to construction sites to produce tile for villa buildings are known from Itter Crescent, Peterborough (OA 2012), East Corby, Northamptonshire (Lambert 2021), and Eccles, Kent (Detsicas 1967). At Eccles, the kilns also supplied tile to the wider region. Whilst it is possible to argue that local production was not necessarily attached to this villa rather than one of the others in the area, or was set up as an independent industry, the quantity of wasters present in the assemblage supports on-site production. The sandy fabrics are very similar to those identified at Redlands Farm (Pringle 1997) and Stanwick villa (Pringle 2000) and it is possible production in the locality was supplying the wider region.

Similarity in certain characteristics such as the rilling on imbrex, similar patterns of combing on flue tiles, some flange profiles in common, and the distinctive base surface finish on many tiles, suggests some influence or a connection between the Harrold tilery and the more local products. Whether this represents individual tilers moving between production areas, tilers from Harrold setting up a temporary satellite production area for the villa building works, or a general diffusion of ideas of standard practice within the region remains uncertain. The linked characteristics seen in the tile may be a feature of the Nene Valley tile industry, contrasting with other regional styles.

Provenance and use

The building material as a whole is typical of a villa assemblage, comprising all the elements that would be required for a masonry building with a tiled roof and which included heated rooms and a bath suite. It is very much concentrated within the enclosures opposite the villa with smaller groups associated with the temple/mausoleum, Building 1320, and the crop processing area to the south (Table 4.30).

Table 4.30 Distribution of the ceramic building material

| | Phase | | | | | | | | | | | | |
| Phase | 3 ER | | 4 MR | | 5 LR | | 4/5 M/LR | | Med–mod | | Total | |
Landscape areas	No.	Wt (g)	No.	Wt (g)	No.	Wt (g)	No.	Wt (g)	No.	Wt (g)	No.	Wt (g)
Building 1320 and spring channel			335	39189	22	6631	6	588			363	46408
Enclosure complex opposite villa			379	64832	1046	182329	30	3363	14	440	1469	250964
Field system and crop processing area west of the spring channel			49	10839	103	31188	3	779			155	42806
Field system east of the spring channel			37	5505	300	54098	9	1096	2	29	348	60728
Late Iron Age/early Roman settlement in Areas 1 and 5	9	860									9	860
Total	9	860	800	120365	1471	274246	48	5826	16	469	2344	401766

The two types of ceramic tile and the stone roofing tile could represent three different phases of construction within the villa or different buildings in the complex or a combination of the two. Without evidence directly related to the villa buildings themselves, any conclusions must be speculative. All groups are present in both middle and late Roman contexts in roughly the same proportions. The bulk of the assemblage concentrated in the enclosure complex opposite the villa is probably a fair representation of the variety of material used in the construction of the villa buildings. There appear to be no significant differences between the material found in Phases 4 and 5, with proportions remaining similar in terms of fabric and form, though roughly three quarters occurred in Phase 5, which no doubt reflects changes occurring in the use of the villa buildings, which are likely to have fallen into disuse during this period. Only a small proportion of the tile can be dated more closely than Roman and most of this was produced during the mid-2nd to mid-3rd century, representing the main period of construction for the villa.

The disposal of tile within this area of enclosures must reflect changes taking place to the villa buildings relating to repairs, refurbishment, demolition or additional building. In both Phases 4 and 5 about a third of the tile has some evidence of burning or heat-discolouration, indicating that surplus tile was being reused in ovens or hearths. The patterns of burning suggest that the main use was as hearth or oven floor surfaces or as furniture within ovens, either as suspended floors, supports, cheek pieces or flue covers. There is little evidence to indicate that the reused tile was built into structures as walling, which usually results in burning only on the exposed edge of the tile. The pattern is similar in relation to the tile deposited in the field system east of the spring channel, where the range of forms follows that in the enclosure complex and a high proportion exhibits evidence of burning and reuse.

The majority of the tile recovered from features associated with late Roman aisled Building 3 comprised well-preserved fragments of tegula and imbrex, together with two pieces of brick and a single flue tile. It is tempting to suggest that the building had a ceramic tile roof, but much of the tile exhibited evidence of burning and it seems more likely that it represents reuse of tile in ovens or hearths. It is possible, therefore, that the tile reflects activity within the building, or that the tile was recycled for a second time for use in the walls or foundations of the building. The few pieces of tile that can be dated are of mid-2nd to mid-3rd century manufacture.

Building 1320 produced a range of CBM with a much higher proportion made in the Harrold shelly fabric, amounting to over three quarters of the fragments (83% by weight), compared with the whole assemblage. This group was dominated by roof tile, including not only standard tegulae and imbrices but also the unusual short imbrices, identified as purpose-made ridge tile, and the imbrex with closed end, or plain antefix. The tegulae included nearly all examples on the site of the late group D form of lower cutaway, though they were considerably outnumbered by the earlier group C cutaways. The tile evidence indicates the building was roofed with ceramic tile, including special ridge tile and imbrex possibly purpose-made for the building. Dating evidence for the building is slight, and although the tile evidence is ambiguous and cannot confirm its construction date with certainty, the dominance of the Harrold fabric suggests that it was constructed at a different date to the main villa buildings, possibly coinciding with the main period of tile production at Harrold during the late-3rd to mid-4th centuries. Certainly, some of the tegulae are of middle Roman type based on the cutaway, but these are dated as late Roman at Harrold (Brown 1994, 79–83, fig. 41.9 and fig. 42.12 and 14). The problem here is that the tile found at Harrold in the late phase kilns could be tile from earlier production reused in the construction of the kilns. No definite tile kilns were found. One possible example, kiln 7, was postulated, but the tile fragments from it cannot be interpreted as products of the kiln as opposed to debris from the kiln structure. Discrepancies between dates for Harrold tile found at Redlands Farm compared to that at the production site have been noted (Pringle 1997), as have differences in size between the tile at Harrold and that found at Milton Keynes (Brown 1994, 83). Too much reliance should not be placed on the dating of tile at Harrold, as the full sequence of production of tile may be under-represented in the excavations. Based on the tile associated with Building 1320, the evidence indicates both middle and late Roman products were used. This could be interpreted in two ways: either as construction in the middle Roman period with repairs taking place in the late Roman period or as construction in the late Roman period partly reusing roofing materials from another building supplemented by some new products as required. Of the stone roofing slabs associated with the building, the two best-preserved examples had been reused as paving in surface 1165, which may support a late reuse of earlier materials.

The crop-processing area in Area 2 produced the smallest group of material, but included the best-preserved examples of brick, though none were complete. These included three lydion bricks from corndrying oven 2039 and two others dumped in ditch 2494. Brick, tegula and flat tile were the most common forms selected for use in the structure of the oven, though only a proportion was directly associated with the structure and about a quarter of the fragments had been burnt. Not all tile reused in the oven would exhibit direct burning if built into the core of the structure and rendered with a clay lining. Much of the fired clay recovered from the oven represents scraps of lining and floor, but also included pieces of flat slab with a variety of impressions on one side including wattles, laths and tiles. This suggest the drying floor was constructed of a mix of these materials: tiles may have been built into the walls projecting over the flue to support a framework of wattles and laths coated with clay to form the surface of the drying floor.

Reused building materials were found in other structures in this area. A few pieces of tile had been used in the threshing floor and the only stone roofing slabs found in this area had been reused in the lining of the stone-lined pit 2129.

Pit 2236 contained a fired clay fragment of perforated oven plate, a form normally associated with pottery production, though it is possible this feature was a more general-purpose oven or was associated in some way with crop processing. The perforated plate may have served as a grate, as is the case in a variety of ethnographic cooking ovens from around the world.

The building material provides evidence of the range of elements used in the main villa buildings, of which the most visible would have been the ceramic and stone roof tile. The dating evidence suggests these were in use at the same time, perhaps on different parts of the villa complex, though it is possible that ceramic and stone roofing were used together to decorative effect. In post-medieval buildings stone roofing slabs are sometimes found used in a few courses over the eaves with ceramic peg tile continuing to the ridge. The evidence from a few red painted or slipped tegulae indicates different coloured tiles were selected to produce further variation in colour in addition to the contrast in colour between the light brown shelly fabric and the red of the sandy fabric. Other varieties of CBM would not have had the visibility of the roofing, but none the less were important elements in the construction of a bath complex and other heated rooms. Ceramic building material was an expensive commodity and when alterations were made to the villa buildings, there is clear evidence of its reuse either in later buildings such as the aisled building or in minor structures such as corndryers or ovens.

Catalogue of illustrated building material and fired clay (Figs 4.13–4.17)

1. **Lydion brick**. Scored signature / tally mark in form of X measuring 130mm high and 140mm wide on upper surface. Linear imprints on base possibly from stacking bricks. Fabric E. L: >260mm; B: 315mm; Th: 50mm. Wt: >5500g. Corndrying oven 2039. Ph. 5.

2. **Bessalis brick**. Fabric E. L: 193mm; B: >120mm; Th: 36–9mm. Wt: 934g. Pit 1409. Ph. 5.

3. **Brick with stab marks**. Possible malting kiln floor brick with four cylindrical perforations through brick 6mm dia set 26–50mm apart and stopping *c* 6mm short of the upper surface. Fabric Sh. L: >120mm; B: >115mm; Th: 42mm. Wt: 519g. Ditch 2495. Ph. 5

4. **Flue tile (*tubulus*)**. Rectangular vent and knife mark and type 3 keying of straight and wavy vertical bands of combing on two adjacent faces. Fabric C. Ht: >120mm; B: >105mm; Th: 17&20mm. Wt: 327g. Ditch 20498. Ph. 5.

5. **Flue tile (*tubulus*)**. Combed keying pattern type 1: straight band of combing. Tile has been chipped roughly to a sub-circular disc. Fabric Sh. L: 72mm; B: 60mm; Th: 14mm. Wt: 68g. Ditch 20604. Ph. 5.

6. **Voussoir tile (*tubulus cuneatus*)**. Combed keying pattern type 3: one straight vertical band of combing with a tight wavy band adjacent and second wavy band after a gap of *c* 30mm. Fabric C/B. L: >120mm; B: >120mm; Th: 20mm. Wt: 275g. Ditch 822. Ph. 5.

7. **Voussoir tile (*tubulus cuneatus*)**. Chipped to circular disc; combed keying pattern type 3 with one straight and one zigzag band. Fabric

Fig. 4.13 Ceramic building material, nos 1–16 (bricks, flue tiles and tegulae)

E/C. Dia: 70mm; Th: 20mm. Wt: 126g. Ditch 20482. Ph. 5.

8. **Flue tile (*tubulus*)**. combed keying pattern type 3: one vertical band of very tight wavy combing and one straight steeply sloping or slightly diagonal band diverging from it. Fabric Sh. Ht: >95mm; B: 135mm; Th: 17mm. Wt: 222g. Ditch 20482. Ph. 5.

9. **Flue tile (*tubulus*)**. Two fragments from one plain face and one with combed keying pattern type 4: two diagonal bands forming an X. Fabric E. L: >132mm (estimated *c* 150mm); Ht: >175mm (estimated *c* 250mm); B: >132mm (estimated *c* 140mm); Th: 19/21mm. Wt: 877g. Layer 1001, south of temple/mausoleum 1320. Ph 4.

10. **Flue tile (*tubulus cuneatus*)**. Combed keying pattern type 5b: three straight bands crossing forming a saltire. Fabric Sh. L: >90mm; B: 167–70mm; Th:17 mm. Wt: 363g. Ditch 20603. Ph. 5.

11. **Flue tile (*tubulus*)**. Combed keying pattern type 14/15/17: three bands of combing running horizontally, vertically and diagonally from the corner: this indicates a rectangular frame around the outside of the tile enclosed a cross or saltire or a series of crosses within. Tile roughly chipped to circular disc from corner of tile. Fabric C/D. Dia: 88 x 94mm; Th: 24mm. Wt: 245g. Enclosure ditch 1007. Ph. 5.

12. **Flue tile (*tubulus*)**. Combed keying pattern type 16/24: Single band of straight combing, running from corner at a shallow diagonal to edge, possibly series of multiple crosses or cross-hatch pattern. Fabric Sh. Ht: >120mm; B: >90mm; Th: 17mm. Wt: 189g. Pit 1045. Ph. 4.

13. **Flue tile (*tubulus*)**. Three joining fragments combed with keying pattern type 20/21 comprised opposed curving bands forming 'onion' pattern enclosed within a square frame of straight bands. Fabric Sh. Ht: >175mm; B: >155mm; Th: 18mm. Wt: 430g. Ditch 20355. Ph. 4.

14. **Voussoir tile (*tubulus cuneatus*)**. Combed keying pattern type 25 combed in U shape. Fabric Sh. Ht: >150mm; B:>70 mm; Th: 20mm. Wt: 194g. Ditch 20590. Ph. 5.

15. **Tegula.** Lower left-hand corner with remains of red painted or slipped surface with part of signature mark possibly end of type 24. Flange type A, lower cutaway type D15 with the end of the flange cut to a bevel. Fabric D. L: >90mm; B: >130mm; Th: 19mm. Wt: 306g. Enclosure ditch 1007. Ph. 5.

16. **Tegula.** Lower right hand corner fragment. Flange A3 and cutaway D16. Fabric Sh. L: >300mm; B: >180mm; Th: 17–19mm. Wt: 1390g. Layer 1001, south of temple/mausoleum 1320. Ph. 4.

17. **Tegula.** Flange profile type A3/B. Fabric E. L: >205mm; B: >155mm. Th: 22mm. Wt: 1084g. Oven 620. Ph. 4.

18. **Tegula.** Lower left-hand corner fragment. Flange profile type B, cutaway C56. Signature mark type 1.3: starting from LH flange, measuring >118mm high, >70mm wide. Handling marks on base of three fingertips dimples. Fabric E. L: >135mm; B: >115mm; Th: 22–7mm. Wt: 678g. Pit 20206. Ph. 5.

19. **Tegula.** Lower right-hand corner. Flange profile type C, lower cutaway D16. Signature mark type 1.2 measuring 70mm high, over 130mm wide (estimated *c* 160mm), starting 40mm from right-hand flange. Fabric C. L: >275mm; B: >255mm; Th: 22mm. Wt: 1375g. Ditch 607. Ph. 4.

20. **Tegula.** Flange profile type D and cutaway C4 with bevelled end. Fabric Sh. L: >225mm; B: >180mm; Th: 18–21mm. Wt: 984g. Enclosure ditch 20348. Ph. 5.

21. **Tegula.** Flange profile type B and cutaway C56. Fabric E. L: >275mm; B: >200mm; Th: 27mm. Wt: 1577g. Oven 620. Ph. 4.

22. **Tegula.** Flange profile type E. Fabric Sh. Th: 16–17 mm. Wt: 224g. Ditch 1095. Ph. 5.

23. **Tegula.** Lower right-hand corner. Flange profile type F and cutaway type C56, signature mark type 24, P-shaped with slightly angled upstroke, narrow loop with tail curving to left in a long arc, 105mm high, >95mm wide, loop 40 x 25mm. Partly made with fingernail scoring base of groove. Wide cut bevel along upper arris of edge. Fabric E. L: >140mm; B: >200mm; Th: 30–8mm. Wt: 1521g. Building 3, cleaning layer 8. Ph. 5.

24. **Tegula.** Fragment from upper edge with punched nail hole. Nail hole 10mm dia centred 25mm from edge. Base of tile damaged by nail. The nail hole has been punched through the arc of a finger groove. Assuming this is the top edge of the tile, it would be an unusual location for a signature mark so may be an accidental mark from handling. Fabric B. L: >65mm; B: >105mm; Th: 22–6mm. Wt: 213g. Ditch 20581. Ph. 5.

25. **Tegula.** Upper left-hand corner with central circular nail hole chipped post-firing, 7mm dia centred 38mm from top edge and 145mm from left-hand edge. Flange profile type D and upper cutaway type A2 made by mould and untrimmed. Also lightly scratched lines on the upper surface forming a cross-hatch – possibly keying for reuse. Fabric Sh. L: >180mm; B: >160 (est. *c* 300mm)' Th: 17–19mm. Wt: 915g. Ditch 1417. Ph. 4.

26. **Imbrex.** Near-complete, six joining fragments. Fabric Sh. L: 385mm; B: 120–50mm; Ht: 72–95mm. Th: 17–21mm. Wt: 1990g. Pit 145. Ph. 5.

27. **Ridge tile.** Complete short length, but one side edge has been deliberately chipped off, possibly for reuse. Fabric Sh. L: 225mm; B: *c* 180mm; Ht: *c* 90–110mm; Th: 20mm. Wt: 1466g. Layer 1001, south of temple/mausoleum 1320. Ph. 4.

Fig. 4.14 *Ceramic building material, nos 17–25 (tegulae)*

28. **Imbrex**. Complete lower end with rilled surface. Fabric C. L: >135mm; B: <140–70mm; Th: 16mm. Wt: 920g Layer 1001, south of temple/mausoleum 1320. Ph. 4.

29. **Fired clay**. Perforated oven/kiln plate. Roughly moulded flat surface, smooth and undulating but with cracks and folds. Underside rough pitted as far as it survives, partly sheared off. Pierced by at least one, possibly two perforations, *c* 35 and 25mm dia. There appears to be a rough straight edge – with small pitting – apparently bonding surface where clay has been pressed up against a gritty surface. Fabric M Fe. L: >75mm; B: >62mm. Th:44mm. Wt: 146g. Pit 2336. Phase 4.

30. **Fired clay**. Circular disc with well finished surfaces, flat slightly concave base, smooth curving vertical edge with angular base and rounded at top joining to upper surface. Base and edge burnt/blackened. Fabric Qf. Dia: 300mm; Th: 20–3mm. Wt: 146g. Enclosure ditch 401. Ph. 5.

31. **Fire bar**. End of rectangular plate or fire bar with flat even moulded surfaces, straight flat side edges and rougher flat end. This is a flat rectangular object which appears to taper to the end. This is too thin to be a pedestal and it is more likely to be the end of a firebar to form the suspended floor of a pottery kiln. Fabric V. L: >90mm; B: 93mm. Th: 23–36mm. Wt: 212g. Ditch 43 (123). Ph. 3.

32. **Metal-casting mould** of circular or possibly oval disc, convex on one side, fired pale buff-grey and black on the inner half. The other side is very smooth and flat with a slightly

Fig. 4.15 Ceramic building material, nos 26–8 (imbrices and ridge tile)

raised circle with dished centre in the middle: the outer margin is 21mm wide and the central circle 28mm dia. Edge narrow and vertical. Fabric QfV. B: 72mm; Th: 8–17mm. Wt: 67g. Ditch 607. Ph. 5.

33. **Signature mark: Type 1.1**. Single hoop starting 25mm from the left-hand flange forming a tall arc 115mm high by >125mm wide (estimated total width *c* 250mm). Overlying the signature mark are two (or possibly three) small shallow dimples taken to be fingertip marks but could be a cat paw print, 32mm wide. Fabric E. L: >155mm; B: >160mm; Th: 14–23mm. Wt: 750g. Ditch 20396. Ph. 5.

34. **Signature mark: Type 21**. Large curving arc starting beside the flange and rising over 90mm high from edge. Tegula lower left-hand

corner fragment with flange type B and lower cutaway C4. Handling: three flattened marks from fingers over the top of the flange. Fabric Sh. L: >150mm; B: >75mm; Th: 21mm. Wt: 407g. Ditch 398. Ph. 5.

35. **Signature mark: type 22**. Partial single finger groove forming an arc with a separate straight vertical finger groove within; >90mm wide, >45mm high, on flat tile, probably tegula. Fabric B/E. Th: 28mm. Wt: 406g. Pit 582. Ph. 5.

36. **Signature mark: type 24**. Single finger groove forming an angled upstroke with tight loop at the top that then continues as a shallow arc to the left 75mm high by >105mm wide (est. *c* 170mm wide). Fabric E. L: >140mm; B: >130mm. Th: 23mm. Wt: 474g. Enclosure ditch 1208. Ph. 5.

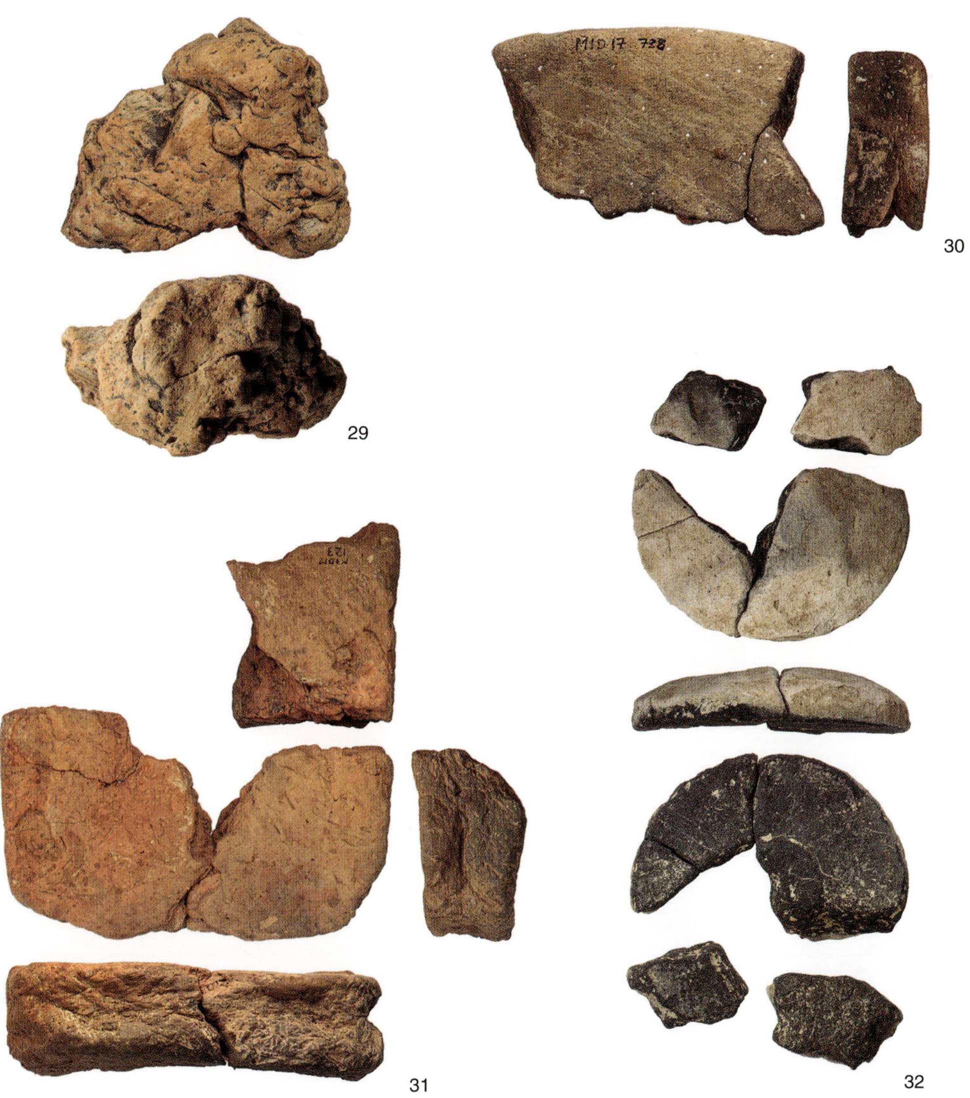

Fig. 4.16 Fired clay, nos 29–32

37. **Signature mark: type 24 variant?** Incomplete, part of a loop above the tile edge facing left rather than right suggests this may be a mirror image of type 24. Fabric C. L: >72mm; B: >87mm; Th: 25mm. Wt: 175g. Ditch 20396. Ph. 5.

38. **Signature mark: type 25**. Three curving finger grooves converging on flat tile/brick. Fabric C/E. Th: 39mm. Wt: 116g. Pit 582. Phase 5.

39. **Signature mark: type 25**. Three curving finger grooves converging very faintly inscribed forming partial arcs probably starting on right-hand side at the tile edge, converging to the left as the fingers curved round the arc. Flat tile/tegula, height of signature: 60mm, width of signature: >80mm. Fabric E. L: :>60mm; B: >80mm; Th: 23mm. Wt: 617g. Circular enclosure ditch 20351. Ph. 5.

40. **Signature marks: type X**. Large scored X, the line running from bottom left to top right looks more like a finger groove (>175mm long), but that from the right-hand side has been scored with a V-shaped stick or tool (>100mm long), Ht: >125mm; intersection at 62mm. Fabric E. L >140mm; B: >140mm; Th: 48mm. Wt: 1120g. Ditch 1385. Ph. 4.

41. **Signature mark: Type 5.1**. Single loop, starting vertically from edge sweeping round to left and crossing over to right, the tail not reaching edge. It appears to be made with stick or tool leaving a V-groove, not a finger mark. Flat tile, probably tegula, with burnt grey upper surface. Fabric C/B. L: >110mm; B: >130mm; Th: 28mm. Wt: 465g. Enclosure ditch 241. Ph. 5.

42. **Paw prints of dog** on tegula. Two prints and part of a third, probably from different feet of

Fig. 4.17 Ceramic building material, nos 33–45 (signature marks)

the same animal. Left hand: >58mm long (including claw) x 46mm wide. Right hand (fore): 36mm wide x 22mm long – 4 pads only smaller than left-hand, which is 45mm wide x 26mm long for same section of foot. Third foot – rear right hand has parts of two pads and claws impacted on top of the tegula flange. Fabric E. Th: 28mm. Wt: 529g. Ditch 960. Ph. 5.

43. **Graffiti on upper surface of tegula**. A series of lines have been scored lengthways, one alongside the flange and three parallel 11 and 13mm apart crossed by four at right angles widthways 17, 33 and 19mm apart. The tile has been scored out pre-firing, presumably by the tilers, possibly as a gaming board. Fabric Sh. L: >145mm; B: >115mm; Th: 22mm. Wt: 504g. Ditch 300. Ph. 4.

44. **Graffiti**. Scratched lines on upper surface of imbrex close to side edge. Fabric B. L: >170mm; B: 85–90mm. Wt: 474g. Corndrying oven 2039. Ph. 5.

45. **Paw print of cat**. Three or four partial cat paw prints. Most complete consists of three toe pads and faint heel pad *c* 34mm long x 24mm wide. Fabric B/C. L: >250mm; B: >135mm; Th: 28mm. Wt: 1365g. Enclosure ditch 20597. Ph. 5.

QUERNS, MILLSTONES AND OTHER STONE OBJECTS *by Ruth Shaffrey*

A total of eleven fragments from a probable six rotary querns and millstones were recovered. Two of these are millstones. A single fragment of lower stone from late Roman pit (SF 88; Fig. 4.18, no. 1) measures 54cm in diameter. Stones with diameters in the range of 50–56cm are likely to have been mechanically powered but retain the potential to have been hand powered (Shaffrey 2015). In this case, the large spindle hole suggests that substantial fittings were used and therefore that it is more likely to have been a millstone. The second millstone comprises four adjoining fragments of a large upper stone of 83cm diameter retrieved from late Roman corndryer 2039 in Area 2 (SF 118; Fig. 4.18, no. 2). Both millstones are made of a coarse feldspathic sandstone from the Millstone Grit.

A further three rotary querns were all found in late Roman contexts. One of these is also made of Millstone Grit and comprises two adjoining fragments found in ditch 1481 (SF 83). A complete lower rotary quern was found in wall 464 (SF 64; Fig. 4.18, no. 3). This is made of Old Red Sandstone and is of a typical Roman form for the region, tapered to the edges and fully perforated. A second fragment of Old Red Sandstone is from an upper rotary quern and was found in pit 957 (SF 86).

Two rounded non-diagnostic fragments of lava, weighing 108g, were found in Phase 4 ditch 20593. These are probably from a rotary quern rather than a millstone.

The three stone types used for querns here, Millstone Grit, Old Red Sandstone and lava, are all typical of the region during the Roman period, and a Millstone Grit quern was also found during the evaluation (MOLA 2015c, 53).

One object is a sandstone whetstone or saddle quern, probably used as a multi-functional tool, bearing smoothed areas and numerous sharpening grooves (SF53; Fig. 4.18, no. 4). It was found in late Roman pit 151.

Discussion

It is clear from the archaeobotanical and structural evidence that crop processing was an important activity at this site, which had corndryers of both middle and late Roman date. Corndryer 2039 contained adjoining fragments from one substantial millstone, and late Roman pit 1224 contained a fragment from another, smaller millstone. These and the fragments from probably four rotary querns suggest a combination of small-scale grinding and centralised processing. Rotary querns have been found at excavated watermills, suggesting they remained useful at centralised locations even when substantial mills were in use (Spain and Riddler 2010).

The millstones were probably employed in a watermill given that the post-medieval Harpole Mill was located in the south-eastern corner of the development area and the river there could clearly power a mill. Structural remains of Roman water-mills are rarely identified in Britain, leaving millstones as the primary form of evidence for them. A watermill at this site could have produced flour for the nearby villa and/or have been part of a wider landscape of organised and centralised grain processing, feeding into a supply network. Locally there are millstones from sites at Wootton Fields (Chapman 2005), Daventry (Northampton-shire Archaeology 2003), Brixworth (Cotswold Archaeology 2018), Boughton (OA 2020), North-ampton (Northamptonshire Archaeology 2008a), Nether Heyford (Steve Young pers. comm.) and Towcester (Brown and Woodfield 1983), which testify to widespread cereal processing at centralised locations. This is most clearly exempli-fied by Burcote Wood, Towcester, where 16 frag-ments of millstones were recovered along with structural remains interpreted as a possible water-mill (Turland 1977; Rod Conlon pers. comm.).

Complete lower rotary quern SF 64 had been placed grinding-side up at the end of a wall or boundary and adjacent to a cobbled surface. These features are difficult to interpret, but the quern had possibly been positioned at a threshold and, if so, the wear to the upper surface could have resulted from it having been walked on. It is clear that the quern had been intentionally placed and it seems likely, given its position in relation to the cobbled surface, that it was intended to be seen. That intention should be seen in the light of the

Fig. 4.18 Querns and millstones

obvious crop-processing emphasis at the site, since the decision to decommission a fully functioning quernstone is not likely to have been one that was taken lightly. Possibly the symbolic attributes of the quern were significant. Various meanings have been attached to querns, from fertility to life and death, and we can only hypothesise about the relevant symbolism, but perhaps their associations with grain and the harvest were key (Watts 2014, 53).

Catalogue of stone objects (Fig. 4.18)

1. **Lower millstone**. Millstone Grit. Large, slightly tapered fragment with spindle hole of 57mm diameter. Pecked all over but very roughly so on the base. The edges are straight and vertical. Dia: 540mm; Th: 25–72mm at the centre. Wt: 6kg. Pit 1224. Ph. 5. SF 88.

2. **Upper millstone**. Millstone Grit. Four adjoining fragments of slightly tapered disc type with large central hole of 130mm diameter. Two smaller holes through the stone are fittings; these are subsquare and *c* 45mm across. Pecked and tooled all over with deep rotational wear on the grinding surface and one long U-shaped smooth groove from sharpening or smoothing a round-sectioned object. This straddles two fragments so the millstone was reused prior to breakage. Dia: 830mm; Th: 47mm. Wt: 9kg. Corndrying oven 2039. Ph. 5. SF 118.

3. **Lower rotary quern**. Old Red Sandstone, pebbly sandstone. Complete tapered type with flat base, straight vertical edges and sloped convex grinding surface of *c* 10°. Pecked all over but worn on the grinding surface. The fully perforated spindle hole measures 27mm in diameter. Dia: 450mm. Wt: 6kg. SF 64. Wall 464. Ph. 4. SF 64.

4. **Whetstone/saddle quern**. Fine-grained micaceous sandstone. Sharpening stone with two concave smooth areas worn very smooth and with several sharpening grooves across the edges. Made from a boulder. One face is damaged (looks recent). Measures 250 x 200 x 110mm. Wt: 6kg. Pit 151. Ph. 5. SF 53.

5. **Upper rotary quern** (not illustrated). Millstone Grit: medium-grained feldspathic sandstone. Adjoining fragments of flat disc type with straight sides that slope in slightly. Pecked grinding surface with some smoothing to the circumference. Circular cylindrical eye of 50mm diameter. Dia: 490mm; Th: 36mm. Wt: 1510g. Ditch 1481. Ph. 5. SF 83.

6. **Upper rotary quern** (not illustrated). Old Red Sandstone: pebbly sandstone with quartz pebbles, mostly <20mm, some with grey-green patches, also some reddish siltstone pebbles. Edge fragment of flat-topped type. Centre is missing. Pecked all over but with the grinding surface worn smooth and with some rotational wear. Straight vertical edges. Burnt/blackened on one edge. Wt: 943g. Pit 957. Ph. 5. SF 86.

Chapter 5

Environmental and osteological evidence and radiocarbon dating

ANIMAL BONE *by Martyn Allen*

Introduction

An assemblage of 4765 animal bones was recorded, of which 4238 were recovered by hand excavation and 527 from environmental soil samples (Tables 5.1–2). The analysis concentrated on material from features dating to Phases 1–5 and any bones from later medieval/post-medieval or undated features were not recorded. The small number of bones from medieval/post-medieval features often derived from furrows and were considered likely to have been disturbed and heavily mixed. Overall, the assemblage was well preserved. Poorly preserved remains generally derived from middle Iron Age contexts, while some from later Roman contexts could indicate a small degree of residuality and redeposition.

Only one bone fragment was identified from an early prehistoric (Phase 1) feature. This was a cattle scapula from early prehistoric pit 4226 and is not considered any further in this report. A total of 250 fragments were recovered from middle Iron Age (Phase 2) features, of which less than one third were identified to species. Most were cattle bones, with some sheep/goat, a small number of pig and horse, and part of a red deer skull.

The majority of the assemblage derives from late Iron Age and Roman features, especially from

Table 5.1 Hand-collected animal bone specimens by phase

Taxon	1	2a	2b	2	3b	3c	3	3–5	4a	4b	4c	4	5a	5b	5c	5	Total
Cattle	1	12	27	9	12	52	7	8	49	2	39	153 (190)	158 (3)	117 (4)	156	19	1018
Sheep/goat		3	12		17	8		4	4	1	6	54	120	64	38	15	346
Sheep						1						1	5	3			10
Pig			1			1 (5)			2		1	14 (120)	36	14	18	5	217
Horse		2	2		2	6	2				2	15	31	18	26 (3)	2	111
cf horse															1		1
Dog						2		2				2	30 (29)	1			66
Cat													1		3		4
Red deer		1									5	1	3	3	15	3	31
Fallow deer																3	3
cf fallow deer														4			4
Fox													2				2
Chicken													2	4			6
cf chicken														1			1
Duck													1		1		2
Woodcock													1				1
Common crane														1			1
cf common crane													1				1
Raven													2				2
Corvid													1				1
Bird												1	1	1			3
Bird?												1					1
Large mammal		16	26		20	28		9	23	7	32	278	255	163	160	60	1077
Medium mammal			15		2	9		9	7	3	4	97	122	54	23	6	351
Small mammal					1		1					1	2		3		8
Unidentified		40	84		25	40	18	7	18	17	27	242	214	111	93	34	970
Total	1	74	167	9	79	152	28	39	103	30	116	1170	1020	563	540	147	4238

Numbers in parentheses represent additional number of bones in associated bone groups

Table 5.2 Animal bone specimens from environmental samples by phase

Taxon	3	3–5	4c	4	5a	5b	5c	Total
Cattle	2						15	17
Sheep/goat						1	10	11
Pig			1	6			20	27
Horse							2	2
Red deer							1	1
Roe deer							3	3
Rodent				6	4		1	11
Chicken				4	1			5
Bird				20				20
Bird?				1				1
Frog			1	13	4		2	20
Pike					1			1
Large mammal		1		1			17	19
Medium mammal	1			47	4		9	61
Small mammal				11				11
Unidentified	1		4	201	27		84	317
Total	4	1	6	310	41	1	164	527

middle Roman (Phase 4) and late Roman (Phase 5) contexts. Around 40 fragments came from Roman contexts that could not be more closely dated to one of these phases. Cattle bones dominated each phase in terms of fragment counts and although sheep/goat and pig remains were better represented when minimum numbers of animals were estimated, cattle continued to be the most frequent animal throughout. Evidence for horned and hornless sheep was identified, the latter being particularly uncommon in Roman Britain, while the discovery of a large and robust horncore suggests that several types of sheep may have been present in the assemblage.

Neonatal remains of cattle, sheep/goat and pig were found in middle and late Roman contexts, suggestive of local breeding and rearing of livestock, while two juvenile bird specimens may relate to chicken husbandry. Horse bones accounted for between 5% and 10% of the assemblage in each of the Roman phases, and several specimens belonging to the late Roman phase displayed butchery marks, including two with saw marks indicative of bone working.

Several associated or articulating bone groups were identified, predominantly from middle and late Roman features. These included a largely complete calf burial, the mixed remains of at least two piglets, and the skeletons of two miniature ('toy') dogs. A small number of articulating horse bones were also identified. Cat bones were also found in late Roman features, and although none were clearly articulated, three were recovered from one ditch and were probably from the same animal.

Remains of red deer, roe deer and fallow deer were all identified, the vast majority from later Roman contexts. Some of these remains clearly reflect local hunting practices, although the fallow deer specimens were all antler and may have been imported to the site. The fallow deer antler had been sawn and represents a rare find from a Romano-British site, given that these animals were not native to Britain and there is only minimal evidence that live herds were kept in captivity at this time. Bird bones were present in small numbers and included duck, woodcock and common crane, which suggest wildfowling by the local community.

Methods

Each fragment was identified to taxon and element where possible with the aid of the author's skeletal reference collection. Refitting fragments were counted as single specimens. Long-bone shaft fragments, ribs and vertebrae were recorded according to a relative size category, either as large-, medium- or small-sized mammals. Elements were recorded according to the anatomical zone present following Serjeantson's (1996) scheme. Specimens with recurring zones were quantified to calculate the minimum number of elements (MNE) present for a particular taxon, and the minimum number of individuals (MNI) was calculated by taking body side into account. Articulating specimens were recorded where present.

Ageing data were collected from the analysis of tooth-wear patterns following Grant (1982) and estimated ages were drawn from comparisons with modern livestock data following the work of Jones and Sadler (2012) for cattle and Jones (2006) for sheep. Pig tooth-wear data were collected and age stages attributed following O'Connor (1988), with estimated ages based upon eruption timings using data collected by Legge (2013). Epiphyseal fusion of post-cranial elements was also recorded, and age estimates were calculated using the timings presented by Sisson and Grossman (Getty 1975).

Measurements were taken using the standards of von den Driesch (1976). Withers heights for cattle, sheep/goats and dogs were calculated using the factors published by von den Driesch and Boessneck (1974), and those for horses using the factors modified from Vitt (1952) by May (1985; after Johnstone 2004, 156). Cattle metacarpals were sexed using the breadth/length ratio formulated by Howard (1963), calculated as the distal breadth divided by the greatest length multiplied by 100 (Bd/GL*100).

Butchery marks were recorded in detail in terms of mark type and location on the bone. Evidence of burning was recorded based on colour (eg black, grey or white, ie calcined). Gnaw marks were recorded where present. Signs of pathology were recorded in detail and possible diagnoses offered with reference to relevant texts (eg Baker and Brothwell 1980; Bartosiewicz with Gal 2013).

Taphonomy and provenance

The assemblage was generally well preserved, except for material from some middle Iron Age features (eg ring gullies 4392/4393 and 4398) and a few later Roman specimens that were probably redeposited. The otherwise good level of preservation allowed for taphonomic markers such as butchery, burning and gnaw marks to be fairly easily seen and recorded.

Just over 3% of the assemblage displayed butchery marks and a detailed analysis of these is provided for each phased group below. Very few butchered specimens were identified from middle Iron Age, late Iron Age/early Roman and poorly dated Roman (Phases 3–5) contexts. Middle Roman contexts produced 40 butchered specimens (2.3%) and 108 specimens derived from late Roman contexts (4.4%). The higher number of butchered bones in later Roman contexts reflects the larger groups of bones from these phases, while the higher percentage of late Roman material perhaps also reflects a better level of preservation and/or fragmentation, allowing for more butchery marks to be observed, or perhaps butchery practices employed during this period more often left physical signs on the bones.

The pattern of burning in the assemblage showed a different chronological pattern to that of butchery. A total of 22 late Iron Age/early Roman specimens, accounting for over 8% of this material, showed signs of burning, and this percentage nearly doubled in the middle Roman group which included 268 burnt specimens (15.4%). In contrast, just over 1% of the late Roman group was found to have been burnt. The pattern is biased by quantities of heavily burnt bones from Phase 4 layer 1001 and pit 1045, which together produced 236 burnt specimens aided by recovery in soil samples. Much of this material could not be identified to species, but it included a pig mandible in pit 1045 and it is possible that much of the medium mammal-sized bones from this feature were also the heavily burnt remains of a pig carcass. Burnt cattle and bird bones were identified from layer 1001. These contexts were, notably, associated with the temple/mausoleum (Building 1320) and probably reflect ritual practices associated with this structure. Other Phase 4 contexts in this area of the site with burnt animal bones also include pits 1036, 1038, 1430, 1433, 1437 and 1440 and layer 558, which overlay wall 1074 of Building 1320.

Gnawing on animal bones was comparatively rare, accounting for less than 1% of the late Iron Age/early Roman and middle Roman material, and 1.5% of the late Roman group. All the gnawed bones were chewed by dogs, except for one red deer phalanx that had possible rodent gnaw marks (Phase 5 ditch 20603). This would suggest that the site was generally kept clear of debris, with animal carcasses being deposited fairly soon after butchery and consumption activities.

The bulk of the assemblage in each phase from the middle Iron Age to the late Roman period derived from ditch fills, and ditch interventions accounted for the greatest number of context groups overall. Over 90% of the middle Iron Age material derived from ditches, while over 80% of the late Iron Age/early Roman and late Roman groups were also recovered from this feature type. The middle Roman group was much more varied in comparison, probably reflecting the greater number of other feature types belonging to this phase that were excavated. The proportion of faunal material from ditch fills accounted for just over 45% in this phase, while pits produced over 30%. Structural features, such as cobbled surface 20045, contained relatively abundant faunal remains, as did layers that were associated with Building 1320. Several pits also associated with Building 1320 also suggest a concentration of activity in this area. However, features associated with the aisled hall farther to the west were less productive, indicating that the deposition of animal remains was much less common there.

Middle Iron Age (Phase 2)

The middle Iron Age assemblage consisted of 250 animal bone specimens, all recovered by hand from Phase 2 features (Table 5.1). Many of these were not identifiable to species and, as mentioned above, much of this group was poorly preserved.

Cattle were the most common taxon, accounting for *c* 70% of the identified livestock remains in this phase (Fig. 5.1), while numerous specimens identified to large mammal size were probably also from cattle. Sheep/goat bones were less common, and pig was represented by one maxilla fragment from ditch 4392. Four horse specimens were represented by two teeth, an astragalus and a distal humerus, each from different ditches.

Evidence of age-at-death was particularly sparse. Tooth-wear data were restricted to two loose lower 3rd molars. One of these was in an early stage of wear on both main cusps, giving an estimated age of 26–36 months, and the other was more heavily worn, indicating an animal that died around 5–10 years old.

Perhaps the most significant find was the partial skull from a red deer stag found in ditch 4382. The antler pedicle was still present, but it is possible that the antler had shed or was about to shed when the animal was killed. It was difficult to be certain of this owing to the poor preservation of the specimen. If the antler had been shed it seems likely that the stag had been hunted soon after the rut, around late autumn/early winter.

Late Iron Age/early Roman (Phase 3)

Faunal remains were recovered from several features. This material was predominantly found in ditch fills located in the western part of the complex and was, for the most part, spatially distinct from the middle and late Roman assemblages recovered from the central and eastern areas of the site.

Taxonomic representation

Cattle bones outnumbered those of sheep/goat by around 3:1 and represented over 60% of the identified livestock remains in terms of NISP (Fig. 5.1). Sheep/goat bones contributed 23%, while pigs and horses contributed 5% and 9% respectively. The late Iron Age/early Roman assemblage was too small to reliably examine minimum numbers of individuals (MNI), although based on the analysis of the middle and late Roman assemblages sheep/goats are likely to have been better represented in terms of MNI owing to higher degrees of fragmentation of larger cattle bones. Quantification by MNI diminishes the problem of bone fragmentation by accounting for the most common element from the skeleton, and therefore gives a better indication of absolute numbers of animals rather than simple counts of bone fragments.

Dogs were the only other taxon represented in this phase, by a complete mandible from ditch 1471 and a canine tooth from ditch 5449. The mandible appeared to be relatively large and robust but had lost all the dentition post-mortem.

Butchery

Butchery data were very limited in this phase. Only three specimens displayed butchery marks, all cattle bones, including a scapula with cuts around the neck, a hyoid bone with fine cut marks on both sides, and a radius that had been chopped through in an axial direction. Hyoid bones are located in the throat, and examples of cattle hyoids with cut marks have been found at other Romano-British sites where they have been interpreted as indicating tongue removal (Allen 2017a, 121–2).

Associated bone group

One group of articulating bones belonging to a young pig were recovered from pit 5524 (see below for definition). This consisted part of a front foot and was represented by four complete metacarpals, all unfused at the distal ends, and a carpal bone. No butchery marks were found on the bones.

Age at death

Ageing data were restricted to two loose third molars from cattle and one loose third molar from a sheep or goat. These were all in early–moderate stages of wear, providing estimated ages of 26–36 months and 40 months–6.5 years for the cattle and 34–43 months for the sheep/goat.

Middle Roman (Phase 4) and late Roman (Phase 5)

The middle and late Roman assemblages form the bulk of the recovered animal bones. These were also distinct in terms of their spatial distribution, mostly deriving from the enclosure ditches and features associated with the structures to the south and south-east of the villa.

Taxonomic representation

Cattle bones dominated in both middle and late Roman phases, contributing 70% and just over 50% of the main livestock taxa remains respectively (Fig. 5.1). This variation is balanced by the higher proportion of sheep/goat bones in the late Roman phase, where they contribute just under 30% of livestock bones compared with less than 20% in the middle Roman phase. Pig and horse bones are also slightly better represented in the late Roman phase, increasing from 7% and 5% in the middle Roman assemblage to 10% and 9% respectively.

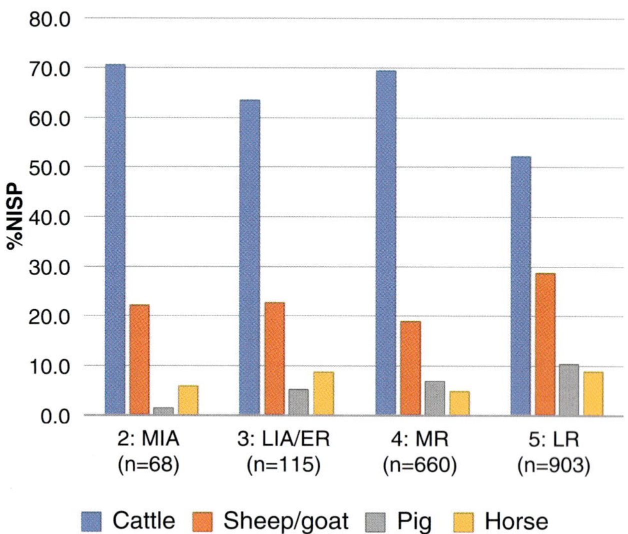

Fig. 5.1 Percentage NISP of the major livestock taxa by phase

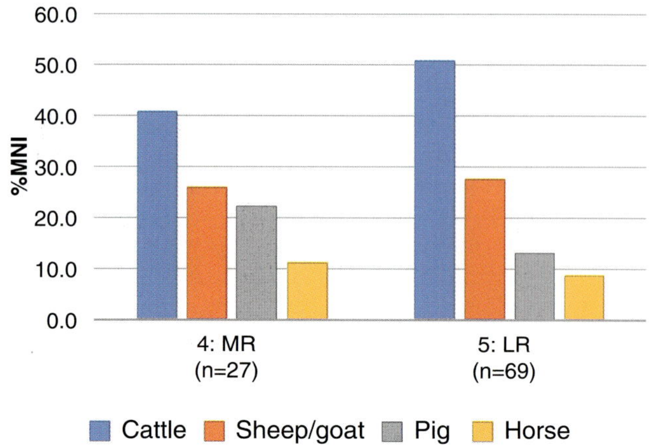

Fig. 5.2 Percentage MNI of the major livestock taxa by phase (middle and late Roman phases only)

Viewing the quantification data in terms of %MNI, sheep/goat, pig and horse remains are all better represented in the middle Roman phase when compared to the NISP counts (Fig. 5.2). Sheep/goats accounted for 26%, pigs for 22% and horses for 11% MNI, while cattle remains still dominated overall, but accounted for just over 40% MNI. As discussed above, the use of MNI diminishes the frequent over-representation of cattle bones, which tend to fragment more than those of smaller mammals.

Perhaps surprisingly, the late Roman data suggest an equally high percentage of cattle in terms of NISP and MNI, with both quantification methods registering 50%. Sheep/goat, pig and horse remains also register fairly similar percentages using both quantification methods. While NISP counts tend to be biased by fragmentation, MNI is biased by low sample sizes which can give a misleading indication of taxa frequencies. The good sample size seen here for the late Roman MNI counts perhaps suggests that the very similar relative frequencies for NISP and MNI are a very good indication of the proportions of each taxon. These data highlight the importance of viewing the results of both quantification methods together.

Only one bone was possibly attributable to goat. This was a large and robust metatarsal from threshing/malting floor 2146. Sheep were distinguished from goats in nine cases – one specimen in the middle Roman assemblage and eight in the late Roman assemblage. These were almost exclusively horncore fragments or skull fragments with surviving parts of horncores. Two potentially different types of sheep were present, including horned and hornless (polled) varieties (Fig. 5.3). The skull of the hornless type was found in Phase 5a ditch 401. It had two small cut marks made when the animal was skinned. Hornless sheep are rarely identified in Romano-British contexts (see below).

Only two dog bones were recovered from Phase 4 features, which contrasts with 31 from Phase 5 features, plus another 29 that constituted two articulated skeletons (Table 5.1). The difference between the number of dog bones in Phases 4 and 5 is possibly due to spatial patterning in dog burial practice and the sampling strategy employed during excavation. Cat bones (four in total) were only found in late Roman features.

The remains of three species of deer were identified in the later Roman period, with red deer specimens present in Phase 4 and 5 contexts, while specimens of roe and fallow deer were found in several Phase 5 features (these are all discussed in more detail below). The roe deer bones were all recovered from sieved samples (Table 5.2). Two fox bones were recovered from ditch 398. Both were tibiae, including a complete example in fill 346 and a proximal half in fill 249.

Twenty-seven bird bones were recorded from middle Roman features. Of these, 25 were recovered from environmental samples and all except four chicken bones were identified as 'bird'. A total of 18 bird bones were recovered from late Roman features, of which 17 were via hand excavation. These included seven chicken bones (including one from a sieved sample), one possible chicken bone, two duck bones, a woodcock bone, one certain and one possible bone of common crane, two raven bones and one corvid bone that was probably raven

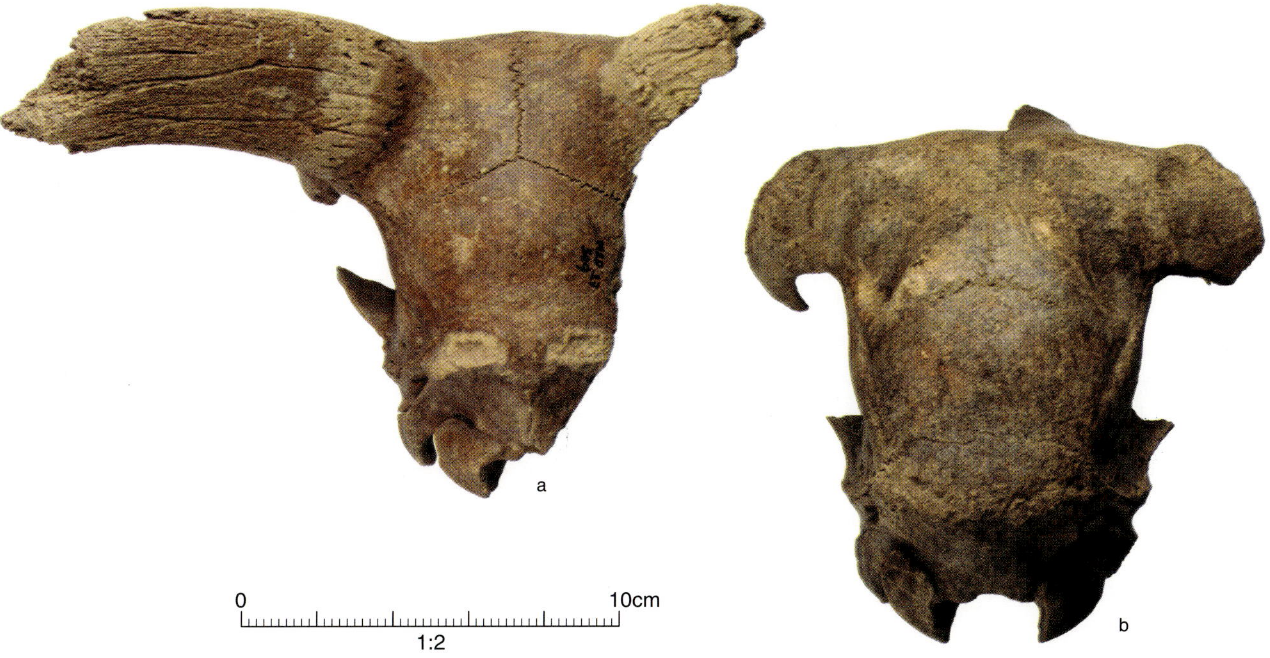

Fig. 5.3 Horned and hornless sheep skulls; a) gully 561; b) ditch 401

as well. The bird bones are discussed in relation to their context below.

A total of 20 frog bones were identified, all from environmental samples: 14 from middle Roman features and six from late Roman features. The majority of these were recovered via sampling of Phase 4 culvert 20002 and included scapula, humerus, urostyle and vertebra specimens. One pike (*Esox lucius*) vertebra from a fish *c* 0.5m long was identified from Phase 5a pit 227.

Cattle

Body-part patterns

Cattle bones were represented by the full range of skeletal elements in the middle and late Roman phases. When body side was accounted for, radius and mandible elements were the most common, representing a minimum of 11 and 35 individuals in each of these phases respectively. Comparison of the minimum number of elements in both phases suggests a high degree of similarity, despite the notably large late Roman sample (Fig. 5.4). Notwithstanding an anomalously high %MNE for radius bones in the middle Roman assemblage, mandibles were generally the best represented element overall. All the major limb bones, the pelvis and the scapula were all well represented. The generally high %MNE of most of the major limb bones suggests that excessive fragmentation was not significantly detrimental to the assemblage. Differential recovery, however, probably accounts for the lower percentages of astragalus, calcaneus and navicular-cuboid bones.

Associated bone groups

'Associated bone group' (ABG) is a term that refers to a collection of animal bones that are found in articulation during excavation, or are thought likely to have been in articulation by the recording

analyst, either a complete skeleton or a partial skeleton (a limb, for example). To be more precise, Morris (2011, 12–13) defines an AGB as one of the following:

1. Animal remains which have been deposited with some portion of the flesh or connective tissue still attached, which has caused them to remain in articulation.
2. Animal remains which had been deposited in articulation but became disarticulated through the taphonomic processes which are then consequently recognised and identified as constituting a single animal by the zooarchaeologist.
3. Animal remains which constitute disarticulated remains when deposited, but are deposited in association, and subsequently identified as being from the same animal by the zooarchaeologist.

Using these criteria, five cattle ABGs have been identified in the Phase 4 assemblage and three in the Phase 5 assemblage (Table 5.3). The Phase 4 group range from a largely complete calf skeleton to two articulating phalanx (toe) bones. The calf skeleton was discovered in pit 1045, entirely from fill 1046 (see Fig. 3.13). A total of 181 fragments belonging to this skeleton were recovered, the majority of which were broken rib, long bone or vertebra fragments, but which included all the major elements except for the skull, suggesting that the head had been removed prior to deposition. The atlas and the axis bones (the two foremost vertebrae) were present, however, although no butchery marks were found anywhere on the skeleton. Despite the absence of teeth, the age of the animal can be refined to around 15 months old owing to the presence of fused proximal radii, an unfused pelvis and a distal humerus that had just begun to fuse.

Other Phase 4 cattle ABGs include the articulating rear limb bones from a neonatal calf found in pit 1435, an articulating humerus and radius from

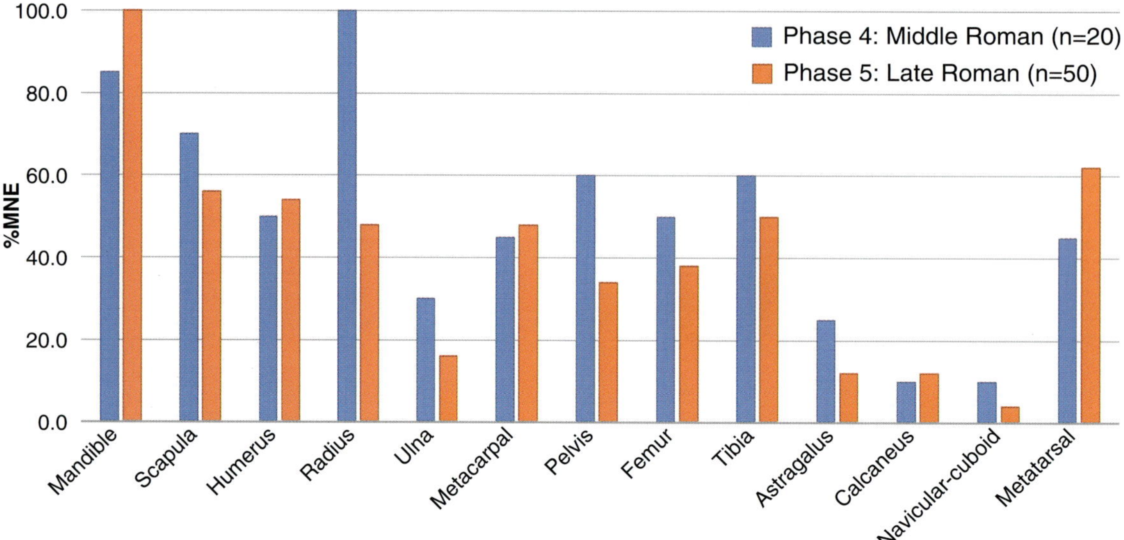

Fig. 5.4 Cattle element representation

Table 5.3 Associated bone groups

Feature	Phase	Taxon	No. frags	Identified remains
Ditch 1495	4	cattle	2	Two phalanges
Ditch 81	4	cattle	7	Articulating atlas, axis and at least five thoracic vertebrae
Pit 1045	4	cattle	181	Largely complete calf skeleton; another fill (1047) of this pit contained a quantity of heavily burnt animal bones
Pit 1435	4	cattle	9	Rear limb bones from a neonate skeleton, also some ribs possibly from same animal
Structure 20035	4a	cattle	2	Articulating humerus and radius
Ditch 20604	5b	cattle	2	Remains of skull and mandible
Ditch 20604	5b	cattle	2	Articulating metatarsal and naviculo-cuboid
Ditch 561	5a	cattle	3	Articulating forelimb (humerus, ulna and radius)
Pit 5524	3c	pig	5	Articulating metacarpals
Pit 2264	4	pig	120	Mixed remains of at least two piglet skeletons consisting of most elements
Ditch 454	5a	dog	7	Partial remains of a toy dog including left and right mandible and several articulating forelimb elements (significant curvature to the humerus)
Ditch 863	5a	dog	22	Skeleton of a toy dog, very similar to the partial skeleton found in ditch 454; elements include scapula, humeri, ulna, radius, vertebrae, pelvis, sacrum, femora and tibiae
Ditch 1481	5b	horse	2	Articulating axis and thoracic vertebra
Ditch 20597	5c	horse	3	Articulating phalanges

cleaning layer 20436 over surface 20042, an articulating atlas and axis and several probably associated large mammal vertebrae in ditch 81 and the two phalanx bones mentioned above from ditch 1495.

The Phase 5 cattle ABGs included an articulating skull and mandible and an articulating naviculo-cuboid and metatarsal in ditch 20604, in fills 20410 and 20411 respectively, and an articulating forelimb in ditch 561.

Butchery

The relatively low degree of fragmentation is partly influenced by the method of butchery employed, which does not appear to have been intensive. A total of 26 cattle bones display butchery marks in the middle Roman assemblage and 52 butchered specimens were identified in the late Roman assemblage. Meat cleavers do appear to have been used in both phases, a distinctive marker of the Roman period often found in urban and military assemblages (Maltby 2007).

Of the butchered middle Roman cattle bones, seven displayed cut marks while 18 had been chopped and one had a clear cleaver mark. Butchered elements included femur, humerus, mandible, metapodial, pelvis, radius, scapula, tibia and ulna specimens. All the main long bones exhibited chop marks, mostly through the proximal or distal ends, suggestive of the carcass being apportioned into joints. The pelvis was similarly found to have been chopped through, dividing the carcass at the hip joint. Scapulae were represented by five specimens, mostly bones that had been chopped at or around the base of the spine.

The same range of elements were found with butchery marks in the late Roman phase, and to these can be added an axis bone that had been chopped from one side when the animal was decapitated, a navicular-cuboid with skinning marks (at the ankle), and a 1st phalanx with similar skinning marks (on the toes). While the number of specimens with cut and chop marks were more equal in this phase, a greater number with other types of cleaver marks were evident. These included a scapula with scoop/blade marks on the medial side of the blade, reflective of defleshing around the shoulder, a mandible with a blade mark on the medial side of the ascending ramus, and three femora with 'scoop' marks down the shaft. The last of these were made when raw meat was removed from the bone. Several long bones had also been split axially to access the marrow, including a metacarpal, a radius and a tibia.

Ageing

Sufficient epiphyseal fusion and dental-wear data were present for the analysis of cattle age patterns in Phases 4 and 5. Epiphyseal fusion occurs when elements in the juvenile skeleton fuse together once they have reached skeletal maturity. For example, all limb bones in the axial skeleton consist of the diaphysis (the main shaft of the bone) and the two epiphyses, one at each end. The timing of this fusion occurs at different ages in different elements and varies according to taxon, but these timings are fairly standard in most species (Getty 1975). Examination of the quantities of different elements that have or have not reached skeletal maturity can build a picture of the slaughter pattern for different livestock.

Table 5.4 shows the pattern of cattle epiphyseal fusion in the Phase 4 assemblage. Here, different elements are grouped into the age stages at which fusion occurs. For example, fusion of the scapula, pelvis and proximal radius tends to occur between

Table 5.4 Cattle epiphyseal fusion data, Phases 4 and 5

		Phase 4			Phase 5		
Fusion stage	*Element*	*Fused*	*Unfused*	*% fused*	*Fused*	*Unfused*	*% fused*
7–15 months	Scapula	7	0		13	2	
	Pelvis	6	2		7	3	
	P radius	12	1		15	1	
	Total	25	3	89.3	35	6	85.4
15–24 months	2nd phalanx	2	1		4	0	
	D humerus	7	0		13	2	
	1st phalanx	5	3		13	0	
	Total	14	4	77.8	30	2	93.8
24–36 months	D tibia	4	2		7	5	
	D metapodial	9	6		19	5	
	Calcaneus	0	2		1	3	
	Total	13	10	56.5	27	13	67.5
36–48 months	P femur	0	7		5	2	
	P humerus	3	1		2	3	
	D radius	5	3		4	4	
	P ulna	0	2		0	0	
	D femur	1	3		4	4	
	P tibia	0	6		2	2	
	Total	9	22	29.0	17	15	53.1

7–15 months in cattle. The presence of two unfused pelvis bones and one proximal radius compares to 25 fused elements in this group, thus giving a percentage fused rate of 89%, suggesting a small but apparent kill-off of livestock at this age. The percentage of fused elements decreases in each of the following age groups, down to 77.8% at 15–24 months, 56.5% at 24–36 months and 29% at 36–48 months. The data nonetheless suggest a kill-off of young cattle in their second, third and fourth years, and possibly younger, indicating that some younger cattle were specifically targeted for culling and consumption at these ages.

Compared to the Phase 4 data, the kill-off rate of young animals in Phase 5 does not appear to have been as high (Table 5.4). While a similar proportion of unfused elements were present in the youngest (7–15 month) age group, the rate remained high (93.8%) in the 15–24 months group, reducing to 67.5% and 53.1% in the 24–36 month and 36–48 month age groups respectively. This would suggest that more cattle were often kept alive to full maturity, with less culling of 'prime beef' stock.

To understand the epiphyseal fusion data further, it is helpful to compare it with the ageing data derived from dental wear. Wear patterns on the occlusal surfaces of the molar teeth in livestock can provide greater resolution in age patterns than epiphyseal fusion because it allows a specific age to be identified rather than the point before or after which an element fuses. In contrast to epiphyseal fusion, the cattle dental-wear data suggest similar cull patterns in Phases 4 and 5, although it should be noted that two Phase 3 specimens were included with the Phase 4 material in order to make use of these and to expand the sample size slightly (Table 5.5). The cull profile indicates that a higher proportion of young calves, those between birth and six months, were culled in

Table 5.5 Cattle dental wear data (number of specimens per age group)

Stage	*Estimated age*	*Phase 3/4*	*Phase 5*
A	Perinatal	0	0
B	0–6 months	0	4
C	5–18 months	1	1
D	16–28 months	2	3
E	26–36 months	1	0
F	34–43 months	0	1
G	40 m–6.5 years	3	4
H	5–10 years	0	0
J	8–16 years	0	3
K	14–20 years +	1	0

Phase 5, while a similar number were culled between 5–28 months. Following this, a second group occurred at 40 months–6.5 years, representing animals immediately following skeletal maturity. Some evidence for more elderly cattle was represented by one Phase 4 specimen at stage K (14–20 years +) and three Phase 5 specimens at stage J (8–16 years), in both cases highlighting survivorship well beyond what might today be considered economically viable.

The presence of some mandibles from very young animals (0–6 years) in Phase 5 and several unfused elements in the earliest-fusing group in both Phases 4 and 5 can be added to by the identification of several neonatal cattle specimens from features dating to both Phases. The partial calf skeleton in pit 1435 represents an animal that must have died at or soon after birth and may have been placed in a purpose-dug feature. Together, these data demonstrate that cattle breeding, birthing and rearing was taking place within the environs of the villa. The group of dental-wear specimens aged around 5–36 months correlate with the epiphyseal fusion data to show that a proportion of the cattle herd were selected for slaughter at a young age. The presence of very young and very old cattle further indicates the presence of a herd maintained on site, rather than livestock necessarily being imported from elsewhere.

Pathology

Cattle specimens displaying pathological markers, ten in total, were only found in Phase 4 and 5 features. These were predominantly arthropathies (joint disease) affecting foot bones. Three 1st phalanges displayed exostoses and/or lipping around the proximal ends, with two also showing at the distal (eg Baker and Brothwell, 1980, 115; Bartosiewicz with Gal 2013, 108). Two metacarpals exhibited splayed distal condyles, while a third displayed exostoses at the proximal end. An astragalus also exhibited exostoses. Such lesions are often caused by excessive strain being placed on this part of the body leading to modifications in the bone structure (ibid.).

A femur showed signs of advanced eburnation over the femoral head, where the thigh bone articulates with the pelvis. This indicates that the animal had been suffering from osteoarthritis for some time (Bartosiewicz with Gal 2013, 108).

A most unusual discovery was a cattle lumbar vertebra that exhibited a relatively large hole about 16mm across, leading from the ventral side of the centrum through to the spinal canal (Fig. 5.5). The hole was smooth throughout and it appears to have been an anomalous development of the nutrient foramina. The trait has not been seen by this author previously, but Baker and Brothwell (1980, 35–6) describe it with regard to medieval examples. It is worth highlighting that the hole in the Panattoni Park specimen appears to have been larger than the largest observed by those authors.

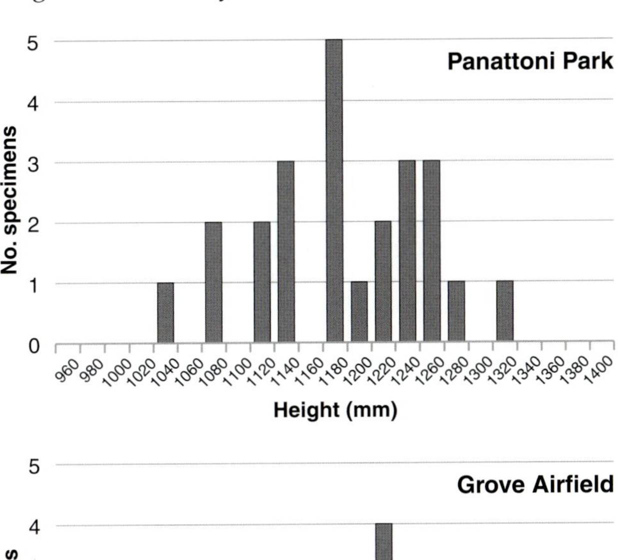

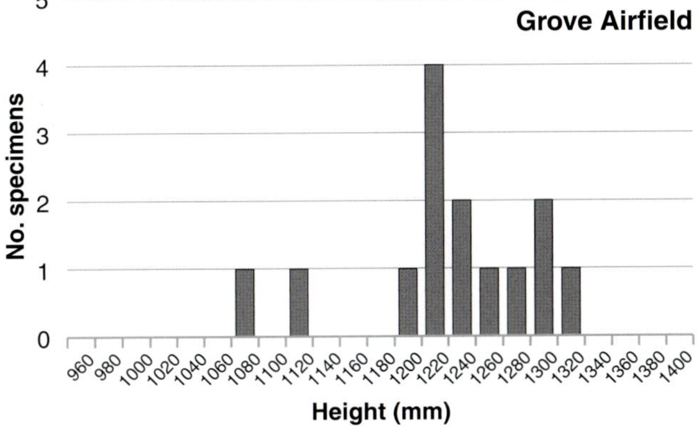

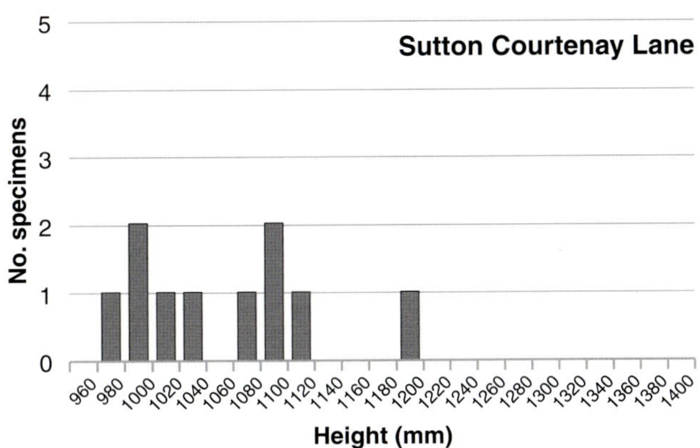

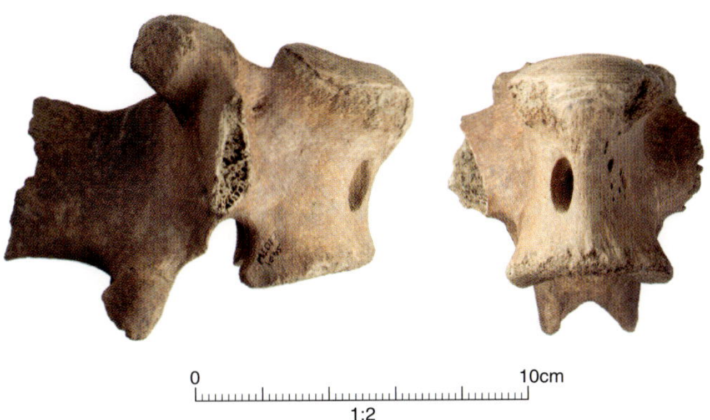

Fig. 5.5 Cattle lumbar vertebra with developmental anomaly in the centrum from pit/ditch terminus 1064

Fig. 5.6 Cattle withers' height data

Size, shape and sex

A large number of measurements were taken from a range of cattle elements, many of which were useful for biometric analyses examining cattle heights and stature, and some have provided information on sexual dimorphism. The data presented below were largely from Phase 4 and 5 specimens, although a small number of Phase 3 specimens are also included. However, the data should be considered broadly as middle to late Roman in date.

Cattle withers' heights were estimated from 24 complete long bones (Fig. 5.6). Most derived from metapodia, although a few radius, tibia and humerus bones were complete enough for estimations to be calculated. Withers' heights ranged from 1043mm to 1331mm with a concentration of individuals in the upper half of the group. These overlapped with the generally shorter cattle found at Sutton Courtenay Lane, Oxfordshire, which were probably dominated by cows, and the fairly tall group from Grove Airfield, Oxfordshire, which are likely to have included more bulls and oxen (OA 2021a; 2021b). The latter two recently analysed assemblages make viable comparisons based on the fact that they are similar in terms of fragment count and levels of preservation and have been recorded by the same author using a consistent methodology. The data would suggest a mixture of cows and bulls in the Panattoni Park assemblage but with a trend towards more males.

Seven metacarpals were sexed on the ratio between the distal breadth (Bd) and the greatest length (GL), which has been shown previously to indicate a division between males and females above or below 30 respectively (Howard 1963). The seven metacarpals gave Bd/GL*100 values of 27.6, 28.0, 30.4, 32.5, 31.6, 33.3 and 37.2, suggesting the presence of five bulls and two cows. Maltby (2010) has shown that other non-complete metacarpals can be added to these sex data by comparing the distal breadth against depth of the distal end at the epiphyseal fusion point (Ddf). Sexed and unsexed cattle metacarpals from Panattoni Park, Sutton Courtenay Lane and Grove Airfield have been compared using this criterion in Figure 5.7, which shows two clusters of specimens. It is worth noting that the Panattoni Park specimen with a Bd/GL*100 value of 30.4 in fact separated into the female group, and thus indicates that specimens close to the 30 mark should be viewed with some caution. This analysis confirms the male-dominated assemblage from Grove, the female-dominated assemblage from Sutton Courtenay Lane and the more mixed Panattoni Park group.

Biometric analysis of other elements also corresponds with the sexual variation found in these three assemblages. Measurements of the distal humerus along the breadth of the trochlea (BT) compared to the height of the trochlea constriction (HTC) present the usual distribution (Fig. 5.8). However, the Sutton Courtenay Lane results cluster predominantly at the lower end of the scale, mostly between 25 and 30mm HTC and 60 and 66mm BT. Both Iron Age and Roman specimens were included in these data to show that there was little change in cattle size over time at that site. Only two Sutton Courtenay Lane specimens were found to be larger than those in the main cluster, both measuring in excess of 30mm BT and 72mm BT. However, these were smaller than all three of the Roman specimens from Grove Airfield and just over half of the Roman group from Panattoni Park. The smaller specimens from Panattoni Park were often larger than those from Sutton Courtenay Lane, while the largest specimens from Grove

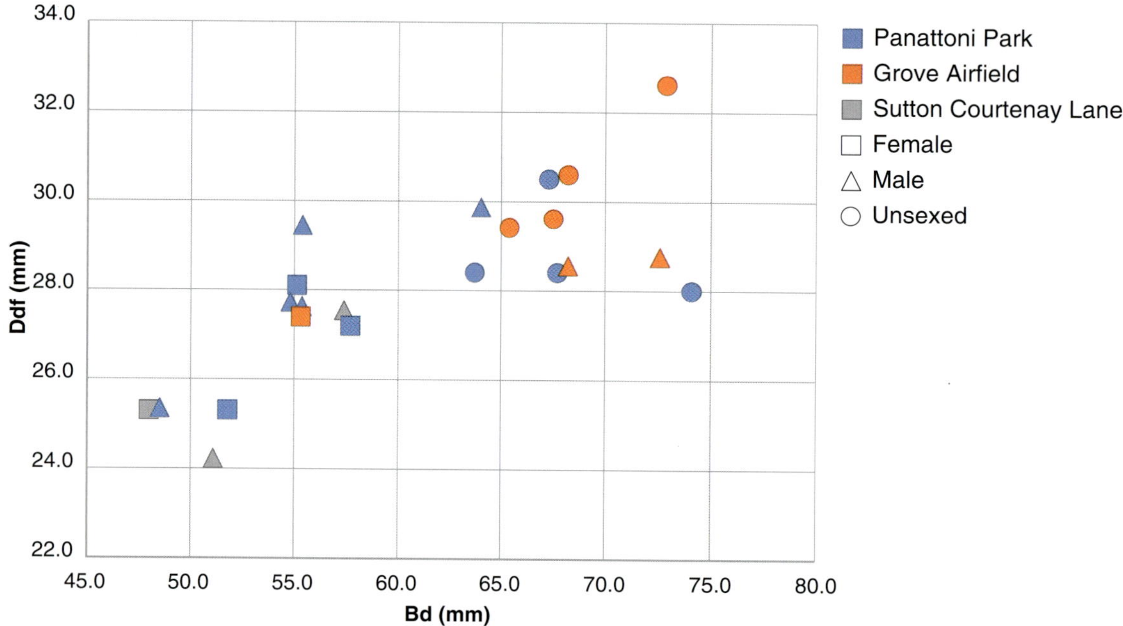

Fig. 5.7 Cattle distal metacarpal measurements from Panattoni Park, Grove Airfield and Sutton Courtenay Lane

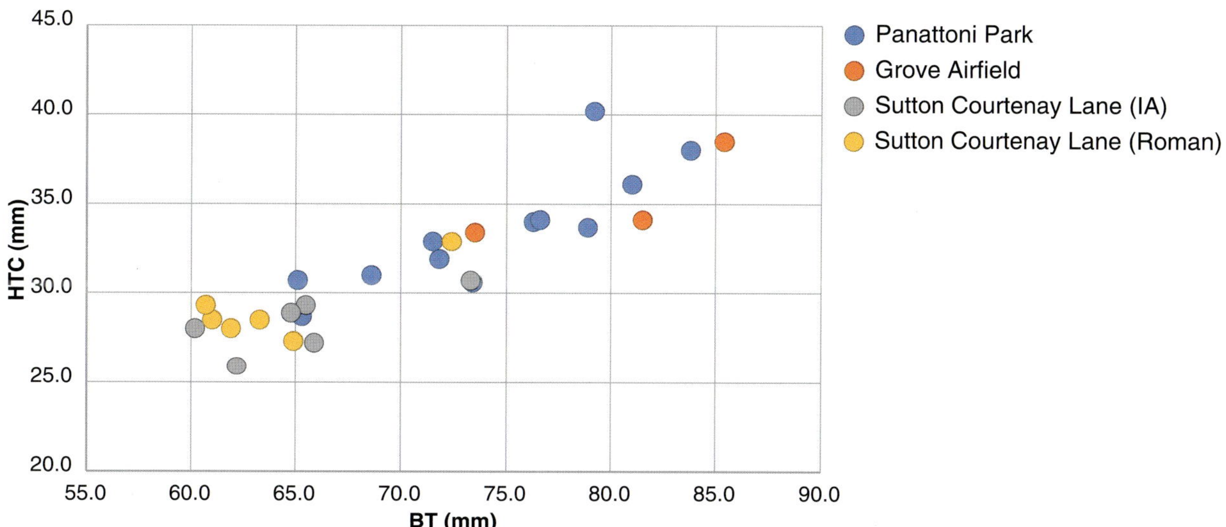

Fig. 5.8 Cattle distal humerus measurements from Panattoni Park, Grove Airfield and Sutton Courtenay Lane

Airfield and Panattoni Park were around 30–50% larger than the majority of the Sutton Courtenay Lane specimens. A similar distribution was observed in the measurements of the distal tibia, although here there was more overlap between specimens from each of the sites. Overall, sexual variation is likely to account for much this difference, as demonstrated above, but it is also possible that improved nutrition and perhaps more intensive breeding may be attributed to the cattle from Panattoni Park and Grove Airfield.

Sheep and goats

Body-part patterns

Sheep/goat bones were represented by a range of elements covering all the main body parts. The relative percentages of surviving elements varied, however, being dominated by mandibles and tibia specimens. In terms of minimum numbers of elements, mandibles are represented by 10 and 37 examples in the middle and late Roman assemblages respectively and tibiae by 6 and 30 examples respectively. When body sides are taken into account, mandibles represent a minimum of 7 and 19 individual animals in each phase.

These two elements are considerably more common than most others in both phases, and the degree of variation is shown in Figure 5.9. The humerus and the radius are relatively well represented, accounting for *c* 30% and 40% MNE respectively. Metatarsals are also fairly well represented, while other bones such as the scapula, metacarpal and pelvis account for around 20% or less. Relatively small bones, such as the calcaneus and astragalus, are very poorly represented, probably owing to recovery bias.

It is worth noting that the %MNE values for both later Roman phases is very similar for each element type. This would suggest that variations between different elements is more a reflection of differential

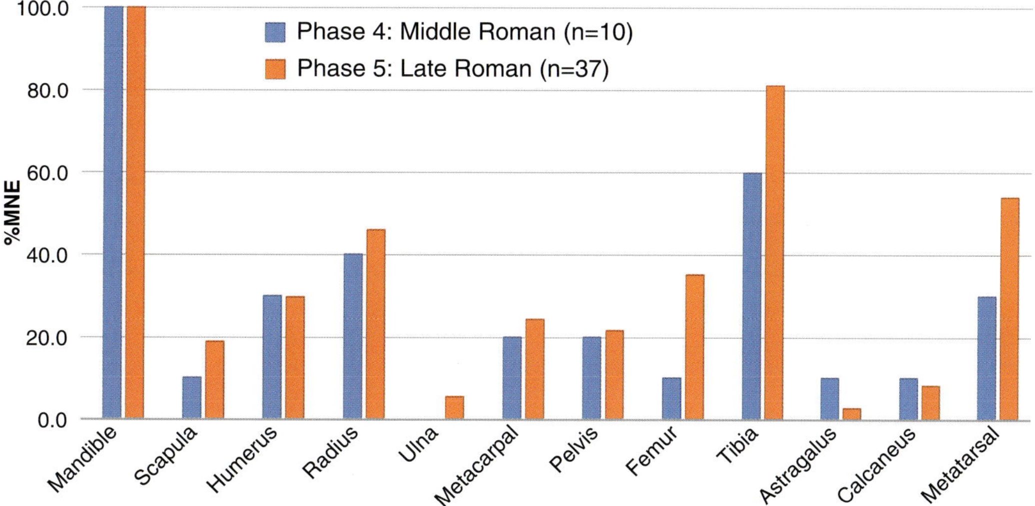

Fig. 5.9 Sheep/goat element representation

recovery and fragmentation than it is to do with any change in carcass processing and disposal practices. No sheep/goat bones were found in articulation.

Butchery

Only two sheep/goat specimens from the middle Roman assemblage displayed butchery marks. One was a horncore that had been chopped at the base and the other a tibia with filleting cuts on the shaft.

A total of 14 late Roman specimens exhibited butchery marks, seven each with cuts and chops. These included skinning marks on a proximal metatarsal at the foot, cuts on an atlas bone in the neck, and cuts on a skull fragment (the hornless sheep). There were cuts that focussed on disarticulating body parts such as on the neck of the scapula and the distal humerus, and defleshing marks mostly on long-bone shafts, notably the tibia and the femur. A sheep skull that had been chopped through the occipital from the posterior side, possibly to access the brain. Chops were also found on radius, pelvis, tibia, astragalus and metatarsal bones.

Ageing

Few data were available to examine epiphyseal fusion in sheep/goats from Phase 4 features (Table 5.6). Some unfused 1st phalanges were identified, suggesting some kill-off of very young animals, although these may have been infant mortalities as indicated by the presence of one neonatal sheep/goat phalanx in pit 2264.

Data from Phase 5 features were more productive (Table 5.6). No clearly neonatal sheep/goat remains were identified in this phase. However, three out of 14 early-stage elements were found unfused, including distal humerus and 1st phalanx specimens. A slightly increased proportion of middle-stage elements were found unfused including distal tibia and distal metapodial specimens, accounting for one-third of this group. For the late-stage elements, over half were found to have been fused, including distal radius, proximal ulna and proximal tibia specimens, suggesting an increase in culling around the third year after birth.

A total of 11 dental specimens provided ageing data from Phase 4 features (Table 5.7). These concentrated at age stages D–F, indicating that the majority of the animals were culled between 10 months and 4.5 years, and predominantly in the third year (stage E), which supports the epiphyseal fusion data. No dental specimens were aged above stage F and only one younger specimen was identified at stage C.

Phase 5 features provided a larger sample of dental specimens, 27 in total. These ranged from specimens at stage C, representing animals culled in their first year, to those at stage H, representing animals aged between *c* 6–11 years. There was a focus on the culling of younger animals at stage C–E, and particularly at stage D, representing livestock culled in their second year. This pattern is similar to the Phase 4 data, which may be biased by the small sample size, but there appears to have been a slight shift towards younger animals in the later phase.

Table 5.6 Sheep/goat epiphyseal fusion data, Phases 4 and 5

Fusion stage	Element	Phase 4			Phase 5		
		Fused	Unfused	% fused	Fused	Unfused	% fused
3–10 months	D humerus	1	0		2	1	
	P radius	0	0		4	0	
	Scapula	1	0		0	0	
	Pelvis	1	0		4	0	
	1st Phalanx	2	3		1	2	
	Total	5	3	62.5	11	3	78.6
15–36 months	D tibia	0	0		5	3	
	D metapodial	2	0		1	1	
	Calcaneus	0	1		2	0	
	Total	2	1	66.7	8	4	66.7
36–42 months	P femur	0	0		1	0	
	D radius	0	1		0	2	
	P ulna	0	0		1	1	
	D femur	0	0		1	0	
	P tibia	0	0		0	1	
	Total	0	1	0.0	3	4	42.9

Table 5.7 Sheep/goat dental wear data (number of specimens per age group)

Stage	Estimated age	Phase 3/4	Phase 5
A	0–1 months	0	0
B	1–3 months	0	0
C	3–12 months	1	5
D	10–24 months	2	11
E	20–36 months	5	5
F	2.5–4.5 years	3	2.5
G	4.5–e. 9 years	0	1
H	e. 6–e. 11+ years	0	2.5
J	e. 8–e. 13+ years	0	0

This pattern demonstrates a higher rate of culling of sheep/goats in their first and second years but with a small survivorship of older animals.

Pathology

Only one sheep/goat specimen exhibited pathological markers. A vertebra from ditch 398 displayed exostoses around both articulating surfaces, particularly at the posterior end. These bony growths are indicative of mild osteoarthritis in the spine.

Size, shape and sex

A small number of measurable sheep/goat bones provided some data with which to compare livestock sizes at Panattoni Park with those from Sutton Courtenay Lane and Grove Airfield. Examination of the height of the trochlea constriction (HTC) versus the breadth of the trochlea (BT) on the distal humerus suggests that the Panattoni Park sheep/goats were relatively large (Fig. 5.10).

The main variation occurred across the BT, which measured in excess of 26mm in all the Panattoni Park specimens, while only one specimen from Sutton Courtenay Lane reached this size. This indicates that sheep/goat breadths varied more than their heights. A similar examination of 'stockiness' was undertaken with the analysis of the breadth (Bd) and depth (Dd) of the distal tibia. Here the three Panattoni Park specimens were almost all larger than Iron Age and Roman specimens from Sutton Courtenay Lane and the Roman specimens from Grove Airfield (Fig. 5.11).

The size patterns shown in both these elements may be somewhat biased by the small sample from Panattoni Park, which would probably overlap with data from the other two sites if more specimens were available. Nonetheless the pattern exhibited by both elements is very similar. Several reasons could account for this, the most likely being sexual variation. Rams may dominate in the Panattoni Park group in comparison with the other two sites, which may have had a higher proportion of females. A high ratio of males is unusual, as it is not in keeping with a locally maintained flock, which would more likely be dominated by females, and it may suggest that sheep/goats were more often selected from flocks based elsewhere. This is perhaps supported by the general lack of neonatal sheep/goats (although see above) and the focus on culling of livestock in their later first and second years, which otherwise appears to be a fairly intensive strategy. Another explanation is that the larger Panattoni Park specimens belonged to goats, although this has not been demonstrated through any clear identifications. Instead, it may represent the presence of a

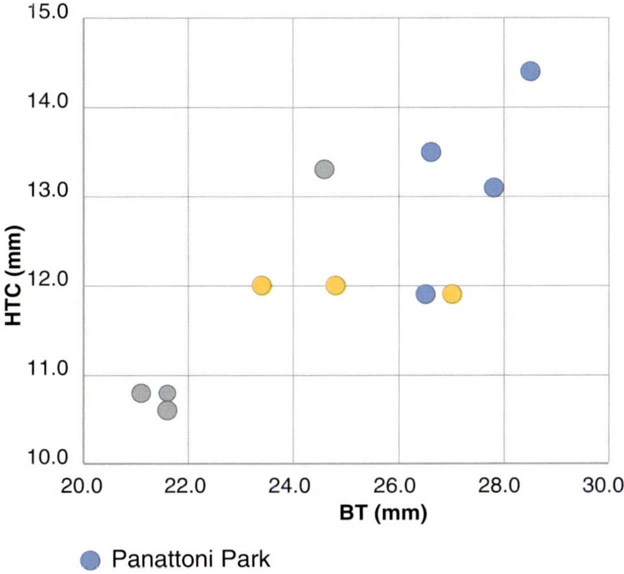

Fig. 5.10 Sheep/goat distal humerus measurements from Panattoni Park and Sutton Courtenay Lane

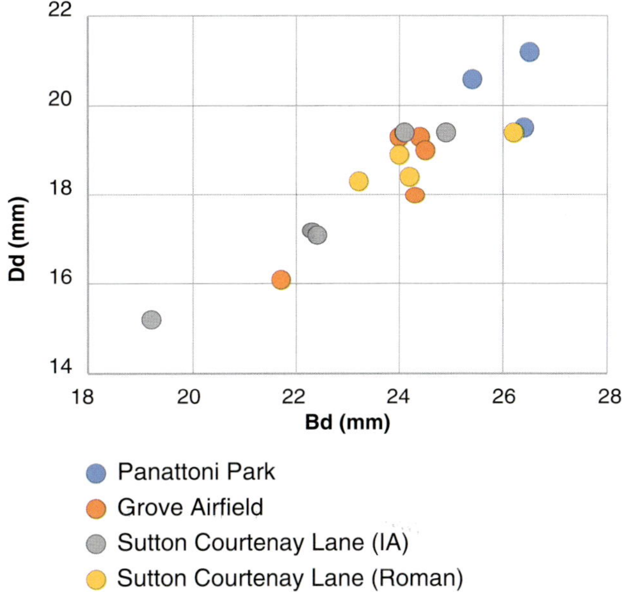

Fig. 5.11 Sheep/goat distal tibia measurements from Panattoni Park, Grove Airfield and Sutton Courtenay Lane

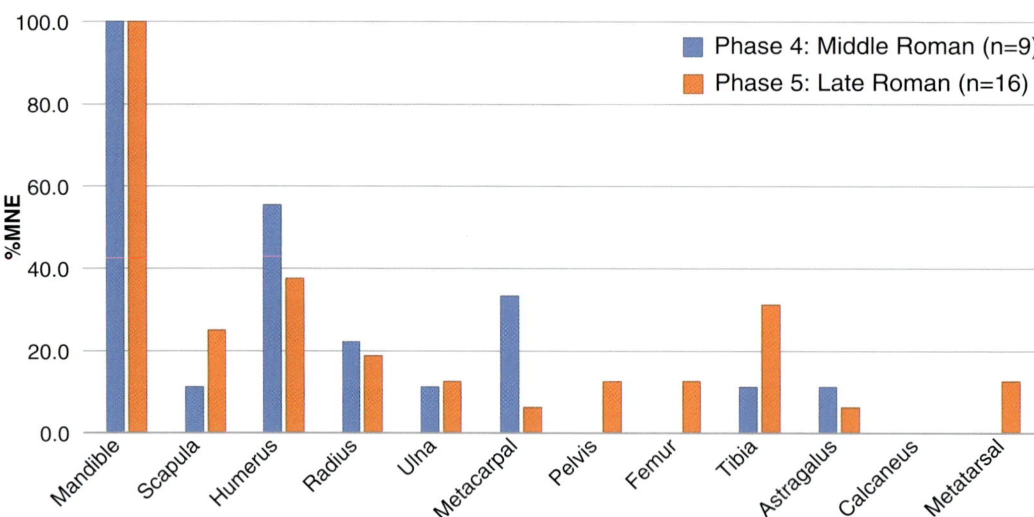

Fig. 5.12 Pig element representation

different type of sheep and the notable discovery of the hornless variety is significant as these are rare for this period. Where present at other sites, these animals have been shown to have been relatively large (eg Maltby 2010, 183).

Pigs

Body-part patterns

The survival and recovery of pig bones varied in terms of the relative abundance of different elements. Material from Phase 4 and 5 features was dominated by mandibles, a trait common in zooarchaeological assemblages owing to the robust character of these elements in pigs. Taking zones and body side into account, mandibles represented a minimum of six individuals in Phase 4 and nine in Phase 5. Comparison of the relative frequencies of different elements in terms of %MNE shows the very low proportion of other elements in comparison with mandibles (Fig. 5.12). Only humerus specimens from Phase 4 deposits registered greater than 40% MNE and just below that figure from Phase 5 deposits. Despite the low representation of post-cranial elements, most pig body parts were present in the assemblage from Phase 5 deposits at least.

Associated bone groups

Phase 4 pit 2264 contained the remains of at least two piglet skeletons that had become comingled following deposition but appear to have been deposited in articulation. All parts of the body were represented, and two individuals were recognised by the identification of two same-sided mandibles and 3rd and 4th metacarpals and metatarsals. Most elements were unfused, but both piglets were aged *c* 5–6 months based on the mandibles, which had the deciduous premolars in slight or medium wear, unworn 1st molars and 2nd molars just visible within the crypt. Some difference in size was noted

in the metapodials and several phalanges, and it is possible that more than two animals were represented amongst the piglet remains.

Butchery

Very few pig bones were found with butchery marks. These included a mandible from Phase 4 ditch 20599 (fill 20448) with a blade mark on medial/ventral side of the ramus, a mandible from phase 5 ditch 1502 (fill 623) that had been chopped through to expose the canine cavity, and a radius from Phase 5 ditch 20399 (fill 20236) with an oblique chop on the shaft.

Ageing

Too few pig post-cranial bones were present to provide reliable information on epiphyseal fusion. However, seven mandibles from Phase 4 deposits and 11 from Phase 5 deposits provided dental-wear data. The two groups were in marked contrast to each other as the cull pattern in the Phase 4 group generally included specimens from very young animals (Table 5.8). Two mandibles were from neonatal pigs and four were from animals that died in the first year, including the two piglets discussed above. Only one mandible was from a slightly older animal, having been culled before the end of its second year.

Table 5.8 Pig dental wear data (number of specimens per age group)

Stage	Estimated age	Phase 4	Phase 5
A	0–1 month	2	0
B	5–6 months	4	0
C	11–14 months	0	5
D	21–24 months	1	2
E	24–36 months	0	2
F	36 months +	0	0
G	6 years +	0	2

These data differ to that from the Phase 5 assemblage, which included no specimens at stage A or B, although post-cranial neonatal bones have been identified from this phase. Five mandibles were recorded at stage C and two each at stages D, E and G. This still represents a fairly intensive cull pattern, with the highest number being slaughtered towards the early part of their second year, but with more surviving into their third year and beyond. It seems unlikely that the difference in culling pattern represents a complete change in pig husbandry and/or slaughter strategy and is perhaps a recovery bias inherent in the small pig sample.

Pathology

A pig mandible from Phase 4a cleaning layer 20436 over surface 20042 had a 1st molar that had been severely impacted by the 4th premolar, which had grown into it because of overcrowding across the molar row. Such overcrowding is often caused by severe malnutrition in the early years of pig development, where teeth develop at a relatively normal rate while the growth of the mandible is stunted (Tonge and McCance 1973). The situation can often be rectified after the first year with proper feeding, but the fact this individual's situation had not improved by the time it died, around the end of its second year, suggests that it had long suffered from malnutrition.

Horses

Body parts

Remains from a minimum of three horses were recovered from Phase 4 deposits. Elements present in this phase included scapula, humerus, radius, metacarpal, calcaneus and metatarsal bones (Fig. 5.13). The Phase 5 assemblage comprised the remains from at least six horses, most commonly represented by the radius. Limb and scapula specimens were also relatively well represented, with

most comprising at least 50% MNE or more. Mandibles were poorly represented, owing to the high degree of fragmentation often occurring in these elements, while pelvis, calcaneus and astragalus bones were also poorly represented.

Associated bone groups

Two articulating groups of horse bones were identified, both from Phase 5 deposits (Table 5.3). These included an axis and thoracic vertebra found in Phase 5b ditch 1481, and 1st, 2nd and 3rd phalanges from a left foot that were found together in Phase 5c ditch 20597. Ditch 20597 also included horse fragments belonging to a left humerus, radius and ulna and right humerus and metacarpal. None of these were clearly articulated, but all may have derived from the same animal. No other horse bones were found in ditch 1481. No butchery marks were found on any of these remains.

Butchery

Butchery marks were recorded on nine horse specimens, all from Phase 5 deposits. Four specimens included cut marks, including a scapula with marks around the neck, a pelvis with a cut on the ridge of the acetabulum, a humerus with a cut on the humeral head and another at the proximal end of the shaft, and a metacarpal with a mark around the proximal end. The metacarpal is clearly indicative of skinning, but the others are all associated with disartiulation and possibly defleshing.

Three specimens had heavier marks possibly caused by a cleaver: an ulna with oblique chops on the medial side and front edge of the olecranon, a metacarpal that had been chopped through axially at the distal end, and a metatarsal that had numerous scoop marks along the medial side of the shaft.

Two specimens exhibited saw marks. Both of these were metapodials that had been sawn horizontally through the mid-shaft on a horizontal alignment. These specimens had clearly been earmarked for bone working.

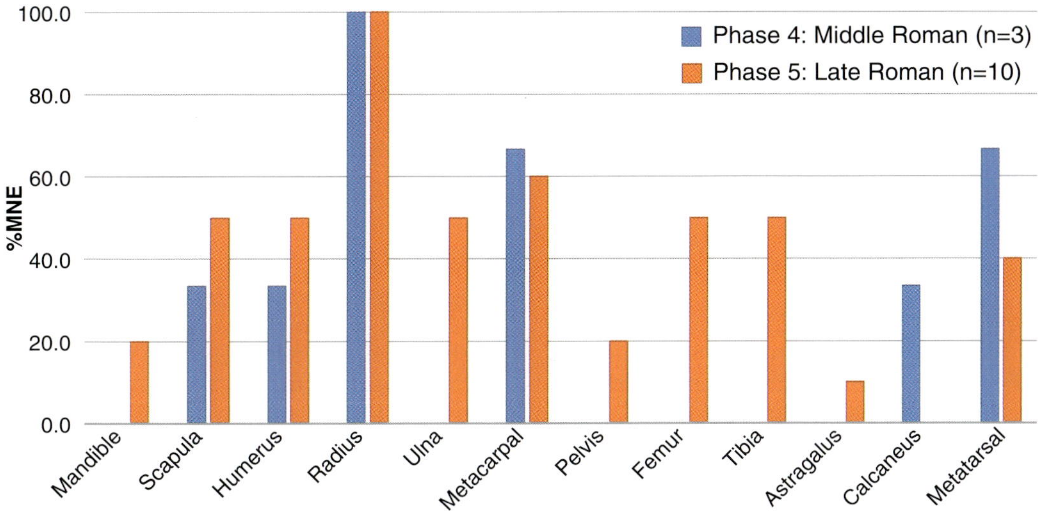

Fig. 5.13 Horse element representation

Table 5.9 Horse epiphyseal fusion data

Phase	Feature	Element	Proximal	Distal
4	Pit 20449	radius	n/a	unfused
5b	Ditch 20592	femur	unfused	n/a
5c	Ditch 20597	humerus	unfused	n/a
5a	Ditch 2513	metapodial	n/a	unfused
5c	Ditch 20603	radius	n/a	unfused
5a	Pit 1224	scapula	unfused	n/a
5c	Ditch 20498	tibia	n/a	unfused
5b	Ditch 20499	tibia	unfused	fused
5b	Ditch 20592	tibia	unfused	fused
5a	Ditch 454	ulna	unfused	n/a
5a	Pit 2129	ulna	unfused	n/a

Ageing

Most of the horse bones were from skeletally mature animals. However, several unfused specimens were found, almost exclusively from Phase 5 deposits (Table 5.9). The youngest specimen represented was a scapula with an unfused articulating surface from an animal no older than 9–12 months (Getty 1975, 272). Following this was an unfused distal metapodial and an unfused distal tibia, bones that mature at 10–18 months and *c* 24 months respectively. All the remaining eight unfused specimens could have derived from young horses up to 3.5 years old. Two specimens, a femur and a tibia, derived from the same fill of ditch 20592 and probably derived from the same animal. All the other specimens were recovered from different contexts and, although elements of one carcass could be distributed across multiple features, it seems likely that most derive from individual animals. The data suggest that foals may have formed a significant element of the local population, indicating nearby rearing and maintenance, if not on-site breeding of horses. A neonatal radius was identified as possibly deriving from a horse, although this could not be confirmed.

Pathology

A horse metacarpal from aisled Building 3 (Phase 5b) exhibited a lesion consistent with osteochondritis around the epiphyseal fusion point at the distal end. A probable horse femur from Phase 5c ditch 20498 exhibited eburnation around the distal condyle and extensive bony lumping on the posterior of the shaft above the condyles. This is suggestive of an advanced stage of osteoarthritis.

Size

Nine complete long bones provided withers' height estimations ranging between 1208.2mm and 1550.7mm (Fig. 5.14). These height data accord well with the heights estimated at Grove Airfield. Both assemblages included a small cluster of shorter horses with heights of around 1180–1240mm and a second cluster around 1300–1400mm. The lower end of this range concurs with the heights recorded

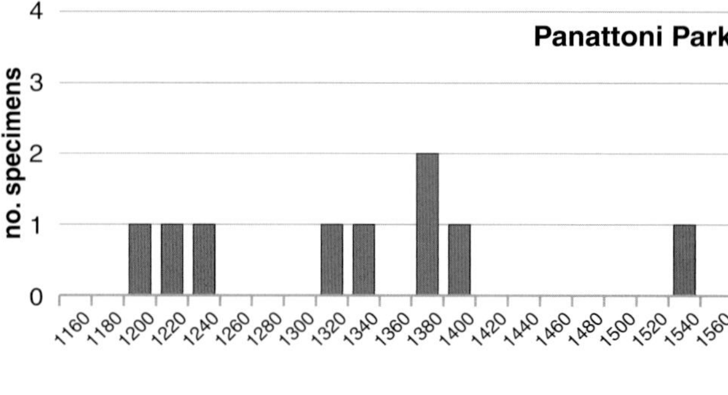

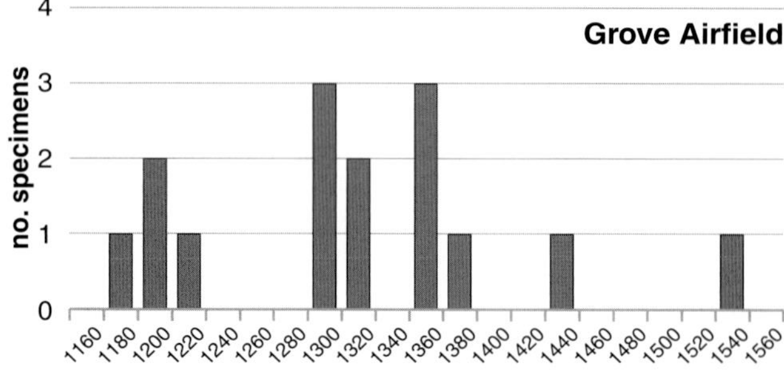

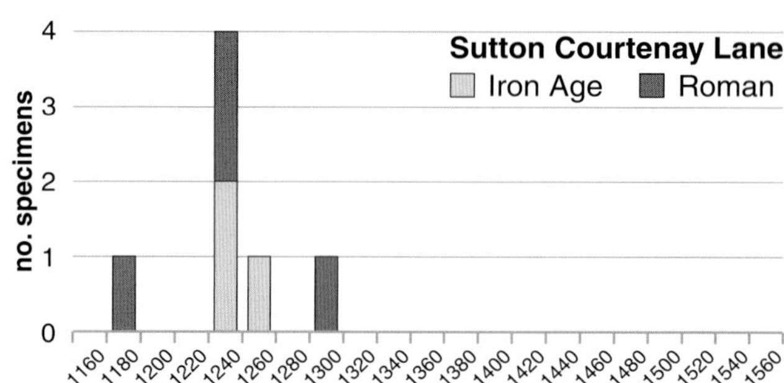

Fig. 5.14 Horse withers' height data

from Sutton Courtenay Lane which, although consisting of a smaller number of specimens, includes both Iron Age and Roman samples.

Examination of metacarpal lengths versus the distal breadths suggests that the horses there were similar in stature to those at Sutton Courtenay Lane, with larger horses more often found at Grove Airfield. The taller withers' heights at Panattoni Park all derive from calculations made on other elements (eg radii, tibiae and metatarsal bones), and this may have some influence on the results.

Dogs and foxes

Dog bones recovered from Phase 4 deposits were restricted to an ulna in ditch 81 and a 3rd metacarpal in ditch 937. From Phase 5 deposits, dog remains amounted to 60 bones from 15 features. Most included single or small numbers of dog specimens, but the majority of the remains belonged to two partially complete skeletons found in ditch 454 and ditch 863. The skeleton from ditch 863 was the more complete of the two, consisting of

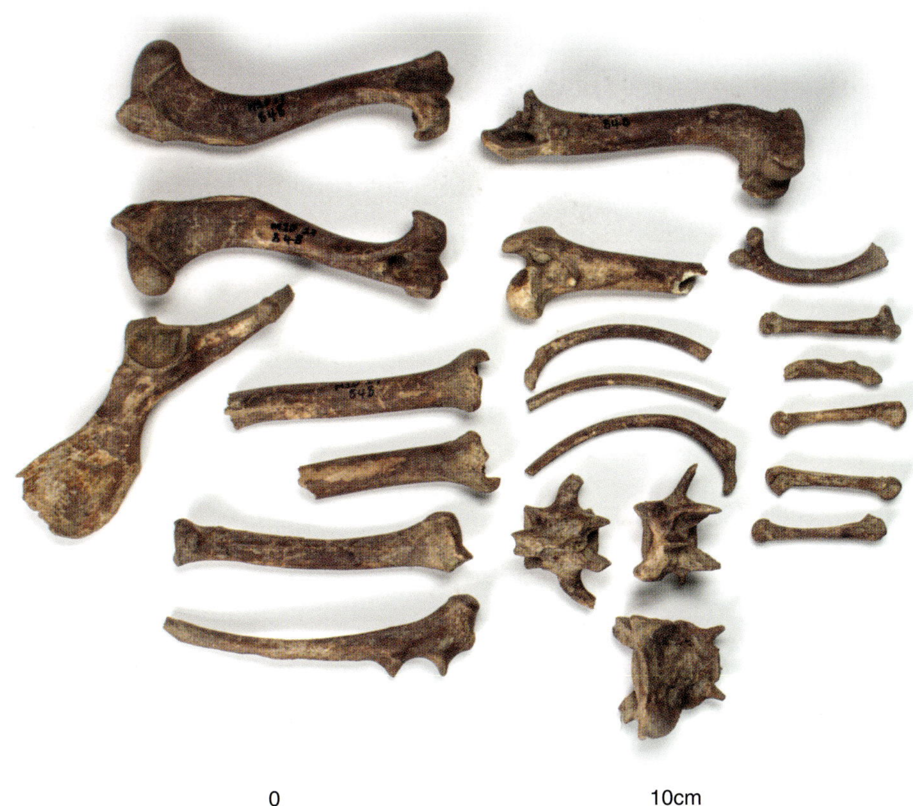

Fig. 5.15 Toy dog skeleton from ditch 863

most of the major limb bones as well as some foot
bones, ribs, pelvis and a fragment of one scapula
(Fig. 5.15). No sign of the skull was discovered
either in the form of cranial/mandible fragments or
teeth. The skeleton from ditch 454 consisted of
mandible fragments and elements of the right
forelimb: the humerus, radius, ulna and two
metacarpals (Fig. 5.16a).

All the bones were exceptionally small, although
each was from skeletally mature animals, and both
were of a 'miniature' type. The size and morphology of the bones in each skeleton were very
similar and all the humeri had a notable curvature.
Withers' heights were calculated as 270.9mm from
the humerus of the ditch 454 individual and
245.4mm and 288.8mm from radius and humerus
respectively from the ditch 863 individual. These
compare to four dog heights estimated from the
Roman assemblage at Grove Airfield that ranged
between 417.9–586.9mm and one dog at 440.9mm
from Sutton Courtenay Lane (OA 2021a; 2021b).
Although ancient dog types cannot be directly
attributed to modern dog breeds, these shoulder
heights compare best with modern Scottish terriers
and Cairn terriers, and these Roman dogs have
clearly resulted from intensive breeding. A radius
and ulna from a miniature dog were also recovered
during the evaluation (MOLA 2015c, 57).

Few other dog specimens were available for
measurement. However, several bones from ditch
398 were notably large and robust. These included

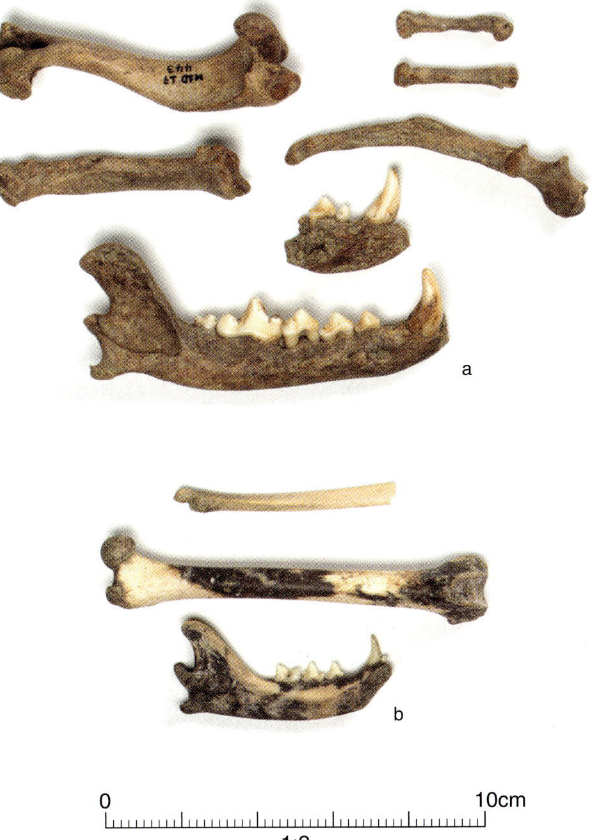

*Fig. 5.16 a) Toy dog bones from ditch 454; b) cat bones
from ditch 20590*

ulna and radius specimens and a tibia with extensive muscle ridges on the posterior side. One of the ulna fragments also exhibited a possible cut mark on the shaft, synonymous with skinning. The presence of two fox right-sided tibiae in this feature perhaps raises the possibility that the large and robust bones were from a wolf. However, this cannot be confirmed without further scientific analysis (eg mDNA). The fox tibiae were identified on morphological grounds as distinct from domestic dogs using Johnson's (2016) criteria. One provided an estimated withers height of 414.9mm, and thus was significantly taller than the two miniature dogs discussed above.

Cats

A complete and skeletally mature cat tibia was recovered from Phase 5a ditch 398. Three cat bones, a mandible, an ulna and a femur, were recovered from Phase 5c ditch 20590 (Fig. 5.16b). The mandible and femur were both complete, while the ulna was represented by the distal end of the shaft. These bones had a fresher appearance compared to the other bones in this context. It is possible that this indicates an intrusive element in the feature, or that it was buried very rapidly and lay fairly undisturbed. No butchery marks were noted on any of the cat bones.

Deer

Red deer was represented by 31 specimens, including five antler fragments and one radius from Phase 4 deposits, plus 12 antler fragments and 13 skull and post-cranial fragments from Phase 5 features.

The Phase 4 antler remains derived from ditches 2495 and 2490. All exhibited saw marks, with those from 2495 representing off-cuts, while the fragment from 2490 was a shed burr that had been sawn across the beam and the first tine. A proximal radius was recovered from Phase 4 ditch 20398. This was fused at the proximal end and showed no sign of butchery.

The Phase 5 antler fragments derived from ditches 960, 20396, 20561, 20597 and 20601. Five of the 12 had been sawn, with one shed example from ditch 20396 sawn close to the base to remove the main beam. However, it is clear from several other specimens that antler from hunted animals was also being exploited. Skull fragments from ditches 607, 20561 and 20597 all included saw marks on surviving antlers. One had been sawn through just above the burr with skinning marks also appearing around the pedicle. Except for a 1st phalanx from ditch 20603 and an upper molar from corndryer 2039, all the other elements were metacarpals and metatarsals from skeletally mature animals. These were recovered from ditch 398, 2487, 4384, 20348, 20396 and 20603, and aisled Building 3.

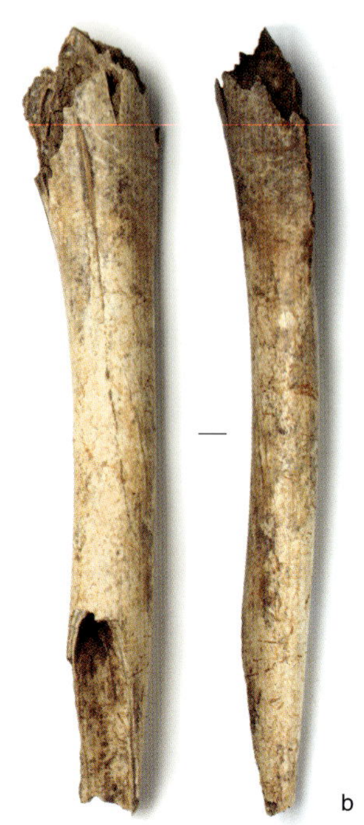

Fig. 5.17 a) Fallow deer antler from ditch 339;
b) common crane humerus from ditch 1095

Three roe deer specimens were all antler fragments recovered via environmental sieving from Phase 5c ditch 20603. One of these had been shed, while another may have been smoothed deliberately on the tine.

Fallow deer were represented by three antler specimens: two tines and a beam fragment recovered from ditch 339. The specimens are fragmentary and have been sawn on the beam in two places (Fig. 5.17a). These are the only clear evidence of fallow deer remains from the site, but there were four antler fragments from ditch 20604, all from the same antler, one of which was quite flat and had a surface texture that may have been fallow or red deer.

Birds

As noted above, bird bones were relatively well represented in Phase 4 and 5 features, in addition to which an owl bone was recovered during the evaluation (MOLA 2015c, 15). Most of the Phase 4 material could not be identified to species and much of it was recovered from sieved samples taken from layer 1001 and pits 1038, 1045, 1430 and 1433. Several of these specimens showed signs of burning, and were either grey or calcined to a white colour. Three specimens were also noted as being from juvenile birds, possibly chickens. These were accompanied by four certain chicken bones from layer 1001, pit 1045 and pit 1437.

Phase 5 features produced a wider range of identified bird species. Chicken bones were recovered from ditches 259, 1095, 1481, 2188 and 20499, and pit 227. These consisted of a range of elements, including humerus, ulna, femur and tarsometatarsus bones. All were skeletally mature except for the ulna from ditch 2188, which derived from a juvenile bird. Two duck bones, both identified as mallards, belonged to this phase: a tibiotarsus from pit 227 and a tarsometatarsus from ditch 20597. A woodcock femur was identified from pit 227, while a common crane humerus was recovered from ditch 1095 (fill 1200). The crane humerus consisted predominantly of the shaft and, although the ends were missing, the specimen was identified by the long and distinctive muscle ridge that appears down the front of the shaft (Fig. 5.17b). A carpometacarpus was tentatively identified as common crane. This specimen, from ditch 401, was only represented by the shaft, but its size and morphology otherwise matched well with crane (cf Cohen and Serjeantson 1996). Corvid bones were represented by two, possibly three, specimens. Raven humerus and radius bones, probably from the same bird, were recovered from ditch 20581. The humerus was complete, while the radius featured only the proximal half. Slightly unusually, the bones derived from the opposite sides of the body. The distal end of a possible raven tarsometatarsal bone was also recovered from ditch 20348.

Discussion

Livestock husbandry

Given the lack of suitable sample sizes from pre-Roman and early Roman phased deposits, it is difficult to examine changes and continuity in livestock husbandry practices over time. Bone fragment counts suggest that cattle were the dominant livestock in each phase, and similar percentages were apparent in terms of the minimum numbers of animals recorded from middle and later Roman deposits. Continuity in cattle exploitation at the site may be attributed to several factors, such as the good availability of local grazing, generational cattle farming within the local community, and the economic advantages of keeping cattle. High proportions of cattle have been found in faunal assemblages recovered from other local Romano-British sites, such as at Pineham Lodge, Upton (Northamptonshire Archaeology 2007) and Piddington (Friendship-Taylor and Friendship-Taylor 2013). Although there are few contemporary local sites with good faunal assemblages, cattle tend to be the most common livestock identified, and this appears to fit a regional pattern, particularly in the later Roman period in the Great Ouse hinterland (cf Allen 2017a, 94–5).

Biometric analyses of cattle bones have indicated that a mixed group of cows and bulls are present in the assemblage. This appears to differ from some other Romano-British rural settlements where a dominance of either bulls or cows was apparent, such as at Grove Airfield and Sutton Courtenay Lane, Oxfordshire, respectively (OA 2021a; 2021b). The mixed sex signature at Panattoni Park suggests the importance of both males and females in the local economy, while in contrast there may have been a focus on dairying at Sutton Courtenay Lane and plough cattle at Grove Airfield, reflecting differing economic concerns. Ageing data indicate a fairly even cull pattern for cattle during the later Roman period with little difference between Phases 4 and 5 and no clear focus on a particular age group. This would suggest a mixed husbandry strategy with breeding, dairying and plough requirements perhaps all being of local importance. This is quite similar to the cattle ageing data from Pineham Lodge, Upton, and perhaps suggests a similar strategy to that site (Northamptonshire Archaeology 2007).

The presence of two sheep types is of interest, with the discovery of a hornless sheep skull from a late Roman feature being of some significance. Most sheep in Iron Age and Roman Britain are thought to have been horned, while hornless sheep are much rarer (Allen 2017a, 99). This may be in part due to the fragmentation of sheep skulls, making it difficult to identify specimens lacking horns. However, if hornless sheep were a prominent type during this period, we should expect them to have been more commonly recognised in zooarchaeological assemblages. Examples have been identified at Winchester, Hampshire, from early and late Roman deposits and in late Roman deposits at Owslebury, Hampshire (Maltby 2010, 181–3), as well as from Springhead, Kent (Grimm and Worley 2011, 28, 35, 46). The identification of a horncore from an especially robust individual may also reflect variation in local breeds, and perhaps the fact that some sheep were being imported from flocks managed in the wider hinterland or even beyond.

Although pig bones were generally rare compared to cattle and sheep, the presence of young animals such as the two piglet skeletons found in Phase 4 pit 2264, as well as neonatal bones in middle and late Roman phases, suggest local breeding and rearing for pork. Pig ageing data varied between Phases 4 and 5, but this is probably a product of the small sample size. The presence of mainly young pigs indicates a fairly intensive culling pattern common to most Romano-British rural assemblages (Allen 2017a, 118–19). Villa sites tend to produce neonatal pig bones more often than other settlement types, perhaps suggesting local specialised production or the purchase of suckling pigs from market (ibid., 119). Pig bones were found in high quantities at Piddington, increasing from 17% in the middle Roman phase to 30% in the late Roman phase and including high numbers of immature bones in these phases, suggesting intensive pig production and consumption by the villa inhabitants (Friendship-Taylor and Friendship-Taylor 2013). An assemblage of *c* 150 foetal and juvenile pig bones was recovered via environmental sieving at Stanwick villa, Northamptonshire (English Heritage 1995). These were not fully analysed but again suggest fairly intensive breeding at a local high-status site. We have little understanding of living conditions for pigs at Romano-British sites, but at Panattoni Park the presence of a mandible from an animal little older than two years old with a heavily impacted 1st molar (caused by the surrounding bone growing much slower than the teeth) suggests that this individual was very malnourished by the time it died. Such evidence perhaps suggests that pigs were living off scraps within the settlement and were not necessarily well kept.

Horse bones were present in middle and late Roman deposits, increasing in frequency in the later phase. The presence of foal bones in Phase 5 deposits points to local horse breeding. One neonatal radius was tentatively identified as horse, while an undeveloped scapula derived from a foal less than a year old, and a distal tibia and metapodials indicated animals less than two years old. Juvenile horse bones are being increasingly recognised on Romano-British rural settlements, particularly at high-status sites such as Stanwick, Northamptonshire (English Heritage 1995). Horse breeding in the Roman period is likely to have been a specialised activity, undertaken by those with the resources and skills to do so (Allen 2017a, 126).

Some variation in horse heights was noted in the assemblage, with some individuals standing *c* 1210–40mm tall and another group standing *c* 1320–1400mm, plus an outlier standing at *c* 1550mm tall. Iron Age horses are often found to have been shorter than 1300mm, while Romano-British horses tended to stand between 1300mm and 1400mm, although examples outside this range are not unusual (ibid., 129). At Roman Winchester, horses generally stood between *c* 1160mm and 1500mm, with taller stock becoming more common following the 2nd century AD (Maltby 2010, 211–12), while horses standing between 1400–1500mm were also identified at Roman Lincoln from a fairly early date, and it has been suggested that these represent imported stock (Dobney *et al*. 1996, 46, 124). Horses standing over 1500mm are much rarer. Examples of animals around the 1550mm mark have been identi-

fied at Haddon, Cambridgeshire (Baxter 2003) and at Grove Airfield (OA 2021b). The Grove Airfield example was estimated from a metacarpal and was argued to represent a gelding, a horse or mule that had been castrated early in life for work purposes (ibid.). Castration has the effect of prolonging the maturation of long bones and allows them to grow longer, potentially producing taller animals. Not only was the Grove Airfield specimen from a notably tall animal, but analysis of its shape showed that it was significantly more slender than all the other horses from the site; in other words, it had grown much taller but had not become correspondingly broader. This could suggest the effects of gelding and/or an animal that was from a different breeding group. The specimen that suggested a height of 1550mm in the Panattoni Park assemblage was a metatarsal and therefore could not be directly compared with the Grove Airfield data in terms of its shape. Nonetheless, the presence of a notably taller horse is significant and adds new information about the presence of such animals in Roman Britain.

Carcass exploitation

Body-part data suggest that livestock carcasses were being processed on site, with most elements being present to some degree. Butchery marks, however, were fairly uncommon, being mostly present on cattle from middle and later Roman features; information on carcass processing was not forthcoming for the earlier material. Some evidence for the use of meat cleavers – an implement fairly commonly used at Romano-British urban and military sites (Maltby 2007) – was identified in the middle and late Roman phases. There is increasing evidence that cleaver butchery was employed at rural sites to a small degree, but rarely was it accompanied by large-scale processing as has been identified at Roman towns (Allen 2017a, 120–1).

Horse bones were rarely found in articulation, as is often the case on Romano-British sites, and it would appear from several butchered specimens that horse carcasses were being processed on site in the later Roman period, particularly in Phase 5. Butchery marks demonstrate that horses were being skinned, with the skins possibly being processed further into hides. Cut and chop marks on other bones indicate that carcasses were being dissected, with some signs of defleshing suggesting the consumption of horse meat. Horse-meat consumption is not widely recognised at Romano-British sites, but evidence is increasing that it may have occurred more often than was previously thought (ibid., 128).

Saw marks on metapodials also demonstrate that horse foot bones were used as raw material for bone working, and this evidence should be seen alongside the evidence for antler working. Although not found in huge numbers, sawn antler fragments were common enough to suggest that local bone and antler working was reasonably important at the site. Substantial deposits of worked bone and antler waste is rare at rural sites and is a much more common occurrence at urban sites (eg Maltby 2010, 218–19; Rees *et al.* 2008, 64–6). The presence of bone- and antler-working waste at Panattoni Park suggests a degree of craftworking specialisation at the site.

Ritual

Evidence for possible ritual practices involving animals has been found in features associated with Building 1320. A concentration of burnt animal bones, notably from two features near this building, may be of significance. These include a total of 236 heavily burnt bones (predominantly of a white or grey colour indicating the high temperature and period of exposure to fire) recovered from Phase 4 layer 1001 and from the middle fill (1047) of pit 1045, along with more burnt material from layer 558, which overlay wall 1074 of Building 1320, and the fills of pits 1036, 1038, 1430, 1433 1437 and 1440. Much of this burnt material could not be identified to species, apart from a few pig bones in pit 1045 that appear to represent the cremated remains of a piglet. Burnt cattle and bird bones were recovered from layer 1001, probably representing debris from carcass burning that did not become deposited in a discrete feature such as a pit.

The placement of animal carcasses or body parts on pyres to accompany human cremations is well known from Roman Britain (Worley 2008; Allen 2018c). Burnt remains interpreted as offerings at Romano-British temples and shrines are less common (King 2005; Allen 2018b), but recent work at Charlwood, Surrey, and Ashwell, Hertfordshire, has recovered notable deposits of burnt animal remains not associated with human burials. Excavations at these sites have suggested the presence of open-air ceremonial sites, rather than rituals focussed in or around buildings (Rainsford *et al.* 2021). Sites with burnt animal remains associated with Romano-British temples include Wanborough, Surrey, the Verulamium 'Triangular Temple', Hertfordshire, and Tabard Square, Southwark (ibid., 194). The evidence of burnt animal remains at Panattoni Park may now be reasonably added to this list in relation to Building 1320.

Further evidence of ritual activity in pit 1045 came in the form of a calf skeleton discovered in the bottom fill (1046), below the concentration of burnt remains found in the middle fill. The relationship between the skeleton and the burnt remains would suggest a structured element to the deposits, with the burnt bones being placed over the top of the calf. Also within this feature group was pit 1435, which contained the articulated remains of a new-born calf. Given the ritual character of the archaeology in this area, the calf burial should also be seen in this context and perhaps represents an animal sacrifice. Structured or placed deposits are typically

found at Romano-British shrines, although the character of the features and associated finds encountered can vary considerably from site to site (Smith 2018a, 121–3). It is possible that the calf burials were an act of votive deposition; King (2005, 359) suggests that some complete or partially articulated animal remains found at Romano-British ritual sites were buried as personal offerings and/or sacrifices. The cremation burial of the piglet could have accompanied such an act. Elsewhere, the presence of two comingled piglet skeletons in pit 2264, and perhaps the neonatal sheep bone found in this feature, may also have been the result of ritualised practise, although no burnt remains were found in this pit.

The discovery of sawn fallow deer antler in ditch 339 may also represent ritual activity. Fallow deer are non-native to Britain and bones of this species are restricted to only a handful of Romano-British sites (Allen 2018a, 99–101; Sykes 2010). The presence of only antler at Panattoni Park does not discount the presence of live animals but it does not provide clear evidence for them, since the antler could easily have been imported (eg Sykes 2010, 53–5). There is historical evidence that fallow deer antlers were used in ritual practices during the Roman period, often being shaved and burnt to produce a distinctive smell, and they were thought to hold healing powers (Allen 2018a, 100). The placement of the fallow deer antler in ditch 339 locates them close to Building 1320 and the associated structured deposits discussed above. While it is possible that the sawn fallow deer antler may simply have been off-cuts from raw material, much like the red deer antler found on site, the fact that this was an item from a probably imported and highly valued animal in this period suggests a greater significance.

Lifestyle and status

Several characteristics of the faunal assemblage point towards local high-status activities. The discovery of two miniature dogs in ditches 454 and 863 is of interest, and the appearance of so-called 'lap' dogs in Roman Britain is often cited as evidence for the intensive breeding and/or importing of specific dog breeds in this period (eg Clutton-Brock 1999, 60). Discoveries of very small dogs have been made at several contemporary rural settlements, including Camp Ground (Higbee 2013) and Longstanton site XX (Evans *et al.* 2006) in Cambridgeshire, and Dicket Mead in Hertfordshire (Rook 1986). These sources refer to the dogs as pets; the possibility that these were working dogs, such as ratters, must remain a possibility, although the two are not necessarily mutually exclusive. Some small dogs have been found deposited in fairly elaborate burial rites or in possible ritual contexts, such as two cremated dogs placed in a shaft at Keston villa, Kent (Fox 1967; Philp *et al.* 1999). No evidence for such ritual beyond the deliberate burial of the dogs is evident at Panattoni Park; however, their recovery in articulation suggests careful placement, perhaps signifying their value to the occupants. The presence of several cat bones in Phase 5 deposits, found in association with each other, if not articulated, suggests that felines may also have been regarded as pets at the villa in this period.

The discovery of deer bones in a reasonable quantity is suggestive of hunting. Wild animal bones rarely occur in sizable numbers on Romano-British sites, and where they do, they tend to be at high-status settlements such as villas or military establishments (Allen 2014; 2018a; Allen and Sykes 2011). There is also evidence that red deer were more commonly hunted in the later Roman period, possibly a reflection of increasing landscape exploitation by high-status groups in the 3rd and 4th centuries AD (Allen 2018a, 104). The discovery of wildfowl remains, notably the presence of common crane, may also be seen in this context (ibid. 109–11). Bones of common cranes have been found at several high-status sites in Roman Britain, including Fishbourne (Allen 2009) and the Tribune's House at Caerleon, where they were recovered in association with bones of red and roe deer, hare and wild boar (Hamilton-Dyer 1993, 133). Together, the wild animal remains provide hints of high-status activity such as hunting and wildfowling, and the addition of venison, duck and crane meat to the dining table suggests more elite tastes.

CHARRED PLANT REMAINS *by Julia Meen*

A total of 50 bulk sediment samples from the site were taken for the recovery of charred plant remains (CPR). The samples were processed using a modified Siraf-style flotation machine, with smaller samples (less than 5 litres in volume) floated by hand using the 'wash-over' technique. Flots were collected onto 250μm meshes and the heavy residues were sieved to 500μm, after which both flots and residues were dried in a heated room. The residues were sorted by eye for artefacts and ecofactual remains. Each flot was then assessed to characterise the nature and condition of charred remains and to identify those samples which had potential to yield significant data that could further the understanding of the site.

Charred plant remains were extracted from each of the 19 samples selected for CPR analysis using a low-power binocular microscope at up to x40 magnification. Several of the samples included highly abundant chaff fragments, necessitating the use of a riffle box to reduce the proportion of the flot that was sorted. For sample 2006, from corndrying oven 2050, and sample 2028, from pit 2129, 25% of the <1mm flot fraction was sorted and the results given include a multiplication by four of the items extracted from that fraction. For sample 2040, from corndrying oven 2323, the whole of the flot was subdivided and the figures provided are from sorting 25% of the whole flot. Remains were identified by comparison with the both the author's own modern comparative seed collection and the collection held at Oxford Archaeology South, and with reference to published guides (eg Cappers *et al.* 2006). Nomenclature for the plant remains follows Stace (2010). Results are shown in Tables 5.10 and 5.11.

Late Iron Age/early Roman settlement in Areas 1 and 5

Significant charred assemblages were recovered from two features associated with the late Iron Age complex that extended across Areas 1 and 5. These are from ditch 1469, which formed part of the boundary of the complex in Area 1 (sample 1), and from pit 671 (sample 10) in the same area.

Although samples from the ditch and the pit contained similar charred remains in terms of cereal taxa, the proportions of the various components are markedly different. The assemblage from ditch 1469 is rich in cereal grain, mostly wheat (*Triticum* sp.) with a little barley (*Hordeum vulgare*), while cereal chaff is rare. In contrast, grain is relatively sparse in the sample from pit 671 and is more evenly split between wheat and barley, while seeds of other plants are very abundant. These include several seeds of flax (*Linum usitatissimum*), which can be cultivated both for fibre (linen) and as an oil crop. In comparison to cereals, which are routinely, albeit accidentally, charred during processing and are generally common on sites of this period, crops such as flax are less frequently preserved archaeologically. However, flax seeds are commonly found in small numbers on sites of this date, and the cultivation of this versatile crop was likely to have been widespread.

Little chaff is present in the sample from pit 671, but notably there are several rachis segments of a free-threshing wheat, some of which are sufficiently well preserved to be identified as bread wheat (*Triticum aestivum*). By the Roman period spelt (*Triticum spelta*) was the dominant type of wheat cultivated in Britain, but a recent synthesis found that free-threshing wheat has been found on almost 30% of late Iron Age/early Roman sites (Lodwick 2017a, 16–17), albeit in small quantities.

Both samples are rich in grass seeds, especially those of meadow grasses/cat's-tails (Poaceae). There are numerous grass stems and root fragments, including swollen basal internodes of onion couch grass (*Arrhenatherum elatius* var. *bulbosum*) in the sample from ditch 1469. Many seed heads of rush (*Juncus* sp.) survived in pit 671, with the abundant tiny seeds they contain fused together during charring. Other abundant seeds include stinking chamomile (*Anthemis cotula*), fat hen (*Chenopodium album*) and common chickweed (*Stellaria media*), small seeds which are produced in large numbers and held densely in seed heads until ripening. Together, these remains are indicative of the uprooting of grasses and whole weed plants, and the burning of these stems perhaps as tinder. This material is delicate and would be quickly consumed in a fire, so that more robust items, such as seeds and grass culm nodes, would be preferentially preserved. The high number of nitrogen-fixing leguminous seeds, both vetches and clovers (*Vicia*/*Lathyrus* and *Trifolium* type), may be a sign of low soil fertility.

Middle to late Roman enclosure complex in Area 1

The middle to late Roman period saw the development of a new enclosure complex, associated with the villa that lies to the north of Area 1, while the previous complex was abandoned. While charred plant remains were generally sparse, two pits contained notable finds: several fruits of beet (*Beta vulgaris*) from pit 1045, and a charred scale of stone pine (*Pinus picea*) from pit 1437.

Although beet is native to Britain, Northamptonshire lies outside its usual coastal range, and the fact that it is charred further strengthens the case for this being a cultivar. Van der Veen *et al.* (2008; 21, 27–8) list beet amongst the crops newly cultivated in the Roman period and note that, although it is never particularly common, it increases in frequency as the Roman period progresses. Carruthers and Hunter-Dowse (2019) suggest that the number of beet records from the Midlands suggest the plant was widely cultivated in the region in the Roman period. It was not until the medieval period that the root of beet was specifically cultivated (Prance and Nesbitt 2005, 73) and so Roman finds must reflect its use as a leafy vegetable. Seeds of beet were also recovered from a middle Roman waterlogged pit at Berryfields, Buckinghamshire (Meen 2019) which contained other artefacts suggestive of ritual deposition.

The pit in which the cone scale of stone pine was discovered was located close to the temple/mausoleum. Although stone pine is not native to Britain, remains of its cones have been found on numerous Romano British sites, often at religious sites (Carruthers and Hunter Dowse 2019). Lodwick (2017b) has recently discussed the significance of pine nut in Roman ritual practices. It is thought that the cones may have been imported to be used as altar fuel (Godwin 1984, 110), but the growing number of discoveries has fed an argument for the trees themselves having been planted in southern Britain to meet this demand (Carruthers and Hunter Dowse 2019). Imported seeds can and do grow healthily in the British climate: a planted cone has successfully matured at the OA offices in Oxford, the tree producing the modern examples shown in Figure 5.18.

Neither of the samples from oven 1247 (samples 19 and 20) are particularly rich in charred plant remains but both include grain, with both wheat and barley present. A high number of detached grain embryos (a structure on the lateral surface of a seed from which the germinating shoot emerges) were recovered from sample 20. Embryos often become detached from cereal grains when the grain has already started to germinate, and in this case the detachment may be a result of damp growing conditions or poor storage.

Middle to late Roman crop-processing area in Area 2

The excavation of four corndrying ovens and a paved surface thought to be a threshing/malting floor led to the hypothesis that this represented a dedicated crop-processing area. The area was extensively sampled to investigate the nature of this activity (Fig. 5.19). Assessment of 19 samples

Fig. 5.18 Cone from a stone pine grown at the OA offices in Oxford

Table 5.10 Charred plant remains from Area 1

			Phase	3		4		5	
			Date	Late Iron Age/ early Roman		Middle Roman		Late Roman	
			Feature	Ditch 1469	Pit 671	Pit 1045	Pit 1437	Kiln/ hearth 1247 stokehole	Kiln/ hearth 1247 flue
			Sample no.	1	10	15	39	19	20
			Context no.	106	711	1047	1438	1134	1133
			Flot vol.	150ml	35ml	650ml	450ml	200ml	5ml
			Sample vol.	40L	24L	20L	10L	30L	6L
Triticum sp.	wheat	grain		752	68	100	4	52	50
Triticum sp.	wheat	tail grain			1			3	
cf *Triticum* sp.	cf wheat	grain						11	4
Hordeum vulgare	barley	grain		53	52			29	4
cf *Hordeum vulgare*	cf barley	grain				3		7	2
Secale cereale	rye	grain						1	
Avena sp.	oat	seed		3	19	1			
Avena/Bromus	oat/brome	seed		22	20	8	1	6	2
Cereale	indet cereal	grain		166	132	24	10	29	27
Cereale	indet cereal	grain fragment		602	203	114	66	394	25
Triticum spelta	spelt wheat	glume base		5	10	28	11	2	
Triticum spelta	spelt wheat	spikelet fork			1	1			
Triticum dicoccum/spelta	glume wheat	glume base		13		26	14	13	
Triticum dicoccum/spelta	glume wheat	spikelet fork		4		10		1	
Triticum aestivum	bread wheat	rachis node			4				
Triticum aestivum/turgidum	free-threshing wheat	rachis node			12				
Triticum aestivum/turgidum	free-threshing wheat	rachis internode			11				
Triticum sp.	wheat	spikelet fork			4				
Triticum sp.	wheat	glume base			52				
Hordeum vulgare	barley	rachis node			20			1F	
Hordeum vulgare	barley	rachis		1	4				
Avena sp.	oat	floret base fragment			1				
Avena sp.	oat	awn fragment		38	25	1	3	2	
Cereale	indet cereal	detached embryo		13	55	1		70	
Cereale	indet cereal	detached coleoptile		8				8	
Cereale/Poaceae	indet cereal/grass	culm fragment			17			14	
Cereale	indet cereal	culm node		1	4				
Pinus pinea	stone pine	cone scale					1		
Papaver sp.	poppy	seed			8			1	
Ranunculus acris/repens/ bulbosus	meadow/creeping/ bulbous buttercup				7	3			
cf *Ranunculus*	cf buttercup	seed						1	
Pisum/Vicia/Lathyrus	pea/vetch/tare	seed		13					
Vicia/Lathyrus	vetch/tare (2mm)	seed		75	110	22	4	5	
Trifolium/Medicago/Melilotus	clover/medick/ melilot	seed		12	25	7	13	9	
Crataegus monogyna Jacq.	hawthorn	stone				3			
cf *Crataegus monogyna* Jacq.	cf hawthorn	stone fragments				1			
Urtica dioica L.	common nettle	seed			5				
Urtica urens L.	small nettle				3				
Corylus avellana L.	hazel	nutshell fragment		1		8			
Linum usitatissimum L.	flax	seed			8				
cf *Linum usitatissimum* L.	cf flax	seed		1	2F				
Linum catharticum L.	fairy flax	seed			1	1			
Linum sp.	flax	seed						1	
Brassica sp.	cabbages	seed		1					
Raphanus raphanistrum L.	wild radish	seed capsule fragment			1			1	
Thlaspi arvense L.	field penny-cress	seed			6				
Persicaria lapthifolia/maculosa	pale persicaria/redshank	seed		3					
Persicaria cf *hydropiper*	cf water-pepper	seed		1					

Table 5.10 continued

			Ditch 1469	Pit 671	Pit 1045	Pit 1437	Kiln/hearth 1247 stokehole	Kiln/hearth 1247 flue
Phase			3	3	4	4	5	5
Date			Late Iron Age/early Roman	Late Iron Age/early Roman	Middle Roman	Middle Roman	Late Roman	Late Roman
Sample no.			1	10	15	39	19	20
Context no.			106	711	1047	1438	1134	1133
Flot vol.			150ml	35ml	650ml	450ml	200ml	5ml
Sample vol.			40L	24L	20L	10L	30L	6L
Persicaria sp.	knotweed	seed		2				
Polygonum aviculare L.	knotgrass	seed	6	33				
Fallopia convolvulus (L.) A. Love	black-bindweed	seed	2	9				
Rumex sp.	dock	seed	12	70	5	40		
Stellaria media (L.) Vill.	common chickweed	seed	6	131	1			
cf *Stellaria media* (L.) Vill.	cf common chickweed	seed		19			2	
Stellaria cf *graminea* L.	cf lesser stitchwort	seed					1	
Stellaria sp.	stitchwort	seed	4			2		
Agrostemma githago L.	corncockle	seed		5				
Agrostemma githago L.	corncockle	calyx fragment	1			1		
Chenopodium sp.	goosefoot	seed	42		2	1	16	
Chenopodium album L.	fat hen	seed	12	>500	2	2		
Atriplex sp.	orache	seed	2	18				
Beta vulgaris L.	beet	seed			6 + 6F			
Hyoscyamus niger L.	henbane	seed				1		
Montia fontana L.	blinks	seed	13	5				
Galium sp.	bedstraws	seed	1	11			1	
Galium aparine L.	cleavers	seed	10	12				
Veronica hederifolia L.	ivy-leaved speedwell	seed		1				
Plantago major L.	greater plantain	seed	1	5				
Plantago media L.	hoary plantain	seed		7				
Plantago lanceolata L.	ribwort plantain	seed		4			2	
Euphrasia/Odontites	eyebright/bartsia	seed	5	13				
cf *Menyanthes trifoliata* L.	cf bogbean	seed		1				
Asteraceae	daisy Family	seed	1	2				
Centaurea sp.	knapweed	seed		1		1		
Anthemis cotula L.	stinking chamomile	seed					1	
Tripleurospermum sp.	mayweed	seed	16	417	1			
cf *Tripleurospermum* sp.	cf mayweed	seed	6	65				
Valerianella dentata (L.) Pollich	narrow-fruited cornsalad	seed		3				
Juncus sp.	rush	seed	2					
Juncus sp.	rush	seed head		47				
cf *Juncus*	cf rush	possible seed heads		8				
Eleocharis sp.	spike-rush	seed		1				
Carex sp.	sedge	seed		30		4		
Poa/Phleum	meadow-grass/cat's-tail	seed	47	734			8	
Lolium type	rye-grass	seed	2	6	24		2	
Bromus sp.	brome	seed	5	8				
Arrhenatherum elatius Var. *bulbosum* (Willd.) St-Amans	onion couch	swollen basal internode	3					
Poaceae	grass (small)	seed	19	130	6	33	2	
cf Poaceae	cf grass (small)	seed						5
Poaceae	grass (medium)	seed	17	51	34	3		
Poaceae	grass (large)	seed	17	15	6			5
Poaceae	grass	culm fragments	94	28		11		
Indet.	root fragment		63		3	2	34	
Indet.	seed			37		2		
Indet.	shell fragments				11		12	

F = Fragment

Table 5.11 Charred plant remains from the crop-processing area

			Phase	4		5	
			Date	Middle Roman		Late Roman	
			Feature	Corndryer 2050		Corndryer 2039	
			Sample no.	2006	2008	2010	2019
			Context no.	2046	2048	2079	2161
			Flot vol.	200ml	15ml	20ml	15ml
			Sample vol.	15L	7L	30L	10L
Triticum sp.	wheat	grain		305	89	50	63
Triticum sp.	wheat	germinated grain		21	3	2	
Triticum sp.	wheat	tail grain		71	3	3	13
cf *Triticum* sp.	cf wheat	grain					
Hordeum vulgare	barley	grain		42		39	4
Hordeum vulgare	barley	germinated grain		19			
cf *Hordeum vulgare*	cf barley	grain					
cf *Hordeum vulgare*	cf barley	germinated grain			1		
Secale cereale	rye	grain		1			
Secale cereale	rye	germinated grain		7			
Avena sp.	oat	seed		8	1	2	2
Avena sp.	oat	germinated seed		6			
Avena/Bromus	oat/brome	seed		41	5	11	14
Avena/Bromus	oat/brome	germinated seed					
Cereale	indet cereal	grain		292	31	39	20
Cereale	indet cereal	grain fragment		816	42	271	20
Cereale/Poaceae	indet cereal/ large grass	grain		21			
Triticum spelta	spelt wheat	glume base		10000	95	13	423
Triticum spelta	spelt wheat	grain attached to glume base					
Triticum spelta	spelt wheat	spikelet fork			4		4
Triticum dicoccum/spelta	glume wheat	glume base					
Triticum dicoccum/spelta	glume wheat	spikelet fork					
Triticum aestivum/ turgidum	free-threshing wheat	rachis node					
Triticum sp.	wheat	spikelet fork			45	5	43
Triticum sp.	wheat	glume base		10000	688	93	888
Triticum sp.	wheat	rachis					14
Hordeum vulgare	barley	rachis node					
Hordeum vulgare	barley	rachis internode					5
Hordeum vulgare	barley	rachis					7
cf *Hordeum vulgare*	cf barley	rachis node					8
Avena sp.	oat	floret base fragment				1	2
Avena sp.	oat	awn fragment		2	2	23	>100
Cereale	indet cereal	detached embryo		79	21	16	55
Cereale	indet cereal	detached coleoptile		377 + 482F	24 + 49F	15 + 8F	16 + 8F
Cereale	indet cereal	culm node					2
Cereale	indet cereal	rachis node				2	
Cereale	indet cereal	rachis internode					
Fumaria officinalis L.	common fumitory	seed				1	
Ranunculus acris/repens/ bulbosus	meadow/creeping/ bulbous buttercup						
cf *Ranunculus*	cf buttercup	seed					
Pisum/Vicia/Lathyrus	pea/vetch/tare	seed					
Vicia/Lathyrus	vetch/tare (2mm)	seed		10	2	4	1
Trifolium/Medicago/ Melilotus	clover/medick/melilot	seed		3		1	6
Urtica dioica L.	common nettle	seed					
Urtica urens L.	small nettle						
Corylus avellana L.	hazel	nutshell fragment					

5
Late Roman

Corndryer 2039		Corndryer 2130			Corndryer 2323	Threshing floor 2146	Stone-lined pit floor 2129	Ditch 2489
2020	2021	2044	2045	2046	2040	2022	2028	2003
2189	2190	2379	2379	2379	2327	2148	2254	2013
(Pot SF 108)	(Pot SF 109)							
2ml	10ml	35ml	5ml	30ml	25ml (25%)	15ml	200ml	80ml
0.5L	3L	10L	8L	10L	8L	8L	32L	32L
13	18	94	54	101	205	75	551	125
	3			3	2	2	11	
					5		44	5
2								
	14	5	10	4		1	55	34
					4			
							2	
	1							
14	20		3	4	12	6		
2	14		3	7	44	18		
						1		
8	19	73	8	202	96	60		269
19		969	25	1138	628	333	1058	349
							171	
4	26	179	2	276	684	750	2441	1334
	1							
				5	14	9	25	2
15	22			877		1626		
	3			33		23		
								1
		11			67		217	66
		526			1137		5310	1429
	3				7			
4	3 + 5F							
	1				1 + 1F		5	
							2F	1 + 3F
2					3	2	9	
	4	13		11	95	22	178	131
6	7	180	3	30	33	62	146	81
9F	12F	20		39 + 49F	20 + 8F	193 + 132F	184 + 11F	80 + 35F
	2					1	5	
2	5							6
1	18							
				1				
								1
						1		
		5		5	1	1	2	11
4	7			3			24	10
								1
								1
								2

Table 5.11 continued

			Phase	4		5	
			Date	Middle Roman		Late Roman	
			Feature	Corndryer 2050		Corndryer 2039	
			Sample no.	2006	2008	2010	2019
			Context no.	2046	2048	2079	2161
			Flot vol.	200ml	15ml	20ml	15ml
			Sample vol.	15L	7L	30L	10L
Linum usitatissimum L.	flax	seed					
Nasturtium officinale W.T. Aiton	water cress	seed					
Brassica sp.	cabbage	seed					
Raphanus raphanistrum L.	wild radish	seed capsule					
Thlaspi arvense L.	field penny-cress						
Polygonaceae	knotweed	seed			1		
Persicaria lapthifolia/ maculosa	pale persicaria/ redshank	seed					
Persicaria sp.	knotweed	seed				2	1
Polygonum aviculare L.	knotgrass	seed		1			
Fallopia convolvulus (L.) A. Love	black-bindweed	seed		5	1	3	1
Rumex sp.	dock	seed		157	7	7	20
Caryophyllaceae	pinks family	seed					
Stellaria media (L.) Vill.	common chickweed	seed					
Stellaria cf *graminea* L.	cf lesser stitchwort	seed					
Stellaria sp.	stitchwort	seed					2
Agrostemma githago L.	corncockle	seed		8 + 9F	1		1
Agrostemma githago L.	corncockle	calyx fragment		249	64	3	15
Chenopodium sp.	goosefoot	seed		15			8
cf *Chenopodium* sp.	cf goosefoot	seed					
Chenopodium album L.	fat hen	seed			2	1	37
Atriplex sp.	orache	seed					1
Galium sp.	bedstraws	seed					
Galium aparine L.	cleavers	seed					
Mentha sp.	mint	seed					
Euphrasia/Odontites	eyebright/bartsia	seed			1		
Asteraceae	daisy family	seed				2	
Cirsium/Carduus sp.	thistle	seed		1			
Centaurea sp.	knapweed	seed					
Anthemis cotula L.	stinking chamomile	seed				7	43
cf *Anthemis cotula* L.	cf stinking chamomile	seed					5
Tripleurospermum inodorum (L.) Sch. Bip.	scentless mayweed	seed					
Tripleurospermum sp.	mayweed	seed		3	4		
Apiaceae	carrot family	seed					1
Juncus sp.	rush	seed					
Cyperaceae	sedge family	seed					1
Eleocharis sp.	spike-rush	seed					1
Carex sp.	sedge	seed		1			
Poa/Phleum	meadow-grass/cat's-tail	seed			3	7	42
Lolium type	rye-grass	seed		138	1		
Bromus sp.	brome	seed		18		4	2
Poaceae	grass (small)	seed		204	10	2	18
Poaceae	grass (medium)	seed		119	21	9	79
Poaceae	grass (large)	seed			11	8	30
Poaceae	grass	culm fragments					
Indet.		seed					1
Indet.		shell fragments					

5
Late Roman

Corndryer 2039		Corndryer 2130			Corndryer 2323	Threshing floor 2146	Stone-lined pit floor 2129	Ditch 2489
2020	2021	2044	2045	2046	2040	2022	2028	2003
2189	2190	2379	2379	2379	2327	2148	2254	2013
(Pot SF 108)	*(Pot SF 109)*							
2ml	10ml	35ml	5ml	30ml	25ml (25%)	15ml	200ml	80ml
0.5L	3L	10L	8L	10L	8L	8L	32L	32L
		1		1	1			
							4	
								1
					1		1	2
					2			
	1							
	2				1		1	1
	4	98	1	25	18	9	105	33
		4						
								1
	1							
	1							1
		3F		1			2	
	1	9		2	2	18	19	2
	4	11		3	6	6	26	12
								6
1				1	20	1	11	11
	1			1	14		7	6
				1				1
					1			
	3							
				1				
					1		4	4
	1							1
	1						1	
2	9	4		5	20		96	44
2	4							
							13	7
	2			2	5	3		
								1
	3							
	1							
3	7		1					
	5			9	29	3	40	11
		10		26		39	32	
1	14	4		6	48	2		
3	8	10			19	3	20	42
1	16	28	2	32	98	23	112	
3	4	13		13	46	20		
	2							
							3	2
							1	5

confirmed that charred plant remains were abundant in these features and further analysis has focused on thirteen of these samples: two from middle Roman corndryer 2050; a total of eight samples from the three late Roman corndryers 2039, 2130 and 2323; and a single sample each from the threshing/malting floor (2146), stone-lined pit 2254 and one of the surrounding enclosure ditches (2489).

As discussed by van der Veen (1989) and more recently by Lodwick (2017a, 55–61), corndryers may have been used for more than one function and the charred remains they contain may have accumulated as a result of various processes, although it is believed that one of their main purposes was for drying harvested grain. This may have been necessitated by a damp growing season, requiring the removal of excess moisture so that the grain did not germinate or rot in storage, and/or to facilitate further processes such as pounding or milling which are impeded by damp grain. However, it is believed that the corndryers were used to produce malt. Malt is grain in which germination is artificially triggered and then halted through kilning, in order to produce fermentable sugars which can then be used to make

beer. The presence of germinated grain, as well as numerous detached embryos and coleoptiles (young shoots) in almost all of the corndryer samples is evidence that malting was occurring at the site. Examples are found in both Phase 4 and Phase 5 samples, suggesting that malting was a function of the crop-processing area over a prolonged period. Malting would require fresh water and a watertight tank in which to steep the grain: the stone-lined pits could potentially have fulfilled this role. Floor 2149 could potentially have been utilised as a malting floor, as it would have provided a suitable surface on which to lay out the germinating grain before it was ready for kilning. Similar stone-lined tanks have been found at other sites with strong evidence for large-scale malting, including Norman Way Industrial Estate in Cambridgeshire (Fosberry and Moan 2018), Springhead roadside settlement and nearby Northfleet villa in Kent (Stevens 2011a) and Whitelands Farm, Bicester (Stevens 2011b).

Evidence from other Roman sites with evidence for malting show that spelt wheat was most commonly used, and the dominance of wheat grain and often abundant spelt wheat chaff from the

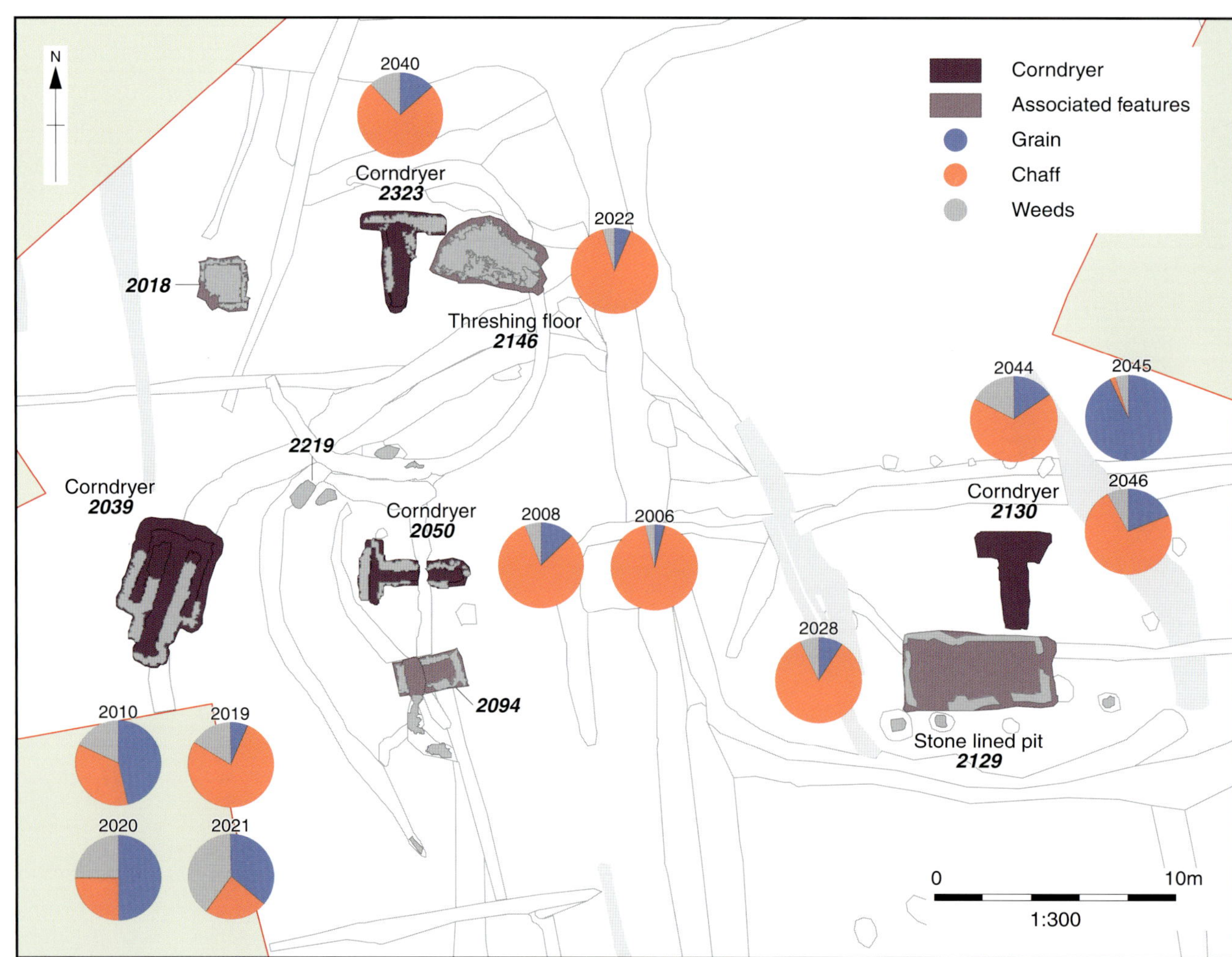

Fig. 5.19 Ratio of grain:chaff:weeds in soil samples from the crop-processing area (chaff is calculated by glume base counts, with one spikelet fork equal to two glume bases)

corndryers indicates that spelt malt was also being produced at the current site. Barley grain is also present, albeit in relatively low quantities, in most of the corndryer samples, although definite examples of germinated barley grains occur only in Phase 4 corndryer 2050. There is occasional evidence for barley being used alongside wheat at contemporary sites, such as Gatehampton Farm, Oxfordshire (Letts 1995), and Beck Row, Suffolk (Fryer 2004). More unusual is the presence of germinated oat (*Avena* sp.) and rye (*Secale cereale*) from the top of the flue in T-shaped corndryer 2050. Using a mixture of grain to produce malt, occasionally seen today in specialist craft beers, was more common in the Anglo-Saxon period, by which time barley was the principal grain used for malt, but is far less commonly found at Roman sites.

Spatial samples have been analysed from close to the T-shaped end of the flue (sample 2046), the middle (sample 2045) and the stokehole end (sample 2044) of Phase 5 corndryer 2130. The results show that material was abundant from the top and stokehole of the flue, but that relatively few charred remains were present in the middle of the flue, and, unlike the chaff-dominated top and basal samples, the middle sample is predominately grain, with almost no chaff or weed seeds. There is a high quantity of fragmented and indeterminate grain in the two richer samples, possibly representing the partially cleaned-out remnants of multiple episodes of use.

Corndryer 2039 was also sampled spatially, and the composition varies between samples. Sample 2019 was taken from a black, apparently *in situ* burnt layer in the base of the corndryer. This layer was rich in spelt what glume bases, with a smaller proportion of weed seeds, and appears to consist of material burnt during the oven's use; the paucity of cereal grains in the layer implies that the material is burnt fuel rather than deriving from the accidental burning of grain during kilning. This is similar to the sample from the base of the flue in corndryer 2323 (sample 2040), which is also rich in spelt chaff. In contrast to the *in situ* basal layer in corndryer 2039, the overlying layer 2079 (sample 2010) was backfill and the mixed nature of this sample – approximately 50% grain, with the remainder split fairly equally between chaff and weed seeds – suggests that the material is a mix of refuse from different episodes of use. The concentration of remains in sample 2010 is comparatively low, only 11 items per litre compared to 184 items per litre in sample 2019. The final two analysed samples are from pots placed inside the stokehole of the corndryer when it went out of use: sample 2020, from pot SF 108, has a similar composition to layer 2079, while the contents of sample 2021, from pot SF 109, are a fairly equal split between grain, chaff and weed seeds. Both assemblages from the pots are of significant size, at 156 and 82 items per litre of sediment respectively.

Both stone-lined tank 2129 and threshing/malting floor 2146 contained abundant charred remains, especially wheat glume bases. The common occurrence of detached coleoptiles in these samples suggests that waste from the removal of glumes and sprouts from part-processed malt may have built up on this surface and in the pit, although it may be a dump rather than an *in situ* accumulation on a primary working surface.

Assessment of the remaining 31 processed samples showed a sharp contrast between the high density of CPR concentrated in this relatively small area and the sparse remains recovered from the rest of the site.

Weed ecology of arable fields

The good condition of the weed seeds in many of the samples allows some insight into the ecology of the arable fields. While seeds of rushes and sedges are common in the sample from late Iron Age/early Roman pit 671, there are few seeds of wetland plants in samples of middle and late Roman date. This may be an indication that drainage had improved. Stinking chamomile (*Anthemis cotula*), a weed typically associated with the cultivation of heavier soils that was found in late Roman corndryers 2039 and 2323 and from surface 2146, further points to agricultural innovation that allowed more difficult soils to be cultivated. Stinking chamomile is absent from the middle Roman corndryer but instead samples from this feature include scentless mayweed (*Tripleurospermum inodorum*). As in the earlier samples, grasses continue to dominate the middle to late Roman weed seed assemblages. Together with dock (*Rumex* sp.), grasses are highly abundant in samples from the top of the flue of corndryer 2020, but much reduced in number at the stokehole end. They are also abundant in corndryer 2323 and in samples from pit 2129 and floor surface 2146.

CHARCOAL *by Julia Meen*

The 50 bulk sediment samples processed for the recovery of charred plant remains were assessed for the presence of charcoal and its potential to yield significant data that would help to answer specific research questions relating to the site. Following this assessment, thirteen samples were selected for further analysis to identify wood taxa present in each sample and ascertain their relative abundance. Identification of wood taxa was attempted for up to 100 items of charcoal from each sample. While this number is desirable for accurately characterising the species mix in a charcoal assemblage, charcoal was not uniformly preserved across the site and samples from some important features – particularly the corndryers – contained fewer fragments of identifiable charcoal, which inevitably resulted in a lower number of fragments being recorded. Identification was based on diagnostic anatomical characteristics, following keys in Schweingruber (1990) and Hather (2016). Charcoal was fractured and examined initially on the transverse section at low magnification using a stereomicroscope, and then on the transverse, radial and tangential sections at up to x400 magnification using a Brunel SPD400 metallurgical microscope. The results of the charcoal analysis are shown in Tables 5.12 and 5.13.

Late Iron Age/early Roman settlement

The charcoal from pit/hearth 5064 (sample 5000) was a mixture of oak and ash, with a smaller amount of willow/poplar (*Salix/Populus*). It is likely that this deposit represents the remains of wood burnt in a domestic setting, in which maintenance of a consistent temperature would not have been as vital as it would have been had it had an industrial function. Regardless, both ash and oak, in particular, have high calorific values and would produce a long-burning, high-temperature fire.

Temple/mausoleum 1320

A number of charcoal-rich pits were situated south of the temple/mausoleum. Assessment of samples from six of the pits showed that charcoal was abundant in pits 1045, 1430 and 1437, in moderate quantity in pits 1433 and 1440, and in relatively low quantity in pit 1435. Initial results suggested a similar composition in each of the pit samples, with oak (*Quercus* sp.) dominant and sparser taxa including hazel (*Corylus avellana*), ash (*Fraxinus excelsior*), hawthorn type (Maloideae) and willow/poplar (*Salix/Populus*).

Both the charred plant remains and charcoal from pit 1045 have been fully recorded, as well as charcoal from pit 1430 and charred plant remains from pit 1437. The charcoal analysis confirmed that oak was the most abundant species in both pits. Pit 1045 contained a strong secondary element of hazel and, to a lesser extent, willow/poplar; all included items of roundwood, suggesting smaller branches as well as trunk wood were being burnt. Pit 1430 contained a similar range of minor taxa, with the exception that here Maloideae roundwood forms a significant part of the assemblage.

Charcoal from burnt rubbish layer 1001, south of the building, was also examined. This layer contained highly abundant charcoal in association with a coin of Hadrian and burnt bones of domestic fowl, the latter indicating that it may have been a ritual deposit. The charcoal assemblage was predominately composed of oak, with a lesser hazel component. There were also small amounts of willow/poplar, ash, field maple (*Acer campestre*) and blackthorn/cherry (*Prunus* sp.). More notable are two fragments of conifer wood. Although it was not possible to identify the conifer wood to genus, yew

Table 5.12 Wood charcoal identifications from Area 1

		Phase 3		Phase 4		Phase 5	
		Late Iron Age/ Early Roman		Middle Roman		Late Roman	
		Pit/hearth 5064	Pit 1045	Rubbish layer	Pit 1430	Hearth 1091	Kiln/hearth 1247
	Sample no.	5000	15	14	37	17	19
	Context no.	5065	1047	1001	1431	1092	1134
	Flot vol.	40ml	650ml	900ml	200ml	40ml	200ml
	Charcoal >4mm	44	200*	500*	300*	23	100*
	Charcoal 4–2mm	300*	500*	1000*	300*	47	500*
Conifer				2			
Prunus sp.	blackthorn/cherry			1			83 (r)
Prunus/Maloideae	blackthorn/cherry/hawthorn type						5
Maloideae	hawthorn/apple/whitebeam				14 (r)		
Quercus sp.	oak	25 (h)	61 (r)	68 (r, h)	67 (r, h)	16 (h)	9
Corylus avellana L.	hazel		22 (r)	20 (r)	6 (r)	26	
cf *Corylus avellana* L.	cf hazel				1	1	
Salix/Populus	willow/poplar	5	13 (r)	5 (r)	3		1
cf *Salix/Populus*	cf willow/poplar				1		
Acer campestre L.	field maple		1	1	4 (r)		
cf *Acer campestre* L.	cf field maple				1 (r)		
Fraxinus excelsior L.	ash	13	3	2	3	7 (s)	1
Ring porous		2					
Diffuse porous		2					
Indet.		3					
Bark					1		1
Total		50	100	100	100	50	100

h = heartwood, r = roundwood, s = sapwood, *= estimated fragment count

Chapter 5

(Taxus baccata) can be ruled out as it does not have tertiary thickenings in the vessels. Aside from yew and juniper, which forms a low scrubby bush, the only native coniferous tree in the British Isles is Scots pine *(Pinus sylvestris)* and, although the diagnostic dentrites could not be observed within the window pits that would confirm this identification, it is the most likely species in this case. Small amounts of *Pinus* pollen were identified from the monolith sequence through the spring channel (Rutherford, below) although, as pine produces abundant pollen and its winged grains can be transported long distances, it does not necessarily show that pine was growing in the immediate vicinity of the site (ibid.). By the Roman period, non-native softwoods were being imported to Britain in the form of barrels, writing tablets and other wooden artefacts, and exotic woods including silver fir and larch are occasionally identified, mostly from urban sites (Smith 2002). The discovery of a cone scale of stone pine *(Pinus pinea)* in pit 1437, which was close to the temple/mausoleum, leaves open the possibility that this non-native conifer was growing at the site (see Charred Plant Remains, above, for further discussion of stone pine).

Enclosure complex in Area 1

The later Roman period saw the continuation and development of the Phase 5 field system. The charcoal from features dating to this period shows a contrast to the assemblages recovered from the earlier pits. The stokehole of oven 1247 contained mostly blackthorn/cherry charcoal, with only a minor oak component, while hearth 1091 produced a mixture of hazel, oak and ash. It is possible that this contrast reflects a distinction between oak-dominated domestic fuels found in the middle Roman pit samples and diffuse porous woods selected for the later kilns. It had been suggested that pit 227 may have had an industrial use, but the charred contents, which comprise only a small number of cereal grains and no identifiable charcoal, do not provide any further evidence to corroborate this theory.

Crop-processing area

In the western half of Area 2 the excavation of four corndrying ovens and a paved surface, thought to be a threshing/malting floor, led to the hypothesis

Table 5.13 Wood charcoal identifications from Area 2

		Phase 4		Phase 5				Roman
		Middle Roman		Late Roman				Roman
	Feature	Corndryer	Corndryer	Corndryer	Corndryer	Ring ditch	Enclosure ditch	Ditch
		2050	2323	2130		2407	20603	20162
	Sample no.	2006	2040	2044	2045	2033	20002	20001
	Context no.	2046	2327	2379		2245	20312	20163
	Flot vol.	200ml	100ml	35ml	5ml	250ml	50ml	20ml
	Charcoal >4mm	21	10		3	20	54	11
	Charcoal 4–2mm	50	90	23	21	98	100	29
Prunus cf *spinosa* L.	blackthorn						1	
Prunus sp.	blackthorn/cherry						10 (r)	
cf *Prunus* sp.	cf blackthorn/cherry					2		
Prunus/Maloideae	blackthorn/cherry/ hawthorn type						2	
Maloideae	hawthorn/apple/ whitebeam					3	12	
Quercus sp.	oak	41	49	20	18	29	29	
Alnus glutinosa (L.) Gaertn.	alder					1		
Corylus avellana L.	hazel				1	7 (r)	10	
cf *Corylus avellana* L.	cf hazel					2	2	
Corylus/Alnus	hazel/alder					6	1	
Salix/Populus	willow/poplar						4	11
cf *Salix/Populus*	cf willow/poplar							4
Acer campestre L.	field maple						4	
Fraxinus excelsior L.	ash	8					22	
cf *Fraxinus excelsior* L.	cf ash						2	
Diffuse porous		1			1			
Indet.			1				1	
Total		50	50	20	20	50	100	15

r = roundwood

that this represented a dedicated crop-processing area dated to the middle and late Roman period. Although spatial samples were taken across the four corndryers, the flots contained very little charcoal suggesting that these structures were regularly cleaned out. Identification was attempted on all suitable charcoal fragments to obtain data on the fuels used to fire the corndryers; suitable material included a small quantity of charcoal from two samples taken from the flue of corndryer 2130, close to the stokehole. Almost all the charcoal proved to be oak and similarly all the identifiable charcoal from what appears to be *in situ* burning in corndryer 2323 was oak. Charcoal was also analysed from late Roman ring ditch 2487 that surrounded corndryer 2323. Although charcoal from this feature was again sparse, it included a more diverse range of taxa than the samples from the corndryers, with hazel, alder, hawthorn type and blackthorn/cherry all present.

Field system east of the spring channel

Abundant charcoal was present in the fills of the system of enclosure ditches that characterise Area 2 East and two samples from these fills have been further analysed. Charcoal from context 20312, a fill of enclosure ditch 20603, comprises a mixture of wood species: most common are oak and ash, followed closely by hazel, hawthorn type and blackthorn/cherry, with smaller amounts of field maple and willow/poplar. This follows a pattern from the site as a whole: that charcoal assemblages from secondary contexts including pits and ditches are mixed, with five or six taxa generally present, in contrast to the almost exclusively oak assemblages from the fills of the corndryers. In general, the pattern of charcoal use suggests that oak was being deliberately selected as fuel to fire the corndryers. As a consistent, reliable heat is required for the kilning of grain, prioritising a single wood fuel which burns at a stable temperature, as oak does, for the corndryers would have been sensible, while the fuel for domestic hearths could afford to be more haphazard. However, the abundance of spelt glumes, particularly in the flue of corndryer 2050, may indicate the use of chaff as a fuel. On a site on which crop processing appeared to have been undertaken on a large scale, large volumes of chaff by-product would have been created and it would have been sensible to recycle it as fuel (van der Veen 1999).

WATERLOGGED PLANT REMAINS FROM THE SPRING OUTWASH CHANNEL AND DITCH 2511 *by Julia Meen*

The geology of the site is such that a spring flows to the surface at the eastern edge of Area 1 to this day. It appears that this spring was regarded as an important feature in the Roman landscape because Building 1320, of possible religious function, seems to have been deliberately orientated so that it faced onto the spring channel. The fills of the spring channel provided an opportunity to recover organic remains preserved through waterlogging, which occurs where ground conditions are permanently saturated, and the resultant lack of oxygen inhibits decay. The channel was investigated through a sondage to the east of Building 1320 and was sampled extensively. A monolith sequence was taken through the channel fills and overlying deposits (1300–1305), while two sets of bulk sediment samples were recovered incrementally from each of the main fills at two locations.

One litre of sediment was processed from each of these bulk samples using the 'wash-over' technique in order to recover waterlogged plant remains (WPR). Flot and residue from each sample were collected separately onto 250µm mesh and retained in sealed plastic bags with water to prevent desiccation.

A subsample from each flot was examined in order to assess preservation. This assessment indicated that both sequences showed comparable results, with good preservation for waterlogged plant remains limited to lower fill 1305. The deposits overlying the channel (1300, 1301 and 1302) proved to be poor in waterlogged plant remains; seeds in these contexts are limited to nettle (*Urtica dioica*) and elder (*Sambucus nigra*) which, on their own, provide limited environmental information. Seeds were also sparse in channel fill 1303, although more diverse than those in the overlying deposits, while initial examination suggested an anthropogenic element to fill 1304, which contained frequent charcoal as well as charred spelt wheat (*Triticum spelta*) chaff. Overall, preservation was better in the second sequence, samples 30–5, and so further work has focused on these: sample 35, from lower fill 1305 and sample 334 from overlying layer 1304. While preservation was less good in layer 1304, the data provides a comparison to that from 1305.

A third sample was also selected for analysis. Ditch 2511 forms part of the enclosure that contains corndryer 2130, and sample 2050 from fill 2501 was found to include frequent waterlogged seeds including aquatic taxa indicative of plants growing in the base of a water-containing ditch, scrubbier vegetation presumably growing on the slopes of the ditch, as well as plants characteristic of more open ground that perhaps reflects wider vegetation in the area around the ditch.

Waterlogged plant remains from the three samples were analysed using the same procedure as was used for charred plant remains (see Meen, above). The entirety of each flot was sorted. Results are shown in Table 5.14.

Spring outwash channel

The seed assemblage in lower fill 1305 is rich and diverse, with almost 4000 individual seeds recorded, comprising more than 40 different species or genera. More than half of these individual seeds are the ubiquitous common nettle (*Urtica dioica*), which flourishes in many types of both natural and disturbed habitat but particularly thrives in nitrogen- and phosphate-rich soils and those disturbed by human activity. Nettles are often abundant on the nutrient-rich alluvium at the edges of streams (Ingrouille 1995, 201, 241). While nettles can often outcompete and suppress less aggressive herbs, the high species diversity suggests that this was not the case here. Removing the nettles and rushes (*Juncus* sp.) from the totals shows more clearly the proportions of seeds from different habitat types, as illustrated in Figure 5.20 (rush seed heads contain many tiny seeds so the presence of only a few seed heads can account for hundreds of seeds). Even with rushes excluded, aquatic and wet ground taxa still form a high proportion of the assemblage, as might be expected from deposits within a stream channel. However, grasses are also common, especially those with larger seeds (greater than 5mm in size). Although it is difficult to classify grass seeds to species or even genera, seeds in this size range may include darnel (*Lolium tementulum*), bromes (*Bromus* sp.) and wild barleys and oats, all of which are common arable weeds. There is also a small but diverse range of other seeds reflecting cultivated or disturbed ground, including swine cress (*Lepidium coronopus*), common chickweed (*Stellaria media*), fat hen (*Chenopodium album*), hemlock (*Conium maculatum*), greater plantain (*Plantago major*) and probable field woundwort (*Stachys* cf *arvensis*). Together, these suggest that arable cultivation was occurring close by, which accords with the identification of a large-scale crop-processing facility on the site.

Returning to the evidence for aquatic plants, these provide evidence for the environment within the spring channel itself. Seeds of water starwort (*Callitriche* sp.) are exceptionally abundant. There are also high numbers of watercress (*Nasturtium officinale*) and aquatic buttercups (mostly crowfoots, *Ranunculus* subgenus *Batrachium*, but also celery-leaved buttercup, *R. sceleratus*). This suggests that the spring waters were clear and mineral rich. Such

taxa are today characteristic of chalk streams, where filtering of the spring waters through the bedrock reduces organic inputs from surface run-off. However, the bedrock at Harpole is siltstone and mudstone, so the spring waters would have been slightly acidic. The near absence of pondweeds (*Potamogeton* spp.) and water plantain (*Alisma plantago-aquatica*) may indicate that the waters from the spring were fairly fast flowing.

The nature of the vegetation growing at the margins of the stream is indicated by the high numbers of marshwort (*Apium* sp.) and frequent rush seeds, although sedge (*Carex* sp.) and bulrush (*Typha* sp.) seeds are rare. The presence of meadow-sweet (*Filipendula ulmaria*), selfheal (*Prunella vulgaris*) and numerous dock (*Rumex* sp.) seeds, as well as the abundant grass caryopses, suggest damp grassland in the vicinity, while seeds of bramble (*Rubus* sp.), elder (*Sambucus nigra*) and hawthorn (*Crataegus monogyna*) hint at a scrubby element.

The richness and diversity of herb macrofossils from layer 1305 matches the pollen evidence from the base of this context. Here, there is an abundance of grass pollen, alongside herbs including meadow-sweet, sedges, dock, carrots (a family which includes marshworts) and buttercups (Rutherford, below). The pollen is therefore indicative of wet grassland used for pasture, an interpretation further strengthened by the presence of fungal spores associated with herbivore dung. However, the higher resolution of pollen sampling reveals a change within context 1305 that is masked in the larger samples taken for macrofossils. It shows that pollen is increasingly of cereal-type, with a reduction in herb diversity. This apparent shift in importance towards arable, rather than pastoral, agriculture in the vicinity of the spring channel probably accounts for the mix of habitat types represented by the water-logged plant remains.

The sample from overlying context 1304 is poorer, both in terms of the overall number of seeds recovered and the number of taxa present, with just over a quarter of the total seeds per litre when compared with context 1305 and only around half

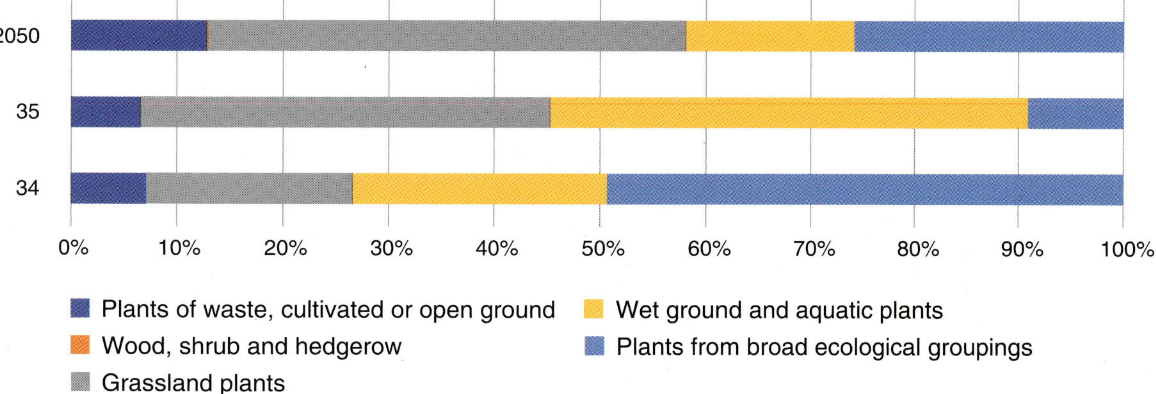

Fig. 5.20 Proportions of seeds from different ecological grouping in each of the selected samples (by total seed numbers; note that seeds of Urtica dioica *and* Juncus spp. *have been excluded)*

Table 5.14 Waterlogged plant remains from the spring outwash channel and ditch 2511

	Feature	Spring outwash channel		Ditch 2511
	Sample no.	34	35	2050
	Context no.	1304	1305	2501
	Flot vol.	70ml	90ml	100ml
	% Sorted	100%	100%	100%
Charred plant remains				
Triticum sp.	wheat grain			1
Triticum spelta	spelt wheat glume base	3	2	6
Triticum sp.	wheat glume base		3	11
Vicia/Lathyrus	vetch/tare	1		
Rumex sp.	dock	1		
Anthemis cotula L.	stinking chamomile	1		
Avena/Bromus	oat/brome			1
Waterlogged plant remains				
Plants of waste, cultivated or open ground				
Triticum spelta	spelt wheat glume base			2
Triticum sp.	wheat glume base			2
Papaver sp.	poppy		1	
Fumaria officinalis L.	common fumitory	1	1	
Aphanes sp.	parsley-piert			1
Urtica dioica L.	common nettle	721	2192	1921
Urtica urens L.	small nettle		2	4
Lepidium coronopus (L.) Al-Shehbaz	swine-cress		3	1
Persicaria sp.	knotweed		6	3
Polygonum aviculare L.	knotgrass		4	7
Rumex acetosella L.	sheep's sorrel		1	1
Stellaria media (L.) Vill.	common chickweed	1	21	25
Chenopodium album L.	fat hen		9	1
Chenopodium sp.	goosefoot			5
Hyoscyamus niger L.	henbane	1	1	
Solanum nigrum L.	black nightshade			1
Plantago major L.	greater plantain	1	20	22
Stachys cf *arvensis* L.	cf field woundwort	2	12	
Lamium purpureum L.	red dead-nettle			2
Sonchus sp.	sowthistle		4	8
Anthemis cotula L.	stinking chamomile		2	
cf *Anthemis cotula* L.	cf stinking chamomile			2
Aethusa cynapium L.	fool's parsley	1		
Conium maculatum L.	hemlock	4	16	3
Wood, scrub and hedgerow				
cf *Prunus* sp.	cf sloe/cherry/plum stone fragments	7	1	
Crataegus monogyna Jacq.	hawthorn stone		1	
Corylus avellana L.	hazel nutshell half			1
Indet.	fruit stone fragment		4	2
Grassland plants				
Linum catharticum L.	fairy flax			1
Stellaria graminea L.	lesser stitchwort			6
Leontodon sp.	hawkbit			2
Poaceae	grass (small)		69	64
Poaceae	grass (medium)	3	93	213
Poaceae	grass (large)	27	440	16
Wet ground and aquatic plants				
Ranunculus sceleratus L.	celery-leaved buttercup		1	
Ranunculus subgenus *Batrachium*	crowfoot	16	35	

Table 5.14 continued

Feature		Spring outwash channel		Ditch 2511
Sample no.		34	35	2050
Context no.		1304	1305	2501
Flot vol.		70ml	90ml	100ml
% Sorted		100%	100%	100%
Filipendula ulmaria (L.) Maxim	meadowsweet		1	1
Nasturtium officinale W.T. Aiton	water cress		83	57
Callitriche sp.	water starwort	13	435	5
Lycopus europaeus L.	gypsywort			1
Apium sp.	marshwort	5	132	32
cf *Cicuta virosa* L.	cf cowbane		15	
Alisma plantago-aquatica L.	water plantain			6
Potamogeton sp.	pondweed		1	
Typha sp.	bulrush	3	1	2
Juncus sp.	rush	181	146	67
Carex sp.	sedge		4	3
Plants from broad ecological groupings				
Ranunculus acris/repens/bulbosus	meadow/creeping/bulbous buttercup	1	5	2
Rubus sp.	bramble	2	1	12
Potentilla sp.	cinquefoil	2		2
Hypericum sp.	St John's-wort			2
Epilobium sp.	willow-herb			1
Lepidium type	pepperwort			3
Rumex sp.	dock		78	81
Cerastium sp	mouse-ear			3
cf *Sagina* sp.	cf pearlwort			1
Silene sp.	campion		1	
Atriplex sp.	orache			1
Solanum sp.	nightshade			4
Stachys sp.	woundwort	11		
cf *Stachys* sp.	cf woundwort	5		
Lamium sp.	dead-nettle	1		
Prunella vulgaris L.	selfheal		2	1
Mentha sp.	mint		1	5
Euphrasia/Odontites	eyebright/bartsia			1
Cirsium arvense (L.) Scop.	creeping thistle		3	9
Cirsium sp.	thistle			13
Cirsium/Carduus sp.	thistle	11	11	3
Lapsana communis L.	nipplewort		11	11
Senecio type	ragwort type			1
Sambucus nigra L.	elder	41	20	1
Apiaceae	carrot family	2	3	1
Daucus carota L.	wild carrot		6	15
Total		1069	3904	2682

the number of species present. This is probably in part due to poorer preservation, as the later samples in the sequence are increasingly poor, but there are clear differences in the vegetation represented which cannot be attributed to differential survival alone. As in primary fill 1305, nettle is highly abundant, and here it is by far the dominant taxon. Other plants associated with disturbance continue to be present, albeit at a low level. These include field woundwort, hemlock and thistles (*Cirsium/Carduus* spp.), while elder seeds increase.

The major divergence with context 1305 is the dramatic reduction in the number of grass caryopses: together with the disappearance of other vegetation indicative of wet grassland, this may point to the land around the channel becoming increasingly waste, with overgrown, nitrate-rich soil and scrubby vegetation. The range of aquatic plants is similar to those in context 1305, although much reduced in number. However, there are no seeds of watercress. Watercress is sensitive to changes in environment: it dislikes stagnant water and shade and prefers clean, alkaline waters. It may be that conditions in the stream had become inhospitable to watercress, possibly due to human activity increasingly encroaching towards the edge of the channel.

Boundary ditch 2511

The analysed sample came from the basal fill of the main N–S aligned boundary ditch. It was noted during excavation that the sides of the ditch appeared eroded, as if water had been flowing quickly through the ditch, and it is likely that the feature would have been an important part of the drainage system that would have made this land, so close to the River Nene, usable despite the risk of seasonal flooding. The sample contains both charred and waterlogged evidence of cereal processing including both grain and glume bases of spelt wheat (*Triticum spelta*), presumably from corndryer 2130 which this ditch encloses. The sample is characterised by abundant grass seeds and a range of plants of disturbed ground, including greater plantain (*Plantago major*), common chickweed (*Stellaria media*), knotgrass (*Polygonum aviculare*), and thistles, including creeping thistle (*Cirsium arvense*), sowthistle, (*Sonchus* sp.), and nipplewort (*Lapsana communis*). Nettles are again by far the most abundant seed present. While the spring channel deposits were dominated by larger grass seeds, here they are more commonly those of an intermediate size and may include fescues (*Festuca* spp.) and rye-grasses (*Lolium* spp.) – grasses commonly seen in contemporary charred assemblages from the site (see Meen, above).

Given this association, and the proximity to the crop-processing area, it may be that the material in the ditch includes crop-processing by-products (ie the smaller arable weeds removed from the harvested crop). The majority of the seeds are smaller than grain size and according to Hillman's (1984) sequence of crop-processing stages they would be removed directly after winnowing, with the coarsest waste elements sieved out, or during a second stage of winnowing following pounding, in which much of the chaff is also separated out. The limited chaff in the sample points to it being from the earlier stage in the sequence. This stage would probably have been carried out close to the point of harvest, to reduce transportation costs; further-more, this processing stage does not require a source of heat and so the by-products are less likely to become accidentally charred and are therefore less archaeologically visible unless waterlogged conditions preserve them (Hillman 1984, fig. 5). This is further evidence that arable cultivation was being practiced close by. Although the area is close to the river and natural drainage is poor (Cranfield Soil and Agrifood Institute 2000), the extensive ridge and furrow that traverses the site shows that the land was successfully drained for arable use in historic times.

INSECTS FROM THE SPRING OUTWASH CHANNEL AND DITCH 2511 *by Enid Allison*

Two samples from deposits within the spring outwash channel in Area 1 and a third from the fill of ditch 2511 were analysed for insect remains. All three deposits are dated to the Roman period.

Methods

The insect samples had volumes of two litres. They were received having been wet-sieved to 0.25mm with separation of organic material by the 'wash-over' method. Since separation was comprehensive, paraffin flotation to extract insect remains was carried out only on the wash-over fraction with recovery on 0.3mm mesh (Kenward *et al.* 1980). Beetle (Coleoptera) and true bug (Hemiptera) sclerites were removed from the paraffin flots onto moist filter paper in a petri dish for identification using a low-power stereoscopic zoom microscope (x10 – x45). Identification was by comparison with modern insect specimens and by reference to standard published works.

Minimum numbers of adult terrestrial beetles and bugs were estimated from the major sclerites. Aquatic beetles and all other groups of insects were recorded semi-quantitatively on a four-point scale: + 1–3 individuals; ++ 4–10 individuals; +++ 11–25 individuals; ++++ 25–99 individuals. Other inverte-brates were simply noted as present, common or abundant. Nomenclature follows Duff (2018) and sources compiled by Bantock and Botting (2018) for Coleoptera and Hemiptera respectively.

To aid interpretation, beetles and bugs were assigned to broad ecological groups based on Kenward *et al.* (1986), Kenward (1997) and Smith *et al.* (2020). Some taxa are included in more than one group, while others are uncoded, either because they occur in a wide variety of habitats and situations or because it was not possible to identify the available sclerites closely enough. Ecological infor-mation was obtained mainly from Bantock and Botting (2018), Cox (2007), Duff (2012; 2016), Luff (1998; 2007), Morris (1990; 1997; 2002; 2008), Southwood and Leston (1959) and White and Hodkinson (1982). Other sources are mentioned where relevant below.

A 'house fauna' consists of beetle taxa predomi-nantly associated with mouldering organic litter and detritus within ancient buildings, such as floor litter, bedding or roofing material, stored fodder and foodstuffs (eg Carrott and Kenward 2001; Hall and Kenward 1990; Kenward and Hall 1995). It is emphasized that the fauna is not confined to human dwellings but could have developed in various buildings containing similar mouldering organic matter, including barns, stables and workshops.

Synanthropic insects are favoured by artificial habitats associated with human occupation and activity. To interpret their significance in particular assemblages, they can be divided into three somewhat arbitrary categories (Kenward 1997; Smith *et al.* 2020). 'Strong' synanthropes are essentially dependent on human activity for survival and are rarely found in natural habitats, 'typical' synanthropes are especially favoured by artificial habitats but can survive in natural situations, and 'facultative' synanthropes are common in natural situations but clearly favoured by man-made habitats.

Proportions for selected terrestrial ecological groups were calculated based on the minimum number of individuals, with all percentages rounded to the nearest whole number. The proportion calculated for each group represents a minimum value since various generalist or uncoded taxa may have exploited similar habitats. The significance of the proportions varies according to group – for example, proportions of decomposers are typically high relative to other taxa on an intensively occupied site and a value of 20% is regarded as low, whereas 20% would be a high to extremely high value for the various groups among the outdoor insects.

The assemblages

General comments

The insect remains were highly fragmented in all three samples. This was especially the case for ground beetles (Carabidae), dung beetles (Scarabaeoidea) and weevils (Curculionidae), and many of the more complete sclerites were torn or rolled. Levels of erosion were generally moderate but a fair proportion of fragments in sample 34 showed more advanced degradation.

Full lists of taxa recorded from each sample are shown in Appendix 1 and the main statistics for each assemblage in Table 5.15.

The spring outwash channel

The samples examined were from silty clays making up the basal fill of the spring outwash channel (1305; sample 35) and the overlying fill (1304; sample 34). The basal deposit contained a higher concentration of insect remains, including a substantial aquatic component. Most of the water beetles were eurytopic, although *Haliplus lineatocollis* and *Limnebius truncatellus* occur most frequently in or by slowly flowing water. Several other taxa are typically associated with exposed wet mud (*Ochthebius dilatatus, O.* cf *minimus, Dryops*), and *Byrrhus* species with mosses. *Prasocuris phellandrii*, a leaf beetle associated with wetland habitats, is primarily found on marsh marigold (*Caltha palustris*) and other Ranunculaceae (Cox 2007, 144). Nettles (*Urtica*) close to the channel were indicated by *Heterogaster urticae, Nedyus quadrimaculatus, Parethelcus pollinarius* and *Brachypterus* while docks were suggested by a dock bug (*Coreus marginatus*). Trees or shrubs were also indicated by *Scolytus*

Table 5.15 Proportions of selected groups of terrestrial beetles (Coleoptera)

Feature	Spring outwash channel		Ditch 2511
Context	1305	1304	2501
Sample	35	34	2050
Minimum terrestrial beetle individuals	212	115	303
Minimum terrestrial beetle taxa	102	70	125
Decomposer component			
Dry decomposers [rd]	2%	3%	2
Foul decomposers [rf]	34%	35%	35%
Eurytopic decomposers [rt]	10%	7%	13%
Total decomposers [rd+rf+rt]	47%	44%	50%
Outdoor component			
Damp ground/waterside [d]	6%	4%	8%
Plant-associated [p]	25%	36%	22%
Outdoor taxa [oa + ob]	68%	78%	69%
Other groups			
Wood-associated [l]	2%	3%	<1%
House fauna [h]	1%	3%	1%
Scarabaeoid dung beetles	33%	34%	33%
Synanthropes [S]			
Strong synanthropes [ss]	0%	0%	0%
Typical synanthropes [st]	0%	1%	<1%
Facultative synanthropes [sf]	9%	6%	12%
Total synanthropes [sf+st+ss]	9%	7%	12%
Strong synanthropes of total synanthropes [ss/S]	0%	0%	0%
Typical synanthropes of total synanthropes [st/S]	0%	14%	3%
Facultative synanthropes of total synanthropes [sf/S]	100%	86%	97%

Ecological codes shown in square brackets are explained in Appendix 1

rugulosus, associated mainly with woody Rosaceae, and *Leperisinus varius*, which primarily bores in ash (*Fraxinus*). There were also poorly preserved remains of either the common woodworm beetle (*Anobium punctatum*) or the closely similar *A. inexpectatum*, found on ivy (*Hedera*). *Barynotus moerens*, a large ground-dwelling weevil, is predominantly found in shaded places with woody vegetation, generally in association with dog's mercury (*Mercurialis perennis*; Morris 1997, 46).

Otherwise, the bulk of the terrestrial beetle assemblage suggested rather open disturbed grassy habitats and grazing land. Beetles with turf-feeding larvae were common (*Agrypnus murinus, Athous haemorrhoidalis, Agriotes* spp., *Phyllopertha horticola*) and *P. horticola* (a small chafer) is characteristic of grassland with a high proportion of 'weeds' (Raw 1951). *Mecinus pyraster* and *Graptus triguttatus* are found on ribwort plantain (*Plantago lanceolata*). *Oxystoma* species feed on vetches (*Vicia* and *Lathyrus*). At least ten species of scarabaeoid dung beetles were recorded (Geotrupinae, Aphodiinae spp., *Onthophagus* spp.), together accounting for a third of the terrestrial beetle fauna, their abundance strongly suggesting that significant numbers of grazing animals were present very close to the channel (Smith *et al.* 2010; 2014). Most dung beetles are not specific to the dung of particular animals, and *Melinopterus prodromus* and *M. sphacelatus* (not distinguished on the fragmentary material represented here) are also attracted to other foul decomposing plant material including settlement waste, but *Onthophagus joannae* and *O. similis* are especially associated with horse or sheep dung (Jessop 1986, 26–7; Skidmore 1991, 149).

A record of *Trox scaber* is of interest. In natural situations it is mainly associated with the nests of hole-nesting birds such as owls, especially if they contain material such as bones or other fairly dry remains of animal origin, and also in dried-out corpses on sandy open ground (Jessop 1986, 14; Duff 2018, 30). In archaeological deposits it often appears to have a connection with ancient buildings, which must have provided a comparable habitat, and with activities such as hide preparation and leatherworking (eg Carrott and Kenward 2001; Hall and Kenward 2011). There were no convincing signs in the insect assemblage for the presence of occupation waste in the deposit, however, and a bird's nest in a nearby tree or an animal corpse might possibly explain its presence here.

Aquatic beetles were much less well represented in the overlying layer 1304 (sample 34), and the significantly more degraded condition of the insect remains might perhaps suggest that waterlogging had been incomplete allowing some aeration of the deposit, possibly seasonally. Vegetation on wet ground likely included reed sweet-grass (*Glyceria maxima*), the main host plant of the wetland weevil *Notaris acridulus*. Most elements of the terrestrial insect assemblage were very similar in implication to the earlier deposit, with a high proportion of scarabaeoid dung beetles (34%) and a similar range of beetles of grassland habitats. Ribwort plantain was specifically indicated by the weevils *Mecinus pyraster*, *Mecinus labilis*, and *Graptus triguttatus*, *Sphaeroderma* species are found on Asteraceae, especially knapweeds (*Centaurea*) and thistles (*Cirsium* and *Carduus*), and nettles were indicated by *Taenapion urticarium*. *Grynobius planus* and *Anobium punctatum* or *inexpectatum* provided hints of dead wood habitats, and by implication perhaps limited amounts of woody vegetation. There were also hints of an anthropogenic element in the make-up of the deposit from a limited range of eurytopic decomposers and a small group of beetles characteristic of a 'house fauna' (*Latridius minutus* group, *Cryptophagus*, *Ptinus*; e.g. Carrott and Kenward 2001; Hall and Kenward 1990;

Kenward and Hall 1995). Although similar relatively dry sheltered conditions suitable for the house fauna might potentially also exist within a dry tree hollow, an anthropogenic influence was also suggested by the plant macrofossil assemblage (Meen, above).

Late Roman ditch 2511

The sample from ditch fill 2501 (sample 2050) produced a large, albeit highly fragmented assemblage of insect remains. A limited range of eurytopic aquatic beetles indicated that the ditch had contained water for at least some of the time, but the assemblage was dominated by terrestrial taxa. Several beetles were indicative of wet waterside mud and moss (*Dryops*, *Platystethus nitens*, *Byrrhus*, *Acidota cruentata*), while *Notaris acridulus*, mainly associated with reed sweet-grass (*Glyceria maxima*), provided an indication of vegetation within the ditch itself or on adjacent wet ground. Evidence for nettles was particularly convincing (*Heterogaster urticae*, shed skins of *Trioza urticae* nymphs, *Taenapion urticarium*, *Nedyus quadrimaculatus*), with some probably growing either within or very close to the ditch, since nymphs of *Trioza urticae* are relatively immobile. Generally, the composition of the insect assemblage indicates that land in the surroundings of the ditch was relatively dry and open, and predominantly disturbed agricultural grassland. Turf-feeding beetles were well represented (*Agrypnus murinus*, *Athous haemorrhoidalis*, *Phyllopertha horticola*) and plant-feeding insects included *Mecinus pyraster* and *Graptus triguttatus* found on ribwort plantain (*Plantago lanceolata*) and *Oxystoma* found on vetches (*Vicia* and *Lathyrus*), while docks (*Rumex*) were indicated by *Rhinoncus pericarpius* and the dock bug (*Coreus marginatus*, represented by three individuals). *Phyllotreta* species are associated with wild and cultivated Brassicaceae, hinting at the presence of disturbed or cultivated ground. Ground beetles (Carabidae) were less fragmented than in the samples from the channel and the most numerous of these was *Poecilus versicolor*, found in grassland and also arable land, especially in damper areas or near water. Other ground beetles were also consistent with an agricultural landscape (*Calathus fuscipes*, *Harpalus rufipes*, *Bembidion obtusum*, *Paradromius linearis*, *Brachinus crepitans*, *Amara* spp.). Scarabaeoid dung beetles made up a third of the terrestrial beetle fauna, the same proportion as in the samples from the channel, strongly suggesting that grazing animals were common in the vicinity of the ditch. There were hints of an anthropogenic influence from a few decomposers including elements of a house fauna and taxa such as *Oxyomus sylvestris*, a scarabaeid beetle that occurs in vegetable refuse of various kinds and dung heaps, rather than in dung lying in fields (Jessop 1986, 19). A ked (*Melophagus ovinus*) puparium is likely associated with this material and records in archaeological contexts are usually indicative of debris from the cleaning of wool.

Conclusion

All three samples produced insect assemblages that were strikingly similar in composition, chiefly indicating open, disturbed grassland used for grazing livestock in the vicinity of both the spring outwash channel and ditch 2511. Scarabaeoid dung beetles were a consistent and major element in the fauna, making up a third of terrestrial beetles in each sample. Trees or shrubs would have been present in the landscape but may have been mainly present along water margins or in the form of hedgerows. Although most of the dung beetles that were closely identified are eurytopic in various kinds of dung, and some will also exploit foul occupation waste, *Onthophagus joannae* and *O. similis*, recorded together in one sample associated with the spring outwash channel, are especially associated with horse or sheep dung on light soils. Debris from wool cleaning, possibly associated with a small house fauna, was suggested by a ked (*Melophagus ovinus*) puparium in the fill of ditch 2511. A limited anthropogenic influence was also suggested in the upper sample from the spring outwash channel.

POLLEN FROM THE SPRING OUTWASH CHANNEL *by Mairead Rutherford*

The analysis was carried out on pollen from a column taken through the spring outwash channel. Pollen counts of 300–500 grains (including trees, shrubs and herbs) were achieved for five samples from the Roman part of the sequence (Fig. 5.21). Pollen data are presented as percentage diagrams using the computer programmes TILIA and TGView (version 2.0.41). The percentage values are based on a total land pollen (TLP) sum that includes trees, shrubs, crops and herbs. Fern spores, pollen of aquatic plants, non-pollen palynomorphs (NPP), microscopic charcoal and deteriorated grains are expressed as percentages of TLP plus the respective sum to which they belong.

Interpretation

The deepest subsample from the bottom of deposit 1305 is floristically rich, the pollen data providing evidence of herb-rich wet grassland that includes a diverse range of plants such as sedges, common knapweed, mints, ribwort plantain, dead-nettles, docks/sorrels, bedstraws, meadowsweets, pollen of the buttercup, daisy, pea, carrot, cabbage, pink and goosefoot families, stitchworts/chickweeds and mugworts. Evidence of wetness is further provided by the recovery of green algae, including *Spirogyra* (HdV-130) and microfossil type HdV-128, both of which have recorded occurrences in shallow, perhaps stagnant water (van Geel 1978). Very low values of cereal-type pollen suggest possible occurrence of wheat/oats, based on grain dimensions. However, the dimensions overlap with those of wild grasses found in wetland areas, for example sweet-grasses (*Glyceria*-type), and therefore the identification cannot be certain (Andersen 1979); however, association with agricultural weeds of disturbed areas such as mugworts, knotgrasses, various plants of the cabbage family (for example, mustards), as well as recovery of charred spelt wheat from the overlying deposit 1304 (Meen, above) may support the idea of arable activity or crop processing in the vicinity. Cereal-type pollen could also have entered the record through discard of animal waste in, for example, hay or straw used for animal fodder.

The main land use suggested by the pollen assemblages from this deepest subsample is, therefore, pastoralism. Wet grasslands containing meadow-rich plant communities would provide ideal environments for pasturing animals, and this interpretation is further supported by the recovery of a range of coprophilous fungal spores, including *Sordaria* (HdV-55A/B), *Cercophora* (HdV-112) and *Podospora* (HdV-368).

Tree and shrub pollen account for 10–15% of the total pollen count and include, in particular, pollen of walnut and ash, with fewer records of birch, oak, hazel-type, alder, pine, willow, heather and hawthorn. Some of these trees/shrubs may have been growing as hedgerows (hawthorn, hazel-type) or on damper ground (alder, willow); some pollen, such as the pine, may have been derived from further afield.

There is also a record in this subsample of parasitic eggs of helminths. These parasites can infect freshwater fishes, dogs, cats and other mammals (Wieckowska-Lüth *et al.* 2020). Parasites may be indicative of water contamination, perhaps as a result of livestock grazing.

The next two subsamples from deposit 1305 are clearly distinguished by increasing values of both cereal-type pollen and walnut pollen, with grass pollen frequencies reduced to *c* 20% of the total pollen count. The dominance of cereal-type pollen is associated with a much less diverse herb assemblage, with very reduced occurrences of pollen of ribwort plantain and a near or complete absence of pollen of docks/sorrels, mugworts, knotgrasses, meadowsweets, pink and goosefoot families. This could imply removal of weeds from areas used for arable cultivation. The abundance of cereal-type pollen may reflect arable activity or use/ processing/discard of cereals locally. The possibility remains, however, that these cereal-type grains represent wild grasses, several species of which live in or on damp ground (Stace 2010).

Damp ground may be inferred from the proximity of the site to a spring line, and palynologically from occurrences of green algal-types *Spirogyra* (HdV-130) and *Botryococcus* (HdV-766), which live in shallow water environments (van Geel 1978). Fungal spores of *Glomus* (HdV-207) may be indicative of disturbed soils adjacent to the site. Records of rare helminths and parasites of the whip-worm *Trichuris* (HdV-530) may be indicative of faecal deposition from animals or people (Jones 1982).

Of the arboreal pollen, the most significant record is that of walnut; pollen of maple/sycamore, ash and beech are also present. Both ash and walnut produce large amounts of pollen, however, and clumping of grains of walnut pollen on slides may indicate that the pollen had not travelled far, implying probably local growth of walnut trees. Beech pollen grains do not travel far, as the grains are heavy and rarely spread far from the canopy; therefore, its presence even in very small quantities may signify local growth (Sidell *et al.* 2000). Likewise, pollen of ash is considered to be under-represented in pollen spectra and its presence is therefore also likely to indicate local growth (Sidell *et al.* 2000). The pollen of maple/sycamore probably refers to the native field maple (*Acer campestre*), known from woods, scrub and hedgerows (Stace 2010). Maple/sycamore is insect-pollinated but after flowering, winged fruits are transported by the wind and therefore could represent trees at some distance from the site (Woodland Trust nd a).

No pollen was present in sandy deposit 1304, but the overlying organic silty clay (1303) yielded relatively rich pollen assemblages. The summary curve shows a decrease in cereal-type pollen and increases in the pollen of herbs; the detailed pollen curves imply increases in common knapweed, thistles, buttercup-types, devil's bit scabious, plantains, docks/sorrels and, in particular, dandelion-types. The overall land-use suggested by the diverse and abundant herb pollen assemblage, is pastoralism. Given the diversity of the pollen of herbs, the relative abundance of dandelion-types is interpreted as indicative of waste or disturbed ground rather than reflecting preferential preservation of more robust pollen grains. Cereal-type pollen is recorded in much lower quantities than from deposit 1305 which may indicate reduced local cultivation or secondary processing, assuming it is not attributable to wild grasses. Non-pollen palynomorphs provide continued evidence for wetter environments and include occurrences of the blue/green algae *Botryococcus* (HdV-766) and *Spirogyra* (HdV-130).

Tree and shrub pollen accounts for *c* 20% of the total land pollen counted from deposit 1303, with walnut remaining the most abundant pollen type, although the numbers decrease from the bottom to the top of the deposit. Grains of maple/sycamore, beech, pine and oak pollen are recorded along with occurrences of rowan. The tree and shrub pollen suggests the probable local occurrence of ornamental trees such as walnut and beech, with pollen from pine and oak possibly derived from a more regional source. Rowans are insect-pollinated, but the seeds are bird-transported and could therefore represent trees growing regionally; however, rowans have an association with myths and symbolism and may have been planted adjacent to dwellings for protection (Woodland Trust nd b).

Overlying the assemblages described above is sandy deposit 1302, in which no pollen was preserved. The pollen subsamples from the overlying fills (1300 and 1301) contained a very different assemblage dominated by sedges, with

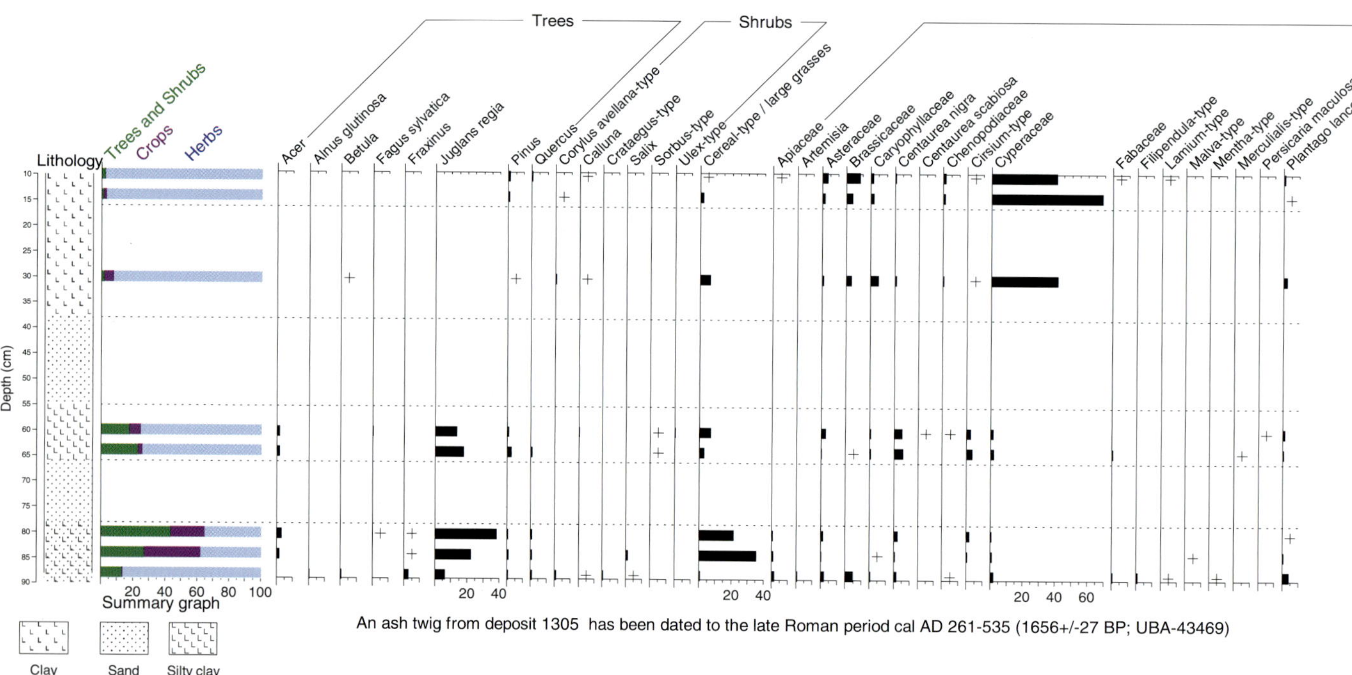

Fig. 5.21 Pollen sequence from the spring channel

fewer records of pollen of grasses and dandelion-type, suggesting rather damp environments and waste/rough ground.

Discussion

Although there are several Roman sites, including villas, that have been excavated in the Northampton area, there are few that have had pollen analysis undertaken, partly presumably because of the unsuitability of sediments. The data from Panattoni Park therefore provide a significant contribution to our understanding of land use and landscape change during a period of late Roman settlement.

The data are interpreted to suggest an initial switch from predominantly pastoral farming to one of cultivation or local processing of crops (assuming the cereal-types reflect cultivated rather than wild grass species). High frequencies of pollen of walnut are interpreted as evidence of the local development of ornamental trees, perhaps growing in the surroundings of the villa or the temple/mausoleum or in a local grove. Other tree types such as beech and possibly maple/sycamore may also have been deliberately planted along with walnut, as part of an ornamental garden. The walnut trees may have been utilised as a food source (walnuts) as well as potentially for flour and oil.

There are occasional records of walnut pollen prior to the Roman period (Long *et al.* 1999; Sidell *et al.* 2000) but it is usually regarded as a Roman introduction (Godwin 1975). Pollen records of walnut are generally from Roman or post-Roman deposits and the records are often of single or a few grains only, which may represent long-distance transport

(Scaife 2001, 123). However, it is perhaps more likely that the abundance of walnut pollen at Panattoni Park, recording values in excess of 35% of the total pollen counted, represent local development, grown deliberately for walnuts and as ornamental trees. This is an important record in the history of Roman palynology, given the proximity of the site to a villa. Walnut pollen was also recorded from Clatterford Roman villa on the Isle of Wight, albeit in much smaller quantities (Scaife 2001). Whilst the cultivation of cereals and herbs requires access to seeds and a plot of land, cultivation of walnut trees implies technical knowledge and longer-term planning (van der Veen *et al.* 2008, 33). Grafted walnut trees generally start to produce nuts after approximately four years and grow best in better drained soils and warmer temperatures, avoiding frosts and strong winds (Royal Horticultural Society 2021). Records of walnuts from plant macrofossil assemblages from Roman Britain suggest that walnut is more commonly found on elite sites (van der Veen *et al.* 2008, 27).

In general, the pollen assemblage from Panattoni Park accords with those from Wollaston, in the Nene Valley east of Northampton, in suggesting a regional palaeoenvironment of largely open landscapes with rough/waste and disturbed ground (Brown *et al.* 2001).

MARINE SHELL *by Rebecca Nicholson*

A small assemblage of 81 individual shells of European flat oyster *Ostrea edulis* L. (1.054kg) was collected by hand from 20 contexts, with an additional 23 valves (0.522kg) extracted from the

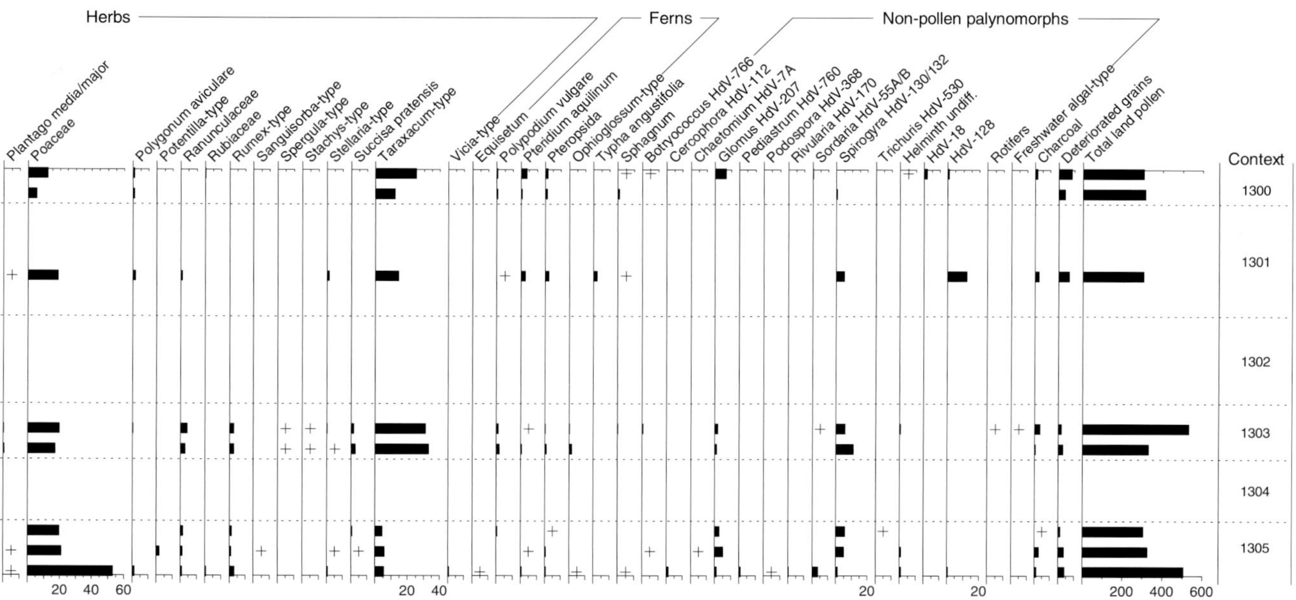

dried residues of sieved soil samples. Several pit fills, those dated being middle Roman (Phase 4), included over 20 valves, but no context included over 30 identifiable shells. All bivalves were quantified (left and right valves were counted separately) and examined for evidence of epibont infestation and encrustations such as those caused by marine worms, sponges and barnacles and for the attachment of juvenile oysters or other shellfish. Shell condition, shell and hinge shape and any unusual characteristics were also recorded together with evidence of marks inflicted during opening and removal of the shellfish (following descriptions and illustrations in Winder 2011). Given the small numbers of shells, measurement was not undertaken.

Most contexts yielded single or small numbers of oyster valves, of variable size and condition, but mostly of the traditional round form. The features with the greatest quantity of shells include middle Roman (Phase 4) pits 1038, 1045 and 1430. Shells were also recovered from rubbish/midden deposit 1001, south of building 1320, also Phase 4.

Typically, the oysters are in fair or poor condition, some being very thin and friable. A few shells have a distinct chalky deposit internally, which may reflect rapid changes in salinity and growth in shallow estuaries or creeks (MacDonald 2011). Some shells have evidence of tunnelling, principally on the exterior, mainly consistent with the marine polychaete worm *Polydora ciliata* (Johnston). There are very occasional examples of infestation in the form of tunnels consistent with those caused by *Polydora hoplura* Claparède. The latter are a significant problem for the modern shellfish industry, causing mudblisters internally, although the shellfish can still be eaten safely. The distribution of *P. hoplura* around the British coastline may be significant as this worm has a south-westerly distribution (Winder 2011) and this may provide an indication of the origin of the shellfish. There are also several instances of holes probably caused by predatory gastropod molluscs such as dogwhelks or sting winkle. At this date it is likely that the oysters were harvested from wild beds which would have been plentiful.

A relatively small proportion of shells have opening notches, indicating that the shellfish were opened when still alive, but it is not clear whether the shellfish were eaten raw or cooked. Certainly in Roman Italy oysters were eaten raw, accompanied by dipping sauces: one recipe is given by Apicius (2009, book 9, recipe 410) which details a dipping sauce made of pepper, lovage, egg yolk, vinegar, liquamen, oil and wine, with honey as an optional addition. There are also recipes which include cooked oysters.

Oysters are present on most Roman military, urban and villa sites in England, which demonstrates the widespread movement inland of these perishable shellfish, presumably packed in pots or tubs with sea water or wrapped in seaweed for transport overland. The small size of the assemblage is consistent with those recovered from other Roman excavations such as those from around the extramural settlement at Alchester, Oxfordshire (Winder 2001; Nicholson 2018), suggesting that oysters were at least an occasional food of those with the means to afford them.

HUMAN SKELETAL REMAINS
by Mandy Kingdom

The human remains recovered from the site comprised three discrete inhumations (skeletons 3006, 6004 and 20575), a femur from an uncertain feature (1420) and a heavily truncated deposit of cremated bone (6006; Tables 5.16–17). All the burials are likely to date from the middle or late Roman periods (Phases 4 and 5), but there was little stratigraphic or artefactual dating evidence other than possibly residual sherds from the backfills. The one exception to this was the cremation, which was accompanied by a Lower Nene Valley white ware flagon/bottle dated to AD 120–230.

Unburnt skeletal remains

Methodology

The skeletal remains were analysed and recorded in accordance with published guidelines (Brickley and McKinley 2004; Mitchell and Brickley 2017). Preservation was recorded with reference to completeness (scored as <25%, 26–50%, 51–75% or 76–100%), degree of fragmentation (scored as low: <25% fragmented; medium: 25-75% fragmented; or high: >75% fragmented) and degree of surface erosion (after McKinley 2004a, 16).

Sex estimation was based on observations of the sexually dimorphic traits of the skull and pelvis (Buikstra and Ubelaker 1994). Age was estimated based on the observation of late-fusing epiphyses (Scheuer and Black 2000) along with the morphology of the auricular surface (Lovejoy *et al.* 1985).

Metrical analysis was carried out to calculate the platymeric index (indicator of proximal femur shape) and platycnemic index (indicator of medio-lateral flatness of the tibia; Brothwell 1981) where possible. It was not possible to employ measurements to estimate the statures for any of the four individuals due to fragmentation of the long bones.

Non-metric traits or minor anomalies of skeletal anatomy that may be genetically or environmentally induced (Mays 2021, 155) were scored as present or absent after Berry and Berry (1967) and Finnegan (1978). All bones were examined macroscopically for evidence of pathology and trauma and, where present, this was described and differential diagnoses explored with reference to standard texts (for example, Aufderheide and Rodríguez-Martin 1998; Ortner 2003; Roberts and Connell 2004).

Table 5.16 Summary of inhumation burials

Grave	Skeleton	Preser-vation	Sex	Age	Metric/non-metric traits	Dental pathology	Skeletal pathology	Notes
1427	1420	Poor	-	Adult	-	-	-	L. femur only
20576	20575	Fair	Indet.	Adult	-	Calculus	Cribra orbitalia, osteo-arthritis, osteophytosis	
3004	3006	Fair	Male	Prime adult (26–35 yrs)	Platymeric; 3rd trochanter on L. femur	-	PNB, osteophytosis, fracture of R. tibial shaft (healed)	Cranium truncated
6005	6004	Fair	Male	Adult	Platymeric; zygo-maticofacial foramen absent; parietal foramen; bilateral mandibular tori	Calculus, AMTL, caries	PNB, spondylosis deformans, osteophytosis	

Preservation

Considering skeleton completeness, bone fragmentation and bone surface condition together, the overall preservation of the skeletons was judged to be poor (skeleton 1420) or fair (skeletons 20575, 3006 and 6003). Skeleton 1420 was just a partial left femur, and skeleton 20575 was approximately 40% complete, with most skeletal regions represented. Skeletons 3006 and 6004 were both approximately 60% complete and had all skeletal regions represented, except for the cranium missing from skeleton 3006. Skeletons 3006, 6004 and 20575 had bone surfaces which were moderately eroded, consistent with McKinley's grade 2 (2004a, 16). More extensive erosion was observed across the femur surface of skeleton 1420, consistent with McKinley's grade 3 (ibid.). Fragmentation was recorded as high for all skeletons, with the epiphyses of the long bones, the crania and pelvises most affected.

Sex and age at death estimation

The assemblage consisted of one individual of unknown sex (skeleton 1420), one of indeterminate sex (skeleton 20575) and two male individuals (skeletons 3006 and 6004). The sex of skeleton 1420 is unknown due to the absence of any sexually dimorphic traits. Skeleton 20575 was recorded as being of indeterminate sex to reflect that fact that sexually dimorphic traits in the pelvis were absent and, in the cranium, observations were limited by its fragmentary nature and mixed traits: the oribital margin suggested a possible male, while the mandible indicated a possible female. Although the cranium was absent from skeleton 3006, this individual was estimated to have been a male based on the morphology of the sciatic notch and auricular surface. These observations are supported by the size of both femoral heads (51mm, M=>47mm; Chamberlain 1994; Bass 2005). Features of the skull and morphology of the sciatic notch, along with the length of the left glenoid cavity (43mm M=>37mm) and right femoral head (51mm M=>47mm) all indicated that skeleton 6004 was biologically male. Age at death estimation was problematic due to the absence or poor preservation of the pelvises. All four skeletons were determined to be adults based on epiphyseal fusion and/or the general size/morphology of the elements present. No additional age information could be obtained for skeletons 1420, 6004 or 20575. Skeleton 3006 was determined to have been a prime adult (26–35 years) based on late-fusing epiphyses (the medial clavicle), and the morphology of a partial left auricular surface, where some striae and course granulation could be observed (Lovejoy *et al.* 1985).

Metrics and non-metrics

The platymeric index for skeleton 3006 and skeleton 6004 were 79 and 84.6, respectively, placing the individuals in the platymeric range (index below 84.9; Brothwell 1981, 88), indicating a flat proximal femur diaphysis (platymeria). The reasons for differences in femur shaft shape are not clear, but ancestry, mechanical stresses and mineral or vitamin deficiency have all been suggested (ibid., 89). The tibial platycnemic index for skeleton 6004 was 75 and therefore eurycnemic (>69.9; ibid., 89), indicating a rounded proximal tibial diaphysis morphology. Again, reasons for variation in the shape of the tibial shaft are unknown, but pathology and mechanical factors are among the possibilities (ibid., 89). These shaft shapes are not uncommon for the Roman period; similar indices have been recorded from other Roman sites, such as at Gill Mill Quarry, Oxfordshire (Webb *et al.* 2018) and the Covenham to Boston pipeline, Lincolnshire (Webb 2015).

All the skeletons could be scored for the presence/absence of cranial and/or post-cranial non-metric traits. Non-metric traits are skeletal variants which cause no symptoms (Mays 1998, 102). Some have a strong genetic component in their aetiology and have been used to study relatedness between individuals, whilst others may be influenced by mechanical factors operating on the bones (Mays 2021, 112, 118). In skeletons 1420 and 20575, no traits were recorded as present, but observations were limited to an incomplete femur from the former, and a patella from the latter. Only the presence/absence of post-cranial non-metric traits could be scored in skeleton 3006; a third trochanter was noted on the left femur. In skeleton 6004, only a limited number of cranial (5) and post-cranial (12) landmarks could be scored; there were no post-cranial traits present and cranial traits included absent zygomaticofacial foramen (right and left), one right parietal foramen (left was recordable) and bilateral mandibular tori (bony overgrowths on the buccal aspect of the mandible in the region of the molar tooth sockets).

Dentition and dental pathology

Two skeletons (6004 and 20575) had dentitions. Only a small portion of the anterior mandible from skeleton 20575 was present and it had suffered post-mortem damage. In addition, there were four loose anterior teeth (both mandibular central incisors and mandibular canines), and all of these had exposed dentine due to attrition. Deposits of calculus (dental plaque) were observed on three of these teeth (both central incisors and the right canine) and, in terms of their extent, were scored as slight to moderate after Brothwell (1981, 155). Skeleton 6004 had three sections of the mandible present with seven observable sockets and a total of fifteen loose maxillary and mandibular teeth. Despite having suffered post-mortem damage, it was possible to observe severe attrition on five teeth (two maxillary – the left first premolar and right second premolar – and three mandibular – both central incisors and the right lateral incisor); only the roots remained. Slight to moderate deposits of calculus (Brothwell 1981, 155) were present on four teeth (maxillary right second premolar, mandibular left second premolar and both mandibular second molars) and a large carious lesion was present on the right mandibular second molar. This had resulted in the loss of half the crown and proximal root and a periapical lesion in the form of a small, smooth walled granuloma (Dias and Tayles 1997) above the tooth socket. It was also evident that four teeth had been lost ante-mortem with near complete re-absorption of the alveola.

The dental pathologies observed in these skeletons are commonly the consequence of carbohydrate consumption, particularly of simple sugars and poor dental hygiene (Lieverse 1999). Dental disease is often accumulative, the relationship between different conditions being a very complex one. For example, a build-up of calculus can lead to inflammation of the gums and/or periodontal ligament (periodontal disease), which in turn can result in ante-mortem tooth loss (Hillson 2000, 249;

Nelson 2016, 472). Similarly, caries is caused by the progressive destruction of dental enamel, dentine and cement by acid produced by acidogenic bacteria within the calculus (Hillson 1996, 269). If severe enough (as seen in skeleton 6004), caries can lead to periapical lesions (Waldron 2009, 238). Periapical lesions are identified as openings or holes in the jaws at the apex of a tooth root. They arise as a result of inflammation of the dental pulp that can occur through trauma, caries or attrition. These cavities may contain granulation tissue (a granuloma), as observed in skeleton 6004, or a fluid filled sac (a periapical cyst), both of which are usually asymptomatic, or, at their most severe, a pus filled sac (an abscess). Differentiation between the types of cavities in dry bone relies on the detection of size differences and morphological differences in their margins and walls (Dias and Tayles 1997).

Skeletal pathology

Skeletal pathology was observed in three of the four skeletons and is discussed below according to primary aetiology (non-specific bone infection, metabolic conditions, joint disease and trauma).

Non-specific infection

Evidence for non-specific bone infection was observed in two individuals, skeletons 3006 and 6004, in the form of periosteal new bone and osteomyelitis. Periosteal new bone (PNB) is commonly observed in archaeological populations and is identified by the presence of fine pitting, longitudinal striations and/or plaque-like new bone formation on the original cortical surface (Roberts and Manchester 2010, 172). These lesions may occur due to infection or as a result of other conditions such as metabolic disease or trauma (Ortner 2003, 88).

Smooth, healed, striated PNB was observed on the medial aspect of both tibial diaphyses of skeleton 6004. Smooth, porotic PNB was also present on the ilium, superior to the acetabular margin of the right innominate bone. In archaeological assemblages, the anterior aspect of the tibia is the most common location for PNB, possibly because this area is more susceptible to recurrent minor trauma due to its close proximity to the skin (Roberts and Manchester 2010, 172). The PNB observed on the ilium may have been associated with inflammation of the ischio-femoral ligament and soft tissues associated with stabilisation of the hip joint. All PNB lesions were healed, indicating that in life the individual's defence system had fought the cause of the inflammatory response (Ortner 2003, 193; Weston 2012, 494).

Healing porotic and partially striated PNB were observed on the anterior aspect of the proximal right tibial diaphysis of skeleton 3006, in association with a well-healed fracture. The fracture callus (healed, remodelled bone) was present just inferior to the nutrient foramen on the tibia diaphysis and had a well-healed cloaca on the medial/posterior boarder, indicative of non-specific osteomyelitis, or bone infection. A cloaca is an opening, or sinus, through the cortex of the bone into the medullary cavity and in life would have served the purpose of draining pus from the bone. Considering the presence of the trauma, it is very likely that the infection had directly entered the body at the site of the fracture (Ortner 2003, 195). The same skeleton also had smooth porotic PNB on the mid-distal diaphysis of the right fibula (medial aspect), probably associated with the trauma and subsequent infection of the lower right leg.

Metabolic disease

Evidence for metabolic disease was observed in skeleton 20575 only, in the form of cribra orbitalia. Cribra orbitalia is identified by the presence of porosity and/or pitting of the orbital roof (eye socket; Stuart-Macadam 1991, 109). The condition is associated with iron deficiency anaemia (Mays 2021, 212; Stuart-Macadam 1991), or megaloblastic anaemia (Walker *et al.* 2009) and may be due to a lack of iron in the diet, iron malabsorption due to parasitic infestation, infection, haemorrhage or a deficiency of vitamins C and B12 (Koztowski and Witas 2012, 406; Walker *et al.* 2009). The porosity observed in the central left orbit of skeleton 20575 was minor and healed, indicating that the individual had recovered from deficiency earlier in their life.

Joint disease

Joint disease was present in all three of the most complete individuals (skeletons 3006, 6004 and 20575) and included spondylosis deformans, osteophytosis and osteoarthritis, conditions which are commonly observed in archaeological human remains (Aufderheide and Rodríguez-Martín 1998, 95). Spondylosis deformans is defined by the presence of coarse pitting and/or new bone growth on the superior and inferior surfaces of the vertebral endplates and is often observed alongside marginal osteophytosis (Rogers and Waldron 1995, 27). Osteoarthritis is a chronic, progressive and non-inflammatory disease that affects any synovial joint in the skeleton and is usually associated with

progressive age (Rogers and Waldron 1995, 32; Aufderheide and Rodríguez-Martí, 1998, 93; Ortner 2003, 545). It was diagnosed by the presence of either eburnation (polished bone from bone-on-bone contact) or at least two of either pitting, osteophytes or bony contour change (Rogers and Waldron 1995, 44).

Spondylosis deformans was observed on the endplates of the remains of the cervical thoracic and lumbar spines of skeleton 6004. In addition, osteoarthritis was observed on at least two superior and inferior thoracic articular facets and a superior lumbar articular facet from skeleton 20575.

Extra-spinal joint disease was observed in the form of osteophytosis on the first metacarpal distal joint surface and on the margin of the proximal articular joint of a distal hand phalanx from skeleton 20575. It was also observed on the lateral aspects of the right and left femoral heads and acetabular margins of skeleton 3006 and on both shoulder and hip joints of skeleton 6004. In the right hip of 6004 eburnation was observed, indicating that the changes were more severe. Marginal osteophytes are common in older individuals and are often part of the aging process (Roger and Waldron 1995, 20). As a major weight-bearing joint, the hip is generally more prone to osteoarthritis than other non-weight-bearing joints (ibid. 32).

Trauma

As mentioned above, skeleton 3006 had a well-healed proximal right tibial shaft fracture with evidence of healed secondary infection. Observation of the healed fracture line suggests this was probably an oblique fracture (Galloway 1999, 195), although this was not confirmed by radiography.

Cremation 6006

Methodology

The cremation deposit was recovered, processed and analysed in accordance with published guidelines (McKinley 2004b). In the field, the deposit was subject to whole-earth recovery. Processing involved wet sieving the deposit to sort it into >10mm, 10–4mm, 4–2mm and 2–0.5mm sized

Table 5.17 Summary of cremation deposit 6006

Deposit	>10mm (% of total weight)	10–4mm (% of total weight)	4–2mm (% of total weight)*	Total weight	Maximum fragment size	Identified elements	Colour	MNI, sex, age
6006	423.2g (66.9%)	171.2g (27.1%)	37.9g (6.0%)	632.3g	65mm (R ulna shaft)	Fragments of: skull vault; vertebral arch; rib; humeral, radial ulnae, femur and tibia shafts; radial head and innominate	White (80%), grey/white (10%), brown/orange (10%)	MNI = 1 Sex unknown Adult unspecified (>18 yrs)

* Estimated from 20g sample of the 24–2mm fraction (total 118.5g)

fractions. The >10mm and 10–4mm sieve fractions were fully sorted, separating the burnt bone from the extraneous material (eg stones). Due to the amount of bone present it was not viable to fully sort the 4–2mm fractions. Instead, a 20g sample from this fraction was sorted and the percentage bone weight calculated. This percentage was then applied to the total weight of the unsorted material to provide more informed bone weight estimates for the fraction (Table 5.17). The smallest fraction size (2-0.5mm) was not sorted but was rapidly scanned for identifiable skeletal remains and artefacts. All bone was analysed to record colour, weight and maximum fragment size. Each sieve fraction was examined for identifiable bone elements and the presence of pyre and/or grave goods. The minimum number of individuals present was estimated based on the identification of repeated elements and/or the presence of juvenile and adult bones within the deposit. Estimation of age was based on the development stage of tooth roots (AlQahtani 2009), observations of completely fused epiphyses (Scheuer and Black 2000) and, more generally, the overall size/morphology of identified bones. Sex estimation was not possible due to the absence of sexually diagnostic features. The bone fragments were also examined macroscopically for evidence of pathology and trauma and where present this was described and differential diagnoses explored with reference to standard texts (as above).

Bone weight

The total bone weight of 632.3g is approximately a third of the weight expected for one individual from a modern cremation (1650g; McKinley 2000, 269). This weight is just within the range that has been reported for archaeologically recovered cremation deposits (600–900g; McKinley 2013, 154).

Fragmentation

There are many factors which may affect the extent of bone fragmentation in a cremation deposit. Some level of fragmentation may occur as a result of excavation and processing, although it is assumed that the impact of this is fairly uniform across all deposits (McKinley 1994). Other factors which may affect fragmentation of the bone are the cremation process itself, as a result of heat-related cracking and fissuring; the collection of the bone from the pyre following cremation; any handling/manipulation of the bone prior to burial; the type of burial (ie urned versus unurned); the burial and backfilling processes; and any post-burial disturbance or truncation (ibid.).

The level of fragmentation within deposit 6006 was relatively low, the highest proportion of bone weight being from the >10mm fraction (423.2g). In addition, the largest bone fragment was a piece of right ulna shaft, which measured 65mm.

Skeletal representation

Due to the low level of fragmentation it was possible to identify over half (55.8%) of the bone fragments to a skeletal region. The greatest proportion of identifiable bone was from the cranium (40.4%), including three adjoining fragments of frontal bone. The high proportion of cranial bone probably reflects the fact that this bone is more easily identified than other bones in cremation assemblages (McKinley 2004b, 11). Bones from the upper limb region were the next most frequently identified included fragments of scapula and fragments of humeral, radial and ulna diaphysis. It was noted that small skeletal elements were poorly represented or absent; for example, only one and a half tooth roots were present and there were no obviously identifiable hand or foot bones.

Colour of the cremated bone

The colour of cremated bone reflects the degree of oxidation and is therefore an indication of the efficiency of the cremation in terms of the quantity of fuel used to build the pyre, the temperature attained in various parts of the pyre, and the length of time over which the cremation was undertaken (McKinley 2004b, 11). Colour may range from brown/orange (unburnt), to black (charred, *c* 300°C), through hues of blue and grey (incompletely oxidised, up to *c* 600°C) to white (fully oxidised, >600°C).

The burnt bone from burial 6006 was predominantly white (80%). Approximately 10% of the fragments (primarily lower long bone fragments) were white/grey, occasionally with black interior surfaces, and approximately a further 10% (including right ulna diaphysis fragments) were a brown/orange colour on the inner surface and a white/grey colour on the cortical surface. The non-white bone may come from those areas of the skeleton where the bone was thicker, with thicker, soft tissue coverage than elsewhere in the skeleton, which, as a result, burnt at a lower temperature (thickness of soft tissue varies across the body and cremation of the bone beneath it cannot commence until it has been removed; McKinley 2013). It is also possible that the non-white bone indicates areas of the pyre which did not reach the required high temperature to obtain full oxidization. It is unlikely that a constant temperature would have been maintained across the pyre or throughout the cremation, the peripheries being cooler than the central areas (ibid.).

Demography

No repeated elements were observed and therefore the deposit is considered to represent a minimum of one individual. The general size and robusticity of partially preserved brow ridges suggested a possible male individual, although this is very tentative owing to the incompleteness and absence of any other sexually diagnostic traits. No specific age indicators were observed, but the size and morphology of the identified fragments were consistent with those of an adult or later adolescent.

Pathology and non-metric traits

Healed smooth striated periosteal new bone was observed on fragments of proximal radius, fragments of tibia and a fragment of unidentified long bone diaphysis. This indicates that the individual had suffered but recovered from non-specific bone inflammation. No non-metric traits were observed.

Discussion

Three of the inhumations were observed to be in a fair condition (skeletons 3006, 6004 and 20575) and one (skeleton 1420) was in a poor condition. Sex estimation could only be attempted for two individuals (skeletons 3006 and 6004, both male) and age at death, for one (skeleton 3006, prime adult). Very limited metrical data could be obtained, and stature could not be estimated due to fragmentation.

Dental and skeletal pathology included calculus, caries, ante-mortem tooth loss, a periapical lesion, non-specific infection, joint disease and trauma. The majority of the dental disease was observed in skeleton 6004, the individual with the most dentition surviving. The non-specific infection observed in skeleton 6004 was well healed, indicating that this individual's defence system was robust enough to overcome the condition, although it is not possible to say what had caused it – it may have been relatively mild trauma, a localised soft tissue lesion (eg leg ulcer) or infection, or other condition of a metabolic or neoplastic nature. The healing periosteal new bone and healed osteomyelitis observed on the right tibia of skeleton 3006 are most likely a consequence of the fracture. The healing periosteal new bone to the anterior diaphysis and the smooth walled cloaca indicate there had been significant infection in and around the fracture. This would have been a nasty and painful fracture. The same individual had bilateral hip osteoarthritis,

possibly secondary to the fracture. Knowledge of the treatment of fractures was well advanced by the Roman period and included traction, splinting of the element, rest to allow for healing, the administration of alcohol, mandrake, henbane and the opium poppy to relieve pain, and wine, vinegar, pitch and turpentine to clean wounds (Roberts and Cox 2003, 161–2). Considering the fracture was well healed and the bone infection was healing or healed, skeleton 3006 had probably received medical treatment and care similar to this for the injury.

The cremation deposit (6006) comprised one adult, tentatively estimated to have been a male, with evidence of healed non-specific infection. The weight of the bone recovered was 632.3g, which is just within the expected range for an archaeologically recovered adult cremation burial (McKinley 2013, 154). However, the deposit was heavily truncated, which has limited the analysis; it is not possible to say how representative the bone is of the bone which was originally deposited. Thus, the osteological findings should be treated with caution. Bone fragments were brown/orange, black/grey and, most often, grey/white, reflecting variation in the temperature attained in different areas of the pyre and/or the duration of firing. This may have been due to a number of factors, such as anatomical differences between the different bone regions and/or the location of body parts in relation to the heat source.

RADIOCARBON DATING *by Andrew Simmonds*

A sample of ash twig preserved by waterlogging in fill 1305 of the spring channel was submitted for radiocarbon dating at the [14]CHRONO Centre for Climate, Environment and Chronology, Queen's University, Belfast, and the resultant date range calibrated using the OxCal 4.4.2 calibration program and the IntCal20 curve (Table 5.18; Bronk Ramsey 2009; Reimer *et al.* 2020). The calibrated date was rounded out to the nearest ten years in accordance with Mook (1986). The result confirmed that the deposit formed during the late Roman period or, less likely, the post-Roman period, and was consistent with the late Roman date of pottery from the overlying layers. A sample of cattle rib from fill 1302 failed to date due to insufficient collagen.

Table 5.18 Summary of radiocarbon dating results

Lab no.	Context	Sample	Material	Radiocarbon age BP	$F^{14}C$	Calibrated date range 95.4% confidence
UBA-43469	1305	35	Wood: *Fraxinus* sp. twig with pith and bark	1656±27	0.8137±0.0028	Cal AD 260–280 (4.7%) Cal AD 340–440 (75.6%) Cal AD 450–480 (5.1%) Cal AD 490–540 (10.0%)

Chapter 6

Discussion

PREHISTORIC AND EARLY ROMAN BACKGROUND

Before the Iron Age

The Nene Valley would have been a significant communication corridor during early prehistory, and the river itself would have provided important resources, but the evidence from Panattoni Park indicates only a minor human presence in the landscape before the Iron Age. In the Mesolithic period, when the flint scatter in Excavation Area 4 was deposited, a large proportion of the county's findspots have a riverine distribution, with a large number of locations on the flanks of the Nene Valley with views over the floodplain, similar to the situation at Panattoni Park (Phillips 2000, 4). Lawrence (Chapter 4) has reconstructed the flint scatter as the debris from a single episode of tool manufacture and use that took place sometime during the early part of the period. The knapper(s) exploited locally available flint cobbles to produce blanks that were then worked into a range of tools, some of which were utilised at the site while others may have been taken away for use elsewhere. Piercers and scrapers may have been used for hide-working, including the creation and maintenance of clothing, and hunting in the surrounding area is attested by the presence of an obliquely blunted point. Such *in situ* evidence is uncommon and provides a rare insight into the everyday routines of Mesolithic populations.

Evidence for the period between the Mesolithic knapping event and the establishment of more substantial settlement in the middle Iron Age was sparse, represented only by unstratified flints, two pits of possible Neolithic date in Area 4 and a single late Bronze Age pit in Area 5. Indeed, the date of the putatively Neolithic pits is not certain, relying as it does on the inclusion of a few flint flakes that could easily have been residual. However, small pits like these, occurring individually or in pairs or large clusters, represent the most common category of Neolithic feature found in Britain (Thomas 1999, 64–74). Locally, a comparable pair of pits has been excavated at Weedon Road, Upton (MOLA 2012) and a single pit containing only a Neolithic core was excavated at Bugbrooke (Northamptonshire Archaeology 2013). Some such pits contain exotic artefacts or objects that appeared to have been deposited in a deliberately structured manner, but the mixed and fragmentary character of the objects recovered from most pits suggests that the material was sourced from a secondary location such as a midden, as may be the case at Panattoni Park and Weedon Road. The limited evidence from these pits indicates that Panattoni Park saw only occasional visits by transient populations during this period and was not the location of any longer-term occupation. This need not, however, mean that the area was not part of a wider landscape that was exploited for natural resources or hunting, and the floodplains of the Nene would have provided opportunities for grazing livestock.

The pit alignment

The character of activity at the site changed completely during the middle Iron Age with the establishment of the long-lived boundary represented by the pit alignment and of the first substantial settlement. This initiated a period of several centuries that was characterised, albeit not necessarily continuously, by increasingly intensive farming of the land and the progressive enclosure of the landscape, which only ended with the abandonment of the villa at the end of the Roman period. The digging of the pit alignment may represent a significant change in attitudes regarding control over the landscape, and occurred at a time when permanent boundaries were first becoming widespread. The unusual form of pit alignments has attracted considerable discussion, largely due to the apparent incongruity between their linearity, which suggests a function as a boundary, and their discontinuous form, which would not provide a functioning barrier to movement of people or livestock. Attempts to resolve this contradiction have tended to argue either that the pits represent the surviving element of an originally more effective barrier, perhaps reinforced by an accompanying fence or bank, or that they had a more symbolic or ritual role. However, as at Panattoni Park, the evidence from the pits typically indicates that they were open features rather than postholes (Barber 1985, 151; Rylatt and Bevan 2007, 220), and evidence for a bank is rare, an example at Gardom's Edge, Derbyshire, comprising only a discrete mound 0.15m high beside each pit (Mellor 2007, 22), and the postulated ritual function is typically left undefined (but see Rylatt and Bevan 2007 for an exception). Of course, in practice a boundary does not necessarily have to present an insuperable barrier to movement in order to be respected, and it is not difficult to envisage boundaries that were intended to be traversed, for example between parts

177

of the landscape that were in different use or that were subject to different rights of access. Environmental evidence is not usually present in useful quantities, but pollen evidence from the alignments at Wollaston indicates that they existed in a largely grassland landscape and it is likely, therefore, that they were used to divide the valley landscape for the purposes of grazing livestock (Meadows 1995; 2009a, 67–70); their permeable form would allow animals to pass through unhindered while still demarcating the limits of individual ownership or rights of access.

The pit alignment at Panattoni Park comprises part of a particularly dense concentration of such boundaries in the part of the Nene Valley west of Northampton (Fig. 6.1), including an example less than 1.2km to the west at Hipwells, Upper Heyford (Seddon and Murray 2000). The boundaries in this area frequently appear to have taken their alignment from the river or its tributaries, to which they lie parallel or perpendicular. A particularly long alignment, for example, may be represented by a group of sites to the east, on the south side of the A4500 at Upton. Two sections of a single alignment were excavated at adjacent sites *c* 100m apart at Weedon Road and Quinton House School (Walker and Maull 2010; Foard-Colby and Walker 2010) and part of an alignment was excavated during the construction of the Cross Valley Link Road *c* 1km west of this (Carlyle 2010). The results of geophysical survey and evaluation in the fields between these sites, at Upton Park (Mason 2011), indicate that the excavated alignments in fact form parts of two converging alignments that extend along the top of the slope overlooking the Nene to the south, one of them being at least 1.3km long. A short distance north of these sites, at South Meadow Road, an alignment had a clear association with a contemporary ditch, from which it extended on a line that would have followed the slope down to meet a tributary of the Nene at a right angle (Speed 2015, 66). Some indication of the way such boundaries parcelled out the landscape is provided by the example of Prologis Park, Pineham, south of the river, where a particularly large complex comprised four pit alignments that divided up a large area of land on either side of a long-lived east–west boundary ditch (MOLA 2017). Neither end of the Panattoni Park alignment was definitely identified, but excavation and geophysical survey indicated that it defined a continuous boundary at least 200m long, extending north–south down the slope of the valley side towards the river, *c* 110m to the south. To the north it continued beyond the development area and to the south it extended into the adjoining fill area, where the pits became increasingly indistinct in the geophysical survey, perhaps because the fills here were closely similar to the alluvium into which they were cut.

Details of the chronology of the alignment and the middle Iron Age settlement were uncertain due to the paucity of material from the pits. This is not uncommon, since the boundaries defined by such alignments often appear to have been situated away from areas of contemporary settlement and consequently did not routinely receive associated artefactual material. In this instance, the alignment clearly predated the late Iron/early Roman enclosures that cut it, but the pottery was not particularly helpful in narrowing down the date, comprising only a handful of small sherds that could be residual and few that were in any way chronologically diagnostic. It may be significant that one of the few probable early Iron Age sherds came from a basal fill. Otherwise, similarly early sherds were recovered from one other pit and from a residual context in a late Iron Age/early Roman enclosure ditch that cut the alignment. Although pottery fabrics did not change substantially between the early and middle Iron Age, the vessels represented by these sherds were of a shouldered form that was not found at the settlement in Area 5 and may indicate that the alignment was created before the settlement. Similar difficulties have been encountered in dating other alignments in the local area. The best-dated example in the area is the Upton alignment, where a sample of hazel charcoal from a lower fill produced a radiocarbon date of 400–200 cal BC (Walker and Maull 2010). A rather earlier date of 1060–920 cal BC was obtained for a sample of charcoal ash from an upper fill in an alignment at Harlestone Quarry, 5km north of Panattoni Park, and was regarded by the excavators as residual material from a nearby area of late Bronze Age settlement (Chapman *et al*. 2017, 66), although the date is not implausibly early. A single sherd of Bronze Age pottery was also the only dating evidence for the alignment at Hipwells (Seddon and Murray 2000). The largest pottery assemblage from any of the local alignments comes from the complex at Prologis Park, where three of the four alignments produced Iron Age pottery, the most diagnostic of which was a jar attributed to the 'late middle Iron Age (250–100 BC)' (MOLA 2017, 48). The dates from these two sites bracket the broad late Bronze Age to middle Iron Age date range that is typically attributed to such alignments (Rylatt and Bevan 2007, 220), and artefactual material from others in the vicinity generally comprises small quantities of pottery with broad Iron Age or late Bronze Age/Iron Age dates. Construction of the Panattoni Park alignment during the early Iron Age or at the start of the middle Iron Age, as indicated by the few diagnostic sherds, would be consistent with this date range.

The use of this boundary to define the western limit of the late Iron Age/early Roman settlement indicates that it was long-lived, spanning several centuries, and this longevity appears to be a notable feature of middle Iron Age boundaries in the Upper Nene Valley, indicating a considerable degree of landscape (and presumably social) continuity. The most closely similar instance was recorded at Prologis Park, where one of the pit alignments was used to define the eastern boundary of the main

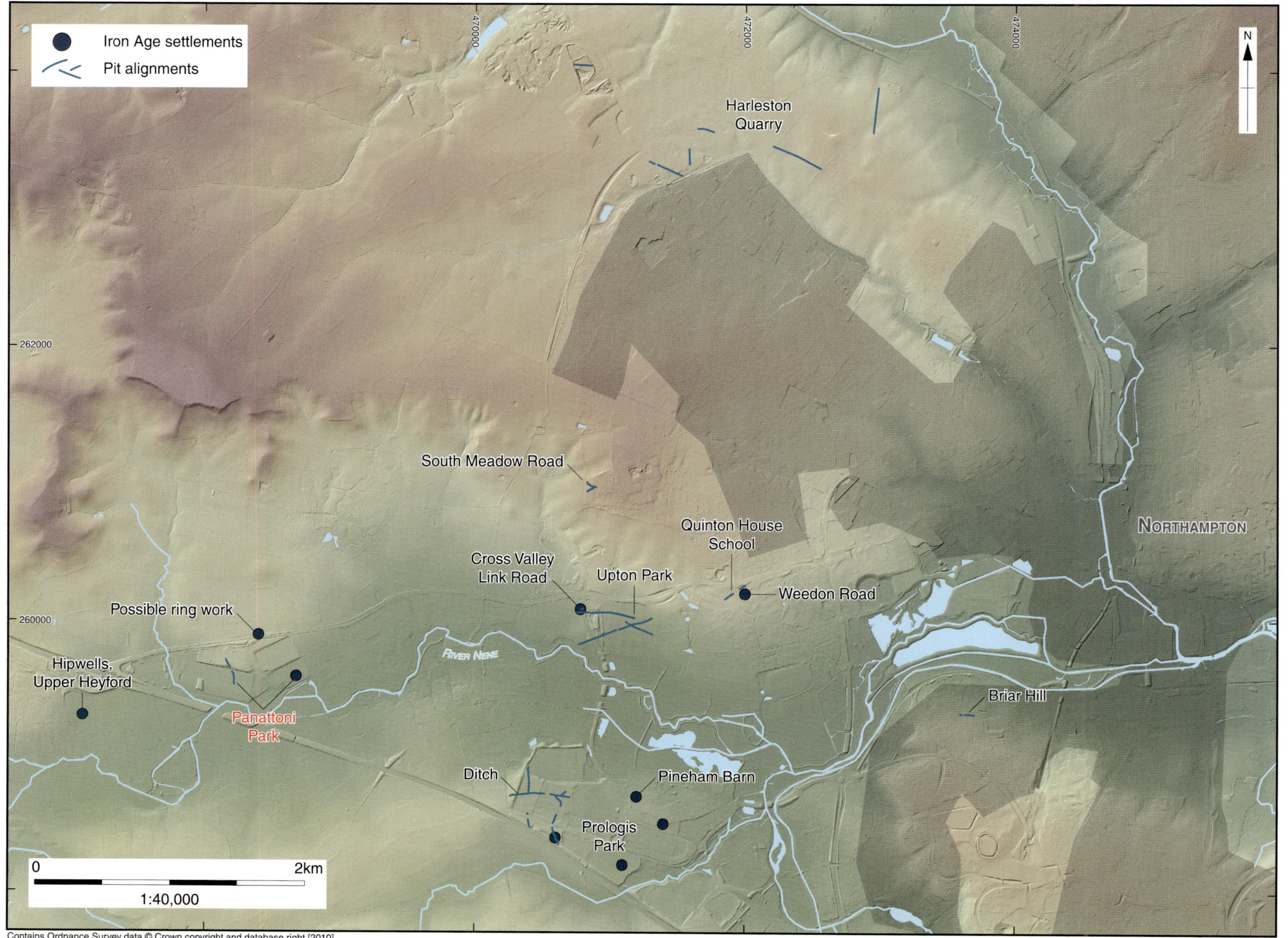

Fig. 6.1 Pit alignments and other Iron Age settlements mentioned in the discussion

domestic enclosure during the middle to late Iron Age and was subsequently perpetuated by the corresponding boundary of the Roman settlement during the 1st to 3rd centuries AD (MOLA 2017). In another example close to this, at Pineham Barn, a long-lived Iron Age boundary ditch that extended for over 1km subsequently had substantial Iron Age settlement enclosures added to either side and, further along its length, formed the northern boundary of a Roman settlement (ULAS 2015). On the north side of the valley at Weedon Road, Upton, the pit alignment and a linear boundary ditch that ran parallel to it provided the alignment for two successive phases of enclosures during the middle and late Iron Age (Walker and Maull 2010). Downstream of Northampton, the largest area of pit alignments examined in the county lies at Wollaston, where one alignment was traced for over 3km and coaxial arrangements divided the land-scape into blocks that continued to be used throughout the Iron Age, with their boundaries becoming marked by ditches later in the period, and the first farmsteads were constructed in the corners of three of these units during the middle/late Iron Age. Some of the boundaries continued as ditches and a major droveway into the Roman period (Meadows 1995; 2009a, 67–70). At Panattoni Park the use of the pit alignment was similarly long-lived and evidently encompassed the occupation of the middle Iron Age settlement in Area 4.

Middle Iron Age settlement

If the construction of the pit alignment represented the first evidence for division of the landscape to facilitate grazing of the floodplain and valley sides, then the construction of the Area 4 settlement may represent the next progression, comprising the first permanent or semi-permanent occupation site. The relationship of the Area 4 settlement, comprising at least seven roundhouses, to the contemporary L-shaped ditches is not well understood, although the geophysical survey provided no evidence that the ditches formed an enclosure around the settlement but indicated that they may instead have formed part of an arrangement of broadly rectilinear boundaries that continued to the south of the excavation area. Rather than being enclosed, the settlement may therefore have been nestled within the angle formed by these two boundaries.

There is good evidence that, like the pit align-ment, the settlement was associated with a continu-ation of a pastoral lifestyle. The settlement is unusual both in its open form and its location at the edge of the floodplain, which was generally not used for settlement (Meadows 2009a, 78). It is possible that its situation and the absence of an enclosure ditch indicate a lack of permanence, and although environmental evidence that might confirm this hypothesis was lacking, a comparable instance is recorded at Farmoor, in the Thames Valley west of Oxford (Lambrick and Robinson 1979). There, three small settlements were situated in wet, open grassland on the floodplain, and aquatic molluscs from ditch fills at two of them indicated they were subject to periodic flooding from the adjacent river that would have rendered year-round occupation impossible. The absence of some common perennial weed species suggested that each farmstead was used for no more than about five years and the excavators argued that they represented short-lived settlements that were used during the spring and summer by groups minding herds grazing on the meadows beside the river. A similar interpretation would be consistent with the evidence at Panattoni Park, although the intercut-ting ring gullies may suggest a longer sequence of use here. The ring gullies have been resolved into a sequence of four roundhouses in subphase 2a and three in subphase 2b, but it is equally possible that they represent a longer sequence, with fewer houses in occupation at any one time. If occupation was indeed seasonal the partial red deer skull may indicate that hunting was carried out in addition to animal husbandry, and that the period of occupa-tion included the late autumn/early winter, when the antler would be shed following the annual rut. It may be significant, therefore, that evidence for cultivation or processing of crops appeared to be completely lacking, since despite extensive excava-tion no deposits with indications of charred plant remains were identified. Furthermore, there was no evidence for crop processing in the form of querns, which is particularly striking on account of the proximity to Hunsbury Hillfort, which the large assemblage of more than 150 querns has made the type-site for beehive querns that characterise middle Iron Age milling practices (Ingle 1993–4). The scarcity of pits, and the complete absence of any of substantial size, further suggests that the settle-ment lacked significant capacity for storing grain. Conversely, there were elements of the settlement that may have been designed for stock manage-ment. The associated boundary ditches may themselves indicate a need to control the movement of livestock, and the adjoining enclosures may have been animal pens. This might also be the reason for the locations of the oval enclosure at the southern end of Phase 2a ditch 4382 and enclosures 4374 and 4380, which abutted the corresponding boundary in Phase 2b, which were situated adjacent to entrances through the boundary, a location where handling of livestock is likely to have been most frequent. The enclosures were too small to function as fields and contained no internal features that might indicate the presence of roundhouses. They were similar to a series of contemporary enclosures at Weedon Road, Upton, where a paucity of plant remains suggested a similar interpretation as a primarily pastoral settlement (Walker and Maull 2010). The animal bone assemblages at Farmoor indicated that the settlements were engaged in dairy farming (Lambrick and Robinson 1979, 134), and cattle were the predominant species at Panattoni Park, accounting for 70% of the remains (by NISP) with smaller numbers of sheep/goat and negligible quantities of pig and horse (Allen, Chapter 5).

The entirely pastoral farming regime suggested here would contrast with practices at most contemporary settlements in the Nene Valley, where mixed farming was the norm; indeed, the insertion of settlements into the landscape at Wollaston was specifically associated with environmental evidence for a changeover from pastoral to mixed agriculture (Meadows 1995; 2009a, 75). Similarly, charred grain and chaff indicates the processing and consumption of wheat crops at Upton and Pineham, the former also producing a saddle quern (Walker and Maull 2010; MOLA 2017). These sites comprise farmsteads within square or rectangular ditched enclosures, which constitute the typical settlement type of the period; of particular note are a contemporary landscape of at least four such settlements at Prologis Park and Pineham Barn (Brown and Carlyle 2007; ULAS 2015). The Panattoni Park settlement is clearly very distinct from these sites and also differs from the few contemporary open settlements known in the county, which are typically much more extensive 'agglomerated settlements' such as Wilby Way and Crick that include pits, four-post storage structures and a wider range of artefactual material (Thomas and Enright 2003; Chapman 1995).

Interpretation of the settlement as entirely pastoral, and possibly seasonally occupied, has significant implications regarding its integration into the wider population of the Upper Nene Valley. Rather than a discrete farmstead, it indicates that the site performed a specialised economic role within a wider community of more varied settlements. This implies that the middle Iron Age community of the valley was very closely integrated, with the more numerous mixed farming settlements perhaps serving as home bases from which some element of the population periodically departed for temporary settlements elsewhere in the local landscape.

Late Iron Age/early Roman settlement

Continuity of occupation through the late Iron Age, and often into the Roman period, appears to be the norm for middle Iron Age settlements in the Nene Valley, and although the settlement in Area 4 did not follow this trend, perhaps because of its suggested status as a seasonally occupied pastoral settlement, continuity of landscape organisation was demonstrated by the longevity of the boundary defined by the pit alignment. The curvilinear gully and L-shaped ditch that comprised the earliest activity (subphase 3a) may indicate that a short-lived episode of open settlement beside the boundary preceded the subsequent ditched complex, but there was insufficient evidence to indicate whether these features were domestic in nature or represented animal pens associated with

continued pastoral farming. The succeeding phase of settlement comprised an enclosure complex that abutted the eastern side of the boundary defined by the pit alignment. The south and east boundaries of the complex were sharply defined, indicating an overall extent of *c* 165m E–W and more than 185m N–S, an area of more than 3ha, the northern limit lying somewhere beyond the northern edge of the excavation areas.

The internal arrangement was less easily discerned, and it was not possible to definitely assign functions to specific parts of the complex. It is possible that the larger ditches that defined successive enclosures 5153 and 5448/5449 at the south-west corner of the settlement indicated that they had a distinct function, possibly as the main domestic focus, which would suggest a similar arrangement to the deeper ditches that enclosed the domestic area of the contemporary and ostensibly similar settlement at Pineham (Northamptonshire Archaeology 2007). However, in contrast to the roundhouse gullies that occupied the corresponding enclosure at Pineham, enclosures 5153 and 5448/5449 contained only two ill-defined groups of postholes, and analysis of the distribution of pottery within the settlement identified no notable concentration in this area (or elsewhere). It is alternatively possible that the enclosures at Panattoni Park formed a field system associated with the prehistoric settlement that Brown excavated immediately to the north, at the top of the slope. The 'red and black butt beakers' that Brown noted from pits there suggest a comparable date, and although the rescue conditions under which the site was recorded, when road-building was actually taking place, did not allow for the identification of structural features such as postholes, the evidence of hearths may indicate domestic occupation.

It is difficult to be certain when occupation at Panattoni Park began, as the late Iron Age 'Belgic' wares that dominated the pottery assemblage were in use both before and after the conquest period. However, the preponderance of these wares in subphase 3b, with only a small quantity of definitely post-conquest pottery, compared to the far greater prevalence of Roman wares in subphase 3c, may indicate that diagnostically Roman wares only began to be used here toward the end of subphase 3b. The paucity of pottery attributed to the late 1st century onward suggests that occupation ceased *c* AD 50/70; this corresponds with a wider pattern of apparent settlement abandonment or shift in the area south and west of the Fens during the period *c* AD 40–60 that has been tentatively associated with the conquest or the Boudiccan uprising (Smith and Fulford 2016, 408–10), although more prosaic socio-economic changes resulting from the imposition of Roman rule is another possible cause.

It is clear from the artefactual and palaeoenvironmental evidence that occupation was of a distinctly different character to that of the middle Iron Age settlement in Area 4. This phase represents the first evidence for the adoption of a mixed farming regime, with cattle continuing to be the most numerous species but now joined by arable cultivation in the form of wheat, barley and flax. In contrast to the earlier settlement, there was evidence for activities beyond mere subsistence, with a spindle whorl and a ceramic firebar indicating production of textiles and pottery (although no wasters were identified within the pottery assemblage). The presence of at least one waterhole represents a facility that was not provided in the Area 4 settlement and may indicate greater permanence. The bow brooch recovered from the waterhole may indicate an increased interest in individual appearance or a change in clothing styles, and the fragment from a 1st-century armilla that was recovered from a late Roman ditch may indicate the presence on the settlement of a military veteran. A concern with status may also be detected in the introduction of vessels with red or orange-brown surfaces and specialised forms for drinking, which would have appeared quite distinct from the darker, buff or brown jars of Iron Age pottery traditions and are likely to have been reserved for display in the context of Continental-style dining, indicating the novel practices that were entering British society at this time.

THE VILLA AND ITS LANDSCAPE

The excavation uncovered the southernmost building of the main complex of the villa and a large area of the associated agricultural landscape to the south and south-east. The alignments of the aisled building and ditched boundaries correspond closely with those recorded by geophysical survey to the north of the A4500, and although none of the boundaries can be traced through both areas it is clear that they form a single coaxial system (Fig. 6.2). The results of the excavation and the geophysical survey demonstrate that the buildings lay within the centre of an area that was delineated to north, west and south by ditched boundaries, with internal subdivisions that presumably indicate differentiation of space for various, primarily agricultural, activities. The excavation has demonstrated that the field systems beyond the villa enclosure were initially limited to a small number of poorly defined enclosures to the east and boundaries associated with an area to the south-east dedicated to crop-processing, which developed during the late Roman period into a more extensive arrangement. The latter began with the construction of an unusual subcircular enclosure (20350) that may have been a compound for livestock, which was subsequently replaced by a complex of rectilinear fields, perhaps representing a shift to arable cultivation or a combination of arable and animal husbandry.

The villa appears to have been founded *de novo*, with no indication of continuity from the early Roman settlement in the western part of the site or

the Iron Age settlement recorded by Brown. This was evident from the arrangement of the new boundaries, which completely disregarded the earlier complex where the two overlapped. The almost total absence of pottery attributable to the late 1st century and the first half of the 2nd century, in particular South Gaulish samian ware and early Central Gaulish forms, suggests that there was a hiatus of at least several decades between the two, and it is quite possible that the features of the preceding settlement were no longer visible on the ground surface when the villa landscape was laid out. Brown suggested a Hadrianic date for construction, based on the recovery of a coin from the foundations of the putative nymphaeum, but the pottery sequence from Panattoni Park would fit better with a date sometime after AD 150. The best dating evidence comes from the temple/mausoleum, where pottery from an associated pit indicates a start date after *c* AD 170, although this building need not have been exactly contemporary with the construction of the main building(s). The single coin of Hadrian was also recovered from the area of the temple/mausoleum, but was stratified above the pit and was therefore probably several decades old when it was brought to the site, perhaps as an offering, and has no bearing on the chronology.

The dating of the end of occupation is subject to the same difficulties that affect other sites at the end of the Roman period due to uncertainties regarding precisely when coinage and Roman pottery ceased to be used and how this relates to their date of final deposition (Meadows 2009b, 112). However, it can be confidently stated that occupation continued to very late in the period, probably extending to the end of the 4th century and perhaps into the 5th. In this respect, the presence of two certain and one possible coin of the last issue regularly represented in Roman Britain, from the period AD 388–402, is significant. One of these came from pit 1224 in the enclosure complex associated with the villa, and several other coins from this complex, including the coin of Julian the Apostate that Brown recovered from the later phase of the nymphaeum cistern, attest to occupation at least as late as the third quarter of the 4th century, while a similar date for activity in the crop-processing area was indicated by the coin from corndrying oven 2039. The latest phase of activity excavated by Brown at the villa itself appears to indicate that occupation continued in a much reduced state, with the nymphaeum building partially demolished and reused as a tannery. Brown ascribed this to the 5th century but was not specific regarding her dating evidence. Perhaps the most intriguing evidence came from the field system east of the spring channel, where the three phases of late Roman enclosures indicated an extended sequence of activity. Pottery from the primary fills of circular enclosure 20350 indicated that activity here started after the middle of the 3rd century, and a date closer to or after the turn of the

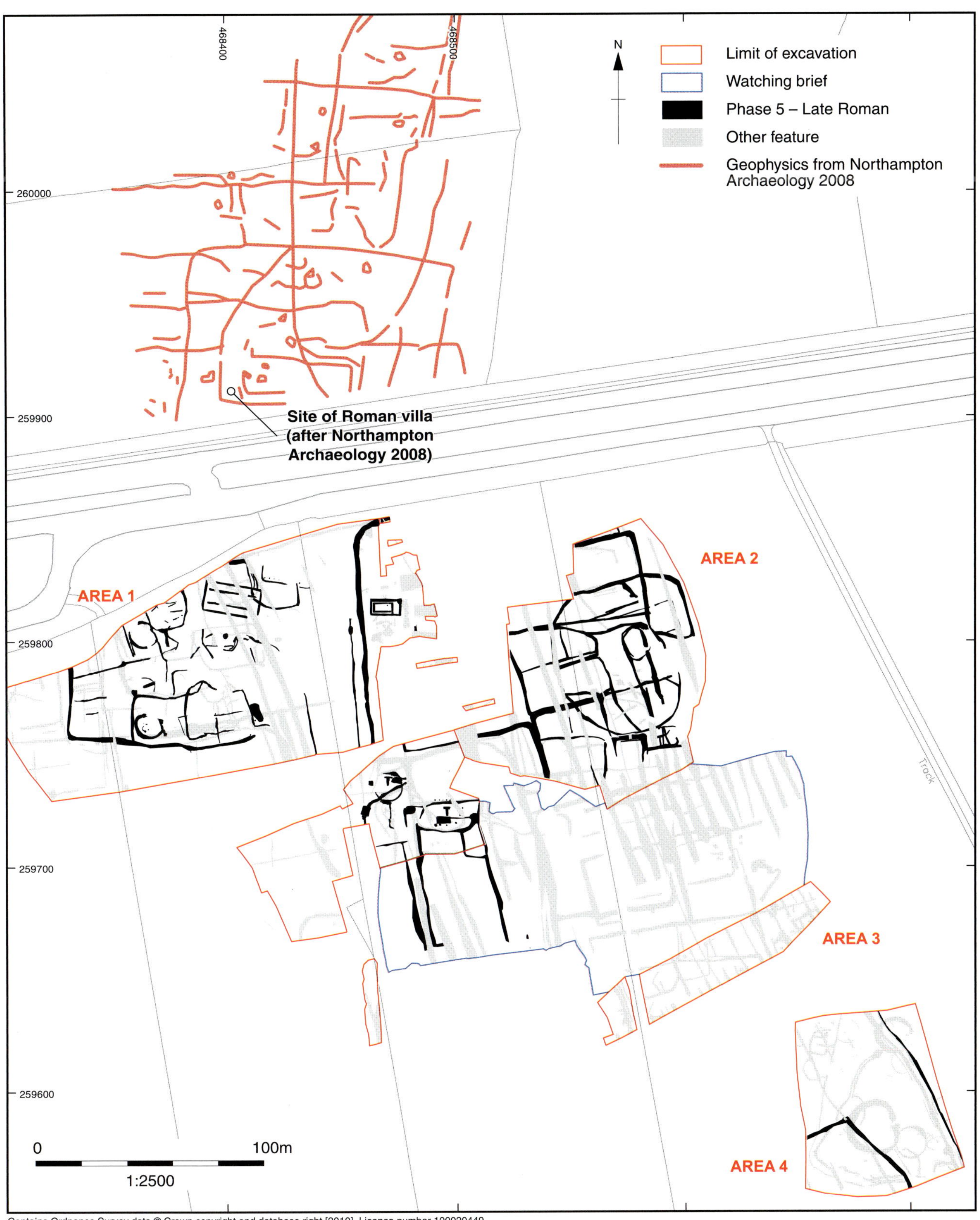

Fig. 6.2 The villa landscape at its greatest extent

4th century may be indicated by both a Nene Valley colour-coated ware jar dated after AD 270 from subdivision 20579 and sherds from a 4th-century dish from Harrold found near the entrance to the enclosure. How late the enclosure continued is less clear, although two coins dated AD 335–41 from ditches and one dated AD 364–78 from cleaning of stone surface 20436 suggest that it was in use for several decades, extending into the middle third of the 4th century. Two coins dated AD 388–402 were recovered from upper fills, and if they were not intrusive so late a date would require the overlying field system to have extended significantly into the 5th century. The field system itself produced little artefactual material that could contribute to dating the sequence beyond confirming a date after *c* AD 350, but the construction of this complex and a subsequent recutting may represent several further decades of activity.

The villa buildings

The A4500 has cut through the main building complex, presumably destroying most of the structures (Fig. 6.2), and it is unfortunate that the brief account in Brown's draft report, which is little more than a summary and concentrates on the nymphaeum area, provides no description of the elements of the villa building that she uncovered. She noted that there was considerable disturbance from the 1899 excavation, which had itself been unable to recover the ground plan due to comprehensive robbing of the foundations (Northamptonshire Exploration Committee 1901–2, 8). It can be inferred from the alignment of the features at Panattoni Park and the results of the geophysical surveys carried out north of the road for CLASP, however, that the complex was cardinally oriented, and it would be usual for the buildings to be arranged around a central courtyard. Building 3 therefore probably represents the southern extent of the complex, with the main house most likely located on the north side, giving it a southerly perspective across the courtyard and the valley beyond. The possible walls and rubble identified by CLASP's geophysical survey (Northamptonshire Archaeology 2008b) and the concentration of stone, tile and tesserae in this location from fieldwalking might therefore indicate the north-western limit of the complex or associated collapse. Brown's reference to having exposed the south-east corner of the building would be consistent with such an arrangement, and additionally suggests that it was a discrete building rather than a series of contiguous ranges. The complex is therefore likely to have comprised the more common arrangement of a group of discrete buildings like the villa at Whitehall Farm, Nether Heyford (CLASP 2012), rather than a courtyard villa similar to the layout suggested by geophysical survey north of Harpole at Road Hill Farm (Northamptonshire Archaeology 2008b, fig. 5). The best-known feature of the main building is the mosaic whose discovery in 1846 had first brought the site to light, and which was drawn at the behest of an Edward Pretty when it was exposed for a second time in 1849 (Fig. 6.3). The mosaic was rectangular and was recorded as having projected dimensions of 5.3m by 4.1m, although one end did not survive (Anon. 1850, 375; 1851). Pretty's interpretation of the central motif as a *Chi Rho*, indicating a Christian origin, has been dismissed as a misinterpretation of an arrangement that is more likely to be simply geometric in origin (Neal and Cosh 2002, 246). In fact, Neal and Cosh described Pretty's rendering of the mosaic as 'so unusual its illustration seems fanciful' but accepted its accuracy on account of the care that had been taken in recording the areas of damage, and its veracity was specifically confirmed in the report of the 1899 excavation (Northamptonshire Exploration Committee 1901–2). The central motif was set within a roundel formed of concentric bands of red, grey and guilloche, within a red octagon. Outside this, four semicircular motifs may have represented scallops or bowls, and the whole was enclosed by concentric borders of thorns, smaller semicircles and a red frame, with plain tesserae beyond. The report of the 1899 excavation described the mosaic as using ceramic tesserae for the red and black elements and limestone for the white parts, and Neal and Cosh noted that stone tesserae in grey and white had been recovered by fieldwalking in 1962. CLASP's more recent fieldwalking produced a total of 1647 tesserae in three distinct sizes, but these need not all derive from the same mosaic as it is possible that the building contained more than one room that was thus furnished.

The location of a possible bath house is suggested by Brown's description of a well-built limestone drain that entered her nymphaeum trench from the north-west and passed east of the nymphaeum building before exiting to the south. Neither the source nor the destination was positively identified, but a function as part of the water supply and drainage for a bath house would be appropriate and the alignment suggests that the structure stood somewhere in the vicinity of the east end of the main house.

Brown described the nymphaeum cistern as being oriented NE–SW, which, if correct, might indicate that it was constructed at an oblique angle to the other buildings. This would represent a further similarity to the villa at Whitehall Farm, where the main house and bath houses were not arranged strictly orthogonally. The building in which it was housed was presumably a discrete structure, and was evidently well appointed, with a paved floor and tiled roof, and the wall plaster was described as being painted yellow and green in the 2nd century and dark red with black transverse lines in the 4th-century rebuild. It probably fronted onto the east or north-east side of the courtyard, and the drain from the putative bath house evidently passed to the rear.

Fig. 6.3 The mosaic, as drawn for Edward Pretty in 1849

More certainty can be attached to the southern end of the building complex, where aisled Building 3 stood. The building had been severely affected by medieval ploughing, but the differences in the construction of the foundations may reflect a composite superstructure, with each of the internal aisle walls supporting a row of wooden posts that divided the central nave from the aisles and took most of the weight of the roof, while the substantial pitched-limestone outer footings supported stone outer walls. An unusual aspect of the building was its location on a significant slope, which dropped by *c* 1m over the length of the building and would have required the east end to have been built up considerably in order to make the wall plates and roof trusses horizontal, giving the structure a distinctive appearance. A partial parallel for such an arrangement can be found in an aisled building associated with the villa at Thurnham, Kent, which was built on the line of a slope, with the post pits dug progressively deeper toward the higher end so that the bases were all level, and evidently surveyed in (Lawrence 2006, 68–9); such structures provide

some indication of the skills of the engineers and surveyors available to Romano-British villa-builders. The aisled form represents a common building type on agricultural settlements, including about a quarter of villas, and served a range of functions that included storage, industrial activity and domestic occupation (Morris 1979, 56–61; Smith 2016b, 66–9). At Panattoni Park the aisled building was clearly a late development and perhaps represents a rationalisation of a part of the complex that was hitherto occupied by a less regular arrangement of ditched enclosures. Aisled buildings were often multifunctional or changed use over time, and in some instances well-furnished domestic rooms were added to transform originally agricultural structures into domestic buildings of some status, but in this instance the extensive truncation of the building precluded any interpretation of its function or structural development.

Only the southern side of the building putatively represented by gully 403/519 and associated postholes survived, but it may have comprised a timber structure similar to barns 2 and 4 at the farmstead at Orton Hall Farm, Cambridgeshire (Mackreth 1996, 55–70). Again, no evidence for function survived, but the comparable structures at Orton Hall Farm were used for crop processing and storage, and a similar interpretation may be appropriate at Panattoni Park. If so, it is possible that the southern end of the building complex, including both this building and Building 3, was primarily devoted to agricultural functions.

Farming at Panattoni Park

The primary role of the villa was as the centre of a farming estate. The limits of its landholding are unknown but must have been far greater than the area enclosed by the ditched field systems that were recorded by the excavation and by CLASP's geophysical surveys north of the A4500, incorporating areas of arable, pasture, woodland and other uses. It may have encompassed subsidiary farmsteads, but its extent was presumably constrained by the lands attached to the Road Hill Farm villa to the north and perhaps by that of the Whitehall Farm villa to the west and the small town at Duston to the north-east. The Raunds survey demonstrated that much of the off-floodplain area was used for cereal cultivation, with the floodplain being reserved for grazing and hay meadows, the latter necessary to maintain stock through the winter months (Parry 2006, 81–3). A similar division may hold true at Panattoni Park, with arable perhaps concentrated on the plateau north of the A4500 and pasture and hay within the valley to the south, the latter representing a continuation of the traditions posited above for earlier periods.

The dominance of cattle among the animal bones, accounting for at least half the assemblage in both the middle and late Roman periods, similarly continues the pattern seen in the Iron Age and the early part of the Roman period and is consistent with husbandry practices elsewhere in the Nene Valley and the wider region beyond (Meadows 2009b, 109). At Stanwick, for example, cattle comprised just under half the animal bone, and at the non-villa farmstead at Orton Hall Farm they represented about 60% of the recovered assemblage (ibid.). At Panattoni Park, as at other sites, sheep were the other main domesticate, with small quantities of pig and horse, and chicken was also present in Phase 5. Ageing data indicated that the pigs were kept primarily for meat, but the cattle and sheep were not slaughtered until maturity, suggesting that meat was not the primary product of either species but that dairy products, traction and wool were also valued, with no evidence for specialisation in any single aspect. The contribution of beef to the meat component of the diet is all the greater when one allows for the greater meat-bearing potential of cattle, Cunliffe (2005, 416) having estimated (albeit in reference to Iron Age animals) that a cow weighed up to 410kg whereas a sheep only weighed about 57kg. Wheat was evidently a staple of the diet and appears to have been almost entirely spelt, although it should be cautioned that remains were scarce outside the crop-processing area, where they may have been biased by deliberate selection of this crop for malting (see below). Even in the few features within the enclosure complex associated with the villa that produced charred plant assemblages, however, the wheat specimens that could be identified to species were spelt, with a small quantity of barley and oat. The balance of arable to livestock within the community's farming strategy is difficult to establish, especially since a significant proportion of the produce may have been exported for consumption elsewhere, with the excavated remains principally representing the portion that was consumed on site. The pollen, insects and waterlogged plant remains from the spring channel are broadly indicative of wet grassland used for pasture, with a possible shift toward arable in the upper part of layer 1305 and a reduction thereafter, but it is difficult to know how large a part of the surrounding area these conditions applied to.

Processing of the harvested crop was one of the areas in which Roman farmers sought to increase efficiency and productivity, through improved technology and centralisation (Allen and Lodwick 2017, 151). In the Nene Valley this phenomenon is represented by a particularly large concentration of evidence for corndrying ovens and mills, and both were present at Panattoni Park. Corndryers have been interpreted as having a role in facilitating the processing of damp grain, either as a routine stage prior to de-husking or to rescue a damp harvest, and although the structures at Panattoni Park appear to have been used for kilning as part of the malting process for production of ale (see below), such structures may have been multifunctional. The Panattoni Park group is the largest complex of ovens in the valley, exceeding the four at Orton Hall Farm (Mackreth 1996, 75–80, 229–30), and may indicate a considerably larger capacity than was available at other settlements. Fulford (2020, 301–2) has interpreted investment in such infrastructure at villas as evidence for the owners exercising increasing control over subordinate settlements and requiring harvests to be brought to the villa for centralised processing. He extended the same argument to the construction of mills, and although no mill building was identified at Panattoni Park, the presence of parts of millstones within pit 1224 and corndrying oven 2039 clearly indicates that such a structure stood somewhere nearby. A watermill was located on the Nene at Redlands Farm, Stanwick (OAU 1992), and it is possible that the mill associated with Panattoni Park was a similar structure, especially since the location of the historic Harpole Mill adjacent to the south-east extent of the development area indicates the suitability of this part of the river for such a use. The mill at Redlands Farm was a simple rectangular stone building, cellared at one end and with a wheel (for which no evidence survived) fed by a stone-lined leat. If the mill was not water-powered, it could have taken a range of forms. The bases of two donkey-powered mills were excavated at Stanwick villa, the better preserved example comprising an oval tread-mill set within a circular mill building and preserving wear-marks from the animals' hooves (Frere 1992, 285), whereas the mill building at Orton Hall Farm was a rectangular structure containing three stone plinths that were interpreted as bases for mills. In the latter instance the mills were probably powered by human labour, as they were too close together to allow room for animals (Spain 1996, 113). While the reuse of a millstone in wall 464 might invite interpretation of this and the associated cobbled surface 463 as part of a mill building, the wall did not appear substantial enough to support such a structure, and the function of these plough-truncated features remains uncertain.

Areas of pasture may have functioned with little or no requirement for ditched boundaries, and this may be reflected in the absence of both contemporary features in the western and southern areas of the excavation and of substantial geophysical anomalies in the area to the south. Ditched boundaries were presumably needed only in areas from which livestock were to be excluded or to which their access was to be controlled. Such locales might include areas of domestic settlement, storage and cultivation. There may also have been dedicated paddocks where livestock were over-wintered, gathered for slaughter, inspection or transit, or brought in for lambing and calving. At Wollaston, for example, trace chemical analysis at one farmstead was able to identify one small enclosure as a stock pen whilst another area might have been a midden (Meadows 2009b, 109). It is likely that the enclosures in the complex associated with the villa had a range of specialised functions, as indicated by the variety in their shape and size. It is possible that accommodation for estate workers was among the roles of this complex, but in the absence of definite structures it is difficult to define the functions of individual enclosures. This was also the area that produced the largest quantity of artefactual material and the widest range of object types, the presence of coins and personal objects such as the bracelet from ditch 1478, the hairpin from Building 3 and the glass counter or gaming piece from ditch 1468 attesting to more than just agricultural activities. Several pieces from quernstones were recovered from this area and may be evidence for either crop processing or the routine milling of flour for domestic consumption, whether immediately or at the adjacent building complex. The association of fragments from the upper part of a rotary quern and a lower millstone with circular enclosure 1245/1246 suggests that these activities may have been particularly focussed within this enclosure, perhaps in association with oven 1247, although the plant remains from the oven did not clarify whether its function was domestic or agricultural. In the northern part of the complex, the whetstone from similar enclosure 241 serves as a proxy for the metal

tools that were used and sharpened here. There was a notable increase in the variety of enclosures and the range and quantity of artefactual evidence between the middle and late Roman periods, which may indicate a corresponding increase in the scale and complexity of activities over time.

The sequence of enclosures east of the spring channel was quite different in form from the complex associated with the villa and appears to have been of a more agricultural character. The initial enclosures, constructed during the middle Roman period, produced no direct evidence regarding their function, but the southern group in particular, arrayed along a boundary ditch, is strikingly reminiscent of arrangements that occur frequently on rural settlements of various types and have been associated with the gathering together of livestock for transit (Smith 2016a, 164). The number of enclosures here is perhaps too small to represent such a large-scale gathering of animals, but an interpretation as livestock pens is nevertheless plausible. These enclosures were superseded by large, circular enclosure 30250 and subsequently by a more coherent complex of rectilinear enclosures, both of which may have been associated with livestock management. Enclosure 20350 is an enigmatic feature with no obvious parallels. Ostensibly similar in form to the small, enclosed farmsteads typical of the Iron Age or the early part of the Roman period, perhaps with a single roundhouse situated within central enclosure 20348/20351, such a form would be extremely unusual in south-eastern Britain for a settlement as late as this. Furthermore, an independent establishment such as a farmstead would not typically be situated in such close proximity to a villa. Given that it was preceded and followed by complexes of agricultural enclosures that are assumed to have belonged to the villa, a similar interpretation may be appropriate. The ceramic assemblage is not large but is indicative of domestic activity, and in fact displays a wider range of vessels than the previous and succeeding phases in this area, and the enclosure may have been a specialised livestock facility with a domestic element, perhaps for a head cowherd or shepherd, within the central enclosure. A few small pieces of plastered mortar were recovered from the southern part of the main enclosure during the evaluation (MOLA 2015c, 52), but the quantity is too small to be certain whether they derive from an otherwise unidentified building or had been transported from a structure elsewhere. The function of structure 20035 is uncertain, but its stratigraphic relationships suggested that it was contemporary with enclosure 20350 and it produced pottery of similar date. A single late 4th-century coin recovered from cleaning may indicate that it continued in use in association with the subsequent field system. Despite their unknown functions, this structure and structure 463/464 in the enclosure complex associated with the villa remind us that the villa's field systems may have been dotted with small buildings and working areas. A further such area may have been situated at the eastern end of the Watching Brief Area, where the geophysical survey indicated a possible circular enclosure *c* 10–12m across that was adjoined to the north by a rectilinear enclosure containing an L-shaped arrangement of closely spaced pits or postholes that was interpreted as a possible timber building (MOLA 2015b, 4). Stripping of this area during the watching brief revealed only an amorphous spread and a linear feature where the circular enclosure should have been and two pits that produced no artefactual material, although a pit here excavated during the evaluation produced roof tile, two fragments of plastered mortar and a glass vessel base (MOLA 2015c, 31, 55).

Enclosure 20350 may have been fairly short lived, lasting only a few decades, and was succeeded by a more extensive complex. The greater area enclosed, and the increased number of subdivisions within the new arrangement, would have accommodated considerably more livestock and allowed closer control over them. Indeed, this phase of the complex is reminiscent of structures that Pryor (1996), albeit in the context of prehistoric farming practice, has termed 'stockyards' – confined spaces where flocks or herds were temporarily kept while animals were sorted, inspected and exchanged. The design of the eastern entrance into the complex, in particular, is typical of such a facility; livestock are typically reluctant to enter a confined space, but the converging arrangement of ditches 20029 and 20396 would have had a funnelling effect that enabled the farmer to drive them through. Perhaps supplemented by fences or temporary hurdles, livestock entering the stockyard could have been held at the entrance for inspection and sorted by removing selected animals via the adjacent break in ditch 20029. Livestock management would have been a constant feature of life at the villa, at which the workers were no doubt expert, and the design of the stockyard and entrance represents a deceptively sophisticated arrangement that facilitated supervision and handling of the animals.

The use of this sequence of arrangements for livestock is consistent with the evidence provided by the pollen, insects and waterlogged plant remains from the nearby spring channel for wet grassland in the vicinity used for pasture, although it is difficult to be certain whether this relates to the enclosure complex. The pollen evidence indicated a possible shift toward arable followed by a subsequent reversion to pasture thereafter, but the sequence of deposits filling the channel cannot be correlated with the chronology of the enclosure complex and so it is not possible to determine whether these changes in the pollen are associated with changes in the arrangement of the enclosures. Supplementary evidence for the cultivation of hay or crops within or close to the complex may also be provided by the mower's tools and scythe or sickle blade recovered from the ditches. It is, of course, perfectly possible that individual enclosures were

reserved for cropping while livestock were corralled in others, or that both activities occurred in the same location, with livestock being introduced after harvesting to graze on the stubble and simultaneously fertilise the field.

A mower's toolkit?

A particularly evocative vignette of the daily life of the community is provided by the group of agricultural tools found in the ditches of the field system east of the spring channel. The placing of the mower's anvil, hammer and spud together in ditch 3076 may represent votive deposition. Anvils of this sort are certainly a common find in hoards, including well-known instances at Silchester, Sandy and Great Chesterford (Evans 1894; Manning 1964; Neville 1856). The tools most likely comprise a group that was used together and may constitute the equipment of a single farm labourer. The anvil was of a portable form and, with the hammer, would have been used for running repairs to scythes and sickles in the field. The body of the anvil comprised a tapered spike that the mower would have driven into the ground, with the horizontal coiled strip preventing it from sinking too far, to provide a surface on which damage to the scythe could be hammered out or the blade sharpened (Rees 2011, 105–6). The spud, on the other hand, represented here by an iron sheath that would have been mounted on a wooden handle, was a more versatile tool and would have been for weeding, breaking up clods of earth, and for cleaning mud from a plough or from other tools.

Ditches are a common location for votive deposits, which occur all across the rural landscape (Smith 2018a, 186), and metalwork, including agricultural tools, was the most frequently deposited material after animal remains and pottery, becoming increasingly popular in the 3rd and 4th centuries (ibid., 189–90). The location of the group in the upper fill of the ditch may indicate that they were deposited when the field system of which it was part was falling out of use during the late 4th or early 5th century. The only associated pottery was a base from a beaker or jar in Oxfordshire colour-coated ware, which could only be broadly dated to sometime after *c* AD 240. The apparent association with the end of the use of the field system could indicate that the tools were placed as part of a rite of closure or abandonment, if they were not simply discarded when the fields ceased to be cultivated. A similar circumstance may surround the deposition of a curving blade probably from a scythe or sickle that was recovered from a ditch 120m to the north within the same field system.

Malting – a Roman cash-crop?

The complex of corndrying ovens and associated features represents a significant investment in crop-processing infrastructure that suggests that malting may have been carried out on a substantial scale. Corndryers are a common occurrence at nucleated settlements and larger rural settlements and are primarily considered to have been used to dry glume wheats prior to de-husking or as part of the malting process (Lodwick 2017a, 55). In the former role they may have made it possible to increase productivity by extending the harvesting season, or by rescuing the crop in the event of wet weather during harvest. Many corndryers may have served more than one function, and this is a possibility for the ovens at Panattoni Park, although the charred plant remains from all the examples here suggest that they were mainly, and perhaps exclusively, used for malting.

The malting process comprises the controlled germination of the grain, followed by heating. Spelt wheat must be malted unthreshed, and thus the grain was germinated as spikelets. For germination or 'chitting' to occur, the grain is soaked or steeped in water, and at Panattoni Park pits 2018, 2094, 2129 and 2135 would have served as steeping tanks. The water for this may simply have derived from groundwater, as the pits filled readily when excavated, or alternatively it may have come from the surrounding enclosure ditches, which probably channelled water that flowed from the spring channel to the north. The River Nene is another possible source, though distance is likely to have precluded its use on any regular basis. Although no evidence survived, it is likely that the sides of pit 2135, which had a stone floor but no side-walls, were revetted with timber and that the bases of the other two pits, which had walls but no floor, were similarly reinforced in order to prevent the water becoming contaminated with soil. It would have been necessary to change the water regularly, perhaps on a daily basis, to prevent spoilage (Dineley 2004, 2), and comparable pits elsewhere are commonly provided with drainage gullies to aid this. The absence of such a facility at Panattoni Park may perhaps be attributed to the proximity of enclosure ditches into which the water may have been bailed. Steeping would have taken up to three days, after which it was necessary to spread the grain thinly on a malting floor to be raked and turned and left for another seven or eight days to complete the germination (ibid., 2–3). Evidence for malting floors rarely survives, but this may have been the function of surface 2146, carefully constructed from flat stones to minimise loss of grain down the cracks between stones. The next stage of the process involved heating the grain to arrest germination, which would have been the function of the corndrying ovens. The spatial associations indicate quite clearly that oven 2050 was used to heat the grain from pit 2094, oven 2130 for pits 2129 and 2135, and ovens 2039 and 2323 may both have been used in conjunction with pit 2018. Charred waste from grain that had been accidentally burnt during heating, and malting by-products that had been used as fuel appear to have

formed a large accumulation spread around much of the working area and became incorporated into the backfills of all the features once they were disused, as well as the associated enclosure ditches. The grain was then rubbed or pounded to remove the chaff, which could again have taken place using surface 2146, to produce a malt suitable for use or storage.

To make ale, the malt was first milled, and it is therefore interesting that two adjoining fragments from a large upper millstone had been placed on the floor of oven 2039, providing a direct link between the malting and brewing processes. The milled grain, or grist, was then mixed with water and heated to produce a mash and convert the starch into sugars. Material evidence for brewing was not identified and it may have been more practical to brew the ale closer to the point of consumption rather than at the malting site. The ale could be flavoured with honey or plants such as meadowsweet (Dineley 2004, 9), and although no certain evidence for its use was found, evidence for meadowsweet growing locally was provided by pollen and waterlogged seeds recovered from the spring channel (Meen and Rutherford, Chapter 5).

The four definite and one possible corndrying oven represent the largest group from the local area, the only comparable quantity being four ovens at the farmstead at Orton Hall Farm (Mackreth 1996, 75–80, 229–30). The excavations at Orton Hall Farm were undertaken between 1964 and 1975, before environmental sampling became common, and so there is no plant remains evidence, but the excavator interpreted the ovens as having been used for malting rather than drying crops. They lacked the common T-shaped form that constituted all but one of the Panattoni Park ovens, and instead comprised large and more complex H-shaped forms and one of reverse-tuning-fork form similar to oven 2039. The ovens were situated within barns that also contained features that were described as vat bases that may have supported wooden containers used for steeping, with wells located outside to provide water. Presumably the floors of the barns served as a malting floor. Such surfaces rarely survive, although a rare example is represented by a rammed chalk floor at a maltings at Mildenhall, Suffolk (Bales 2004). Another farmstead at Parnwell Way, Peterborough, likewise included an elaborate oven, which combined an H-shaped form with a T-shape, with a common stoke-hole, and here charred malting waste was recovered from the oven and had been dumped into an adjacent enclosure ditch (Webley 2007). Beyond the Nene Valley, good examples of malting complexes combining steeping tanks and ovens have been found at Weedon Hill (Wakeham and Bradley 2013) and Berryfields (Biddulph *et al.* 2019), both in Buckinghamshire. The maltings at the farmstead at Weedon Hill comprised a timber building that contained an axially located oven, with a stone-lined steeping tank set to one side that was drained by a gully.

Water was supplied by a natural stream. At Berryfields, located on Akeman Street near the Roman small town at Fleet Marston, a steeping pit that, like pit 2135, had a stone base but no side walls, was drained via a short gully into a nearby sump and was associated with an oven of simple 'long hearth' form. Charred germinated grain and other malting by-products were recovered in quantity from environmental samples collected from the steeping tank and from unrelated features in the vicinity, suggesting that, as at Panattoni Park, debris from the malting activity extended across the surrounding area.

A key question regarding malting and brewing is whether the product was intended for trade or for immediate consumption. The scale of production is key to understanding this but is very difficult to ascertain, not least because the capacity of the facilities is unknown. Experiments carried out with a reconstruction of a corndrying oven in 1975, albeit in relation to using it to dry corn rather than for malting, indicated that it was only effective in drying a thin layer of grain in each firing (Reynolds and Langley 1979), but no comparable information is available for the efficiency for malting. Furthermore, we do not know whether sites with multiple steeping pits and ovens indicate a larger total capacity or structures that were in use successively. At least three units can be identified in the malting facility at Panattoni Park, middle Roman steeping pit 2094 and oven 2050 being succeeded in the late Roman period by pit 2018 and ovens 2039 and 2323, while a separate unit was established to the east comprising pits 2129 and 2135 and oven 2130. The malting facilities evidently spanned a considerable period of time. Dating such structures is hampered by the reliance on material from backfill deposits, but a date for the end of the middle Roman unit is provided by pottery from oven 2050, which indicated that it was probably backfilled between AD 150 and the end of the 3rd century, while late Roman pottery from pit 2018 and the coin from the use-layer in oven 2039 indicate that this unit was in use into the final third of the 4th century. Dating evidence from the eastern unit was less useful, but pottery from pit 2129 indicates that it was backfilled after *c* AD 270. Taken together, the dating evidence indicates that the malting complex probably functioned for at least a century, and possibly more than two, but is not able to demonstrate whether the units were sequential or contemporary.

The uncertainties regarding the capacity of the malting structures and the number of structures in use at any one time make definite conclusions regarding the destination of the ale impossible. It is possible that, as Mackreth (1996, 230–1) argued for the malting complex at Orton Hall Farm, brewing was carried out purely to provide drink for the estate workforce. Roman authors make clear the appetite of the peoples of north-western Europe for ale (Pliny *NH* XIV.29; Tacitus *Germania* I:23.1), and it is likely that it was the staple drink for most of the population. On settlements without identifiable structures for malting, such installations were presumably unnecessary because brewing was conducted at a small scale for immediate household consumption, but this leaves open the question of whether the much greater capacity of the complexes at larger sites such as Panattoni Park and Orton Hall Farm merely reflect the larger workforce at these centres or represent production on a more industrial scale for trade as a 'cash crop' to supplement the main agricultural produce. In support of the latter interpretation, Stevens *et al.* (2011, 242) have drawn attention to the correlation between settlements with malting complexes and a location in proximity to the Roman road network. The proximity of Margary's route 17 (Margary 1967, 187–8), which lies only 3km away and runs north-west from Northampton to a junction with Watling Street at *Bannaventa*, would have provided an opportunity to trade malt to be turned into beer at the town or at settlements elsewhere, making Panattoni Park a strong candidate for this interpretation.

Religion and burial

The results of the excavation and Brown's earlier investigation have produced significant evidence for religious life at the villa. A particularly interesting aspect of this is the possibility that two different spheres of practice and belief are represented. On the one hand, construction of the nymphaeum and the temple/mausoleum, and the practice at the latter of rites that involved the use of exotic plants, indicate that the villa residents had an active interest in classical religious and/or funerary practice and the attendant specialised religious structures. No doubt one element of this was the opportunity to present their sophistication and to express an identity as part of an empire-wide elite which shared common cultural and religious values that distinguished them from the bulk of the population. The concept of differential Roman identities held and expressed by different elements of the population has been considered in detail by Mattingley, who emphasised the role that contrasting religious practice could play in expressing distinct community identities (Mattingley 2006, 520). In contrast to this self-consciously formal expression of religious identity are deposits of possible religious character that were interred in pits and ditches at 'non-religious' locations around the settlement. Following Mattingley's argument, these deposits may represent the religious activity of a different element of the villa population. These practices may have been more closely associated with ensuring agricultural success; they would have been more familiar to rural communities throughout the province and may have been rooted in indigenous beliefs of greater antiquity (Smith 2016c, 653). A noteworthy absence, particularly given the late date to which occupation of the villa continued, is that of any evidence for Christianity.

The temple/mausoleum

The difficulty in defining the function of the building is evident from the composite term that has been applied to it. Temples and mausolea comprised two very distinct categories of building in the Roman world and their functions did not usually overlap, since the ritual pollution that burials entailed would not have been tolerated within religious sanctuaries (Esmonde Cleary 2000, 133). There is considerable structural similarity between the two, however, and straightforward classification based on form is further hindered by architectural diversity within each category. Similarly, the archaeological residues of ritual activities at both types of building can appear very similar and are therefore not helpful in distinguishing them. This perhaps indicates that there was a significant overlap both in the forms of the rituals and in the symbolic concepts behind them. In some instances mausolea can be distinguished from temples by the provision of facilities for burials, such as the large central burial chamber within the building at Bancroft, where evidence for pedestal scars for supporting lead coffins or stone sarcophagi survived on the *opus signinum* floor (Williams and Zeepvat 1994), but burials could alternatively be placed above ground, meaning that demolition of the monument would have removed any archaeologically detectable evidence for the associated burials.

Despite the taboo mentioned above, there are instances in Britain where human remains were deposited at temples. The most striking of these is the pair of skulls that was built into the foundations of the cella of the temple at Cosgrove villa (Quinnell 1991, 21), and the skeleton of an adult male was embedded in mortar beneath the ambulatory floor immediately inside the entrance of the temple at Bourton Grounds, Buckinghamshire (Green 1965, 359, 366). An adult male was also buried within the ambulatory at Cosgrove, although in this case the burial may have post-dated the building (Quinnell 1991, 21). Two human bones were also found amongst deposits of animal bone at the open-air shrine at Ashwell, Hertfordshire (Rainsford *et al.* 2021). The association of the human femur with Building 1320 is rather ambiguous because the feature from which it was recovered was shallow and poorly defined and did not survive well enough to make clear whether it represented a deliberate formal burial. In any case, given the parallels from other sites, the presence of the bone need not indicate that the building was primarily funerary in character.

Whatever the precise role of the building, it was evidently constructed for the benefit of the villa owners and would have served as a monumental reminder of the elite status and Continental values to which they ascribed and, if it was funerary in character, to commemorate the individual(s) buried within. It is likely that the building represented a location that they, and perhaps also other members of the community, would have visited periodically for ceremonies and/or ritual meals (see below).

The architecture of the temple/mausoleum

Temples in Britain vary from imitations of classical forms, exemplified by the Temple of Claudius at Colchester (de la Bédoyère 1991, figs 131 and 132), to more irregular arrangements including the circular building at Hayling Island (King and Soffe 2008) and the octagonal Shrine of Apollo at Nettleton (Wedlake 1982). Such large and elaborate structures are rare, however, and mainly limited to urban and military settlements and sites of a specifically sacred character, and the most common form in rural contexts is the Romano-Celtic temple, defined by a concentric ground plan conventionally interpreted as accommodating a tower-like central structure, or cella, surrounded by a colonnaded ambulatory with a lower roof that abutted the cella wall (Lewis 1965). Buildings definitely identified as mausolea are typically at the smaller end of the range and often comprise a simple square single-celled structure like the example recently excavated at Priors Hall, Corby (Lambert 2021; OA 2021c), or have an ambulatory forming a similar arrangement to a Romano-Celtic temple, as at Bancroft and Cosgrove (Williams and Zeepvat 1994; Quinnell 1991). One element that is common to many instances of both temples and mausolea is a surrounding precinct, or temenos, that separated the site from the profane activities in the outside world. At the Corby mausoleum, for example, a stone wall enclosed a temenos that measured *c* 17m by 14m (OA 2021c, 10). No such structure was present at Panattoni Park, perhaps because the building was in any case already located at some distance from any other structures, or because ditch 339, which divided the building and associated activity from the villa and its adjacent enclosures, was considered to be a sufficient boundary.

The Rural Settlement of Roman Britain Project identified eight villas with stone-built mausolea (Smith 2018b, 249), while 28 villas possessed some form of sacred site, representing just under 10% of excavated villas (Smith 2018a, 152). Villas associated with buildings comparable to Building 1320 are therefore quite scarce. The East Midlands appears to have contained a particular concentration of villas with such monuments (Esmonde Cleary 2000, 134), however, to which Building 1320 may now be added. In addition to the building at Corby described above, temples or mausolea of Romano-Celtic form are known at the villas at Cosgrove (Quinnell 1991) and Bancroft (Williams and Zeepvat 1994). In addition to these instances, although not associated with villas, a burial in a stone sarcophagus that was excavated in 1908 at the nearby small town of Duston was surrounded by 'roughly built stone walls 4 feet thick', which presumably represents a mausoleum of some form although the shape was not determined (RCHME 1985), and a small rectangular shrine with an ambulatory around three sides is known at the roadside settlement at Stanwick (Crosby and Muldowney 2011). None of these buildings is an exact parallel for Building 1320, since they are generally square or only slightly longer than they are wide, whereas Building 1320 is distinctly rectangular. There is little doubt regarding its interpretation as a religious structure of some form, however, on account of its association with the spring channel and artefactual and ecofactual evidence for ritual activity (see below).

Much rests on whether the concentric wall circuits were contemporary, defining an ambulatory and therefore a variation on the typical Romano-Celtic form, or represent successive rectangular buildings of different sizes constructed in the same location. Definite evidence pertaining to this is sadly lacking due to the almost complete truncation of the foundations. The former circumstance is suggested by the arrangement of the surviving robber trenches, which appear to indicate that the inner cell was integral to the N–S cross-wall, which was certainly of one build with the outer circuit, but no stonework survived at the junction between the inner cell and cross-wall to demonstrate their relationship conclusively. If contemporary, the two wall circuits would form the footprint of a building with an ambulatory around the sides and rear, with the cross-wall being the original east end – the only surviving stratigraphic relationship in the stonework proved that the eastern end of the building was a later addition. In contrast to the buildings mentioned above, however, which had wide ambulatories that were capable of defining a space that could be readily accessed, the wall circuits of Building 1320 were nowhere more than 0.5m wide. This was presumably not a functional space and is more likely to indicate an ornamental portico, the outer circuit comprising a dwarf wall supporting a colonnade. The addition of the extension to the east end may represent the construction of a porch, providing a more elaborate entrance and perhaps housing a flight of steps by which the cella was accessed, as was the case at Bourton Grounds (Green 1965, 358). The stone surface in front of the building may have been where people gathered or where rites were conducted.

The chronology of the construction and use of the building are problematic due to the absence of datable material stratified within its fabric and the rather wide date ranges attributed to the pottery from superficial layers and associated pits. This material provides a general indication of activity beginning in the 2nd century, with an ambiguous end date perhaps in the 4th century. A Dragendorff 79 dish with a name stamp of Beliniccus III from a layer over the building may indicate a start date no earlier than AD 160–200 and is consistent with the pottery from pit 1041 – possibly the earliest feature in the pit group associated with the building – which included a Nene Valley white ware flagon and several sherds from a South Spanish Dressel 20 amphora, indicating a date after *c* AD 170. If this

represents the approximate construction date, it would be quite closely contemporary with construction at Bancroft, which was attributed to the second half of the 2nd century (Williams and Zeepvat 1994, 89–102), and at Cosgrove, where the stone temple replaced a mid-2nd century timber precursor during the late 2nd century (Quinnell 1991, 21). The date of the end of the building is more open-ended and it is in practice impossible to be certain whether the small quantity of late Roman material represents continuity or decline in activity. Activity of some sort continuing into the 4th century is certainly indicated by the Oxfordshire white ware mortarium and Nene Valley ware colour-coated necked jar/bowl recovered from cleaning of the building, and the ceramic evidence indicates that this was also when the rough stone surface was laid down to provide access across the adjacent part of the infilled channel. These few sherds are scant evidence from which to posit activity on any significant scale, although the relative isolation of the building precludes the possibility that they got here incidentally from occupation elsewhere. Smith (2008; 2018a, 136) has demonstrated that the majority of pagan religious sites continued in use until at least the end of the 4th century and has argued that the fate of each individual site depended on the fortunes of the settlement with which it was associated rather than on the anti-pagan policies of Christian emperors. In the latter respect, the late date to which the villa continued provides a context for continuation of the temple/mausoleum. Coin evidence from Cosgrove and Bourton Ground indicates that these sites certainly continued to the end of the 4th century, but elsewhere the mausoleum at Corby was turned into a tile kiln during the 3rd century (OA 2021c, 9) and the temple/mausoleum at Bancroft was systematically demolished during the mid-4th century (Williams and Zeepvat 1994, 89–102). There was no evidence to provide a definite date for the addition of the porch, but Poole (Chapter 4) has noted that the ceramic roof tiles include both middle and late Roman pieces and it is possible that this distinction represents material from the original construction and the later extension.

Evidence for ritual activity at the temple/mausoleum: the location and environs of the building

The location of the building was certainly not incidental and was undoubtedly selected very carefully. It is commonly noted that mausolea associated with villas were placed at some remove from the villa buildings, often in prominent topographical positions that rendered them very visible, particularly from the principal residence (Esmonde Cleary 2000, 131; Smith 2018b, 249). The latter point clearly does not apply to Building 1320, which was sited on slightly lower ground than the villa. Instead, it appears to have been deliberately placed beside the spring channel that flows from an unknown source in the vicinity of the A4500 immediately to the north. The importance of springs in Romano-British religion is demonstrated by the well-known extensive religious complexes that were built around the hot-water spring at Bath, Somerset (Cunliffe and Davenport 1985), and the source of the River Ebbsfleet at Springhead, Kent (Andrews *et al.* 2011), and the association at Panattoni Park is strengthened by the evidence from the associated stone surface 861/862 that the building's entrance faced toward the channel, only *c* 5m away. A particularly close parallel for the relationship between Building 1320 and the spring channel is provided by Building 400035 at Springhead, a rectangular stone-founded temple that was built in the mid-2nd century and measured 13.5m by 5m, aligned on the head of the River Ebbsfleet less than 5m away (ibid., 61–5). The significance of water and water sources to the religious life of the community at Panattoni Park is also emphasised by the presence of the putative nymphaeum. The contemporaneity of Building 1320 and the channel is demonstrated by a radiocarbon date of cal AD 260–540 obtained for a waterlogged ash twig from the channel's basal fill (1305; Table 5.18) and the base of an Oxfordshire colour-coated ware bowl and a rim sherd from a 4th-century shell-tempered dish recovered from middle fill (1304). In addition to this, the building is the only nearby source for the small group of beetles characteristic of a 'house fauna', associated with mouldering organic litter and detritus within ancient buildings, that was recovered from the latter deposit (Allison, Chapter 5). By the time stone surface 1297/1306 was laid down, probably during the 4th century, the channel was evidently fully silted and no longer flowing, but was still wet enough to require the surface to provide a dry crossing. The channel evidently underwent a period of inactivity during the medieval period when the ridge and furrow earthworks that cross the site were formed, since medieval furrows would not have formed across an area that was too wet to cultivate, but has since reactivated, the outflow resulting in the erosion of the earthworks in this area.

The building may have been associated with an ornamental garden or grove, which provided the pollen of walnut, beech and possibly maple/sycamore that was recorded from the channel fills. The abundance of walnut pollen leaves no doubt that it was grown in the immediate vicinity and represents an important discovery for understanding the introduction of the plant into Britain. Walnut is native to a large area that extends from the eastern Mediterranean to the Himalayas and is usually regarded as a Roman introduction to Britain. The Rural Settlement of Roman Britain Project records only seven occurrences scattered from Castleford in Yorkshire to Neatham in Hampshire, comprising three roadside settlements, a military vicus, a villa, a farmstead and industrial site associated with lead extraction, in addition to which there is a record from the villa at Clatterford,

Isle of Wight. In all these cases walnut was represented by the nut, preserved by charring or waterlogging, and it is impossible to be certain whether they were grown locally or transported as nuts. The pollen evidence at Panattoni Park is therefore the first definite instance of the tree being grown in Britain. Why it was grown is less certain. It is possible that walnut and the other tree species evidenced here were entirely ornamental and were cultivated as part of a formal garden of the sort common on high-status sites throughout the empire (Lodwick 2018). Alternatively, the nuts may have been regarded as an exotic food crop, which perhaps better suits the types of sites at which they have been cited elsewhere in Britain, or as appropriate for use in ritual or funerary practices, as at Doncaster where an example was burnt as a pyre good with a cremation burial (ArcHeritage 2013). The stone pine scale recovered from one of the pits in the group to the south of the building may represent another plant species that was cultivated as part of the garden, but given that the cones were widely traded from their natural range around the Mediterranean basin and that examples in Britain are limited to the cones and kernels, which are robust enough for long-distance transportation, rather than the plants themselves (Lodwick 2015; 2018, 57), it is perhaps more likely that it arrived by other means. There is plentiful evidence that the cones were imported to sacred sites for use in religious and funerary rituals (see below).

Evidence for ritual activity at the temple/mausoleum: votive deposits and ritual feasting

The material recovered from deposits overlying the building and from the group of pits to the south provides rare evidence for the character of some of the rites that were performed here. Two distinct depositional processes are represented, comprising individual acts of votive deposition and deposits of material that may have accumulated from successive episodes. The first category is represented by the burial of individual calves in pits 1045 and 1435, perhaps representing the dedication of sacrificed animals. Aldhouse-Green (2001, 24) has discussed how the interment of such offerings in subsurface pits may have been intended to remove them from the human world, both physically and metaphorically, in order to transfer them to the divine. The calf in pit 1435 was represented only by the articulating rear limb bones, but the pit occurred early in the stratigraphic sequence and much of it had been cut away by the digging of subsequent pits, so it is quite possible that the animal was more complete when originally deposited. The calf in pit 1045 was complete except for the skull, which had presumably been removed during the sacrifice and taken for use elsewhere; the use of skulls for special purposes is clearly demonstrated by the three ox skulls that Brown found cemented into the entrance to the nymphaeum and by a horse skull beneath the threshold of a building at Bourton Grounds (Green

1965, 361), and a comparable burial of a headless animal, in this instance a pig, was excavated within the circular shrine at Bancroft (Williams and Zeepvat 1994, 107–9). The calf was only the first element of a more complex sequence of deposition that comprised the burial within the middle fill of the pit of burnt bone that included the cremated remains of a piglet and at least one burnt chicken bone. The remains in this pit thus provide vivid evidence for the sacrifice of animals of three different species, one of them beheaded and the other two cremated.

King (2005, 357) has argued that animal bone assemblages from British temples may indicate some seasonality to the rituals at which they were sacrificed, which varied between sites but with a concentration in autumn and sometimes spring, perhaps representing ceremonies related to important festivals in the agricultural cycle in what was a primarily agrarian society. The ages of the animals in pit 1045 provide some interesting information regarding the seasonality and temporality of the burial sequence here. The calf was aged *c* 15 months at death, so assuming that the calving season during the Roman period was around March, as it is now, the animal was killed and deposited in the pit in summer, probably in June/July. The piglet is more problematic, as it could not be accurately aged and birthing seasons for pigs are less consistent and can occur twice a year. However, if the animal was aged around 5–6 months, as the two piglets in pit 2264 were, and assuming that domestic pigs in Roman Britain mated around April/May, as wild boar in northern Europe traditionally do, then slaughter and deposition may have occurred anywhere from a few weeks to a couple of months after that of the calf. This is speculative due to the uncertainties regarding the piglet, but suggests that although the burials may have been inserted in a single episode, it is alternatively possible that they were deposited in the same pit some time apart. If true, such a sequence might relate to deposition at set seasonal festivals or (if the building was a mausoleum) perhaps anniversary rituals and feasting to commemorate the dead.

The material from other pits in the group and from overlying layer 1001 was more mixed and comprised much burnt animal bone, as well as pottery and ceramic roof tiles. The tile was probably incorporated incidentally, but the bone and pottery are likely to derive from activities directly associated with the temple/mausoleum. A direct link between these deposits and the building was demonstrated by both their spatial proximity and the recovery of similar burnt bone from cleaning layer 558, which comprised objects encountered while removing overburden from the substantial foundation (1071) of the north-east corner of the building. Due to the high level of fragmentation only a small number of bones could be identified to species, but mammals and birds were both present, including instances of individual cattle and chicken bones. The deposits were mixed and homogenous, and in the absence of any indication of discrete deposits of individual animals it seems plausible that the material from layer 1001 represented an accumulation of material on the ground surface that had built up from successive rituals, or a rubbish heap. The bones from the pits were similar in composition, perhaps indicating that they were derived from periodic clearing away of material from similar surface accumulations.

The bone from these deposits was quite different from that recovered from elsewhere on the site, which derived from butchery and consumption of animals associated with domestic occupation. The mixed condition of the domestic assemblage contrasted with the bones associated with the temple/mausoleum, which was consistently and heavily burnt (predominantly to a white or grey colour) in a manner that indicates deliberate and careful burning at a high temperature, more analogous to the rite of cremation in human funerals than to the accidental burning that might result during cooking. Deposition of burnt animal remains at temples was not the norm, with most deposits interpreted as votive offerings being unburnt, and King's (2005) survey indicated that it was characteristic specifically of Mithraea and other eastern cults. Since his survey, however, an extremely large assemblage has been excavated at an open-air shrine at Ashwell, Hertfordshire, apparently dedicated to a previously unattested native goddess named Senuna, and a smaller assemblage has been recovered from limited trenching of the ditch of a ritual enclosure at Charlwood, Surrey (Rainsford *et al.* 2021). Both assemblages are much larger than that at Panattoni Park and have been interpreted as debris from 'ritual activity in a feasting or festival setting' (ibid., 193). The smaller scale of the assemblage associated with Building 1320 would be consistent either with an accumulation of individual sacrifices or as detritus from ritual meals with a smaller participation than those sites, reflecting its status as a private monument associated with the villa rather than a public temple. Animals that had been offered for sacrifice were certainly routinely consumed in ritual meals, accounting for the fragmented and butchered condition of the bones from most temple sites (King 2005, 363), and a context for similar consumption at mausolea is provided by the tradition of regular graveside meals to commemorate the dead (Alcock 1980, 63–4; Weekes 2016, 438–9). Such ritualised feasting at Building 1320 was also indicated by the oyster shells from some of the pits and by the composition of the pottery assemblage from this area, which demonstrated a greater emphasis on forms designed for eating and drinking, including flagons, beakers and bowls. The two near-identical wide-mouthed jars are particularly interesting since they may have been supplied and used as a pair (Biddulph, Chapter 4), whether in rituals or associated meals. Such meals would not, of course, have produced bone that was as thoroughly incinerated as the deposits in question, but it is possible that after the meal the remains were incinerated as part of a ritual cleansing or purifying of the sanctuary. It therefore remains an open question whether the animal bone represents the sacrifice of burnt offerings or debris from ritual feasting.

The evidence provided by the complete animals buried in pits 1045 and 1435 and the bones that could be identified to species in the other deposits indicates that only domestic species had been provided for sacrifice or consumption, and this is typical of British temples, with domesticates constituting the vast majority of animal remains from sites elsewhere (King 2005, 357). It would appear that it was not considered necessary or desirable to acquire hunted or exotic species for such purposes. The detailed make-up of assemblages varies between sites, with different species appropriate to specific deities, and there is some evidence that individual temples adopted a traditional or accustomed set of sacrificial practices. The assemblage at Charlwood, for example, is heavily focused towards sheep, whereas the range of animals burnt at Ashwell is substantial, including both domestic and wild taxa and a small amount of human bone. It is likely that the animals slaughtered at Building 1320 were sourced locally, probably from the settlement's own flocks and herds.

The use of exotic plant materials in rites at the building was indicated by the stone pine cone scale in pit 1437. The charred condition of the scale may result from it having been deliberately burnt as incense, a practice well-attested as a part of Roman rituals (King 2005, 362; Lodwick 2015). Pine cones could also be placed as votive offerings, as is demonstrated by a wall painting at a villa at Boscoreale, near Pompeii, which shows one placed on an altar with other fruit, and a complete unburnt cone from a stone pine that was recovered from a deposit of possible ritual material within a ditch at the villa at Clatterford, Isle of Wight (Busby *et al.* 2001, 110) and another from a waterhole at Claydon Pike, Gloucestershire (Robinson 2007, 361–2), may be evidence that their use in Britain did not always involve burning. As evergreens, they were associated with immortality and fertility and clearly had a role in Mithraism and other eastern religions, with excavated examples from the Mithraea at London (Grimes 1968) and Carrawburgh (Richmond and Gillam 1951) and the Triangular Temple at Verulamium (Wheeler and Wheeler 1936, 119), but examples have also been found at other temples including the Springhead complex (Stevens 2011a) and the shrine at Westhawk Farm, Kent (Pelling 2008), as well as high-status non-temple sites. As a symbol of immortality and rebirth they were also appropriate to funerary contexts and appear as a subject on several British tombstones (Alcock 1980, 54), and a charred kernel has been recovered from a middle to late Roman cremation burial at Horcott Quarry, Gloucestershire (Lodwick and Challinor 2017). The occurrence at Building 1320 would therefore be appropriate regardless of whether it was a temple or a mausoleum.

'Special deposits' in non-religious locations

The deposition of objects in ostensibly non-religious contexts within settlements for spiritual reasons appears to have been quite common in the Roman period and was probably a continuation of Iron Age traditions (Cunliffe 1995; Hill 1995). In general, a smaller range of materials was deposited than at formal shrines, since coins, personal items and specifically religious objects are less common and most deposits comprise animal remains or pottery vessels with a smaller proportion of tools, querns and suchlike (Smith 2016c, 653; 2018, 189–90). The deposition of objects that formed a part of everyday domestic life or were associated with agricultural production was presumably deliberate and reflected the range of activities that the community wished to address through these rites. Accordingly, the evidence for such deposits at Panattoni Park contrasts with the activity at the nymphaeum and temple/mausoleum, with their classical-style buildings, religious feasting and exotic imported material such as stone pine cones, and appears less overtly formal. However, despite their smaller scale and more humble offerings, these depositional events may have been approached with their own formality and reverence. Since the materials involved are everyday objects, identifying ritualised deposition is not straightforward, but perhaps the difficulty in distinguishing between religious and mundane categories may be entirely appropriate, representing a blurring of a distinction that did not exist to the population placing such deposits.

The strongest candidate for a ritual deposit of (sacrificed?) animal remains is the pair of piglets in pit 2264. The deposit shares elements with the animal burials associated with the temple/mausoleum, in the selection of young animals and the use of burial within a subsurface pit to dedicate them to whatever deity was being invoked. Although a more mundane interpretation is possible, such as the disposal of incidental livestock mortalities, there is no reason to think that the crop-processing area, where the pit was situated, was used for handling livestock, and as discussed above, there are other areas of the site where the boundaries are more likely to have been designed for such activities. Smith (2016c, 653–4) has drawn attention to the widespread presence of dogs in ritualised deposits, and burials of complete or partial dogs at Silchester and other sites played a key role in Fulford's argument that Iron Age-style special deposits formed a significant element of religious practice within Roman settlements (Fulford 2001). In this context, the remains of a substantially complete (though headless) miniature dog recovered from ditch 863, and the mandible and articulated leg from a similar individual from ditch 454, both within the enclosure complex immediately south of the villa, invite interpretation as possible ritual deposits. In this instance, however, certainty is impossible, and it must be acknowledged that deposition within a ditch pit might denote more casual disposal of natural deaths in contrast to deliberate burial within a purpose-dug pit.

Metal tools and quernstones were also considered appropriate objects of deposition in special deposits. As noted above, the cache of mower's tools in ditch 3076 may represent a ritual deposit and includes items that can be paralleled in hoards elsewhere, although there was insufficient evidence to be confident of the status of this particular group. The role of quernstones in converting grain into flour made them potent symbols of death, regeneration and new life (Peacock 2013, 166), and accordingly they were a common inclusion in special deposits throughout the Iron Age and Roman periods. Some of the quernstones at Panattoni Park were evidently incidental inclusions, such as the fragments in the fill of ditch 20593, but a few instances were deposited in potentially significant contexts. Chief among these was a complete lower rotary quernstone which had been placed flat with the grinding surface upward and may have marked a threshold through wall 464, which was associated with a cobbled floor. Although the function of the structure was not established, the stone was evidently placed in a symbolically significant liminal location and would have been readily visible to anyone passing through the entrance. The large upper millstone that had been placed within corndrying oven 2039 was similarly positioned with the grinding side upward and may have been deliberately situated close enough to the end of the flue to be visible to workers at the stokehole. Roasting and milling were clearly associated, as successive stages in malting or flour-processing, but there was no reason for them to be carried out at the same location and no other evidence was found for a mill in the crop-processing area. A location on the river is more likely, in which case the stone must have been carried some distance to be deposited on the base of the oven flue, either being incorporated into the structure or placed shortly after the oven ceased to be used. It was uncertain whether feature 957 was the terminus of ring ditch 1245 or a pit dug at the end of the ditch, but either way it may have represented a significant location in which to deposit rotary quern fragment SF 86.

Other burials

While it is possible that Building 1320 represents the final resting place of the villa owner(s), the burials found within the field system east of the spring channel are likely to be those of individuals at the opposite end of the social spectrum. Only three inhumation burials and a single cremation burial were uncovered, and given this small number of graves, the main burial area for the community attached to the villa must lie elsewhere, perhaps to the north of the main building complex, albeit that not all of the population need necessarily have practiced funerary rites that involved formal burials. Such small numbers of burials, scattered among the fields and enclosures around the settlement, are a common occurrence at villas and farmsteads of the period, and are often characterised as 'backland burials' (Esmonde Cleary 2000; Pearce 1999), although some villas were associated with more formal cemeteries. At Wootton Fields, for example, seven inhumations in three locations both within and outside the villa enclosure were interpreted as possibly forming separate cemeteries (Chapman *et al.* 2005, 95), although this is a somewhat grandiose term for such small groups, and perhaps they would be better viewed as small concentrations of backland burials similar to grave 6005 and cremation burial 6007 at Panattoni Park. Where formal cemeteries have been more certainly defined in association with villas, they may be situated some distance from the main building complex. In two large examples in Cambridgeshire, for example, the cemetery associated with the Whitehills villa, Huntingdon, lay 200m away (Nicholson 2006), while antiquarian excavations at Litlington are recorded as having uncovered a cemetery of 250 inhumations and 80 cremation burials within a walled enclosure some 350m from the villa (Wessex Archaeology 2010, 3).

The small number of burials from Panattoni Park provide only very limited evidence for the community's funerary practices. None were buried in coffins and the only grave goods were the urn and ancillary vessel accompanying cremation burial 6007, which represent a typical combination of vessels for such a burial, albeit that cremation burials were less commonly provided with vessels in the Central Belt than they were further south and east (Smith 2018b, 266–7). All the burials were adults, at least two being male, and the presence of non-specific infections, cribra orbitalia and degenerative joint disease, as well as a healed fracture of the right tibia of skeleton 3006, were consistent with Rohnbogner's (2018, 340) characterisation of the Roman rural population as 'a physically active population involved in agricultural and domestic labour'. The burials are thus broadly unremarkable, although the selection of these individuals for burial may in itself mark them out from members of the community whose funerary rites may have left no archaeologically detectable evidence (Pearce 2016, 355).

Panattoni Park and the Nene Valley

The villa formed part of a dense network of contemporary settlements in the Nene Valley, which is reasonably well understood due to the concentration of archaeological excavations undertaken in advance of development and gravel quarrying (Fig. 6.4). They range from large villas to more humble farmsteads, as well as the walled towns at Water

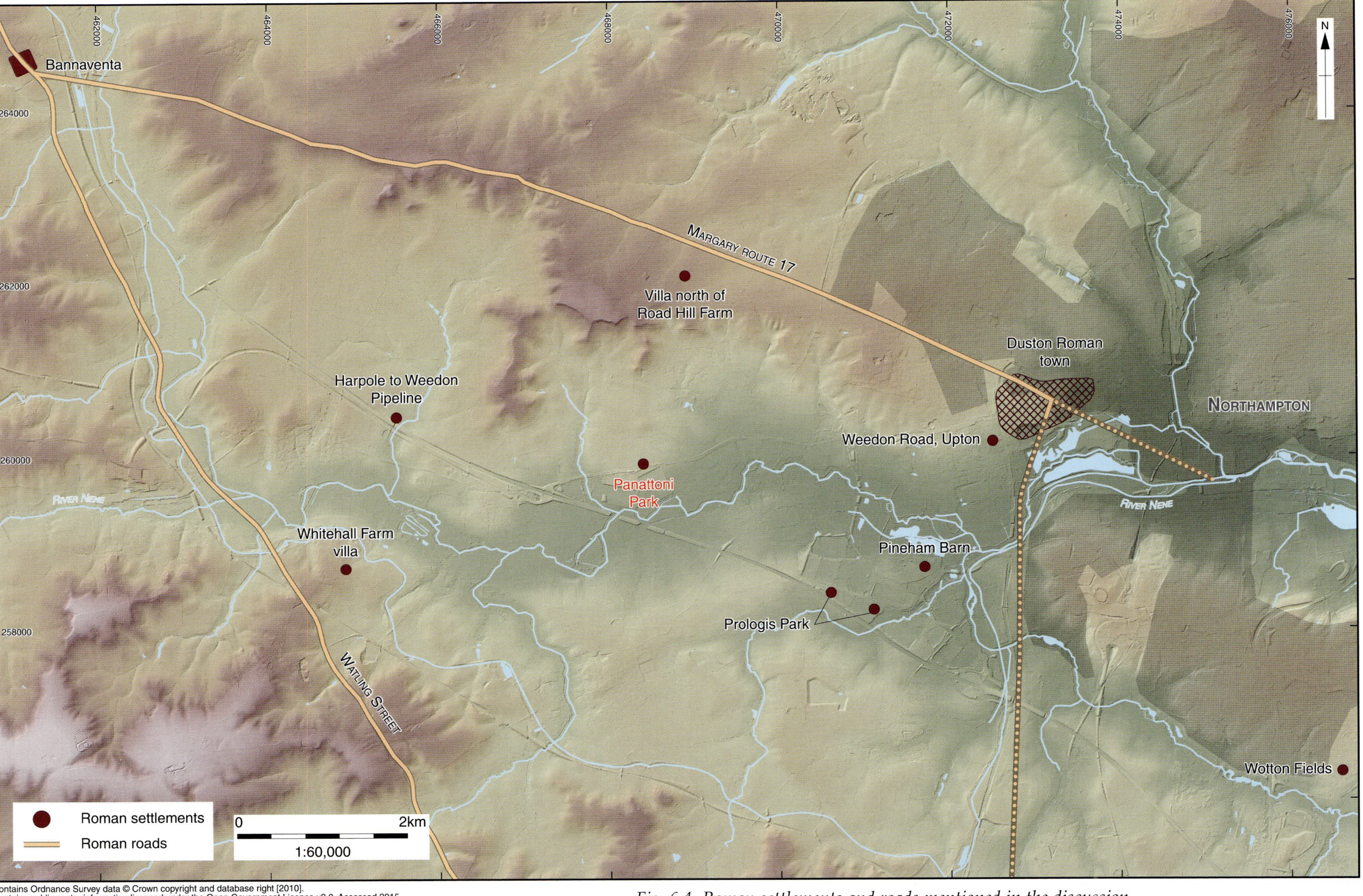

Contains Ordnance Survey data © Crown copyright and database right [2010].
Contains public sector information licensed under the Open Government Licence v3.0. Accessed 2015.
Initial evaluation and Geophysical survey carried out by Museum of London Archaeology.

Fig. 6.4 Roman settlements and roads mentioned in the discussion

Newton and Irchester and smaller nucleated settlements including the nearby one at Duston. It is clear from the architectural evidence – the stone buildings, the mosaic that initiated interest in the site, the nymphaeum and the temple/mausoleum – that the villa was toward the upper end of the social scale and comprised a high-status dwelling for members of the local elite (Allen and Smith 2016, 33). The villa appears to have been established as such from the outset in the 2nd century, in contrast to some excavated villas in the county that developed from late Iron Age predecessors (eg Ashley: Taylor and Dix 1985; Brixworth: Woods 1972; Piddington: Friendship-Taylor and Friendship-Taylor 2013; Stanwick: Neal 1989; Weekley: Jackson and Dix 1988). However, data from the Rural Settlement of Roman Britain Project for the Central Belt region indicates that it is these precocious developments that are unusual rather than the circumstance at Panattoni Park, although the Nene and Ouse Valleys do appear to contain a concentration of such early villas (Smith 2016a, 158–9). The armilla that was recovered from a late Roman ditch may be relevant to the origin of the villa, perhaps indicating an association with a military veteran, whether one posted to Britannia from elsewhere or returning from a posting abroad. Retired soldiers from the British garrison would have numbered in the region of 800–1600 each year, and a significant proportion of these must surely have chosen to invest in property in the province in which they had served (Smith and Fulford 2016, 410).

In contrast to the structural evidence, however, the artefactual evidence for the status of the villa's occupants is less obvious. Indeed, the range and quality of objects found is unremarkable and would not be out of place on a farmstead of lesser pretentions. For example, there was nothing to compare with the range of metal finds and 20–30 glass vessels from the Whitehall Farm villa, and Biddulph (Chapter 3) has shown that only the temple/mausoleum area produced a pottery assemblage with a 'high-status' signature, characterised by vessels for eating and drinking in a formal social context. This may be because the main buildings were not situated within the excavation area, and may have been destroyed when the A4500 was upgraded in 1966; if refuse from the villa buildings was routinely disposed of close to where it was generated, this might explain the absence of such remains from the excavated areas. It is possible, therefore, that the pottery and other objects from the enclosure complex associated with the villa represent the material cultural of the estate workforce rather than the villa's residents, as the material from other parts of the excavation undoubtedly do. This would be consistent with the emphasis here on cooking and storage vessels as opposed to forms used for fine dining, and has an interesting analogue in the argument above for the presence of two separate spheres of religious practice relating to these distinct elements of the villa community. The

pottery recovered by CLASP's fieldwalking of the corresponding enclosure complex on the north side of the A4500 had a similar profile.

One area in which evidence for an elevated status was identified was in the diet of the villa community. Although predominantly beef eaters, as seems to have been the norm throughout the valley, pigs were evidently being reared at the settlement. This may have enabled them to be consumed more frequently than on other site types, especially if the presence of bones from piglets indicates the eating of suckling pigs, which may have been regarded as something of a delicacy (Allen 2017a, 119). The presence of bones from deer and wildfowl is also likely to represent the consumption of occasional delicacies that occur infrequently on non-villa sites and were presumably not available to most of the population, and may also be evidence for hunting, an activity reserved for the elite (Allen 2018a, 119). If the fragments of fallow deer antler represent the presence of live animals rather than importation of antlers alone, they comprise rare evidence for a species that is not native to Britain, but which is known to have been imported for emparkment at high-status residences (ibid., 99–101).

Some of the economic strategies evidenced at the villa are also typically only found at higher-status settlements and would not have been available to groups with less substantial resources. The possibility that malting was carried out to supplement income from more conventional produce was discussed above, and whatever its specific function, the complex of stone-lined pits and ovens clearly represents a significant investment in crop-processing infrastructure. The presence of bone- and antler-working waste, too, suggests a degree of craftworking specialisation that is rare on rural settlements below villa status, whether because this was where the greatest demand was situated or because smaller settlements did not produce a sufficient supply of raw material to support these crafts (Allen 2017b, 216–18). Antler working may have been concentrated in the enclosure complex east of the spring channel, as most of the sawn pieces were recovered from this area, both during the excavation and the evaluation (MOLA 2015c, 55), although there was no single concentration that indicated a precise location for the activity. The recovery of only a small number of sawn examples may indicate that the activity at Panattoni Park was at a fairly non-intensive level, in contrast to the evidence for specialised manufacture of gaming pieces at Stanwick (English Heritage 1995) and a small workshop within the roadside settlement at Higham Ferrers (Lawrence and Smith 2009). In total contrast to these economic strategies, the small size of the two miniature dogs whose remains were recovered from ditches in the enclosure complex associated with the villa may indicate that they served no economic function at all and instead were kept simply as pets.

The evident disparity in the status of the different

settlements in the valley naturally invites interpretation as a stratified system with the villas comprising estate centres and smaller settlements dependent farms, with the Panattoni Park settlement being in the former category. Such an arrangement has been tentatively posited to describe the relationship between four artefact-poor farmsteads that were excavated at the edge of the floodplain at Wollaston and three nearby settlements with stone buildings that are known only from cropmarks (Meadows 2009b, 101–4). In practice, as Meadows acknowledges, specific tenurial relationships are almost impossible to demonstrate from archaeological evidence, although the possible evidence discussed above for centralised processing of agricultural production at Panattoni Park, in the form of the corndrying ovens, probable mill and stockyard, may suggest that produce was being gathered from settlements elsewhere. However, it is impossible to prove that this comprises a tied relationship with, for example, the farmsteads at Weedon Road, Upton or Pineham. The significance of the nearby roadside settlement at Duston is uncertain. Villas tend to cluster around the larger towns, a pattern that is commonly attributed to their role as residences of the urban elite, but recent research has tended to view the smaller roadside settlements primarily as working agricultural villages rather than centres of urbanisation (Dawson 2019; Smith and Fulford 2019). In this case Duston is unlikely to have provided a significant market for produce from the villa and may have had little or no role in the administration of the local area. On the other hand, the roadside location of the settlement suggests that it was engaged in trade with passing traffic and perhaps housed a station of the Imperial postal system, and so it may have provided a locus via which trade from the villa accessed the road network and the world beyond.

AFTER THE VILLA

No Anglo-Saxon material has been found associated with the villa. Brown assigned a 5th-century date to the final phase of activity in her excavation, comprising the tannery within the former nymphaeum, but stated that this was 'of the later RB occupation', and clearly interpreted this as the final phase of Roman activity rather than evidence for an Anglo-Saxon presence. Occupation in a similarly reduced state has been recorded at several other villas in the area, including nearby at Whitehall Farm, where the east wing of the winged corridor villa was demolished and overlain by a timber hall and cobbled yard (Brown and Foard 2004, 78) and Redlands Farm, where occupation continued after both wings had been levelled, the hypocaust had fallen into disuse, and an infant cemetery had been inserted into one of the former rooms (OAU 1992, 65). This final stage of occupation at the latter site may have been contemporary with three Anglo-Saxon sunken-featured buildings that were dug into the villa courtyard, and similar evidence was recorded at Orton Hall Farm, where the excavator argued that there was no break in occupation between the Roman farmstead and the succeeding Anglo-Saxon settlement, comprising two timber halls, a granary and a single sunken-featured building (Mackreth 1996, 237). Possible evidence for continuity of occupation between the two periods has also been recorded at Wollaston, where ditches associated with a villa west of the village produced early Anglo-Saxon pottery from the upper fills and sunken-featured structures were excavated nearby (Chapman and Jackson 1992). Generally, however, Roman settlements in the Nene Valley do not appear to have continued into the Anglo-Saxon period, whose small-scale society presumably had little need for estate centres like Panattoni Park. It would appear that following the end of Roman occupation in the late 4th/early 5th century the villa was simply forgotten and remained exclusively agricultural throughout the historic period, with activity represented only by the ridge and furrow earthworks and the construction of Harpole Mill on the adjacent part of the Nene. Only the accidental discovery of the mosaic in 1846 brought it back to light.

Appendix 1

Insects and other invertebrates
from the spring channel and ditch 2511

Context	1305	1304	2501
Sample	35	34	2050
Sample volume	2L	2L	2L
ANNELIDA			
Oligochaeta sp. (earthworm) egg capsules	P	P	P
CRUSTACEA			
Daphnia sp. ephippia	P	-	-
Cladocera sp(p). ephippia	P	P	P
Ostracoda spp. carapaces	-	P	P
INSECTA			
DERMAPTERA (earwigs)			
Dermaptera sp. [u]	+	-	+
HEMIPTERA: HETEROPTERA (true bugs)			
Coreidae (shield bugs)			
Coreus marginatus (Linnaeus) [oa-p]	1	-	3
Pentatomidae (shield bugs)			
Dolycoris baccarum (Linnaeus) [oa-p]	-	-	1
Pentatoma rufipes (Linnaeus) [oa-p]	1	-	1
Anthocoridae (minute pirate bugs)			
Anthocoridae sp. [u]	-	-	1
Lygaeidae (ground bugs)			
Drymus sp. [oa-p]	-	-	1
Heterogaster urticae (Fabricius) [oa-p]	1	-	1
Scolopostethus cf *affinis* or *thompsoni* [oa-p]	-	1	1
Lygaeidae spp. [oa-p]	2	-	-
Saldidae (shore bugs)			
Saldidae sp. [oa-d]	-	-	1
HEMIPTERA: HOMOPTERA			
Aphrophoridae (spittle bugs)			
Aphrophora alni (Fallén) [oa-p]	1	1	-
Cicadellidae (planthoppers)			
Megophthalmus sp. [oa-p]	1	-	-
Delphacidae (leafhoppers)			
Auchenorhyncha spp. [oa-p]	6	3	4
Auchenorhyncha spp. (nymphs) [oa-p]	-	-	+
Psylloidea (jumping plant lice)			
Trioza urticae (Linnaeus) (nymphs) [oa-p]	-	-	+
Psylloidea sp. nymph skin [oa-p]	-	+	-
COLEOPTERA (beetles)			
Haliplidae (crawling water beetles)			
Haliplus lineatocollis (Marsham) [oa-w]	+	-	-
Dytiscidae (diving beetles)			
Agabus bipustulatus (Linnaeus) [oa-w]	+	+	-
Agabus or *Ilybius* spp. [oa-w]	+	+	+
Colymbetes fuscus (Linnaeus) [oa-w]	+	+	-
Hygrotus inaequalis (Fabricius) [oa-w]	+	-	-
Hydroporinae spp. [oa-w]	+	-	-
Carabidae (ground beetles)			
Nebria brevicollis (Fabricius) [oa]	1	-	-
Notiophilus sp. [oa]	-	1	-
Carabus violaceus Linnaeus [oa]	-	-	1
Carabus spp. indet. [oa]	-	1	1
Clivina sp. [oa]	1	1	-
Trechus obtusus or *quadristriatus* [oa]	1	-	-
Bembidion (*Philochthus*) *guttula* or *mannerheimi* [oa]	-	-	2
Bembidion (*Phyla*) *obtusum* Audinet-Serville [oa]	-	-	1

Context	1305	1304	2501
Sample	35	34	2050
Sample volume	2L	2L	2L
Bembidion spp. [oa]	2	1	1
Brachinus crepitans (Linnaeus) [oa]	-	-	1
Poecilus versicolor (Sturm) [oa-d]	-	-	5
Pterostichus diligens or *strenuus* [oa]	-	-	1
Pterostichus sp. [oa]	-	-	1
Amara spp. [oa]	-	-	2
Harpalus rufipes (De Geer) [oa]	-	-	1
Harpalus or *Ophonus* sp. [oa]	1	-	-
Ophonus sp. [oa]	-	-	1
Calathus fuscipes (Goeze) [oa]	3	1	-
Paranchus albipes (Fabricius) [oa-d]	-	1	-
Paradromius linearis (Olivier) [oa]	-	-	1
Carabidae spp. [ob]	2	-	3
Helophoridae (grooved water scavengers)			
Helophorus grandis Illiger [oa-w]	-	+	+
Helophorus aequalis or *grandis* [oa-w]	+	-	-
Helophorus spp. [oa-w]	+++	+	+
Hydrochidae			
Hydrochus sp. [oa-w]	+	-	-
Hydrophilidae			
Laccobius sp. [oa-w]	+	-	-
Hydrobius fuscipes (Linnaeus) [oa-w]	+	+	+
Hydrophilinae spp. [oa-w]	-	+	-
Sphaeridium sp. [rf]	-	-	2
Cercyon ?melanocephalus (Linnaeus) [rf-sf]	1	-	-
Cercyon pygmaeus (Illiger) [rf-st]	-	-	1
Cercyon ustulatus (Preyssler) [oa-d]	-	1	-
Cercyon spp. indet. [u]	-	2	1
Cryptopleurum minutum (Fabricius) [rf-st]	-	1	-
Megasternum concinnum agg. (Marsham) [rt-sf]	5	1	2
Histeridae (clown beetles)			
Onthophilus striatus (Forster) [rt-sf]	-	1	1
Histerinae sp(p). [rt]	1	1	4
Hydraenidae			
Hydraena testacea Curtis [oa-w]	-	-	+
Hydraena spp. [oa-w]	+	-	+
Limnebius truncatellus (Thunberg) [oa-w]	+	-	+
Ochthebius bicolon or *dilatatus* [oa-w]	-	-	+
Ochthebius dilatatus Stephens [oa-w]	+	-	-
Ochthebius c.f. *minimus* [(Fabricius) oa-w]	+	-	-
Ptiliidae (featherwing beetles)			
Ptenidium sp. [rt]	-	-	1
Acrotrichis sp. [rt]	3	-	1
Leiodidae			
Choleva or *Catops* sp. [u]	-	-	1
Silphidae (sexton beetles)			
Phosphuga atrata Linnaeus [u]	1	1	1
Silphidae sp(p). [u]	3	1	3
Staphylinidae (rove beetles)			
Omalium spp. [rt]	1	1	2
Acidota cruentata Mannerheim [oa]	-	-	1
Lesteva longoelytrata (Goeze) [oa-d]	4	1	5
Metopsia clypeata (Müller) [rt]	-	-	1
Pselaphinae spp. [u]	-	-	1
Sepedophilus sp. [u]	1	-	-
Tachyporus spp. [u]	1	-	4
Tachinus spp. [u]	2	1	3
Mycetoporus sp. [u]	-	1	-
Aleochara spp. [rt]	-	-	2
Cordalia obscura (Gravenhorst) [rt-sf]	-	-	4
Cordalia or *Falagria* sp. [rt-sf]	1	-	-
Aleochariinae spp. [u]	-	-	7
Carpelimus ?bilineatus or *erichsonii* [rt-sf]	-	-	4
Carpelimus sp. [u]	1	-	3
Platystethus cornutus group [oa-d]	1	-	1
Platystethus nitens (Sahlberg) [oa-d]	2	-	8

Context	1305	1304	2501
Sample	**35**	**34**	**2050**
Sample volume	**2L**	**2L**	**2L**
Platystethus arenarius (Geoffroy in Fourcroy) [rf]	2	-	-
Anotylus nitidulus (Gravenhorst) [rt-d-sf]	2	-	2
Anotylus rugosus (Fabricius) [rt-sf]	2	1	1
Anotylus sculpturatus group [rt-sf]	1	-	9
Anotylus tetracarinatus (Block) [rt-sf]	-	-	1
Stenus spp. [u]	2	1	1
Lobrathium multipunctum (Gravenhorst) [u]	1	-	-
Rugilus sp. [rt]	-	-	1
Othius sp(p). [rt]	-	1	1
Gyrohypnus sp. indet. [rt]	-	-	1
Xantholinus gallicus or *linearis*[rt-sf]	2	-	1
Staphylininae spp. [u]	7	1	6
Geotrupidae (dor beetles)			
Geotrupini sp. [oa-rf] (*Geotrupes* s.l.)	1	1	1
Trogidae (hide beetles)			
Trox scaber (Linnaeus) [rt-sf]	1	-	-
Scarabaeidae (dung beetles and chafers)			
Acrossus rufipes (Linnaeus) [oa-rf]	2	-	1
Agrilinus ater (De Geer) [oa-rf]	2	-	11
Agrilinus ?ater (De Geer) [oa-rf]	-	1	-
Aphodius fimetarius (Linnaeus) [ob-rf]	-	-	7
Aphodius ?fimetarius (Linnaeus) [ob-rf]	3	3	-
Melinopterus prodromus or *sphacelatus* [ob-rf]	54	27	72
Nimbus contaminatus (Herbst) [oa-rf]	3	2	6
Oxyomus sylvestris (Scopoli) [rt-sf]	-	1	2
Aphodiinae spp. [ob-rf]	2	3	1
Onthophagus joannae Goljan [oa-rf]	2	-	-
Onthophagus similis (Scriba) [oa-rf]	1	-	-
Onthophagus spp. indet. [oa-rf]	-	2	1
Phyllopertha horticola (Linnaeus) [oa-p]	1	1	1
Scirtidae (marsh beetles)			
Contacyphon sp. [oa-d]	-	-	1
Dascillidae (orchid beetles)			
Dascillus cervinus (Linnaeus) [oa-p]	-	1	-
Byrrhidae (pill beetles)			
Byrrhus sp. [oa]	3	4	3
Dryopidae (long-toed water beetles)			
Dryops sp. [oa-d]	1	-	1
Elateridae (click beetles)			
Agrypnus murinus (Linnaeus) [oa-p]	5	4	4
Agriotes spp. [oa-p]	6	-	-
Athous haemorrhoidalis (Fabricius) [oa-p]	1	1	2
Athous haemorrhoidalis (Fabricius) larval apex	+	-	+
Elateridae spp. and sp. indet. [ob]	3	2	4
Cantharidae (soldier beetles)			
Cantharidae spp. [ob]	-	-	2
Ptinidae (spider and woodworm beetles)			
Ptinus sp. [rd-sf-h]	-	1	-
Grynobius planus (Fabricius) [l]	-	1	-
Anobium inexpectatum or *punctatum* [l]	2	2	-
Anobium punctatum (De Geer) [l-sf]	-	-	1
Cryptophagidae (silken fungus beetles)			
Cryptophagus sp. [rd-sf-h]	-	1	-
Atomaria spp. [rd-sf-h]	3	-	4
Kateretidae (short-winged flower beettles)			
Kateretes sp. [oa-p-d]	1	-	-
Brachypterus sp. [oa-p]	1	-	-
Nitidulidae (sap and pollen beetles)			
Meligethes sp. [oa-p]	1	-	1
Coccinellidae (ladybirds)			
Coccinellidae sp. [oa]	-	-	1
Corylophidae			
Corylophidae sp. [rt]	-	-	1
Latridiidae (minute brown scavenger beetles)			
Latridius minutus group [rd-st-h]	-	1	-
Enicmus sp. [rd-sf]	2	-	3

Context	1305	1304	2501
Sample	35	34	2050
Sample volume	2L	2L	2L
Corticariinae spp. [rt]	2	1	3
Latridiidae sp. [u]	-	-	1
Chrysomelidae (seed and leaf beetles)			
Prasocuris phellandrii (Linnaeus) [oa-p-d]	2	-	-
Sphaeroderma sp. [oa-p]	-	1	-
Chaetocnema arida group [oa-p]	1	-	-
Psylliodes sp. [oa-p]	-	-	1
Longitarsus sp. [oa-p]	2	-	4
Phyllotreta nemorum group [oa-p]	-	-	1
Phyllotreta spp. [oa-p]	2	1	5
Chrysomelidae spp. and sp. indet. [oa-p]	2	-	2
Apionidae			
Taenapion urticarium (Herbst) [oa-p]	-	1	3
Oxystoma sp(p). [oa-p]	3	1	1
Apionidae spp. and sp. indet. [oa-p]	11	1	19
Erirhinidae (wetland weevils)			
Notaris acridulus (Linnaeus) [oa-p-d]	-	1	1
Curculionidae (weevils)			
Mecinus labilis (Herbst) [oa-p]	-	2	-
Mecinus pascuorum (Gyllenhal) [oa-p]	-	-	1
Mecinus pyraster (Herbst) [oa-p]	1	1	-
?Mecinini sp. [oa-p]	1	2	-
Ceutorhynchus sp. [oa-p]	-	1	1
Nedyus quadrimaculatus (Linnaeus) [oa-p]	1	-	2
Parethelcus pollinarius (Forster) [oa-p]	1	-	-
Rhinoncus pericarpius (Linnaeus) [oa-p]	-	-	1
Rhinoncus sp. indet. [oa-p]	1	-	-
Ceutorhynchinae spp. [oa-p]	2	2	-
Graptus triguttatus (Fabricius) [oa-p]	2	4	4
Strophosoma sp. [oa-p]	-	-	1
Barynotus moerens (Fabricius) [oa-p]	1	-	-
Barynotus sp. [oa-p]	1	2	-
Otiorhynchus sp. [oa-p]	-	-	1
?*Otiorhynchus* sp. [oa-p]	1	-	-
Sitona spp. [oa-p]	2	2	1
Entiminae sp. [oa-p]	-	-	1
Hypera sp. [oa-p]	1	-	-
Hyperinae sp. [oa-p] large	2	3	3
Hylesinus varius (Fabricius) [l]	2	-	-
Scolytus rugulosus (Müller) [l]	1	-	-
Curculionidae spp and sp. indet. [oa-p]	7	5	3
Coleoptera spp. and sp. indet. [u]	1	2	2
DIPTERA (flies)			
Chironomidae sp(p). larval head capsules	++	-	-
Melophagus ovinus (Linnaeus) puparia	-	-	+
Diptera spp. adults	+	-	+
Diptera spp. puparia	++	-	++
HYMENOPTERA (bees, wasps and ants)			
Formicidae sp(p).	+	-	+
Hymenoptera Parasitica sp.	+	-	-
TRICHOPTERA (caddis flies)			
Trichoptera sp. wing fragments	+	-	-
Trichoptera sp. larval fragments	+	-	-
ARACHNIDA			
Acarina spp. (mites)	P	-	-
Aranae sp. (spiders)	-	P	P
Total adult terrestrial beetles and bugs	225	120	317

Ecological codes shown in square brackets are: d - damp ground/waterside, h - house/building, l - wood/timber, oa - outdoor taxa not usually found within buildings or in accumulations of decomposing matter, ob – probable outdoor taxa, p- plant-associated, sf - facultative synanthropes, st - typical synanthropes, t - tree/shrubs, u - uncoded, w - aquatic. Minimum numbers were estimated for adult beetles (Coleoptera) and bugs (Hemiptera). Abundance of aquatic taxa and other insects has been recorded semi-quantitatively as + 1–3, ++ 4–10, +++ 11–50. Other invertebrate groups have been recorded as (P), common (C) and abundant (A)

Bibliography

ACBMG, 2007 *Ceramic building material: minimum standards for recovery, curation, analysis and publication*, Archaeological Ceramic Building Materials Group, https://www.archaeological ceramics.com/uploads/1/1/9/3/11935072/ ceramic_building_material_guidelines.pdf, accessed 24 March 2021

Alcock, J P, 1980 Classical religious belief and burial practice in Roman Britain, *Archaeol J* **137**, 50–85

Aldhouse Green, M, 2001 *Dying for the gods: human sacrifice in Iron Age and Roman Europe*, Stroud

Allen, M G, 2009 The re-identification of great bustard (*Otis tarda*) from Fishbourne Roman Palace, Chichester, West Sussex, as common crane (*Grus grus*), *Env Archaeol* **14(2)**, 184–90

Allen, M G, 2014 Chasing Sylvia's stag: placing deer in the countryside of Roman Britain, in *Deer and people* (eds K Baker, R Carden and R Madgwick), Oxford, 174–86

Allen, M, 2017a Pastoral farming, in Allen *et al.* 2017, 85–141

Allen, M, 2017b Animal products, in Allen *et al.* 2017, 216–20

Allen, M, 2018a The social context of animals and exploitation of wild resources, in Smith *et al.* 2018, 78–119

Allen, M, 2018b Ritual use of animals, in Smith *et al.* 2018, 192–99

Allen, M, 2018c Animals in burials, in Smith *et al.* 2018, 271–5

Allen, M, and Lodwick, L, 2017 Agricultural strategies in Roman Britain, in Allen *et al.* 2017, 142–77

Allen, M, Lodwick, L, Brindle, T, Fulford, M, and Smith, A, 2017 *The rural economy of Roman Britain*, Britannia Monogr **30**, London

Allen, M, and Smith, A, 2016 Rural settlement in Roman Britain: morphological classification and overview, in Smith *et al.* 2016, 17–43

Allen, M, and Sykes, N, 2011 New animals, new landscapes and new worldviews: the Iron Age to Roman transition at Fishbourne, *Sussex Archaeol Collect* **149**, 7–24

Allison, P, Pitts, M, and Colley, S (eds), 2018 Big data on the Roman table: new approaches to tablewares in the Roman world, *Internet Archaeol* **50**, https://intarch.ac.uk/journal/issue50/ index.html, accessed 1 April 2021

AlQahtani, S, 2009 *Atlas of tooth development and eruption*, London

Andersen, S Th, 1979 Identification of wild grasses and cereal pollen, *Danm Geol Unders* 1978, 69–92

Anderson-Whymark, H, 2008 *The residue of ritualised action: Neolithic deposition practices in the Middle Thames Valley*, BAR Brit. Ser. **466**, Oxford

Anderson-Whymark, H, 2013 The flint, in *Opening the wood, making the land: the archaeology of a Middle Thames landscape. The Eton College Rowing Lake Project and the Maidenhead, Windsor and Eton Flood Alleviation Scheme, volume 1: Mesolithic to early Bronze Age* (T G Allen, A Barclay, A M Cromarty, H Anderson-Whymark, A Parker and M Robinson), Thames Valley Landscapes **38**, Oxford, 513–20

Andrews, P, Biddulph, E, Hardy, A, and Brown, R, 2011 *Settling the Ebbsfleet Valley: High Speed 1 excavations at Springhead and Northfleet, Kent. The late Iron Age, Roman, Saxon and medieval landscape, volume 1: the sites*, Oxford and Salisbury

Anon., 1850 Proceedings of the Association, *J Brit Archaeol Assoc* **5**, 337–78

Anon., 1851 On a Roman pavement discovered at Harpole, in Northamptonshire, *J Brit Archaeol Assoc* **6**, 126–7

Apicius, 2009 *Cooking and dining in Imperial Rome* (trans. J D Vehling), Project Gutenberg, https:// www.gutenberg.org/ebooks/29728

ArcHeritage, 2013 Excavations at Waterdale, Doncaster: excavation report, https://doi.org/ 10.5284/1029314, accessed 7 October 2021

Aufderheide, A C, and Rodríguez-Martin, C, 1998 *The Cambridge encyclopedia of human paleo-pathology*, Cambridge

Baker, J R, and Brothwell, D R, 1980 *Animal diseases in archaeology*, London

Bales, E, 2004 *A Roman maltings at Beck Row, Mildenhall, Suffolk*, East Anglian Archaeology Occ Pap **20**, Bury St Edmunds

Bamford, H, 1985 *Briar Hill: excavation 1974–1978, Northampton*, Northampton Development Corporation Archaeological Monograph **3**, Northampton

Bantock, T, and Botting, J, 2018 *British bugs*, www. britishbugs.org.uk/

Barber, J, 1985 The pit alignment at Eskbank Nurseries, *Proc Prehist Soc* **51**, 149–66

Barclay, A, 2001 Later prehistoric pottery, in A Barclay, A Boyle and G D Keevill, A prehistoric enclosure at Eynsham Abbey, Oxfordshire, *Oxoniensia* **66**, 127–39

Barnett, C, McKinley, J I, Stafford, E, Grimm, J M, and Stevens, C J, 2011 *Settling the Ebbsfleet Valley. High Speed 1 excavations at Springhead and Northfleet, Kent: the late Iron Age, Roman, Saxon, and medieval landscape, volume 3: late Iron Age to Roman human remains and environmental reports*, Oxford and Salisbury

Bartosiewicz, L, with Gal, E, 2013 *Shuffling nags, lame ducks: the archaeology of animal disease*, Oxford

Bass, W, 2005 *Human osteology: a laboratory and field manual*, Columbia, Missouri

Baxter, I, 2003 Animal bone, in *A late Iron Age farmstead and Romano-British site at Haddon, Peterborough* (M Hinman), BAR Brit. Ser. **358**, Oxford, 99–103

Berry, A C, and Berry, A J, 1967 Epigenetic variation in the human cranium, *J Anatomy* **101**, 361–79

BGS, nd *Geology of Britain viewer*, British Geological Survey, http://mapapps.bgs.ac.uk/geologyof britain/home.html, accessed 7 September 2020

Biddulph, E, 2008 Form and function: the experimental use of Roman samian ware cups, *Oxford J Archaeol* **27(1)**, 91–100

Biddulph, E, Brady, K, Simmonds, A, and Foreman, S, 2019 *Berryfields: Iron Age settlement and a Roman bridge, field system and settlement along Akeman Street near Fleet Marston, Buckinghamshire*, Oxford Archaeology Monograph **30**, Oxford

Biddulph, E, Seager Smith, R, and Schuster, J, 2011 *Settling the Ebbsfleet Valley. High Speed 1 excavations at Springhead and Northfleet, Kent. The late Iron Age, Roman, Saxon and medieval landscape, volume 2: Late Iron Age to Roman finds reports*, Oxford and Salisbury

Blinkhorn, E, and Little, A, 2018 Being ritual in Mesolithic Britain and Ireland: identifying ritual behaviour within an ephemeral material record, *J World Prehist* **31**, 403–20

Blinkhorn, P, Jackson, D and Chapman, A, 2015, The Iron Age potter from the Long Dole, in Masefield *et al.* 2015, 44–8

Booth, P, nd Oxford Archaeology Roman pottery recording system: an introduction, unpubl. Oxford Archaeology South, Oxford, updated November 2019

Booth, P, Evans, J, and Hiller, J, 2001 *Excavations in the extramural settlement of Roman Alchester, Oxfordshire, 1991*, Oxford Archaeology Monograph **1**, Oxford

Booth, P M, and Simmonds, A, 2018 *Gill Mill: later prehistoric landscape and a Roman nucleated settlement in the Lower Windrush Valley at Gill Mill, Near Witney, Oxfordshire*, Thames Valley Landscapes **42**, Oxford

Bradley, P, 1999 The worked flint, in *Excavations at Barrow Hills, Radley, Oxfordshire. Volume 1: the Neolithic and Bronze Age monument complex* (A Barclay and C Halpin) Thames Valley Landscapes **11**, 211–27

Brickley, M, and McKinley, J I (eds), 2004 *Guidelines to the standards for recording human remains*, IFA Paper No. **7**, Reading

Brickstock, R J, 2004 *The production, analysis and standardisation of Romano-British coin reports*, Swindon

Brodribb, G, 1987 *Roman brick and tile*, Gloucester

Brothwell, D, 1981 *Digging up bones*, Oxford

Bronk Ramsey, C, 2009 Bayesian analysis of radiocarbon dates, *Radiocarbon* **51**, 337–60

Brown, A, 1994 A Romano-British shell-gritted pottery and tile manufacturing site at Harrold, Bedfordshire, *Bedfordshire Archaeol* **21**, 19–107

Brown, A E, and Woodfield, C, 1983 Excavations at Towcester, Northamptonshire: the Alchester Road suburb, *Northamptonshire Archaeol* **18**, 43–141

Brown, A G, Meadows, I, Turner, S D, and Mattingly, D J, 2001 Roman vineyards in Britain: stratigraphic and palynological data from Wollaston in the Nene Valley, England, *Antiquity* **75**, 745–57

Brown, G, 1967 Harpole, in *Excavations Annual Report 1966*, **6**, Ministry of Public Works, London

Brown, J, and Carlyle, S, 2007 Northampton, Upton, Pineham North, *SMA* **37**, 19–20

Brown, T, and Foard, G, 2004 The Anglo-Saxon period, in *The archaeology of Northamptonshire* (ed. M Tingle), Northampton, 78–101

Buikstra, J E, and Ubelaker, D H, 1994 *Standards for data collection from human skeletal remains*, Arkansas Archaeological Survey Research Series No. **44**, Arkansas

Busby, P, de Moulins, D, Lyne, M, McPhillips, S, and Scaife, R, 2001 Excavations at Clatterford Roman villa, Isle of Wight, *Proc Hampshire Field Club Archaeol Soc* **56**, 95–128

Butler, C, 2007 A Mesolithic site at Street Lane, Street, East Sussex, *Sussex Archaeol Collect* **145**, 7–31

Cappers, R T J, Bekker, R M, and Jans, J E A, 2006 *Digital seed atlas of the Netherlands*, Groningen Archaeological Studies **4**, Eelde

Carlyle, S, 2010 An Iron Age pit alignment near Upton, Northampton, *Northamptonshire Archaeol* **36**, 75–87

Carrott, J, and Kenward, H, 2001 Species associations among insect remains from urban archaeological deposits and their significance in reconstructing the past human environment, *J Archaeol Sci* **28**, 887–905

Carruthers, W J, and Hunter Dowse, K L, 2019 *A review of macroscopic plant remains from the midland counties*, Historic England Res Rep **27/2019**, Portsmouth

Chamberlain, A, 1994 *Human remains*, London

Champness, C, Donnelly, M, Ford, B, and Haggart, A, 2015 Life at the floodplain edge: terminal upper palaeolithic and Mesolithic flint scatters and early prehistoric archaeology along the Beam River, Dagenham, *Trans Essex Soc Archaeol Hist* **73**, 55–61

Chapman, A, 1995 Crick, *SMA* **25**, 37–9

Chapman, A, 2005 The querns and millstones, in Chapman *et al.* 2005, 105–6

Chapman, A, Clarke, J, and Foard, A, 2017 A Bronze Age and Iron Age landscape at Harlestone Quarry, Northampton, *Northamptonshire Archaeol* **39**, 37–67

Chapman, A, and Jackson, D, 1992 Wollaston

Bypass, Northamptonshire, Salvage Excavations 1984, *Northamptonshire Archaeol* **24**, 67–75

Chapman, A, Thorne, A, and Upson-Smith, T, 2005 A Roman villa and an Anglo-Saxon burial at Wootton Fields, Northampton, *Northamptonshire Archaeol* **33**, 79–112

CLASP 2012 *Whitehall Roman villa and landscape project*, Community Landscape Archaeology Survey Projects, https://claspweb.org.uk/WHITEHALL/index.html, accessed 23 September 2021

CLASP, nd a *Local people:local past*, Community Landscape Archaeology Survey Projects, https://claspweb.org.uk/LOCAL/index.html, accessed 23 September 2021

CLASP, nd b Harpole 1: Romano-British and late Iron Age pottery by fabric, *CLASP: Community Landscape Archaeology Survey Project*, https://claspweb.org.uk/LOCAL/DATABASES_AND_REPORTS/harpole1/har1_pottery.html, accessed 30 March 2021

Clifton-Taylor, A, 1987 *The pattern of English building*, London

Clutton-Brock, J, 1999 *A natural history of domesticated mammals*, 2nd edn, Cambridge

Cohen, A, and Serjeantson, D, 1996 *Manual for the identification of bird bones from archaeological sites*, London

Cool, H E M, 1983 A study of the Roman personal ornaments made of metal, excluding brooches, from southern Britain, unpubl. PhD thesis, Univ. Wales

Cooper, L, Jarvis, W, Bayliss, A, Beamish, M, Bronk Ramsey, C, Browning, J, and Macphail, R, 2017 Making and breaking microliths: a middle Mesolithic site at Asfordby, Leicestershire (R Macphail), *Proc Prehist Soc* **83**, 43–96

Cotswold Archaeology, 2018 Saxon Rise 2. Northampton Road, Brixworth, Northamptonshire: post-excavation assessment and updated project design, unpubl. report **17046**, Cotswold Archaeology, Kemble, 88–91

Cox, M L, 2007 *Atlas of the seed and leaf beetles of Britain and Ireland*, Newbury

Cranfield Soil and Agrifood Institute, 2000 *Soilscapes*, http://www.landis.org.uk/soilscapes/

Crew, P, 2004 Perforated tiles from corn driers and malt kilns, *British Brick Society Information* **95**, 4–12

Crosby, V, and Muldowney, L, 2011 *Stanwick Quarry, Northamptonshire. Raunds Area Project: phasing the Iron Age and Romano-British settlement at Stanwick, Northamptonshire (excavations 1984–1992): volume 1*, Engl Heritage Res Dept Rep **54**, Portsmouth

Crummy, N, 1979 A chronology of Romano-British bone pins, *Britannia* **10**, 157–63

Crummy, N, 2005 From bracelets to battle-honours: military armillae from the Roman conquest of Britain, in *Image, craft and the Classical World: essays in honour of Donald Bailey and Catherine Johns* (ed. N Crummy), Monographies

Instrumentum **29**, Montagnac, 93–105

Cunliffe, B W, 1995 *Danebury: an Iron Age hillfort in Hampshire, volume 6, a hillfort community in perspective*, CBA Res Rep **102**, York

Cunliffe, B, 2005 *Iron Age communities in Britain*, 4th edn, London

Cunliffe, B, and Davenport, P, 1985 *The temple of Sulis Minerva at Bath, vol 1: the site*, Oxford University Committee for Archaeology Monograph **7**, Oxford

Cunliffe, B, and Poole, C, 1991 *Danebury: an Iron Age hillfort in Hampshire, vol. 5: the excavations, 1979–1988: the finds*, CBA Res Rep **73**, London

Davies, A, 2018 *Creating society and constructing the past: social change in the Thames Valley from the late Bronze Age to the middle Iron Age*, BAR Brit. Ser. **637**, Oxford

Davies, A, 2020 Prehistoric pottery, in Apex Park, Daventry, Northamptonshire: Archaeological Excavation Report, unpubl. report, Oxford Archaeology, Oxford, https://library.oxfordarchaeology.com/5865/

Davies, A, Webley, L, and Boothroyd, J, 2022 A middle Bronze Age enclosure and other prehistoric to early medieval activity at Nerrols Farm, Cheddon Fitzpaine, *Somerset Archaeol Natur Hist* **164**, 14–41

Dawson, M-J, 2019 Rethinking small town market status in Roman Britain: a review of the data for five case studies in the Thames Valley region, unpubl. PhD thesis, Univ. Kent

Deegan, A, and Foard, G, 2008 *Mapping ancient landscapes in Northamptonshire*, London

De la Bédoyère, G, 1991 *The buildings of Roman Britain*, London

Detsicas, A P, 1967 Excavations at Eccles, 1966, *Archaeol Cantiana* **82**, 162–78

Dias, G, and Tayles, N, 1997 'Abscess cavity' – a misnomer, *Int J Osteoarchaeol* **7**, 548–54

Dineley, M, 2004 *Barley, malt and ale in the Neolithic*, BAR Int. Ser. **1213**, Oxford

Dobney, K, Jaques, D, and Irving, B G, 1996 *Of butchers and breeds: report on vertebrate remains from various sites in the city of Lincoln*, Lincoln Archaeological Studies **5**, Lincoln

Donnelly, M, Grant, R, Kennard, L, Lawrence, T, and Souday, C, 2019 The flint, in Bexhill to Hastings Link Road: post-excavation assessment and updated project design, unpubl. report, Oxford Archaeology, Oxford

Duff, A G, 2012 *Beetles of Britain and Ireland, volume 1: Sphaeriusidae to Silphidae*, privately printed

Duff, A G, 2016 *Beetles of Britain and Ireland, volume 4: Cerambycidae to Curculionidae*, privately printed

Duff, A G (ed), 2018 *Checklist of beetles of the British Isles*, 3rd edn, Iver

Eckardt, H, 2002 *Illuminating Roman Britain*, Monographies Instrumentum **23**, Montagnac

Eckardt, H, 2011 Heating and lighting, in *Artefacts*

in Roman Britain: their purpose and use (ed. L Allason-Jones), Cambridge, 180–93

English Heritage, 1995 Raunds Area Project: Iron Age and Romano-British Project, English Heritage Report

Esmonde Cleary, S, 2000 Putting the dead in their place: burial location in Roman Britain, in *Burial, society and context in the Roman world* (eds J Pearce, M Millett and M Struck), Oxford, 127–42

Evans, C, Mackay, D, and Appleby, G, 2006 *Longstanton, Cambridgeshire: a village hinterland (I, II and III), 2004, 2005 and 2006 investigations*, unpubl. report, Cambridge Archaeological Unit, Cambridge, https://doi.org/10.5284/1021795

Evans, J, 1894 On some iron tools and other articles formed of iron found at Silchester in the year 1890, *Archaeologia* **54**, 139–56

Evans, J, 2001a Material approaches to the identification of different Romano-British site types, *Britons and Romans: advancing an archaeological agenda* (eds S James and M Millett), CBA Res Rep **125**, 26–35, York

Evans, J, 2001b Iron Age, Roman and Anglo-Saxon pottery, in Booth *et al.* 2001, 263–383

Finnegan, M, 1978 Non-metric variation of the infracranial skeleton, *J Anatomy* **125**, 23–37

Foard-Colby, A, 2008 A Bronze Age cremation burial from Upton, Northampton, *Northamptonshire Archaeol* **35**, 15–26

Foard-Colby, A, and Walker, C, 2010 Iron Age settlement and medieval features at Quinton House School, Upton, Northampton, *Northamptonshire Archaeol* **36**, 53–73

Fosberry, R, and Moan, P, 2018 Romano-British spelt malting on the Cambridgeshire Fen edge: excavations at Norman Way Industrial Estate, Over, *Proc Cambridge Antiq Soc* **107**, 15–30

Fox, N P, 1967 The ritual shaft at Warbank, Keston, *Archaeol Cantiana* **82**, 184–91

Frere, S S, 1992 Roman Britain in 1991: sites explored, *Britannia* **23**, 255–308

Friendship-Taylor, R M, and Friendship-Taylor, D E, 2013 Iron Age and Roman Piddington: 11th interim report and phase descriptions of the late Iron Age settlement, military phase, Roman villas, and Saxon phases at Piddington, Northants, Upper Nene Archaeol Soc report

Fryer, V, 2004 Charred plant remains and other macrofossils, in *A Roman maltings at Beck Row, Mildenhall, Suffolk* (E Bales), East Anglian Archaeology Occas Pap **20**, Ipswich, 49–54

Fulford, M, 2001 Links with the past: pervasive 'ritual' behaviour in Roman Britain, *Britannia* **32**, 199–218

Fulford, M, 2020 The countryside of Roman Britain: a Gallic perspective, *Britannia* **51**, 295–306

Galloway, A, 1999 *Broken bones: anthropological analysis of blunt force trauma*, Springfield, Illinois

Getty, R, 1975 *Sisson and Grossman's the anatomy of the domestic animals*, Philadelphia

Godwin, H, 1975 *The history of the British flora*, 2nd edn, Cambridge

Godwin, H, 1984 *History of the British flora: a factual basis for phytogeography*, 2nd edn, Cambridge

Grimes, W, 1968 *The excavation of Roman and medieval London*, London

Goodburn, R, 1984 The non-ferrous metal objects, in *Verulamium excavations vol 3* (S S Frere), Oxford University Committee for Archaeology Monograph **1**, Oxford, 18–68

Grant, A, 1982 The use of tooth wear as a guide to the age of domestic ungulates, in *Ageing and sexing animal bones from archaeological sites* (eds B Wilson, C Grigson, S and Payne), BAR Brit. Ser. **109**, Oxford, 91–108

Grauer, A L (ed.), 2012, *A companion to paleopathology*, Chichester

Green, C W, 1965 A Romano-Celtic temple at Bourton Grounds, *Rec Buckinghamshire* **17**, 356–66

Grimm, J, and Worley, F, 2011 Animal bone, in Barnett *et al.* 2011, 15–52

Hall, A R, and Kenward, H K, 1990 *Environmental evidence from the Colonia*, Archaeology of York **14(6)**, London

Hall, A, and Kenward, H, 2011 Plant and invertebrate indicators of leather production: from fresh skin to leather offcuts, in *Leather tanneries: the archaeological evidence* (eds R Thomson and Q Mould), London, 9–32

Hall, D, 1985 Survey work in eastern England, in *Archaeological field survey in Britain and abroad* (eds S Macready and F H Thompson), Soc Antiquaries Occas Pap **6**, London, 25–44

Hamilton-Dyer, S, 1993 The animal bone, in Excavations in the *Scamnum Tribunorum* at Caerleon: the Legionary Museum Site 1983–5 (J D Zienkiewicz, J Hillam, E Besly, B M Dickinson, P V Webster, S A Fox, S Hamilton-Dyer, A E Caseldine and P A Busby), *Britannia* **24**, 132–6

Hammer, Ø, Harper, D A T, and Ryan, P D, 2001 PAST: Paleontological statistics software package for education and data analysis, *Palaeontologia Electronica* **4(1)**, http://palaeo electronica.org/2001_1/past/issue1_01.htm, accessed 30 March 2021

Hancocks, A, and Willis, S, 2015 Pottery, in *The Iron Age and Romano-British settlement at Crick Covert Farm, Northamptonshire. Excavations 1997–8 (DIRFT volume 1)* (G Hughes and A Woodward), Oxford, 101–4

Hancocks, A, and Woodward, A, 2015 Prehistoric pottery, in *The Iron Age and Romano-British Settlement at Crick Covert Farm: excavations 1997–1998* (G Hughes and A Woodward), Oxford, 204–31

Harding, J, and Healy, F, 2008 *The Raunds Area Project: a Neolithic and Bronze Age landscape in Northamptonshire*, London

Harding, P, 1990 The worked flint, in *The Stonehenge environs project* (J C Richards), London

Hartley, B R, and Dickinson, B M, 2008 *Names on terra sigillata: an index of makers' stamps and signatures on Gallo-Roman terra sigillata (samian ware), vol, 2 (B to Cerotcus)*, Bulletin of the Institute of Classical Studies Supplement **102-02**, London

Hartley, B R, and Dickinson, B M, 2009 *Names on terra sigillata: an index of makers' stamps and signatures on Gallo-Roman terra sigillata (samian ware), vol. 5 (L to Masclus I)*, Bulletin of the Institute of Classical Studies Supplement **102-05**, London

Hather, J G, 2016 *The identification of northern European woods: a guide for archaeologists and conservators*, Abingdon

Hawkes, C F C, and Hull, M R, 1947 *Camulodunum: first report on the excavations at Colchester, 1930–1939*, Reports of the Research Committee of the Society of Antiquaries of London, no. **14**, Oxford

Hayden, C, Simmonds, A, Lawrence, S, and Masefield, R, in prep. *Great Western Park, Didcot, Oxfordshire: Phase 1 excavations, 2010–2012*, Thames Valley Landscapes, Oxford

Healy, F, 1988 *The Anglo-Saxon cemetery at Spong Hill, North Elmham, part 6: occupation during the seventh to second millennia BC*, East Anglian Archaeol **39**, Gressenhall

Henderson, A M, 1949 Small objects in metal, bone, glass, etc, in *Fourth report on the excavations of the Roman fort at Richborough* (J P Bushe-Fox), Rep Research Committee Soc Antiqs London No. **15**, London, 106–60

Higbee, L, 2013 Animal bones, in *Process and history. Romano-British communities at Colne Fen, Earith: an inland port and supply farm* (C Evans), The Archaeology of the Lower Ouse Valley **2**, Cambridge, 116–33

Hillman, G, 1984 Reconstructing crop husbandry practices from charred remain of crops, in *Farming practice in British prehistory* (ed. R Mercer), Edinburgh, 123–62

Hill, J D, 1995 *Ritual and rubbish in the Iron Age of Wessex*, BAR Brit. Ser. **242**, Oxford

Hillson, S, 1996 *Dental anthropology*, 3rd edn, Cambridge

Hillson, S, 2000 Dental pathology, in *Biological anthropology of the human skeleton* (eds M A Katzenberg and S R Saunders), New York, 249–86

Holmes, M, Yates, A, Chapman, A, and Wolframm-Murray, Y, 2012 A middle Neolithic enclosure and mortuary deposit at Banbury Lane, Northampton: an interim report, *Northampton-shire Archaeol* **37**, 19–28

Hooley, D, 2001 Copper alloy and silver objects, in *The Romano-British 'small town' at Wanborough, Wiltshire* (A S Anderson, J S Wacher and A P Fitzpatrick), Britannia Monograph **19**, London, 75–116

Howard, M M, 1963 The metrical determination of the metapodials and skulls of cattle, in *Man and cattle: proceedings of a symposium on domestication at the Royal Anthropological Institute, 24–26 May 1960* (eds A E Mourant and F E Zeuner), London, 91–100

Hull, G, 2001 A late Bronze Age ringwork, pits and later features at Thrapston, Northamptonshire, *Northamptonshire Archaeology* **29**, 73–92

Inall, Y L, 2015 In search of the spear people: spearheads in context in Iron Age eastern Yorkshire and beyond, unpubl. PhD thesis, Univ. Hull

Ingle, C, 1993–4 The quernstones from Hunsbury Hillfort, Northamptonshire, *Northamptonshire Archaeol* **25**, 21–34

Ingrouille, M, 1995 *Historical ecology of the British flora*, London

Inizan, M-L, Reduron-Ballinger, M, Roche, H, and Tixier, J, 1999 *Technology and terminology of knapped stone*, Nanterre

Jackson, D, 1994 The Iron Age hillfort at Borough Hill, Daventry: excavations in 1983, *Northamptonshire Archaeology* **25**, 63-7

Jackson, D, 2001 The prehistoric pottery, in G Hull, A late Bronze Age ringwork, pits and later features at Thrapston, Northamptonshire, *Northamptonshire Archaeology* **29**, 78–82

Jackson, D, 2005, The Iron Age pottery, in Iron Age Settlement at Swan Valley Business Park, near Rothersthorpe, Northampton (M Holmes and P Chapman), *Northamptonshire Archaeology* **33**, 35–40

Jackson, D A, and Dix, B, 1988 Late Iron Age and Roman settlement at Weekley, Northants, *Northamptonshire Archaeol* **21**, 41–93

Jessop, L, 1986 *Dung beetles and chafers. Coleoptera: Scarabaeoidea*, Handbooks for the identification of British insects **5(11)**, London

Johnson, E, 2016 A skeletal comparison of domestic dog (*Canis familiaris*), red fox (*Vulpes vulpes*), badger (*Meles meles*) and domestic cat (*Felis catus*), unpubl. report, Univ. Exeter

Johnstone, C J, 2004 A biometric study of equids in the Roman world, unpubl, PhD Thesis, Univ. York

Jones, A K G, 1982 Human parasite remains: prospects for a quantitative approach, in *Environmental archaeology in the urban context* (eds A R Hall and H K Kenward), CBA Res Rep **43**, London, 66–70

Jones, G G, 2006 Tooth eruption and wear observed in live sheep from Butser Hill, the Cotswold Farm Park and five farms in the Pentland Hills, UK, in *Recent advances in ageing and sexing animal bones* (ed D Ruscillo), Oxford, 155–78

Jones, G, and Sadler, P, 2012 Age at death in cattle: methods, older cattle and known-age reference material, *Env Archaeol* **17(1)**, 11–28

Kenward, H, 1997 Synanthropic decomposer insects and the size, remoteness and longevity of archaeological occupation sites: applying concepts from biogeography to past 'islands' of human occupation, in *Studies in Quaternary entomology: an inordinate fondness for insects*, Quaternary Proceedings **5**, 135–52

Kenward, H K, and Hall, A R, 1995 *Biological evidence from 16–22 Coppergate*, Archaeology of York **14(7)**, York

Kenward, H K, Hall, A R, and Jones, A K G, 1980 A tested set of techniques for the extraction of plant and animal macrofossils from waterlogged archaeological deposits, *Sci and Archaeol* **22**, 3–15

Kenward, H K, Hall, A R, and Jones, A K G, 1986 *Environmental evidence from a Roman well and Anglian pits in the legionary fortress*, Archaeology of York **14(5)**, London

King, A C, 2005 Animal remains from temples in Roman Britain, *Britannia* **36**, 329–69

King, A, and Soffe, G, 2008 Hayling Island: a Gallo-Roman temple in Britain, in *Ritual landscapes of Roman south-east Britain* (ed. D Rudling), Oxford, 139–51

Koztowski, T, Witas, H W, 2012 Metabolic and endocrine diseases, in Grauer 2012, 401–19

Lambrick, G H, and Robinson, M A, 1979 *Iron Age and Roman riverside settlements at Farmoor, Oxfordshire*, CBA Res Rep **32**, Oxford Archaeological Unit Report **2**, Oxford

Lambert, P, 2021 Building a Roman villa: a Romano-Celtic temple-mausoleum and evidence of industry at Priors Hall, Corby, *Curr Archaeol* **370**, 18–25

Lawrence, S, 2006 *The Iron Age settlement and Roman villa at Thurnham, Kent*, Channel Tunnel Rail Link Oxford Wessex Archaeology Joint Venture Integrated Site Report Series, https://doi.org/10.5284/1008824

Lawrence, S, and Smith, A, 2009 *Between villa and town: excavations of a Roman roadside settlement and shrine at Higham Ferrers, Northamptonshire*, Oxford Archaeology Monograph **7**, Oxford

Legge, A J, 2013 'Practice with science': molar tooth eruption ages in domestic, feral and wild pigs (*Sus scrofa*), *Int J Osteoarchaeol*, https://onlinelibrary.wiley.com/pb-assets/assets/10991212/Anthony_Legge_Final_Paper.pdf

Letts, J, 1995 Charred plant remains, in *Lithics and landscape: archaeological discoveries on the Thames water pipeline at Gatehampton Farm, Goring, Oxfordshire, 1985–92* (T G Allen), Thames Valley Landscapes **7**, Oxford

Lewis, M J T, 1965 *Temples in Roman Britain*, Cambridge

Lieverse, A R, 1999 Diet and the aetiology of dental calculus, *Int J Osteoarchaeol* **9**, 219–32

Lodwick, L, 2015 Identifying ritual deposition of plant remains: a case study of stone pine cones in Roman Britain, in *TRAC 2014: proceedings of the twenty-fourth annual Theoretical Roman Archaeology Conference* (eds T Brindle, M Allen, E Durham and A Smith), Oxford, 54–69

Lodwick, L, 2017a Arable farming, plant foods and resources, in Allen *et al.* 2017, 11–84

Lodwick, L, 2017b Evergreen plants in Roman Britain and beyond: movement, meaning and materiality, *Britannia* **48**, 135–73

Lodwick, L, 2018 Ornamental gardens and plants, in Smith *et al.* 2018, 55–7

Lodwick, L, and Challinor, D, 2017 *Pinus pinea* (stone pine) and other charred plant remains from cremation burials 3343 and 4593, in *Horcott Quarry, Fairford, and Arkell's Land, Kempsford: Prehistoric, Roman and Anglo-Saxon settlement and burial in the Upper Thames Valley in Gloucestershire* (C Hayden, R Early, E Biddulph, P Booth, A Dodd, A Smith, G Laws and K Welsh), Thames Valley Landscapes **40**, Oxford, 357–8

Long, A J, Scaife, R G, and Edwards, R J, 1999 Pine pollen in intertidal sediments from Poole Harbour, UK: implications for late Holocene sediment accretion rates and sea-level rise, *Quaternary Int* **55**, 3–16

Lovejoy, C, Meindl, R, Pryxbeck, T, and Mensforth, R P, 1985 Chronological metamorphosis of the auricular surface of the ilium: a new method for the determination of age at death, *American J Physical Anthropol* **68**, 15–28

Luff, M L, 1998 *Provisional atlas of the ground beetles (Coleoptera, Carabidae) of Britain*, Huntingdon

Luff, M L, 2007 *The Carabidae (ground beetles) of Britain and Ireland*, Handbooks for the identification of British insects **4(2)**, 2nd edn, London

MacDonald, J, 2011 Microstructure, crystallography and stable isotope composition of *Crassostrea gigas*, unpubl. PhD thesis, Univ. Glasgow

Macdonald, P, 2000 The ironwork (excluding brooches), in *Cadbury Castle, Somerset: the later prehistoric and early historic archaeology* (J C Barrett, P W M Freeman and A Woodward), English Heritage Archaeol Rep **20**, London, 122–32

Mackreth, D F, 1996 *Orton Hall Farm: a Roman and early Anglo-Saxon farmstead*, E Anglian Archaeol **76**, Manchester

McKinley, J I, 1994 Bone fragment size in British cremation burials and its implications for pyre technology and ritual, *J Archaeol Sci* **21**, 339–42

McKinley, J I 2000 Cremation burials, in *The eastern cemetery of Roman London. Excavations 1983–1990* (B Barber and D Bowsher), MoLAS Monograph **4**, London, 264–77

McKinley, J I, 2004a Compiling a skeletal inventory: disarticulated and co-mingled remains, in Brickley and McKinley 2004, 14–17

McKinley, J I 2004b Compiling a skeletal inventory: cremated human bone, in Brickley and McKinley 2004, 9–13

McKinley, J I 2013 Cremation: excavation and analysis, in *The Oxford handbook of the archaeology of death and burial* (eds S Tarlow and L Nilsson Stutz), Oxford, 147–72

McKinley, J I, and Roberts, C A 1993, *Excavation and post-excavation treatment of cremated and inhumed human remains*, IFA Technical Paper **13**, Birmingham

McSloy, E R, 2015a, Prehistoric pottery, in Masefield *et al.* 2015, 198–207

McSloy, E R, 2015b, The late prehistoric pottery, in Masefield *et al.* 2015, 76–83

Maltby, M, 2007 Chop and change: specialist cattle carcass processing in Roman Britain, in *TRAC 2006: Proceedings of the 16th Annual Theoretical Roman Archaeology Conference* (eds B Croxford, N Ray, R Roth and N White), Oxford, 59–76

Maltby, M, 2010 *Feeding a Roman town: environmental evidence from excavations in Winchester, 1972–1985*, Winchester

Manning, W H, 1964 A Roman hoard of ironwork from Sandy, Bedfordshire, *Bedfordshire Archaeol J* **2**, 50–7

Manning, W H M, 1985 *Catalogue of Romano-British iron tools, fittings and weapons in the British Museum*, London

Margary, I D, 1967 *Roman roads in Britain*, London

Marney, P T, 1989 *Roman and Belgic pottery from excavations in Milton Keynes, 1972–1982*, Buckinghamshire Archaeological Society Monograph **2**, Aylesbury

Martin, P, and Hall, D, 1980 Brixworth, Northamptonshire: new evidence for early prehistoric settlement and agriculture, *Bedfordshire Archaeol J* **14**, 5–14

Masefield, R, Chapman, A, Ellis, P, Hart, J, King, R, and Mudd, A, 2015 *Origins, development and abandonment of an Iron Age village (DIRFT vol. 2): further Archaeological investigations for the Daventry International Rail Freight Terminal, Crick and Kilsby, Northamptonshire 1993–2013*, Oxford

Mason, P, 2011 Archaeological evaluation at Upton Park, Weedon Road, Northampton, January to March 2011, upubl. Report, Northamptonshire Archaeology, Northampton

Mattingley, D, 2006 *An imperial possession: Britain in the Roman Empire, 54 BC–AD 409*, London

May, E, 1985 Wideristhöhe und Langknochenmaße bei Pferd: ein immer noch aktuelles Problem, *Zeitschrift für Säugertierkunde* **50**, 368–82

Mays, S, 2021 *The archaeology of human bones*, London

Meadows, I, 1995 Wollaston, *SMA* **25**, 41–5

Meadows, I, 2009a The late Bronze Age and the Iron Age, in Meadows *et al.* 2009, 68–88

Meadows, I, 2009b The Roman and early Saxon periods, in Meadows *et al.* 2009, 89–124

Meadows, I, Boismier, W A, and Chapman, A, 2009 *Synthetic survey of the environmental archaeological and hydrological record for the River Nene from its source to Peterborough, part 1: the archaeological and hydrological record*, Northampton

Meen, J, 2019 Waterlogged plant remains from pit 3067, in *Berryfields: Iron Age settlement and a Roman bridge, field system and settlement along Akeman Street near Fleet Marston, Buckinghamshire* (E Biddulph, K Brady, A Simmonds and S Foreman), Oxford Archaeology Monograph **30**, Oxford, 140–8

Mellor, V, 2007 Prehistoric multiple linear ditches and pit alignments on the route of the Oakham Bypass, Rutland, *Trans Leicestershire Archaeol Hist Soc* **81**, 1–33

Millett, M, Revell, L, and Moore, A, 2016 *The Oxford handbook of Roman Britain*, Oxford

Mitchell, P D, and Brickley, M, (eds) 2017 *Updated guidelines to the standards for recording human remains*, Reading

MOLA, 2012 Archaeological excavation at Sites F and G, Weedon Road, Upton, Northamptonshire May–July 2012, unpubl. report, Museum of London Archaeology, London, https://doi.org/10.5284/1078731, accessed 24 September 2021

MOLA, 2015a Archaeological desk-based heritage assessment for land at M1dway J16, Northamptonshire, unpubl. report, Museum of London Archaeology, London

MOLA, 2015b Archaeological geophysical survey of the proposed development at M1dway J16, Northamptonshire, unpubl. report, Museum of London Archaeology, London

MOLA, 2015c Archaeological evaluation at M1dway J16, Northamptonshire, unpubl. report, Museum of London Archaeology, London

MOLA, 2016 Written scheme of investigation for a programme of earthwork survey and archaeological excavation on land at M1dway J16 Northamptonshire, unpubl. report, Museum of London Archaeology, London

MOLA, 2017 Archaeological excavation on land at Pineham, Zone H, Northamptonshire, September 2015 to May 2016: assessment report and updated project design, unpubl. report, Museum of London Archaeology, London https://doi.org/10.5284/1053645, accessed 24 September 2021

Monteil, G, 2020 Samian, in *Farmsteads and funerary sites: the M1 Junction 12 Improvements and the A5–M1 Link Road. Central Bedfordshire archaeological investigations prior to construction, 2011 and 2015–16* (J Brown), Oxford, 416–17

Mook, W G, 1986 Business meeting: recommendations/resolutions adopted by the Twelfth International Radiocarbon Conference, *Radiocarbon* **28**, 799

Morris, E, 1994 Pottery, in C M Hearne and M J Heaton, Excavations at a late Bronze Age settlement in the Upper Thames Valley at Shorncote Quarry near Cirencester, 1992, *Transactions of the Bristol and Gloucestershire Archaeological Society* **117**, 34–43

Morris, J, 2011 *Investigating animal burials: ritual, mundane and beyond*, BAR Brit. Ser. **535**, Oxford

Morris, M G, 1990 *Orthocerous weevils, Coleoptera: Curculionoidea (Nemonychidae, Anthribidae, Urodontidae, Attelabidae and Apionidae)*, Handbooks for the identification of British insects **5(16)**, London

Morris, M G, 1997 *Broad-nosed weevils, Coleoptera: Curculionidae (Entiminae)*, Handbooks for the identification of British insects **5(17a)**, London

Morris, M G, 2002 *True weevils (Part 1), Coleoptera:*

Curculionoidea (Subfamilies Raymondionyminae to Smicronychinae), Handbooks for the identification of British insects **5(17b)**, London

Morris, M G, 2008 *True weevils (Part 2), Coleoptera: Curculionidae, Ceutorhynchinae*, Handbooks for the identification of British insects **5(17c)**, London

Morris, P, 1979 *Agricultural buildings in Roman Britain*, BAR Brit. Ser. **70**, Oxford

Neal, D S, 1977 Northchurch, Boxmoor and Hemel Hempstead Station: the excavation of three Roman buildings in the Bulbourne Valley, *Hertfordshire Archaeol* **4**, 1–136

Neal, D, 1989 The Stanwick villa, Northants: an interim report on the excavations of 1984–88, *Britannia* **20**, 149–68

Neal, D S, and Cosh, S R, 2002 *Roman mosaics of Britain, vol. I: northern Britain incorporating the Midlands and East Anglia*, London

Nelson, G C, 2016 A host of other dental disorders, in *A companion to dental anthropology* (eds J D Irish and G R Scott), Chichester, 471–83

Neville, R C, 1856 Description of a remarkable deposit of Roman antiquities of iron, discovered at Great Chesterford, Essex, in 1854, *Archaeol J* **13**, 1–13

Nicholson, K, 2006 A late Roman cemetery at Watersmeet, Mill Common, Huntingdon, *Proc Cambridge Antiq Soc* **95**, 57–90

Nicholson, R A, 2018 Marine shell, in *Footprints from the past. The south-eastern extramural settlement of Roman Alchester and rural occupation in its hinterland: the archaeology of east-west rail Phase 1* (A Simmonds and S Lawrence), Oxford Archaeology Monograph **28**, Oxford, 229–30

Northamptonshire Archaeology, 2003 Excavation of Roman features at Plot 1, Middlemore Farm, Daventry, Northamptonshire, https://doi.org/10.5284/1002262, accessed 23 March 2021

Northamptonshire Archaeology, 2007 Archaeological excavation at Pineham North, Upton, Northampton, December 2006, settlement 2: assessment report, Northamptonshire Archaeology Report **06/177**, Northamptonshire Archaeology, Northampton, https://doi.org/10.5284/1002245

Northamptonshire Archaeology, 2008a A Romano-British 'ladder' enclosure at Milton Ham, Northampton: assessment report and updated project design, Northamptonshire Archaeology, Northampton, https://doi.org/10.5284/1005371, accessed 23 March 2021

Northamptonshire Archaeology, 2008b Geophysical Surveys at Barn Close And Harpit, Harpole, Northamptonshire, January 2006–December 2007, Northamptonshire Archaeology, Northampton, https://doi.org/10.5284/1004829, accessed 7 April 2021

Northamptonshire Archaeology, 2013 Archaeological trial trench evaluation of land at Ace Lane, Bugbrooke, Northamptonshire, Northamptonshire Archaeology, Northampton, https://doi.org/10.5284/1042492, accessed 29 September 2021

Northamptonshire Exploration Committee, 1901–2 Roman villa at Harpole, *J Northamptonshire Nat Hist Soc and Field Club* **11**, 7–8

OA, 2012 An Iron Age settlement and Romano-British villa complex at Itter Crescent, Peterborough: post-excavation assessment, unpubl. report, Oxford Archaeology, Oxford https://library.oxfordarchaeology.com/3406

OA, 2018 M1dway J16, Northamptonshire: post-excavation assessment report and updated project design, unpubl. report, Oxford Archaeology, Oxford

OA, 2020 Buckton Fields Phase 2, Northampton: post-excavation assessment report and updated project design, unpubl. report, Oxford Archaeology, Oxford

OA, 2021a Grove Airfield, Grove, Oxfordshire: archaeological excavation report, unpubl. report, Oxford Archaeology, Oxford, https://library.oxfordarchaeology.com/5916

OA, 2021b Sutton Courtenay Lane, Sutton Courtenay, Oxfordshire: archaeological excavation report, unpubl. report, Oxford Archaeology, Oxford

OA, 2021c A Roman temple-mausoleum, tile and pottery manufactories and associated industries at Zone 3, Area A, Priors Hall, Corby: post-excavation assessment and updated project design, unpubl. report, Oxford Archaeology, Oxford https://library.oxfordarchaeology.com/search/corby/6144

OAU, 1992 Redlands Farm, Stanwick, Northamptonshire. Recording action: major excavations 1989–1990, unpubl. report, Oxford Archaeology, Oxford, https://doi.org/10.5284/1023758

O'Connor, T P, 1988 *Bones from the General Accident Site, Tanner Row*, The Archaeology of York **15**: the animal bones, London

Ohnuma, K, and Bergman, C A, 1982 Experimental studies in the determination of flake mode, *Bull Inst Archaeol Univ London* **19**, 161–71

Ortner, D J, 2003 *Identification of pathological conditions in human skeletal remains*, London and San Diego

Orton, C, and Hughes, M, 2013 *Pottery in Archaeology*, 2nd edn, Cambridge

Parry, S, 2006 *Raunds Area Survey: an archaeological study of the landscape of Raunds, Northamptonshire 1985–92*, Oxford

Peacock, D, 2013 *The stone of life: the archaeology of querns, mills and flour production in Europe up to c. 50 AD*, Southampton Monographs in Archaeol **1**, Southampton

Pearce, J, 1999 The dispersed dead: preliminary observations on burial and settlement space in rural Roman Britain, in *TRAC 98: proceedings of the eighth annual Theoretical Roman Archaeology*

Conference (eds P Baker, C Forcey, S Jundi and R Witcher), Oxford, 151–62

Pearce, J, 2016, Status and burial, in Millett *et al.* 2016, 341–62

PCRG 2010 *The study of prehistoric pottery: general policies and guidelines for analysis and publication* (3rd ed.), Prehistoric Ceramics Research Group: Occasional Papers **1** and **2**

PCRG, SGRP and MPRG 2016 *A standard for pottery studies in archaeology*, Prehistoric Ceramics Research Group, Study Group for Roman Pottery and Medieval Pottery Research Group booklet

Pelling, R, 2008 Charred and waterlogged plant remains, in *The Roman roadside settlement at Westhawk Farm, Ashford, Kent. Excavations 1998–9* (P Booth, A-M Bingham and S Lawrence), Oxford Archaeology Monograph **2**, Oxford

Perrin, J R, 1999 Roman pottery from excavations at and near to the Roman small town of Durobrivae, Water Newton, Cambridgeshire, 1956–58, *J Roman Pottery Stud* **8**, 1–141

Perrin, J R, 2006 Romano-British pottery, in *Raunds Area Survey: an archaeological study of the landscape of Raunds, Northamptonshire 1985–94* (S J Parry), Oxford, 84–91

Perrin, R, 2018 Iron Age and Roman pottery, in *Late Iron Age and Roman settlement at Bozeat Quarry, Northamptonshire. Excavations 1995–2016* (R Atkins), Oxford, 71–106

Phillips, G, 2000 *An archaeological resource assessment of the Mesolithic in Northamptonshire*, East Midlands Archaeological Research Framework, https://researchframeworks.org/emherf/wp-content/uploads/sites/6/2018/11/2.Northants Meso.pdf

Philp, B, Parfitt, K, Willson, J, and Williams, W, 1999, *The Roman villa at Keston, Kent*, Dover

PKRB, nd *The pottery kilns of Roman Britain by Vivien Swan*, https://romankilns.net/, accessed 30 March 2021

Pliny, 1968 *Natural History*, trans. H Rackham, Cambridge, Massachusetts

Poole, C, 2009a Ceramic building material, in *Trade and prosperity, war and poverty: an archaeological and historical investigation into Southampton's French Quarter* (R Brown and A Hardy), Oxford Archaeology Monograph **15**, Oxford

Poole, C, 2009b Ceramic building material, in Lawrence and Smith 2009, 263–72

Poole, C, 2009c Fired clay from Owslebury, Hampshire, unpubl. report

Poole, C, 2011 Ceramic building material and fired clay, in Biddulph *et al.* 2011, 313–50

Poole, C, 2020 Ceramic building material and fired clay, in An early Roman lime kiln and later Roman agricultural processing at Maylands Gateway, Hemel Hempstead: archaeological excavation report, unpubl. report, Oxford Archaeology, Oxford, https://library.oxford archaeology.com/5807/

Poole, C, and Shaffrey, R, 2011 Roman ceramic building material, in *Winchester, a city in the making: archaeological excavations between 2002 and 2007 on the sites of Northgate House, Staple Gardens and the former Winchester Library, Jewry Street* (B Ford and S Teague), Oxford Archaeology Monograph **12**, Oxford, 290–3

Prance, G, and Nesbitt, M (eds), 2005 *The cultural history of plants*, New York

Pre-Construct Geophysics, 2003 Fluxgate gradiometer survey: land at Harpole, Northamptonshire, https://claspweb.org.uk/LOCAL/GEOPHYS/har1_geophys_web.pdf, accessed 23 September 2021

Pringle, S, 1997 Rounds Iron Age and Romano-British Project: report on the tile and brick from Redlands Farm Roman villa, unpubl. report

Pringle, S, 2000 Rounds Iron Age and Romano-British Project: report on the tile and brick from Stanwick villa, unpubl. report

Pryor, F, 1996 Sheep, stockyard and field systems: Bronze Age livestock populations in the fenlands of eastern England, *Antiquity* **70**, 313–24

Quinnell, H, 1991 The villa and temple at Cosgrove, Northamptonshire, *Northamptonshire Archaeol* **32**, 4–66

Rainsford, C, King, A C, Jones, S, Hooker, R, and Burleigh, G, 2021 Cremated animal bone from two ritual/ceremonial sites in Britannia, in *Roman animals in ritual and funerary contexts: proceedings of the 2nd meeting of the Zooarchaeology of the Roman Period Working Group, Basel, 1st–4th February 2018* (eds S Deschler-Erb, U Albarella, S Valenzuela-Lamas and G Rasbach), Wiesbaden, 185–99

Raw, F, 1951 The ecology of the garden chafer *Phyllopertha horticola* (L.) with preliminary observations on control measures, *Bulletin of Entomological Research* **42**, 605–46

RCHME, 1982 *An inventory of the historical monuments in the county of Northampton. Volume 4: archaeological sites in south-west Northampton shire*, London

RCHME, 1985 *An inventory of the historical monuments in the county of Northampton. Volume 5: archaeology and churches in Northampton*, London

Reece, R, 1991 *Roman coins from 140 sites in Britain*, Cotswold Studies **4**, Cirencester

Rees, H, Crummy, N, Ottaway, P J, and Dunn, G, 2008 *Artefacts and society in Roman and medieval Winchester: small finds from the suburbs and defences, 1971–1986*, Winchester

Rees, S, 2011 Agriculture, in *Artefacts in Roman Britain: their purpose and use* (ed. L Allason-Jones), Cambridge

Reimer, P J, Austin, W E N, Bard, E, Bayliss, A, Blackwell, P G, Bronk Ramsey, C, Butzin, M, Cheng, H, Edwards, R L, Friedrich, M, Grootes, P M, Guilderson, T P, Hajdas, I, Heaton, T J, Hogg, A G, Hughen, K A, Kromer, B, Manning,

S W, Muscheler, R, Palmer, J G, Pearson, C, van
der Plicht, J, Reimer, R W, Richards, D A, Scott,
E M, Southon, J R, Turney, C S M, Wacker, L,
Adolphi, F, Büntgen, U, Capano, M, Fahrni, S M,
Fogtmann-Schulz, A, Friedrich, R, Köhler, P,
Kudsk, S, Miyake, F, Olsen, J, Reinig, F,
Sakamoto, M, Sookdeo, A, and Talamo, S, 2020
The IntCal20 Northern Hemisphere Radiocarbon
Age Calibration Curve (0–55 cal kBP),
Radiocarbon **62**, 725–57

Reynolds, P J, and Langley, J K, 1979 Romano-
British corn-drying oven: an experiment,
Archaeol J **136**, 27–42

Richmond, I, and Gillam, J, 1951 The temple of
Mithras at Carrowburgh, *Archaeol Aeliana* **29**, 1–
92

Roberts, C, and Connell, B, 2004 Guidance on
recording paleopathology, in Brickley and
McKinley 2004, 34–9

Roberts, C A, Cox, M, 2003 *Health and disease in
Britain: from prehistory to the present day*, Stroud

Roberts, C, and Manchester, K, 2010 *The archaeology
of disease*, 3rd edn, Ithaca, New York

Robinson, M, 2007 The environmental archaeology
of the Cotswold Water Park, in *Iron Age and
Roman settlement in the Upper Thames Valley:
excavations at Claydon Pike and other sites within
the Cotswold Water Park* (eds D Miles, S Palmer,
A Smith and G P Jones), Thames Valley
Landscapes **26**, Oxford, 355–64

Rogers, J, Waldron, T, 1995 *A field guide to joint
disease in archaeology*, Chichester

Rohnbogner, A, 2018 The rural population, in
Smith *et al.* 2018, 281–345

Rook, T, 1986 The Roman villa at Dicket Mead,
Lockleys, Welwyn, *Hertfordshire Archaeol* **9**, 79–
175

Royal Horticultural Society, 2021 *Walnuts*, https://
www.rhs.org.uk/advice/profile?PID=546,
accessed 20 March 2021

Rylatt, J, and Bevan, B, 2007 Realigning the world:
pit alignments and their landscape context, in
The later Iron Age in Britain and beyond (eds C
Haselgrove and T Moore), Oxford, 219–34

Saville, A, 1980 On the measurement of struck
flakes and flake tools, *Lithics* **1**, 16–20

Saville, A, 1981 Honey Hill, Elkington: a
Northamptonshire Mesolithic site, *Northamptonshire Archaeol* **16**, 1–13

Saville, A, 1990 *Hazleton North: the excavation of a
Neolithic long cairn of the Cotswolds-Severn group*,
London

Scaife, R, 2001 Pollen analysis of valley fen peats of
Romano-British date, in Busby *et al.* 2001, 119–24

Scheuer, L, and Black, S, 2000 *Developmental
juvenile osteology*, Oxford

Schweingruber, F, 1990 *Microscopic wood anatomy*,
3rd edn, Birmensdorf

Scott, E, 1993 *A gazetteer of Roman villas in Britain*,
Leicester Archaeology Monograph No. **1**,
Leicester

Seager Smith, R, Brown, K M, and Mills, J M, 2011
The pottery from Springhead, in Biddulph *et al.*
2011, 1–134

Seddon, G, and Murray, J, 2000 Hipwells, Upper
Heyford, Northamptonshire: an archaeological
evaluation, unpubl. report, Hertfordshire
Archaeological Trust, Hertford

Serjeantson, D, 1996 The animal bones, in *Refuse
and disposal at Area 16 East Runnymede: Runnymede Bridge Research Excavations, volume 2* (eds S
Needham and A Spence), London, 194–222

Shaffrey, R, 2009 Other worked stone, in Lawrence
and Smith 2009, 254–7

Shaffrey, R, 2015 Intensive milling practices in the
Romano-British landscape of southern England:
using newly established criteria for distinguishing millstones from rotary querns,
Britannia **46**, 55–92

Shennan, S, 1997 *Quantifying archaeology*, 2nd edn,
Edinburgh

Shepherd, J D, 1998 *The temple of Mithras, London:
excavations by W F Grimes and A Williams at the
Walbrook*, London

Sidell, J, Wilkinson, K, Scaife, R, and Cameron, N,
2000 *The Holocene evolution of the London Thames:
archaeological excavations (1991–1998) for the
London Underground Limited Jubilee Line Extension
project*, MoLAS Monograph **5**, London, 1–144

Simmonds, M, Hosfield, R, Branch, N, and Black,
S, 2019 From findspot to site: a spatial examina-
tion of the Mesolithic resource in Surrey, *Surrey
Archaeol Collect* **102**, 1–22

Skidmore, P, 1991 *Insects of the British cow-dung
community*, Field Studies Council Occas Pub **21**,
Shrewsbury

Smith A, 2008 The fate of pagan temples in south-
east Britain during the late and post-Roman
period, in *Ritual landscapes of south-east Britain*
(ed. D Rudling), Norfolk and Oxford, 171–90

Smith, A, 2016a The central belt, in Smith *et al.*
2016, 141–207

Smith, A, 2016b Buildings in the countryside, in
Smith *et al.* 2016, 44–74

Smith, A, 2016c Ritual deposition, in Millett *et al.*,
641–59

Smith, A, 2018a Religion and the rural population,
in Smith *et al.* 2018, 120–204

Smith, A, 2018b Death in the countryside: rural
burial practices, in Smith *et al.* 2018, 205–80

Smith, A, Allen, M, Brindle, T, and Fulford, M,
2016 *The rural settlement of Roman Britain*,
Britannia Monograph **29**, London

Smith, A, Allen, M, Brindle, T, Fulford, M,
Lodwick, L, and Rohnbogner, A, 2018 *Life and
death in the countryside of Roman Britain*, Britannia
Monograph **31**, London

Smith, A, and Fulford, M, 2016 Conclusions: the
rural settlement of Roman Britain, in Smith *et al.*
2016, 385–420

Smith, A, and Fulford, M, 2019 The defended vici
of Roman Britain: recent research and new
agendas, *Britannia* **50**, 109–47

Smith, D, Hill, G, Kenward, H, and Allison, E, 2020 Development of synanthropic beetle faunas over the last 9000 years in the British Isles, *J Archaeol Sci* **115**, https://doi.org/10.1016/j.jas.2020.105075

Smith, D, Whitehouse, N, Bunting, M J, and Chapman, H, 2010 Can we characterize 'openness' in the Holocene palaeoenvironmental record? Modern analogue studies of insect faunas and pollen spectra from Dunham Massey deer park and Epping Forest, England, *The Holocene* **20(2)**, 215–29

Smith, D, Nayyar, K, Schreve, D, Thomas, R, and Whitehouse, N, 2014 Can dung beetles from the palaeoecological and archaeological record indicate herd concentration and the identity of herbivores? *Quaternary International* **341**, 1–12

Smith, W, 2002 *A review of archaeological wood analyses in southern England*, English Heritage Centre for Archaeology Report **75/2002**, Portsmouth

Southwood, T R E, and Leston, D, 1959 *Land and water bugs of the British Isles*, London

Spain, R J, 1996 The millstones, in Mackreth 1996, 105–13

Spain, R, and Riddler, I, 2010 The millstones, in *The Roman watermills and settlement at Ickham, Kent* (P Bennett, I Riddler and C Sparey-Green), The Archaeology of Canterbury new Series **V**, Canterbury, 277–85

Speed, G, 2015 A pit alignment, Iron Age settlement and Roman cultivation trenches west of South Meadow Road, Upton, Northampton, *Northamptonshire Archaeol* **38**, 53–71

Stace, C, 2010 *New flora of the British Isles*, 3rd edn, Cambridge

Starmer, G H, 1970 A check list of Northamptonshire wind and watermills, *Bull Industrial Archaeol in CBA Group 9* **12**, 11–38

Starmer, G H (ed.), 1971 Reports from the individual counties of CBA 9: Northamptonshire, *Bull Industrial Archaeol in CBA Group 9* **15**, 9–14

Starmer, G, 2002 Northamptonshire watermills survey, 2001–2002

Stevens, C, 2011a Charred remains from Springhead, in Barnett *et al.*, 95–105

Stevens, C, 2011b Charred plant remains, in Prehistoric, Romano-British and Saxon activity at Whitelands Farm, Bicester, Oxfordshire (J Martin), *Oxoniensia* **76**, 226–33

Stevens, C, Grimm, J, and Worley, F, 2011 Agriculture, food and drink, in Andrews *et al.* 2011, 236–43

Stone Roofing Association, 2014 *Historic Sources of Collyweston Slate*, http://www.stoneroof.org.uk/historic/Historic_Roofs/Collyweston_Slate.html, accessed 3 October 2020

Stuart-Macadam, P, 1991 Anaemia in Roman Britain: Poundbury Camp, in *Health in past societies: biocultural interpretations of human skeletal remains in archaeological contexts* (eds H Bush and M Zvelebil), Oxford, 101–13

Swift, E, 2000 *Regionality in dress accessories in the late Roman west*, Monographies Instrumentum **11**, Montagnac

Swift, E, 2012 Object biography, re-use and recycling in the late to post-Roman transition period and beyond: rings made from Romano-British bracelets, *Britannia* **43**, 167–215

Sykes, N J, 2010 Fallow deer, in *Extinctions and invasions: the social history of British fauna* (T P O'Connor and N J Sykes), Oxford, 51–8

Tacitus, 2010 *The Agricola and the Germania*, trans. H Mattingly, London

Taylor, S, and Dix, B, 1985 Iron Age and Roman settlement at Ashley, Northants, *Northamptonshire Archaeol* **20**, 87–112

Thomas, A, and Enright, D, 2003 Excavation of an Iron Age settlement at Wilby Way, Great Doddington, *Northamptonshire Archaeol* **31**, 15–69

Thomas, J, 1999 *Understanding the Neolithic*, London

Timby, J, 2000 The ceramic tile, in *Late Iron Age and Roman Silchester: excavations on the site of the forum-basilica* (M Fulford and J Timby), Britannia Monograph **15**, London, 116–20

Timby, J, 2007 The Iron Age and Roman pottery, in *Iron Age and Roman settlement on the Northamptonshire Uplands. Archaeological work on the A43 Towcester to M40 Road Improvement Scheme in Northamptonshire and Oxfordshire* (A Mudd), Northamptonshire Archaeology Monograph **1**, Northampton, 88–118

Timby, J, 2010 The Roman pottery, in Walker and Maull 2010, 38–42

Tomber, R, and Dore, J, 1998 *The National Roman Fabric Reference Collection: a handbook*, MoLAS Monograph **2**, London

Tonge, C H, and McCance, R A, 1973 Normal development of the jaws and teeth in pigs, and the delay and malocclusion produced by calorie deficiencies, *J Anatomy* **115**, 1–22

Turland, R E, 1977 Towcester, Wood Burcote, *Northamptonshire Archaeol* **12**, 218–23

ULAS, 2014 *Roman 'smoke-house' found at Pineham, Northamptonshire*, University of Leicester Archaeological Services, https://ulasnews.com/2014/02/03/roman-smoke-house-found-at-pineham-northamptonshire, accessed 17 September 2021

ULAS, 2015 Archaeologists return to Pineham, Northamptonshire, University of Leicester Archaeological Services, https://ulasnews.com/2015/04/20/archaeologists-return-to-pineham-northamptonshire/, accessed 28 September 2021

van der Veen, M, 1989 Charred grain assemblages from Roman-period corn driers in Britain, *Archaeol J* **146**, 302–19

van der Veen, M, 1999 The economic value of chaff and straw in arid and temperate zones, *Vegetation Hist and Archaeobotany* **8**, 211–24

van der Veen, M, Livarda, A, and Hill, A, 2008

New plant foods in Roman Britain: dispersal and social access, *Env Archaeol* **13(1)**, 11–36

van Geel, B, 1978 A palaeoecological study of Holocene peat bog sections in Germany and the Netherlands based on the analysis of pollen, spores and macro-and microscopic remains of fungi, algae, cormophytes and animals, *Review of Palaeobotany and Palynology* **25** 1–120

Vitt, V O, 1952 Loshadi Pezyryksich kuganov, *Sovetskaja Archeologija* **16**, 163–205

von den Driesch, A, 1976 *A guide to the measurement of animal bones from archaeological sites*, Peabody Museum Bulletins **1**, Harvard

von den Driesch, A, and Boessneck, J, 1974 Kritische Anmerkungen zur Widerristhöhenberechnung aus Längenmassen vor- und frühgeschichtlicher Tierknochen, *Säugetierkundliche Mitteilungen* **22**, 325–48

Waddington, C, 2000 Recent research on the Mesolithic of the Millfield Basin, Northumberland, in *Mesolithic lifeways: current research from Britain and Ireland* (ed. R Young), Leicester Archaeological Monograph **7**, Leicester

Wakeham, G, and Bradley, P, 2013 A Romano-British malt house and other remains at Weedon Hill, Aylesbury, *Rec Buckinghamshire* **53**, 1–45

Waldron, T, 2009 *Palaeopathology*, Cambridge

Walker, C, 2014 Historic environment desk-based assessment Midway Park, Junction 16, M1, Northamptonshire, unpubl. report, Iain Soden Heritage Services, Long Buckby

Walker, C, and Maull, A, 2010 Excavation of Iron Age and Roman settlement at Upton, Northampton, *Northamptonshire Archaeol* **36**, 9–52

Walker, P L, Bathurst, R, Richman, R, Gjerdrum, T, and Andrushko, V A, 2009 The causes of porotic hyperostosis and cribra orbitalia: a reappraisal of the iron-deficiency-anemia hypothesis, *American J Physical Anthopol* **139**, 109–25

Warry, P, 2006 *Tegulae manufacture, typology and use in Roman Britain*, BAR Brit. Ser. **417**, Oxford

Watts, S, 2014 The symbolism of querns and millstones, in *Seen through a millstone* (ed. L Selsing), AmS-Skrifter **24**, 51–64

Webb, H, 2015 Specialist report on the human remains, in Covenham to Boston Pipeline, Lincolnshire

Webb, H, Loe, L, Clough, S, and Gibson, M, 2018 Human remains, in Booth and Simmonds 2018, 503–35

Webster, P, 1996 *Roman samian pottery in Britain*, London

Webley, L, 2007 Prehistoric, Roman and Saxon activity on the Fen hinterland at Parnwell Way, Peterborough, *Proc Cambridge Antiq Soc* **96**, 79–114

Wedlake, W J, 1982 *The excavation of the shrine of Apollo at Nettleton, Wiltshire, 1956–1971*, Soc Antiq Res Rep **40**, London

Weekes, J, 2016 Cemeteries and funeral practices, in Millett *et al.* 2016, 425–47

Wessex Archaeology, 2010 Litlington, Cambridgeshire: archaeological evaluation and assessment of results, unpubl. report, Wessex Archaeology, Salisbury, https://doi.org/10.5284/1010258, accessed 13 July 2021

Wessex Archaeology and Jacobi, R M, 2014 *Palaeolithic and Mesolithic lithic artefact (PaMELA) database*, https://doi.org/10.5284/1028201

Weston, D, 2012 Nonspecific infection in paleopathology: interpreting periosteal reactions, in Grauer 2012, 492–512

Wheeler, R E M, and Wheeler, T V, 1936 *Verulamium: a Belgic and two Roman cities*, Soc Antiq London Res Rep **11**, London

White, A, and Baily, C, 1847 Proceedings of the Association, *J Brit Archaeol Assoc* **2**, 334–94

White, I M, and Hodkinson, I D, 1982 *Psylloidea (Nymphal stages) Hemiptera Homoptera*, Handbooks for the identification of British insects **2(5b)**, London

Whittle, A, Healy, F, and Bayliss, A, 2011 *Gathering time: dating the early Neolithic enclosures of southern Britain and Ireland*, Oxford

Wickenden, N P, 1992 *The temple and other sites in the north-eastern sector of Caesaromagus*, Chelmsford Archaeological Trust Report **9**, CBA Res Rep **75** London

Wieckowska-Lüth, M, Kirleis, W, and Schmütz, K, 2020 *Non-pollen palynomorphs database*, Kiel University Institute for Prehistoric and Proto-historic Archaeology, www.wikis.uni-kiel.de/non_pollen_palynomorphs, accessed 25 October 2020

Wilkinson, D, 1992 Oxford Archaeological Unit field manual, unpubl. document, Oxford Archaeology, Oxford

Williams, J H, and Shaw, M, 1981 Excavations in Chalk Lane, Northampton, 1975–1978, *Northamptonshire Archaeol* **16**, 87–136

Williams, R J, and Zeepvat, R J, 1994 *Bancroft: a late Bronze Age/Iron Age settlement, Roman villa and temple-mausoleum*, Buckinghamshire Archaeol Soc Monograph **7**, Milton Keynes

Willis, S, 2004 Samian pottery, a resource for the study of Roman Britain and beyond: the results of the English Heritage funded samian project. An e-monograph, *Internet Archaeol* **17**, https://doi.org/10.11141/ia.17.1, accessed 30 March 2021

Wilson, D R, and Wright, R P, 1967 Roman Britain in 1966: sites explored, *J Roman Stud* **57**, 174–202

Winder, J, 2001 Oyster shell, in Booth *et al.* 2001, 416

Winder, J M, 2011 *Oyster shells from archaeological sites: a brief illustrated guide to basic processing*, http://oystersetcetera.files.wordpress.com/2011/03/oystershellmethodsmanualversion11.pdf

Woodfield, P, 2010 The Delapré Roman kiln field, Northampton, *Northamptonshire Archaeol* **36**, 97–112

Woodward, A, and Hancocks, A, 2006 Iron Age

pottery, in *Iron Age, Roman and Saxon occupation at Grange Park: excavations at Courteenhall, Northamptonshire, 1999* (L Jones, A Woodward and S Buteux), BAR Brit. Ser. **425**, Oxford, 75–89

Woodland Trust, nd a *Maple, field*, A–Z of British trees, https://www.woodlandtrust.org.uk/trees-woods-and-wildlife/british-trees/a-z-of-british-trees/field-maple, accessed 4 January 2021

Woodland Trust, nd b *Rowan*, A–Z of British trees, https://www.woodlandtrust.org.uk/trees-woods-and-wildlife/british-trees/a-z-of-british-trees/rowan, accessed 4 January 2021

Woods, P J, 1972 *Brixworth excavations*, Wellingborough

Worley, F, 2008 Taken to the grave: an archaeozoological approach assessing the role of animals as crematory offerings in first millennium AD Britain, unpubl. PhD thesis, Univ. Bradford

Young, C J, 1977 *The Roman pottery industry of the Oxford region*, BAR Brit. Ser. **43**, Oxford

Index